The Lancashir

A bibliographical account of books on topography, biography, history, science, and miscellaneous literature relating to the county palatine, including an account of Lancashire tracts, pamphlets, and sermons printed before the year 1720. With collations, & bibliographical, critical, & biographical notes on the books and authors

Henry Fishwick

Alpha Editions

This edition published in 2019

ISBN : 9789353895143

Design and Setting By
Alpha Editions
email - alphaedis@gmail.com

THE

LANCASHIRE LIBRARY

A BIBLIOGRAPHICAL ACCOUNT OF BOOKS ON TOPOGRAPHY, BIOGRAPHY, HISTORY, SCIENCE, AND MISCELLANEOUS LITERATURE RELATING TO THE COUNTY PALATINE

INCLUDING

An Account of Lancashire Tracts, Pamphlets, and Sermons printed before the Year 1720.

WITH

Collations, & Bibliographical, Critical, & Biographical Notes on the Books and Authors

BY

LIEUT.-COL. HENRY FISHWICK, F.S.A.

AUTHOR OF 'THE HISTORY OF THE PAROCHIAL CHAPELRY OF GOOSNARGH,' 'THE HISTORY OF THE PARISH OF KIRKHAM,' ETC.

LONDON: GEORGE ROUTLEDGE AND SONS

WARRINGTON: PERCIVAL PEARSE

1875

PREFACE.

A PREFACE is often only an apology, or, at the best, an explanation of the *raison d'être* of the work prefaced. In the present instance no apology can be required, as every student of the wide-spread literature of Lancashire must have felt and acknowledged the absolute want of a book to cover the ground which the "Lancashire Library" professes to occupy. A well-known French author said that "when he wanted a book he wrote it," and I will at once admit that I have been actuated by the same feelings; for as I have wandered farther and farther in the byeways of the literature of our county, I have been the more convinced that no accurate knowledge of its richness and value could be gained until some one had prepared a complete catalogue embracing all the necessary particulars.

This work I have ventured to undertake, whether successfully or not is for the reader to decide.

Under the title of the "Literature of Lancashire" I have not included books which were published in the county, or were written by Lancashire men, *yet do not in any way refer to the county.*

Works to be included in my list must be written about or refer to Lancashire places, persons, or things. The only exception to this rule has been made in the case of some few theological pamphlets printed in the 17th century, which are so curious and valuable that their admission will not be regretted.

As a rule Tracts and Pamphlets printed since 1720 are excluded, because after that date their number is so great (and many of them so perfectly valueless), that to have included them would have defeated the object in view. As a book of this kind is essentially a work of reference, every care has been taken, by means of alphabetical and chronological arrangement, as well as by the addition of copious Indices, to render its contents accessible with the least possible trouble.

I have now only to record my sense of gratitude to those gentlemen who have kindly rendered me assistance by the loan of books or the forwarding of collations, and also to express my thanks to the custodians of the various Lancashire Public Libraries for the facilities which they have afforded me in consulting the volumes in their keeping.

H. F.

CARR HILL, ROCHDALE.

CONTENTS.

PART I.

	PAGES
TOPOGRAPHY	1-189

PART II.

BIOGRAPHY AND FAMILY HISTORY	190-238

PART III.

POETRY, FICTION, AND MISCELLANY	239-289

PART IV.

WORKS PARTLY RELATING TO LANCASHIRE	290-332

PART V.

TRACTS AND PAMPHLETS PRINTED BEFORE 1720	333-379

PART VI.

SERMONS AND THEOLOGICAL TREATISES	380-420
ADDENDA	421-423
GENERAL INDEX	425-436
INDEX OF AUTHORS	437-443

THE LANCASHIRE LIBRARY.

PART I.—TOPOGRAPHY.

An HISTORICAL ACCOUNT of the TOWNS of ASHTON-UNDER-LYNE, STALYBRIDGE, and DUKINFIELD. By EDWIN BUTTERWORTH, Busk, near Oldham. Ashton: printed by T. A. Phillips, stationer, etc., Old Cross. 1842. *Foolscap octavo.*

Title as above, Preface, and History, 177 pp., Index, v. pp. Sells for 5s. 6d.

Edwin Butterworth, the youngest son of James Butterworth, the author of the History of Oldham, etc., was born 1st October 1812, and died at Oldham, 19th April 1848. A monument to his memory is in Greenacre's Cemetery. He edited several of his father's works.

A HISTORY and DESCRIPTION of the TOWN and PARISH of STOCKPORT, ASHTON-UNDER-LYNE, MOTTRAM-LONG-DEN-DALE, and GLOSSOP. With some Memoirs of the late F. D. Astley, Esq., of Dukinfield; and extracts from his Poems, with an Elegy to his memory. By JAMES BUTTERWORTH. Manchester: printed by W. D. Varey, St. Ann's Square. 1827. *Octavo.*

Title, Dedication, Preface, and History of Ashton, 86 pp. 2d Title, View of Glossop Church, and Dedication, and History of Glossop, pp. 87-132. View of Mottram Church, 3d Title, Dedication, and History of Mottram, pp. 133-210. View of Parish Church of Stockport, 4th Title, Dedication, Preface, and History of Stockport, pp. 211-375. View of Dukinfield Lodge, 4th Title, Dedication, and Memoirs, 110 pp. Addenda, viii. pp. Frontispiece, View of Ashton-Under-Lyne Church. Sells for 5s. 6d.

The History of Ashton was first published in 1823. This work is generally known as the "History of the Four Townships."

James Butterworth, born on the 28th August 1771 at a place called Pitses, in the hamlet of Alt, parish of Ashton in Lancashire. His father, who was also called James, married Jane Ogden of Low Side, Oldham. They had eleven children, of whom James was the youngest. In early life he (the author) was a hand-loom weaver, and afterwards a schoolmaster. One of his scholars was the late Edmund Buckley, sometime M.P. for Newcastle. He married Hannah Boyton, and had ten children. He died the 23d November 1837. Many of his MSS. are preserved in the Oldham Lyceum. See EDWIN BUTTERWORTH, p. 1.

GEOLOGICAL SKETCHES and OBSERVATIONS on VEGETABLE FOSSIL REMAINS, etc., collected in the Parish of ASHTON-UNDER-LYNE from the GREAT SOUTH LANCASHIRE COAL-FIELD, etc. etc. Also an attempt to explain the Original Formation of the Earth on a Theory of Combination. Illustrated with numerous woodcuts, etc. By CHARLES CLAY, M.R.C.S.E., Ashton-under-Lyne.

[Quotation, four lines.]

London: published by H. Johnson, 44 Paternoster Row; Bancks and Company, Manchester, and Davis, Stalybridge. 1839. *Octavo.*

Title as above, Dedications, Preface, and Explanation of Lithographed Plate, ix. pp. Geological Sketch and Index, 150 pp. Frontispiece, Folding Lithographic Plate of Fossils. Published at 6s. 6d. Sells for 3s. 6d.

ILLUSTRATION of the CUSTOM of a MANOR in the NORTH of ENGLAND during the FIFTEENTH CENTURY. With occasional remarks on their resemblance to the Incidents of Ancient Scottish Tenures. By SAMUEL HIBBERT, M.D., F.R.S., F.S.A.E., etc. Edinburgh: printed by Alexander Smellie, printer to the University. 1822. *Quarto.*

Title as above. Address to Reader, 3 pp. Illustration of the Custom, etc., 28 pp. (exclusive of folding plate of arrangement of forms in Kirk of Assheton). Documents connected with the foregoing Illustrations of the Custom of the Manor of Assheton-under-Lyne in the fifteenth century, 23 pp. (This forms the Appendix). *Quarto.*

Originally read before the Society of Scottish Antiquaries. A copy of this, somewhat scarce work, is in the Manchester Free Library.

The BLACK KNIGHT of ASHTON. Being an account of a visit to Ashton-under-Lyne to witness the annual ceremony of Riding the Black Lad; with some Tales and Songs by the Way. Manchester. 1870. *Octavo.*

Title, Black Knight, etc., 62 pp. Published at 6d.

Written by Mr. W. E. A. Axon, author of "Folk Lore and Folk Speech of Lancashire."

A Short Sketch of the RISE and HISTORY of the BAPTIST CHURCH, BACUP, and of the Churches at Clough Fold, Rodhillend, Rawden, Salendine Nook, Accrington, Blackburn, Cowling-Hill, Goodshaw, and a Short Account of the Several Ministers, particularly Messrs. Mitchell, Crosley, Moore, Piccop, Lord, Turner, Holden, Nuttall, Ashworth, etc. By James Hargreave. Rochdale: printed and sold by Joseph Littlewood. 1816. *Foolscap octavo.*

Title as above, Preface, and Contents, iv. pp. A Short sketch, 119 pp. Somewhat scarce. A copy is in the author's library. See Memoir of John Hirst.

James Hargreaves also published "An Address to the Heads and Members of Families on the Neglect of Family Religion, with appropriate Extracts from the Acts of Parliament," etc.

BARROW-IN-FURNESS. Its RISE and PROGRESS, with brief SKETCHES of its leading industries. By Francis Leach, B.A., editor of the *Barrow, Furness, and North Western Daily Times.* Barrow-in-Furness: *Daily Times Office,* Victoria Buildings, Strand; Manchester, J. Heywood, Deansgate; Liverpool, Mawdesley, Castle Street, etc. All rights reserved. 1872. *Foolscap octavo.*

Title as above, Dedication, Index, and Barrow-in-Furness, etc., 128 pp. Appendix, 32 pp. Illustrated with a Folding Map of Barrow, and six Plates.

A HISTORY of the ANCIENT CHAPEL of BIRCH in Manchester Parish, including a Sketch of the Township of Rusholme, for the convenience of which Township the Chapel was originally erected, together with notices of the more ancient local Families, and particulars relating to the descent of their Estates. By the Rev. John Booker, M.A.,

F.S.A. of Magdalene College, Cambridge, Curate of Ashurst, Kent. Printed for the Chetham Society. MDCCCLIX. *Foolscap quarto.*

Chetham Society's[1] Title, and List of Council, 3 pp. Title as above, Preface, List of Illustrations, and Half-title, 7 pp. A History of Birch Chapel, Appendix, and Index, 253 pp. Errata, etc., 1 p. List of Illustrations:—Birch Chapel, Frontispiece; Portrait of Major-General Birch, p. 50; Slade Hall, p. 134; St. James' Church, Birch, p. 158.

The Rev. John Booker has contributed several other valuable local histories to the Chetham series. See *Post.*

BISPHAM. See Thornber's Blackpool (*Post*).

BLACKBURN, Lancashire. CHRONOLOGICAL NOTES of prominent HISTORICAL EVENTS in the Town and Parish of Blackburn, from A.D. 448 to A.D. 1860, with the census of 1851 and 1861. By WILLIAM DURHAM. Blackburn: printed and sold by Charles Tiplady, 53 Church Street; sold also by J. Walkden, J. H. Haworth, Ed. Wharton, and all Booksellers. 1861. *Post duodecimo.*

Title as above, Dedication, List of Mayors, and Chronological Notes, 32 pp.

This small pamphlet is inserted here, being the only local work which covers the same ground.

A brief HISTORY of the rise and progress of the LANCASHIRE CONGREGATIONAL UNION, and of the BLACKBURN INDEPENDENT ACADEMY. By R. SLATE. London: Hamilton, Adams, and Co., etc. 1840. *Octavo.*

Title as above and History, 148 pp. Frontispiece, "View of the Lancashire Independent College, near Manchester." Sells for 2s. 6d.

BLACKBURN as it is. A TOPOGRAPHICAL, STATISTICAL, and HISTORICAL ACCOUNT of the Borough of BLACKBURN, in

[1] The Subscription to the Chetham Society is £1 per annum, for which a Member is entitled to three volumes. Works are not sold to the public, and consequently many of the older volumes, when offered second-hand, fetch a high price.

the Hundred of Blackburn (Lower Division), in the County Palatine of Lancaster; its antiquities and modern improvements, including a correct copy of the Charter granted in the reign of Queen Victoria, Biographical Sketches of Eminent Men, etc., a Directory for 1852, with a list of the streets, etc. By P. A. WHITTLE, F.S.A., author of the "Ancient and Modern History of Preston," "Marina," or a History of Southport, Lytham, and Blackpool, etc. etc.

We have a deep concern in preserving from destruction the manners and thoughts of the past, the leading conceptions of all remarkable forms of civilisation, the achievements of genius or virtue, and the benevolent improvements of men.

Preston: printed by H. Oakey, Fishergate; and sold by James Walkden, J. H. Haworth, Charles Tiplady, William Wood, Edward Wharton, and William Fish, Booksellers, Blackburn, and by the principal Booksellers in Lancashire. MDCCCLII. *Octavo.*

Title as above, Dedication, Preface, and Introduction, ix. pp. Blackburn as it is, and Index, p. 11 to p. 400. Frontispiece, Arms of the Borough. Sells for 5s. 6d.; large paper, 12s. 6d. (only a few printed).

A HISTORY of the ANCIENT CHAPEL of BLACKLEY, in MANCHESTER PARISH, including Sketches of the Townships of Blackley, Harpurhey Moston, and Crumpsall, for the convenience of the which several Hamlets the Chapel was originally erected; together with Notices of the more Ancient Local Families, and Particulars relating to the descent of their Estates. By the Rev. JOHN BOOKER, M.A., F.S.A. of Magdalene College, Cambridge, Curate of Prestwich. Manchester: George Simms, St. Ann's Square. 1855. *Foolscap quarto.*

Title as above, Dedication, Preface, and List of Illustrations, viii. pp. A History, 217 pp. Errata or Slip. No Index.

LIST OF ILLUSTRATIONS.

Blackley Chapel . . . *Frontispiece*
Blackley Hall . . . p. 19
Booth Hall . . . p. 28
Blackley Chapel in 1736 . . . p. 60
Apartment in Lightbourne Hall . . p. 176
Hough Hall . . p. 187
Reputed Birthplace of Bishop Oldham . p. 200
Crumpsall Hall . p. 210

A DESCRIPTION of BLACKPOOL in LANCASHIRE, frequented for Sea-bathing. Birmingham: printed by Pearson and Rollason; sold by R. Baldwin, Paternoster Row, London, and also by Bailey and Hudson at Blackpool. MDCCLXXXIX. Price 1s. [By WILLIAM HUTTON.] *Octavo.*

Title and Description, 55 pp.

Now very scarce; a copy is in the Manchester Free Library. 720 Copies were printed.

A DESCRIPTION of BLACKPOOL in Lancashire, frequented for Sea-bathing. By W. HUTTON, F.A.S.S. The Second Edition. London: printed by and for J. Nichols and Son, Red Lion Passage, Fleet Street; and sold by F. C. and J. Rivington, St. Paul's Church-yard, and J. Payne, Castle Street, St. Martin's. 1804. *Octavo.*

Half-title, Title as above, and Preface, vi. pp. A Description, pp. 9-86. Published at 2s. 6d.

A second impression of this edition was "printed by Henry Moon Kirkham, and sold only by G. Cooke, Blackpool, price 1s." The advertisement to which states that "the first impression being disposed of, and as many Ladies and Gentlemen during the last Season were disappointed in not gratifying their curiosity in reading it, it is now reprinted."

Half-title, Title, Advertisement, and Description, 54 pp.

Copies of both these are in the Manchester Free Library.

This impression was nearly all destroyed by fire, and a Third Edition was issued. Printed by and for Nichols and Son, etc. etc. 1817. *Octavo.*

Title and Preface to 3d Edition, iv. pp. A Description, 49 pp.

It is stated to be a "very small impression." This Description of Blackpool will also be found in Hutton's Collected Works. Now sells for 3s. 6d.

An HISTORICAL and DESCRIPTIVE ACCOUNT of BLACKPOOL and its neighbourhood—viz. Layton, Carlton, Poulton, Main's Hall, Singleton, Thornton, Burn Hall, Rossal, Bispham, Martin, Lytham, Southshore, etc. etc. etc. By WILLIAM THORNBER, M.A., Incumbent of Blackpool. "Modo te Thebis, modo ponit Athenis." Poulton: printed and published for the author by Smith, Market Place; and sold by Clarke, Preston, Stirzaker, and at the Promenade, Blackpool. MDCCCXXXVII. *Foolscap octavo.*

Title as above, Dedication, iv. pp. Preface and Contents, vi. pp. Historical Account, pp. 5-345. Woodcut of Celtic Metal Axe. Errata, 2 pp. Blackpool Charities, 4 pp. Sells for 4s. 6d., and is now rather difficult to procure.

An Historical and Descriptive ACCOUNT of BLACKPOOL, LYTHAM, and SOUTHPORT. By a popular writer. Embellished with three beautiful Engravings. London: Whittaker and Co. [1831]. *Octavo.*

Title as above. Title for History of Blackpool, and Preface, iv. pp. History of Blackpool, 72 pp. Title to History of Lytham, and Preface, iv. pp. History of Lytham, 88 pp. Title to History of Southport, Preface, "Baths and Promenade," and History of Southport, 160 pp. These are three works bound together with a general Title-page. They were all written by P. WHITTLE (see *Post*). Sells for 7s. 6d.

A GUIDE from BLACKPOOL and FLEETWOOD to FURNESS ABBEY, with a ground plan of the ruins. Fleetwood: published by W. Porter, Dock Street and Market Street, Blackpool. 1847. 32*mo.*

Title as above, and Guide, 34 pp. Sells for 2s. 6d.

PORTER'S GUIDE to BLACKPOOL, FLEETWOOD, LYTHAM, etc., with a Directory of Blackpool, and a Map of the district. Sixth edition. Blackpool and Fleetwood: W. Porter, steam printer, *Chronicle* and *Herald* Office. MDCCCLXVI. *Octavo.*

Title as above, and Preface, 111 pp. Introduction and Guide, 86 pp. Directory, etc., 46 pp. Map of the Fylde district; map of Blackpool (folding). Engraving of the pier at Blackpool. Sells for 3s. 6d.

BOLTON. The RISE and PROGRESS of NONCONFORMITY in BOLTON. An HISTORICAL SKETCH of a CONGREGATION of PROTESTANT Dissenters assembling first in Deansgate, and afterwards in Bank Street. In Four Lectures delivered at the close of the year 1853. By FRANKLIN BAKER, M.A., Minister of the Chapel. (Ps. cxxxvii.) London: E. T. Whitfield, 178 Strand. 1854. *Octavo.*

Half-title, Title as above. List of Ministers, Address, and Contents,

viii. pp. Lectures, 116 pp. Frontispiece, Bank Street Chapel, Bolton. Sells for 3s. 6d.

A HANDBOOK of the History and Topography of BOLTON. By JOHN D. BRISCOE. Entered at Stationers' Hall. Bolton: printed by Thomas Morris, Oxford Street. MDCCCLXI. *Duodecimo.*

Title as above, Preface, Introduction, and Handbook, 48 pp. Frontispiece, View of Bolton from Bury Road. Sells for 3s.

The HISTORY of GREAT and LITTLE BOLTON. "Veluti in speculum." Manchester: printed by C. W. Leake, No. 5 Half Street; published by Mr. Kell, bookseller, Deansgate, Bolton; Messrs. Clark, Market Place, Manchester. Price Sixpence. [1824].

General Introduction, xii. pp. Ancient and Original History of Lancashire, Chapter I., p. 1 to p. 14. History of Bolton, p. 15 to p. 398. Frontispiece, View of Bolton Dispensary, 1823.

No more of this work was published. No Title-page was printed. It was published in parts. The above is from the paper cover of No. 1. The Introduction is dated, "Little Bolton, Sep. 15th, 1824." Very scarce. A copy is in the Bolton Free Library.

John Brown was the author of "The Basis of Mr. Samuel Crompton's claims to secure remuneration for his discovery of the Mule Spinning Machine" (see *Post*), and from Mr. French's Life of Crompton it appears that on the failure of his efforts to obtain the compensation for Crompton, he committed suicide in his lodgings in London.

A CHRONOLOGICAL HISTORY of BOLTON from the Earliest Known Records to 1870. Compiled from the *Bolton Chronicle*. By JAMES CLEGG. Entered at Stationers' Hall. Bolton: printed at the *Chronicle Office*, Knowsley Street. MDCCCLXX. *Foolscap octavo.*

Title and History, 41 pp. Sells for 2s.

This is perhaps, strictly speaking, a pamphlet; but will be found useful to the Topographer.

BOLTON-LE-MOORS and the Townships in the Parish. An HISTORICAL, STATISTICAL, CIVIL, and MORAL ACCOUNT of the Corporate and Parliamentary Borough of Bolton, in the Division of the Hundred of Salford, County Palatine of Lancaster, including a curious description of the PARISH of DEANE, in the Wapentake and Hundred of Salford, Barony of Manchester. By P. A. WHITTLE, F.A.S.—R., author of the ancient and Modern History of Preston, etc. etc.

[Two Quotations.] Bolton: printed by John Crompton, Bradshaw-gate. MDCCCLV. *Octavo.*

Title as above, Preface, Introduction, xxi. pp. History of Bolton, 434 pp. Dedication, Corrigenda, and Contents, iv. pp. Published in 10 parts. Sells for 6s.

PROCEEDINGS of the BOLTON TOWN-COUNCIL. Alderman James Barlow, Mayor. Bolton: printed at the *Chronicle Office*, Knowsley Street. MDCCCLXVIII. *Octavo.*

Title 1 p. Proceedings, 336 pp. Appendix, xxxix. pp.

The above, and the succeeding Volumes (to the present date) are in the Bolton Public Library.

BROUGHTON (near Preston). See Account of Fernyhalgh, etc. By P. WHITTLE. (*Post*).

HISTORY of the PAROCHIAL CHURCH of BURNLEY; its Endowments, its Records, and its Incumbents; with a Description of the Towneley and Stansfield Chapels, and an Appendix containing Accounts of all the District Churches within the Chapelry. By T. T. WILKINSON, F.R.A.S., Member of the Manchester Literary and Philosophical Society; of the Historic Society of Lancashire and Cheshire, etc. etc. Burnley: T. Sutcliffe, St. James' Street. London: Longman and Co. MDCCCLVI. *Foolscap quarto.*

Title as above. Dedication, Contents, and Preface, ix. pp. History, Appendix, and Index, 124 pp.

PLATES.

St. Peter's Church, 1853.
Interior of St. Peter's Church. (Looking East).
Interior of St. Peter's Church. (Looking West).
Cross in Godly Lane, etc.

Published at 5s., afterwards reduced to 3s. 6d.

We are indebted to Mr. Wilkinson for several important Lancashire Books. (See *Post.*) Relating to Burnley he wrote—" The Grammar School,"

16 pp. 8vo, and "Ancient Mansions near Burnley, their History, and their Owners," 24 pp., 12mo.

Thomas Turner Wilkinson, the son of William Wilkinson, farmer, was born at Abbott House, Mellor, near Blackburn, on the 17th March 1815. For many years he was Second Master of the Burnley Free Grammar School. He died 6th February 1875, and was buried at Burnley. A long list of the numerous books and papers from his pen appeared in the "Preston Guardian," 13th February 1875.

BURY GRAMMAR SCHOOL, the ORIGINAL Book of Statutes, and TRANSCRIPTS of DOCUMENTS relating to the BURY GRAMMAR SCHOOL. Printed by Crompton, bookseller, Fleet Street. MDCCCLXIII. *Octavo.*

Title, etc., and Index, 36 pp. Sells for 1s. 6d.

CARTMEL PARISH and PARISH CHURCH, and Sermons preached therein. By the Rev. WILLIAM FOLLIOTT, B.A., author of the "Christian's Dream." London: Wertheim and Mackintosh. 1854. *Duodecimo.*

Title as above, Dedication and Contents, vi. pp. Cartmel Parish, etc., and Appendix, 134 pp.

Illustrated with a View of Cartmel Church, and a folding Plan of Cartmel Town. Sells for 2s. 6d.

An ACCOUNT of the PARISH of CARTMELL. By the Rev. THOMAS DURHAM WHITAKER, LL.D., F.S.A., Vicar of Whalley. London: printed by and for Nichols, Son, and Bentley, Red Lion Passage, Fleet Street; and Thomas Edwards, Bookseller, Halifax. 1818.

PLATES.

Choir of Cartmel[1] Church.
Monument of Harrington Family.
North-East View of Cartmel[1] Church.

Title as above, 1 p., Account, 10 pp. Large paper. Very scarce. This was a separate issue of the sheets used for History of Whalley. (See *Post.*)

A copy is in the Author's Library. See Grange. *Post.*

[1] In these cases spelt with one 'l.'

An HISTORICAL and DESCRIPTIVE ACCOUNT of the PARISH of CHORLEY, including in it the Situation, Extent, Rivers, Mines, Minerals, Manufactures, Markets, Fairs, Gentlemen's Seats, Public Charities, Antiquities, Civil and Ecclesiastical Jurisdictions, etc. etc. With a Sketch of the most remarkable places in the neighbourhood; to which is added a Directory or a List of the Gentry, Clergy, Professional Men, Manufacturers, and Tradesmen of every description, and men holding responsible situations in the said Parish, etc.; and an Account of all the Coaches which pass through Chorley daily; and a List of Carriers by land and water. Chorley: Printed and published by C. Robinson, Market Street. 1835. *Duodecimo.*

Title as above, Preface, iv. pp. Description, etc., 48 pp. The compiler admits that "much of the historical part has been copied from Baines' 'History of Lancashire.'"

CHORLEY TOWN and PARISH of—See Mannex and Co.'s "History of Preston," etc. *Post.*

ANCIENT CHARTERS and other Muniments of the BOROUGH of CLITHERO, in the County Palatine of Lancaster. From the original Documents, with Translations and Notes by J. HARLAND, "Guardian" Office, Manchester. 1851. Privately printed for the Mayor and Corporation of Clithero, by Cave and Sever, Palatine Buildings, Hunt's Bank, Manchester. *Royal octavo.*

Half-title. Title as above. Dedication to Thomas Garnet, Esq., of Low Moor, Clithero, Mayor, and to the Aldermen and Burgesses of the Borough of Clithero; and Introduction, viii. pp. Charters, etc., 55 pp. Sells for 5s. 6d.

The name of John Harland, F.S.A., will frequently be found in the pages of "The Lancashire Library." He was the son of John Harland of Hull, and Mary, his wife, daughter of John Breasley of Selby, and was born at Hull 27th May 1806. He came to Manchester in 1830 to accept an offer of a post on the staff of the "Manchester Guardian," where he resided until his death on the 23d April 1868. Amongst his miscellaneous writings are "On the Find of Six Thousand Pennies at Eccles." (*The Reliquary.*) "On Local and other Names and Words." (*The Reliquary*); and "Some Account of Seats and Pews in Old Parish Churches of the County Palatine of Lancaster." (A pamphlet of 16 pp.)

CHORLTON. See J. Booker's History of Chapel of Didsbury, etc. (See below).

MEMORIALS of OLDHAM'S TENEMENT at CRUMPSALL, in the Parish of Manchester. The BIRTHPLACE of HUGH OLDHAM, Bishop of Exeter, and Founder of the Manchester Free Grammar School. Manchester: Sidney Smith, printer. 1864. *Super-royal folio.*

Title as above, 1 p. Memorials, etc. 2 pp. [By T. BAKER.]

PHOTOGRAPHS.

1. Cottage at Crumpsall in which Hugh Oldham was born.
2. Fresco upon the inner wall of Hugh Oldham's Cottage.
3. Coat of Arms in Hugh Oldham's Cottage.

A copy of this is in the Manchester Free Library.

Description of the Parish of DEAN. See Bolton, page 9.

A HISTORY of the ANCIENT CHAPELS of DIDSBURY and CHORLTON, in Manchester Parish, including Sketches of the Townships of Didsbury, Withington, Burnage, Heaton, Reddish, Levenshulme, and Chorlton-cum-Hardy. Together with notices of the more ancient local families, and particulars relating to the descent of their estates.

By the Rev. JOHN BOOKER, M.A., F.S.A., of Magdalene College, Cambridge, Curate of Prestwich. Printed for the Chetham Society. MDCCCLVII. *Foolscap quarto.*

Chetham Society's Title (vol. XLII.), and List of Council, 3 pp. Title as above, Preface, List of Illustrations, and Half-title, 7 pp. History of Chapel of Didsbury, 238 pp. Half-title and History of Chorlton Chapel, and Index, 239 pp. to 337 pp. The 14th Report and List of Members, 8 pp.

HISTORICAL and DESCRIPTIVE NOTICES of DROYLSDEN, Past and Present. By JOHN HIGSON, Author of "The Gorton Historical Recorder," etc. Manchester: printed for the Author by Beresford and Southern, 32 Corporation Street. 1859. *Foolscap octavo.*

Title as above, Dedication, Table of Contents, Preface, etc., 8 pp. Notices, p. 9 to p. 170.

ILLUSTRATIONS.

Clayton Hall, *Frontispiece.* | Droylsden Educational Institute.

John Higson, eldest son of Daniel and Letitia Higson, was born at Whiteley Farm, Gorton, 25th July 1825. He was educated partly at Ardwick, and afterwards at the Gorton Old School. For nearly twenty years he was cashier of the Victoria Mills, Droylsden, and afterwards of Springhead Spinning Company. In 1848 he married Elizabeth Caroline, daughter of John Green. He died 13th December 1871, and was buried in Droylsden Churchyard. John Higson was a large contributor to the local newspapers, and at the time of his death had completed a "Glossary of Lancashire Words and Phrases," and had in an advanced state a "History of Lees and Neighbourhood," beside which he left a large amount of valuable MSS.

The ANCIENT PARISH CHURCH of ECCLES. Its ANTIQUITY, ALTERATIONS, and IMPROVEMENTS. Eccles: A. Shuttleworth, printer and bookbinder, Market Place. 1864. *Octavo.*

Title as above, and Ancient Parish Church, 82 pp. This was written by JOHN HARLAND. Sells for 1s. 6d.

The HISTORY of ECCLES and BARTON'S CONTENTIOUS GUISING WAR. I. An Account of the Heathens and Ancient Christians observing the first of May, having some resemblance with Guising. II. Some fictitious Debates bordering near the Matter of Truth; with an Account of these Guisings, from the first rise to the present time, between Eccles and Barton. With several entertaining remarks. By F. H** R** G** N.

> Barton and Eccles they will not agree,
> For envy and pride is the reason you'll see;
> France and Spain with England are the same,
> And a great many more compose th' ill-natur'd train.
> You neighbours that over each other do crow,
> And now and then turn out to make a great show;
> Like England and America do make a great noise.
> Be wise, for it only diverts our girls and boys.

Price 3d. *Octavo,* 19 pp. The History, etc., commences on the reverse of the Title, p. 2, and appears to have been printed in

1778, but no printer's name appears. A copy of this (which is believed to be unique), is in the possession of William Harrison, Esq., of St. John's, Isle of Man.

The HISTORY of EVERTON, including familiar Dissertations on the People, and Descriptive Delineations of the several and separate Properties of the Township. With a Map, Plates, and Woodcuts. By ROBERT SYERS.

"History is the roast beef of literature on which all minds may feed advantageously; but those who are fond of feasting on literary fricasees, truffles, and trifles, seldom relish a dish so plain; and yet off all modern dishes that intellect feeds on history is the most nutritious."—*Ethic Scraps.*

Liverpool: published by G. and J. Robinson, Castle Street, and D. Marples, Lord Street. 1830. *Octavo.*

Title as above, Preface, and Contents, 16 pp. History and Appendix, 479 pp. Errata, etc., 1 p.

Map of Liverpool in 1790.

PLATES.

The Beacon, to face p. 56. | The New Cemetery, p. 210.
West View of Church, p. 282.

Sells for 15s. A valuable History.

Mr. Picton says (see "Liverpool Memorials"), that the "account of localities and people are charming for the *bonhomie* and minuteness of the pictures." Robert Syers was long resident in Everton.

An ACCOUNT of ST. MARIE'S CHAPEL at FERNYHALGH, in the Township of Broughton, Parish of Preston, Hundred of Amounderness, County Palatine of Lancaster. To which is added many curious Notices respecting BROUGHTON CHURCH, and the Families of the Singletons and the Langtons, etc.; also "The Duties of a Good Priest." By P. A. WHITTLE, F.S.A., author of the "History of Preston," etc. Preston: Printed for the Author by Henry Oakey, Fishergate. MDCCCLI. *Foolscap octavo.*

Title as above. Prefatory Remarks, and Account, etc., 54 pp. Sells for 2s. 6d.

The BIRTHPLACE of TIM BOBBIN or the PARISH of FLIXTON. By EDWIN WAUGH, Author of "Sketches of Lancashire Life," "Poems and Lancashire Songs," "Rambles in the Lake Country," etc. etc. [Quotation from Wordsworth, 4 lines.] London: Simpkin, Marshall, and Co.; Manchester: John Heywood, 141 and 143 Deansgate. *Duodecimo.*

Title as above, and The Birthplace, 61 pp. Published at 1s.

HANDBOOK to the ABBEY of ST. MARY'S, FURNESS, in Lancashire. Ulverston: Published by Stephen Soulby, King Street. MDCCCXLV. [? G. H. Barber.] *Octavo.*

Title as above. Preface and Contents, iv. pp. Hand Book, 77 pp. Illustrated with Woodcuts, and the following

PLATES.

Plan of the Abbey. | Furness Abbey Church.
Guest Hall, Chapel.

The matter of the book is professedly "principally derived from the 'Annales Furnesienses.'"

ANNALES FURNIENSIS. HISTORY and ANTIQUITIES of the ABBEY of FURNESS. By THOMAS ALCOCK BECK, Esq. London: Payne and Foss, Pall Mall; M. A. Nattali, Bedford Street, Covent Garden; S. Soulby, Ulverston. MDCCCXLIV. *Royal quarto.*

Title as above, Dedication, Contents, List of Plates, and Preface, xi. pp. Annales, 403. Appendix and Contents, cxi. pp.

LIST OF PLATES.

1. South-East View of Furness Abbey.
2. Plan " " "
3. North Doorway.
4. North View (double plate).
5. Western Tower.
6. Effigies in the North Aisle.
7. View of Sidelia (double plate).
8. Effigies in the Chancel.
9. West View of Transept.
10. Tombstones and Panels.
11. South-East View.
12. Entrance to Chapter House.
13. Section through Chapter House.
14. South-West View (double plate).
15. East End of Guest Hall.
16. East and North View of Guest Hall.
17. Guest Hall Chapel.
18. Bas-reliefs in the Manor-house (three plates).

21. Abbot's Private Chapel, and Hawkshead Hall.
22. Illuminated facsimile from the Chartulary.
23. Facsimile of Abbot's Deed of Surrender.
25. Heads of Stephen and Maud.

A valuable work, of which only 250 copies were printed. Published at £7 : 7s., and now sells for from £5 to £7.

GEOLOGICAL FRAGMENTS, collected principally from Rambles among the Rocks of FURNESS and CARTMEL. By JOHN BOLTON, Ulverston. 1869. *Royal octavo.*

Plates. Sells for 4s. 6d.

FURNESS, and FURNESS ABBEY, or a Companion through the Lancashire part of the Lake District. By FRANCIS EVANS.

"At secura quies et nescia fallere vita."
Virgil.

(and four following lines).

Ulverston: Published by D. Atkinson, King Street; Whittaker and Co., London. MDCCCXLII. *Foolscap octavo.*

Half-title, Title as above, Preface, and Contents, x. pp. Furness, etc., and Errata, 254 pp.

PLATES.

Ulverston, from the North.	*Frontispiece.*
Map of Furness.	To face page 1.
Conishead Priory.	" " 166.
Furness Abbey, from the East.	" " 195.
Ground Plan of Furness.	" " 199.

Published at 6s. 6d.

SKETCH of FURNESS and CARTMEL, comprising the Hundred of Lonsdale North of the Sands. By CHARLES M. JOPLING. London: Whittaker and Co., Ave Maria Lane. Ulverston: Stephen Soulby. MDCCCXLIII. *Octavo.*

Title, Preface, and Contents, 6 pp. Sketch, 256 pp. Appendix, 19 pp., and Index, 2 pp.

ILLUSTRATIONS.

An engraved Frontispiece, containing two Views of Furness Abbey.
A Map of Furness and Cartmel.
A Geological Map of Furness and Cartmel.
The Guest's Chapel, Furness Abbey, page 32.

Bowness Chapel, p. 25.
The North Front, p. 147.
Conished Priory, p. 147.
The Hall, Conished Priory, p. 148.
Pile Castle, p. 163.
Halker Hall, p. 268.

Published at 6s. 6d.

A GLOSSARY of the WORDS and PHRASES of FURNESS (North Lancashire). With Illustrative Quotations, principally from the old Northern Writers. By J. P. MORRIS, F.A.S.L. Corr. Mem., Anth. Soc. of Paris. [Quotation from Higden's Polychronicon.] London: J. Russell Smith. Carlisle: George Coward. MDCCCLXIX. *Duodecimo.*

Half-title, Title as above, Dedication, Preface. List of Abbreviations, etc., xvi. pp. Glossary, 114 pp. Published at 3s. 6d.

FURNESS ABBEY and the Neighbourhood. By JAMES PAYN. Fourth Edition. Windermere: John Garnett. London: Simpkin, Marshall, and Co. *Duodecimo.*

Title as above, and Contents, v. pp. Guide, 76 pp.

PLATES.

Furness Abbey.
Plan of the Abbey.
Folding Map of the Duddon, etc.

The 1863 edition, with Photographs, was published at 15s.; the edition of 1869 (as above), at 10s. 6d. Mr. Payn also wrote a small "Handbook to the English Lakes."

The ANTIQUITIES of FURNESS, or an ACCOUNT of the ROYAL ABBEY of ST. MARY'S in the VALE of NIGHTSHADE, near DUTTON in FURNESS. Belonging to the Right Honourable Lord George Cavendish. London: printed for the Author by T. Spilsbury, in Cook's Court, Carey Street, Lincoln's Inn, and sold by J. Johnson, in St.

Paul's Churchyard, J. Ridley, in St. James' Street, and S. Leacroft, at Charing Cross. MDCCLXXIV.

Title as above, Dedication, signed "T. WEST, Titeup in Furness." List of Subscribers and Contents, xviii. pp. (unnumbered). Explanation of the Ground Plan, 2 pp. Descriptive View of Furness, lvi. pp. Antiquities of Furness, 288 pp. (exclusive of Title). Appendix, cxxxvi. pp. (unnumbered).

PLATES.

Ground Plan (folding), of Furness Abbey.
Plan (folding), of the Liberties of Furness.
A View of the Abbey. A Seal of the Abbey.

Sells for 12s. 6d.

The ANTIQUITIES of FURNESS. Illustrated with Engravings. By THOMAS WEST. A New Edition, with Additions, by WILLIAM CLOSE, Ulverston : printed and sold by George Ashburner, and may be had of R. S. Kirby, London House Yard; Messrs. Lackington, Allen, and Co., London; H. Mozley, Gainsborough; Wilson and Spence, York; Troughton and Gore, Liverpool; Thompson and Sons, Manchester; Ware, Whitehaven. 1805. *Octavo.*

Title as above, Dedication, Preface, Advertisement, Contents, Errata, etc., xvi. pp. A Descriptive View, Antiquities, and Appendix, 426 pp. Index, vi. pp.

PLATES.

North-West View of the Abbey, to face title-page.		
Map,	"	p. 1.
North-East View of the Abbey, to face pp. 69 or 359.		
Ground Plan,	"	71 or 74.
Antiquities,	"	190.
View of Dalton Castle,	"	346.
View of Pile of Fouldrey,	"	369 or 373.

Sells for 5s. 6d.

Thomas West was a lay priest of the Society of Jesus, and afterwards a Guide to the Lakes. He died at Sizergh in Westmoreland in 1779.

A small Guide to Furness Abbey was published by D. Atkinson in 1861, which consists of 28 pp., with six woodcuts.

The HISTORY of the PAROCHIAL CHAPELRY of GOOSNARGH, in the County of Lancaster. By HENRY FISHWICK, F.H.S. Manchester: Charles Simms and Co. London: Trübner and Co. MDCCCLXXI. *Foolscap quarto.*

Title as above, Preface, Contents, and List of Illustrations, vii. pp. History, Appendix, General Index, and Index of Names, 239 pp. (Errata on slip.)

LIST OF ILLUSTRATIONS.

Goosnargh Church (South-West View). *Frontispiece.*
Goosnargh Church (South-East View), facing p. 19.
The Singleton Tomb, facing p. 23.
The Church of Whitechapel, facing p. 46.
Goosnargh Hospital, „ p. 128.
Portrait of Alexander Rigby, „ p. 146.
Bulsnape Hall, „ p. 152.
Figure over the Door of "Ashes," facing p. 164.
Arms of Fishwick, p. 154.*[1]
Arms of Parker, p. 189.*
Arms of Newsam, p. 193.*
Inscription on Whinney Clough Barn, p. 181.
Inscription in St. Anne's Well, p. 184.

LIST OF FOLDING PEDIGREES.

Caterall of Little Mitton and Goosnargh, Fishwick of Bulsnape, Hesketh of Whitehill, Midgeal of Blakehall, Newsam of Newsam Hall, Parker of Whittingham House, Rigby of Middleton, Singleton of Chingle Hall, and Whittingham of Whittingham.

Published at 15s. Large paper copies (100 printed), published at 30s.

The GORTON HISTORICAL RECORDER, or a Concise, Chronological, Ecclesiastical, Municipal, Biographical, and Domestic History of the Chapelry. Illustrating the Rise and Progress of the "Mesne Manor" and its inhabitants from the earliest to the present

[1] The (*) refers to Pedigrees facing the pages named.

time. By JOHN HIGSON. Droylsden: published by John Higson, Market Street. [1852]. *Foolscap octavo.*

Title as above, Preface, Introduction, and Recorder, 227 pp. Sells for 2s. 6d.

GUIDE to GRANGE and its Neighbourhood, with Notes on CARTMEL PRIORY CHURCH, Lancashire. Cartmel: printed by H. Brockbank. *Duodecimo.*

Title as above, Guide, and Directory, 36 pp. Sells for 1s.

Merely a local Guide-book of no historical value.

An HISTORICAL DESCRIPTION of the Town of HEYWOOD and Vicinity. By EDWIN BUTTERWORTH. [Arms of Heywood]. Heywood: V. Cook, printer, Market Place. 1840. *Post octavo.*

Title as above, Introduction, and Description, 40 pp. Scarce. Sells for 3s. 6d.

HORNBY. A Verbatim REPORT of the CAUSE Doe Dem TATHAM *v.* WRIGHT, tried at the Lancaster Lammas Assizes, 1834, before Mr. Baron Gurney and a Special Jury. BY ALEXANDER FRASER of Clifford's Inn, the accredited reporter in the case. VOL. I. Lancaster: published by William Barwick and by Arthur Fisher, Kirby, Lonsdale; sold in London by Simpkin and Marshall, Oliver and Boyd, Edinburgh, Banks and Co., Manchester, and Marples and Co., Liverpool. 1834. *Octavo.*

Title as above, and Report, 371 pp.

VOL. II. Title, 1 p. Report, 360 pp.

This celebrated "Will Case" was to recover possession of the Manor of Hornby and Tatham, and other lands in Lancashire. Sells for 7s. 6d.

The HISTORY of the PARISH of KIRKHAM, in the County of Lancaster. By HENRY FISHWICK, Esq., F.R.H.S., author of "The History of the Parochial Chapelry of Goosnargh." Printed for the Chetham Society. MDCCCLXXIV. *Foolscap quarto.*

Chetham Society. Title (Vol. XCII.) and List of Council, iii. pp.
Title as above, Introduction, Contents, and List of Illustrations, vii. pp.

History of Kirkham, Appendix, General Index, and Index of Names, 230 pp. (Errata on Slip).

ILLUSTRATIONS.

North View of Kirkham Church, *Frontispiece.*
Arms of Clegg, p. 128.
„ Westby. On Pedigree facing p. 174.

FOLDING PEDIGREES.

Westby of Mowbrick, facing p. 174
Parker of Bradkirk, „ „ 180
Harrison of Bankfield, facing p. 189
Skilicorne of Prees, „ „ 191
Hesketh of Mains, facing p. 197

GLEANINGS from the MENAGERIE and AVIARY at KNOWSLEY HALL. Knowsley. 1846.

Title as above, Preface, and Gleanings, xiv. pp. Coloured Plates from Drawings by E. Lear. Vol. I. [Edited by J. E. GREY.] *Imp. folio.*

Vol. II. 1850.

Title and Preface, iv. pp. Gleanings, and List of Plates, 76 pp. 62 Plates from Drawings by W. HAWKINS (many of them coloured).

This magnificent work was printed for private circulation only. Sells for £12 : 12s. A copy is in the Liverpool Free Public Library.

A PICTURESQUE TOUR of the ENGLISH LAKES, containing a description of the most romantic scenery of CUMBERLAND, WESTMORELAND, and LANCASHIRE, with Accounts of Antient and Modern Manners and Customs, and Elucidations of the History and Antiquities of that part of the country, etc. etc. Illustrated with 48 coloured Views drawn by Messrs. T. H. FIELDING and J. WALTON.

Published by R. Ackermann at his Repository of Arts, 101 Strand. 1821. *Royal quarto.*

The VIEWS in Lancashire are—

North-West View of Furness Abbey.
Coniston Waters.
Copper Mill in Coniston Fell.
Yewdale Crags, Esthwaite Water.
Esthwaite Water.
Ferry on Windermere.

Station on Windermere.
Windermere from above Troutbeck.
Low Wood Inn.
Windermere from Troutbeck Lane, with Langdale Pikes.
Windermere Head.
Stockgill Force.
Skelwith Force.

Published at £6 : 6s. Sells for £1 : 10s. A Second Edition in 1821.

This work is generally known as "Ackermann's English Lakes." See "Wilkinson's Lakes." [*Post.*]

ALLISON'S NORTHERN TOURISTS' GUIDE to the LAKES of CUMBERLAND, WESTMORELAND, and LANCASHIRE, wherein the Mountains, Lakes, and Scenery are correctly described, and the Stages and Favourite Excursions distinctly pointed out. Seventh Edition, with very considerable additions. Penrith: printed by J. Allison; sold also by Longman and Co., Paternoster Row, London, etc. * * * 1837. *Duodecimo.*

Title as above, Advertisement, Introduction, a Tabular View of the Lakes, Altitudes of Mountains, Waterfalls, and Table of Distances, xii. pp. Guide and Contents, 168 pp. Sells for 2s. 6d.

A COMPANION to the LAKES of CUMBERLAND, WESTMORELAND, and LANCASHIRE, in a Descriptive Account of a Family Tour and an Excursion on Horseback, comprising a Visit to Lancaster Assizes. With a new, copious, and correct Itinerary. By EDWARD BAINES jun. London: printed for Hurst, Chance, and Co., and for Wales and Baines, Liverpool; J. Baines and Co., Leeds, and sold by all booksellers in Lancashire, Kendal, Keswick, Penrith, Carlisle, etc. 1829. *Duodecimo.*

Preface and Contents, xi. pp. Companion, 271 pp. Itinerary and Index, 49 pp.

This is the First Edition; the Second was published in 1830, the Third Edition in 1834, and the Fourth in 1836.

BLACK'S PICTURESQUE GUIDE to the ENGLISH LAKES, including the Geology of the District. By JOHN PHILIPS, M.A., LL.D., F.R.S., F.G.S., Professor of Geology in the University of Oxford. Outline Views by Mr. FLINTOFT. Illustrations by BIRKET FOSTER. Eighteenth Edition. Edinburgh: Adam and Charles Black. 1874. *Foolscap octavo.*

Title as above, Preface, Contents, etc., xxv. pp. Guide and Index, 293 pp. A Map and 5 Charts. 11 Outline Views of Mountains, and 15 Woodcuts. Published at 5s.

ADAM'S POCKET and DESCRIPTIVE GUIDE to the LAKE DISTRICT of LANCASHIRE, Westmoreland, and Cumberland. A Complete Companion for the Tourist to the Attractive Scenery, Picturesque Antiquities, Mountains, Lakes, and Waterfalls of this celebrated region. By E. T. BLANCHARD, author of Adam's "Guide to London," the "Environs," and the "Watering Places of England." Embellished with a new and accurate Map, and Illustrative Engravings, by F. G. DELAMOTTE. Price One Shilling. London: W. J. Adam, 59 Fleet Street, and Bradshaw's Guide Office. [1852]. *Duodecimo.*

Title as above, Preface, and Contents, viii. pp. Guide and Index, 126 pp. Published at 1s.

A FORTNIGHT'S RAMBLE to THE LAKES in WESTMORELAND, LANCASHIRE, and CUMBERLAND. By a RAMBLER. [Quotations from Thompson]. The Second Edition. London: printed for J. Nichols, Red Lion Passage, Fleet Street. 1795. *Octavo.*

Title as above, References, Dedication, Preface, and Contents, xxxiii. pp. The Ramble, 286 pp. Poems, p. 287 to p. 292.

This Edition was published at 5s., and sells for 4s. 6d. The First Edition, which is rather scarce,[1] was printed in 1792, and the Third Edition in 1810, which contains a portrait of William Noble of Bampton, and sells at 4s. 6d. Lowndes says that this book contains the earliest account of the Beauty of Buttermere. The author of this book was Joseph Budworth, the son of Joseph Budworth, innkeeper, of Manchester. He was Lieutenant in the Manchester Royal Volunteers, which served at Gibraltar. He died 4th September 1815.

Budworth was the author of a poem entitled "Windermere." Lon-

[1] In the Preface to the Third Edition the author states that of the First Edition as many copies having been sold as paid his expenses, and there being many inaccuracies in it, he had the "remaining copies disfigured, and made an exchange of them at a celebrated Literary Repository in Cockspur Street."

don : printed for J. Cadell jun. and W. Davies (successor to Mr. Cadell) in the Strand. 1798.

Price One Shilling. 28 pp. ; and "The Siege of Gibraltar," a Poem.
For notice of him, see "Manchester School Register," Vol. I.

A SURVEY of the LAKES of CUMBERLAND, WESTMORELAND, and LANCASHIRE, together with an Account, Historical, Topographical, and Descriptive, of the adjacent country, to which is added a Sketch of the Border Laws and Customs. By JAMES CLARKE, Land Surveyor. London : printed and published for the author, and sold by him at Penrith, Cumberland ; also by J. Robson and J. Faulder, New Bond Street, P. W. Fores, No. 3 Piccadilly ; the Engraver and J. Neele, 352 Strand, London ; T. Bull and J. Marshall, Bath ; Rose and Drury, Lincoln ; Todd, Stonegate, York ; Ware and Son, Whitehaven ; C. Elliot, Edinburgh, and most other booksellers in the kingdom. MDCCLXXXVII. [Entered at Stationers' Hall, according to Act of Parliament]. *Folio.*

Title as above, Dedication, and Introduction, xlii. pp. Half-title, Contents, The Survey and Appendix, 193 pp.

PLATES.

Plan of Town of Penrith (folding)	p. 10
" " Roads between Penrith and Ullswater (folding) .	p. 22
Views from Penrith Beacon (folding)	p. 23
Ancient Ornament	p. 42
Map of Derwentwater (folding)	p. 86
" " Roads, etc., between Penrith and Keswick (folding) .	p. 92
" " " " " Keswick and Broadwater (folding)	p. 94
" " Broadwater (folding)	p. 102
" " Roads between Keswick and Ambleside (folding) .	p. 126
" " Southern part of the Lake of Windermere (folding) .	p. 154
" " Northern " " " .	"

Published at 18s. Now very scarce. Sells for about £1 : 10s., but copies have sold for a much higher price. There is a copy in the Manchester Free Library.

P. CROSTHWAITE'S PLANS of the LAKES of LANCASHIRE, Cumberland, and Westmoreland, with a short description to each Map. These were published in 1783-1788, and republished in 1794 and 1809.

No Title page, but on the Maps (which include views of Churches, Houses, Roman Remains, etc.) P. Crosthwaite describes himself as "Admiral at Keswick Regatta, who keeps the museum at Keswick, and is Guide, Pilot, Geographer, and Hydrographer to the Nobility and Gentry who make the Tour of the Lakes."

The Plans are curious and interesting; they were probably first issued separately, and afterwards bound together. Sells for 5s. A copy is in the Manchester Free Library.

A TOUR to the principal SCOTCH and ENGLISH LAKES. By JAMES DENHOLM, of the Drawing and Painting Academy, Argyle Street, Author of the History of Glasgow, Member of the Philosophical and Philotechnical Societies of that City. [Quotation from Akinside.] Glasgow: Printed by R. Chapman for A. Macgown, Bookseller. 1804. *Octavo.*

Title as above, Preface, and Contents, vi. pp. Tour, 306 pp. Contains a Map of the District. Sells for 2s. 6d.

A DESCRIPTION of the SCENERY in the LAKE DISTRICT, intended as a Guide to Strangers. By the Rev. WILLIAM FORD, sometime Curate of Wythburn, Keswick. Illustrated with Maps and Plates. London: William Edwards, 12 Ave Maria Lane; Charles Thurnam, Carlisle; John Sinclair, Dumfries. MDCCCXXXVIII. *Duodecimo.*

Title as above, Advertisements, Contents, and Itinerary, vii. pp. Introduction, ix. pp.. Description and Index, 175 pp.

This went through several Editions. The 12th was published in 1849 by Groombridge at 4s., and another in 1850 at 1s. 6d.

The Tourists' New Guide, containing a DESCRIPTION of the LAKES, MOUNTAINS, and SCENERY in CUMBERLAND, WESTMORELAND, and LANCASHIRE, with Account of their Buildings, Towns, and Villages. Being the result of Observations made during a residence of eighteen years in Ambleside and Keswick. By WILLIAM GREEN. In 2 volumes. Vol. I. Kendal: Printed and Published by

R. Lough and Co., and sold by them at the "Chronicle Office," Finkle Street, etc. etc.[1] 1819. *Octavo.*

Title as above, and Preface, xi. pp. Index, viii. pp. Guide, 461 pp.

VOL. II.

Title and Index, ix. pp. Guide, 507. List of Excursions, lv. pp.

Illustrated with 24 aquatints. Published at £2 : 2s. Sells for 6s. 6d.

A DESCRIPTION of a Series of PICTURESQUE VIEWS in the NORTH of ENGLAND. Drawn from Nature, and engraved by WILLIAM GREEN. Manchester : Printed at C. Nicholson and Co.'s Office, 4 Palace Street. 1796. *Post octavo.*

Title as above, Introduction, and Description, 16 pp. Sells for 3s. 6d.

A Description of 60 Studies from Nature, etched in the Soft Ground by WILLIAM GREEN of Ambleside, after Drawings made himself in Cumberland, Westmoreland, and Lancashire, comprising a General Guide to the Beauties of the North of England. London, 1810. *Duodecimo.*

Title, Introduction, and Description, 132 pp. Sells for 3s. 6d.

Reprinted with Etchings in 1814.

Seventy-eight Studies from Nature (in Cumberland, Westmoreland, and Lancashire). Engraved by WILLIAM GREEN, from Drawings made by himself. London, 1809.

Letterpress, 22 pp.

Copies of W. Green's Works are in the Manchester Free Library.

RAMBLES in the LAKE DISTRICT. July 1857. Reprinted from "The Albion," Liverpool. By HARRY HARDKNOT. [H. SHIMMIN.] London : Whittaker and Co., Ave Maria Lane. Liverpool : "The Albion" Office ; H. Young, South Castle Street. 1857. 18*mo.*

Title as above, Dedication, and Rambles, 68 pp. Sells for 1s. 6d.

[1] A long list here of other Booksellers.

SELECT VIEWS of the LAKES in Cumberland, Westmoreland, and Lancashire. From Drawings made by P. HOLLAND. Engraved by C. ROSENBERG.

To Daniel Daulby, Esq. (a Lover of the Arts), the following Views, which owe their Publication to his suggestion and Friendship, are respectfully inscribed by his obliged servant, P. HOLLAND.

Liverpool, Aug. 1, 1792. *Oblong quarto.*

Title as above, followed by 21 Views, with a short description of each of them, printed on the opposite page. Sells for 5s. 6d.

The LAKES of LANCASHIRE, WESTMORELAND, and CUMBERLAND, delineated in 43 Engravings, from Drawings by JOSEPH FARINGTON, R.A.; with DESCRIPTIONS, HISTORICAL, TOPOGRAPHICAL, and PICTURESQUE; the result of a Tour made in the Summer of the Year 1816. By THOMAS HARTWELL HORNE. London, 1816.

Title as above, and Preface, viii. pp. The Lakes, 96 pp.

Map of the Lakes. *Frontispiece.*
South View of Lancaster . . . . Page 2
East View do. 3
Bowness and Lake Windermere 9
Windermere (from Bowness) 10
Do. from Calgarth Park 14
Do. from Low Wood 14
Head of Windermere 15
Ambleside 18
Waterfall at Ambleside 19
Culleth Force 21
Coniston Lake 22
Hawkeshead and Esthwaite Water 23
Waterfall at Rydall 26
Rydal Mere 27
Grassmere 28
Thirlmere 32
Derwent Water from Brough Top 34
Keswick and Skiddaw 36
View on the road from Keswick to Borrowdale . 39

East side of Derwentwater . . . . Page 40
Lowdore Waterfall 41
Skiddaw and Derwentwater 42
The Grange in Borrowdale 43
Castle Crag and Bowderstone 44
Wastdale Village 50
Muncaster Castle and Eskdale 51
Honister Crag 52
Buttermere and Crummock Water 53
Village of Lowswater 55
Cockermouth 56
Maryport 56
Bassenthwaite Lake 57
Saddlebeck and R. Rothay 60
Scene at Nunnery 68
Ulswater from Pooley Bridge 69
Water Millock, and the Lower End of Ulswater . 70
Ulswater and Liulph's Tower 71
Head of Ulswater from Gobarrow Park . . . 73
Head of Patterdale and Helvellyn 76
North-East View of Carlisle 84
View at Gilsland Spa 88
Brougham Castle 94
Hawswater 95

The Engravings are by Middiman, Scott, Byrne, Pye, Landseer, etc. Published at £12 : 12s. in boards. Sells for 15s.

A DESCRIPTIVE TOUR and GUIDE to the Lakes, Caves, Mountains, and other Natural Curiosities in Cumberland, Westmoreland, Lancashire, and a part of the West Riding of Yorkshire. By JOHN HOUSMAN, Esq. The Sixth Edition, embellished with superb Engravings. Carlisle: printed by and for F. Jollie and Sons, and sold by Longman, Hurst, and Co., London, and all other Booksellers. 1814. *Duodecimo.*

Title as above, Advertisement, and Index, viii. pp. Tour, 264 pp. Sells for 3s. 6d.

The First Edition was published in 1800 as part of a work entitled "A Topographical Description of Cumberland, Westmoreland, Lancashire, and a part of the West Riding of Yorkshire," in *octavo,* and contained Title, Address Dedicatory, Index, and Distances of Places, xii. pp. Description, 536 pp. Addenda and Errata, 2 pp.

The Descriptive Tour [1800] contained Title, etc., viii. pp. and 226 pp., and the following

PLATES.

North View of Furness Abbey, *Frontispiece.*
Map of the Soils (coloured and folded), p. vi.
Map of Cumberland Lakes (folded), p. 91.
Map of Lancashire and Westmoreland Lakes (folded), p. 226.

The following editions have appeared :—The second, Carlisle, 1803. The third, 1808. The fourth, 18 . The fifth, 1814. The sixth, as before detailed.

The latter editions, in addition to the Plates before named, contained Plans of Kendal and Lancaster, Views of Ulswater, Borrowdale, Wastwater, Derwentwater, and Basenthwaite.

JENKINSON'S PRACTICAL GUIDE to the ENGLISH LAKE DISTRICT. With Maps. London: Edward Stamford, 6 and 7 Charing Cross, S.W. 1872. *Foolscap octavo.*

Title as above, Preface, Contents, Introduction, Geology, etc., lxiv. pp. Guide and Index, 335 pp. Sells for 3s. 6d.

LEIGH'S GUIDE to the LAKES and MOUNTAINS of CUMBERLAND, WESTMORELAND, and LANCASHIRE. Illustrated with a Map of the Country, and Map of Windermere, Derwentwater, Borrowdale, Ullswater, Grasmere, Rydal Water, and Langdale. Third edition, carefully revised and corrected. London; printed for Leigh and Son, 421 Strand. MDCCCXXXV. Price Seven Shillings. *Royal* 18*mo.*

Title as above, Contents, and Preface, viii. pp. Guide and Index, 160 pp. First edition published in London, N. D. A fourth edition in 1840 at 6s. 6d.

The LAKE COUNTRY. By E. LYON LINTON. (Vignette.) With a Map and One Hundred Illustrations, drawn and Engraved by W. J.

Linton. London: Smith, Elder, and Co., 65 Cornhill. 1864. *Royal octavo.*

Title as above, Contents, List of Illustrations, Preface, Half-title, the Lake Country, Early History, xxx. pp. The Lake Country, and Appendices, 351 pp. Published at 21s., reduced to 10s. 6d.

The SCENERY and POETRY of the ENGLISH LAKES. A Summer Ramble. By CHARLES MACKAV, LL.D., Author of 'Legends of the Isles,' 'The Salamander,' etc. etc. With Illustrations from original Sketches, drawn on Wood by W. Harvey, J. Gilbert, D. H. M'Kewan, D. Cox jun., W. C. Smith, G. Fennel, W. Dickes, W. P. Smith, and E. Gilks. Engraved by Thomas Gilks. London: Longman, Brown, Green, and Longmans, Paternoster Row. MDCCCXLVI. *Post Octavo.*

Title and Preface, ii. pp., 2d Title, with Portraits of Wordsworth, Southey, and Coleridge.

Introductory Matter, xxvi. pp., the Scenery, etc., 235 pp., Tinted Frontispiece (View of Scale Force), and eight large Wood Engravings (not paged), viz.—

Coniston Old Man, page 57.
Colwith Force, „ 63.
Ulleswater, „ 67.
Airey Force, „ 70.
Furness Abbey, „ 100.
Lodore Fall, „ 135.
Stanley Gill, „ 149.
Returning from Border Incursion, 204.

Re-published in 1852 at 7s. 6d. Sells for 4s. 6d.

A Complete GUIDE to the ENGLISH LAKES. By HARRIET MARTINEAU. Illustrated from Drawings by T. L. Aspland and W. Banks. And a Map, coloured Geologically by John Ruthven. To which are added an Account of the Flowering Plants, Ferns, and Mosses of the District; and a complete Directory. Windermere: John Garnett. London: Whittaker and Co. *Duodecimo.*

Half-Title, Engraved Title, Title as above, v. pp. Preface (dated 1855), iii. pp. Contents, ii. pp. Index, iv. pp. List of Illustrations and Guide, 233 pp. Sells for 4s. 6d.

The ENGLISH LAKES, PEAKS, and PASSES from Kendal to Keswick. By GEORGE KING MATTHEW. Kendall: J. Richardson, Printer and Bookseller, "Times" Office, Highgate. 1866. *Foolscap octavo.*

Title as above, and Introduction, x. pp. English Lakes, 207 pp. Index, iv. pp. Folding Map and four Plates of Peaks and Passes.

Rydal Water, *Frontispiece.*

Windermere.	Ferry Vale and Hotel,
Ambleside.	Windermere.

HANDBOOK for WESTMORELAND, CUMBERLAND, and THE LAKES. With a Map. Second Edition. Revised. London: John Murray, Albemarle Street. 1869. *Post octavo.*

Title as above, Preface, Contents, and Introduction, xxxix. pp. Handbook and Index, 134 pp.

The right of Translation reserved. Published at 6s.

A Concise DESCRIPTION of the ENGLISH LAKES and adjacent Mountains, with General Directions to Tourists, Notices of the Botany, Mineralogy, and Geology of the District. Observations on Meteorology, the Floating Island on Derwent Lake, and the Black-lead Mine in Borrowdale. By JONATHAN OTLEY. Keswick: published by the author; by Simpkin and Marshall, Stationers' Hall Court, London, and Arthur Foster, Kirby, Lonsdale. 1838. Sixth Edition. *Duodecimo.*

Title as above, Preface, Contents, and Explanation of Map, viii. pp. The Description and Index, 184 pp.

Folding Map of District sells for 2s. 6d. The First Edition was published at Keswick in 1803, and the Fourth in 1830. Published at 5s.

HANDBOOK to the ENGLISH LAKES. BY JAMES PAYN. Whittaker and Son, London. 1859. 12*mo.* Price 1s. 6d.

LAKE SCENERY of England. By J. B. PYNE. (View of Dungeon Gill Force). Drawn on Stone by T. PICKEN. Published by Day and Son, Lithographers to the Queen, London. *Quarto.*

Half-title, Engraved Title as above, iv. pp. Introduction, vii. pp. List of Plates, i. p. The rest is unpaged. Contains 25 Tinted Plates, exclusive of Woodcuts. [1859].

Published at 21s., Coloured Plates, 42s.

The First Edition was published in 1854 by Ackermann in Folio at £6 : 6s. Proofs, £9 : 9s.

ASCENTS and PASSES in the LAKE DISTRICT of England, being a new Pedestrian and General Guide to the District. By Herman Prior, M.A., late Scholar of Trinity College, Oxford.

"ὀρέων αιπεινὰ κάρηνα
και πηγας ποτομῶν και πισεα ποιηεντα."

London: Simpkin, Marshall, and Co.; Windermere, J. Garnet. 12*mo.*

Title as above, Dedication, and Preface, ix. pp. Contents, v. pp. Introduction and Guide, 269 pp. Index, v. pp. Folding Map of the District.

Published in 1865 at 5s.; reduced in 1871 to 3s. 6d.

A JOURNEY made in the Summer of 1796 through HOLLAND and the WESTERN FRONTIER of GERMANY, with a return down the Rhine. To which are added OBSERVATIONS during a TOUR to the LAKES of LANCASHIRE, WESTMORELAND, and CUMBERLAND. By Ann Radcliffe. London: printed for G. G. and J. Robinson, Paternoster Row. 1795. *Quarto.*

Title as above, Contents, etc., x. pp. Journey, 500 pp.

The writer of the above is best known as the author of "The Mysteries of Udolpho." The above-named work is now scarce. Lowndes only quotes the sale of one copy, which fetched £1 : 3s. A copy is in the Warrington Public Library.

GUIDE to the LAKES of LANCASHIRE, WESTMORELAND, and CUMBERLAND. By John Robinson, D.D., of Clifton, Westmoreland. 1819. *Post octavo.*

Published at 15s. Sells for 4s. 6d.

The ENGLISH LAKE SCENERY from Drawings by T. L. ROWBOTHAM, with descriptions by the Rev. W. J. LOFTIE.

Illustrated with Six Chromo Facsimile of Original Drawings. London: Marcus Ward and Co., 67 Chandos Street, Strand, and Royal Ulster Works, Belfast. 1874. *Quarto.*
Published at 7s. 6d.

The LAKES of ENGLAND. London: published by Sherwood and Co., Paternoster Row; and Hudson and Nicholson, Kendal. 1836. *Duodecimo.*

Title as above, Preface (dated London, April 15, 1836), List of Plates (42), with Map of the Lakes, xii. pp. Contents, 2 pp. The Lakes, 165 pp. (including a List of Subscribers). Engraved Title with a Vignette. Dedicated to the Right Honourable George, Earl of Egremont. By GEORGE TATTERSALL.

The Illustrations are etched on Steel by Mr. W. F. Topham, from original drawings by the author, of which five only refer to Lancashire.

A GUIDE to the MOUNTAINS, LAKES, and N.W. COAST of ENGLAND, descriptive of Natural Scenery, Historical, Archælogical, and Legendary. London: E. Stanford. 1860. *Small octavo.*

Title as above. Scenery, 243 pp., with a Map.
By the Rev. MACKENZIE E. C. WALCOTT, B.D.

RAMBLES in the LAKE COUNTRY and its Borders. By EDWIN WAUGH.

> "And so by many winding nooks he strays
> With willing sport to the wild ocean."
> SHAKSPEARE.

London: Whittaker and Co. 1861. 12*mo.*

Title and Contents, ii. pp. Rambles and Notes, 267 pp. Published at 5s.

A GUIDE to the LAKES. Dedicated to the Lovers of Landscape Studies, and to all who have visited, or intend to visit, the Lakes of Cumberland, Westmoreland, and Lancashire. By the author of "The Antiquities of Furness."

> "Quis non malarum, quas amor curas habet,
> Hæc inter obliviscitur?"

London: printed for Richardson and Urquhart, under the Royal Exchange; and W. Pennington, Kendal. 1778. *Post octavo.*

Title as above, i. p. A Guide, 203 pp. Errata, i. p.

This is the First Edition of Thomas West's "Guide to the Lakes." Published at 2s. 6d. A copy is in the author's library. The Eleventh Edition is as under.

A GUIDE to the LAKES in CUMBERLAND, WESTMORELAND, and LANCASHIRE. By the author of "The Antiquities of Furness." [THOMAS WEST].

> "For Nature here,"
> (And four following lines). *Paradise Lost.*

The Eleventh Edition. Kendal: printed for W. Pennington; and sold by J. Richardson, Royal Exchange, London. 1821. Price 7s. *Octavo.*

Title as above, Preface, Advertisement, and Table of Lakes, vii. pp. Guide, 312 pp.

Frontispiece, Tinted View of Grasmere. Folding Map. Sells for 2s. 6d.

The other Editions were as follows, viz.—Second, 1779; Third, 1784; Fourth, 1789; the Fifth in 1793; the Sixth in 1796; the Seventh in 1799; the Eighth in 1802; the Ninth in 1807 (published at 6s.); and the Tenth in 1812.

The DESCRIPTIVE PART of Mr. WEST'S GUIDE to the Lakes in Cumberland, Westmoreland, and Lancashire. Kendal: printed by W. Pennington; and sold by J. Richardson, Royal Exchange, and W. Clarke, New Bond Street. London. 1809. Price 3s. *Duodecimo.*

Title as above, Advertisement, and Table of the Lakes, iv. pp. A Guide to the Lakes, 149 pp.

The following 16 Views of the Lakes in Cumberland and Westmoreland, drawn by J. SMITH and J. EARNES, engraved (in aquatinta) by S. ATKEN, are often bound with West's "Guides to the Lakes." They were published at £1 : 1s.—

1. Vale of Lonsdale.
2. Coniston.
3. Windermere Great Island.
4. „ from Calgarth.
5. Elter Water.
6. Stock Gill Force.
7. Upper Cascade, Rydal.
8. Rydal Water.
9. Grasmere Lake.
10. Leathes Water.
11. Derwentwater from Castle-Crag.
12. Derwentwater from Ormathwaite.
13. Buttermere.
14. Lowes Water.
15. Ullswater, Upper End.
16. „ towards Gowbarrow.

SELECT VIEWS in CUMBERLAND, WESTMORELAND, and LANCASHIRE. By the Rev. JOSEPH WILKINSON, Rector of East and West Wretham, in the County of Norfolk, and Chaplain to the Marquis of Huntly. London: published for the Rev. Joseph Wilkinson by R. Ackermann at his Repository of Arts, 101 Strand. 1810.

Harrison and Rutter, printers, 373 Strand. *Royal folio.*

Title as above, Contents, and Dedication, vi. pp. Introduction, xxxiv. pp. Views (and letterpress at the end of volume), 46 pp.

Contains 48 tinted chalk Etchings. The Lancashire Views are—

The Vale Lun.
South View of Furness Abbey.
Penny Bridge between Ulverston and Coniston.
Coniston Water.
Coniston Head.
View of Banks of Coniston Water.
Esthwaite Water.
View of Winandermere.
View on Winandermere.

Published at £6 : 6s. Sells for 21s. A Second Edition published in 1821.

The Introduction was written by William Wordsworth, and published as part of his works in 1820.

TOURS to the BRITISH MOUNTAINS, with the Descriptive Poems of Lowther and Emont Vale. By THOMAS WILKINSON. [4 lines of Poetry.] London: printed for Taylor and Hessey, 93 Fleet Street, and 13 Waterloo Place, Pall Mall. 1824. *Octavo.*

Title as above, Advertisement, and Preface, viii. pp. Tours, etc., 320 pp.
Only a portion of this volume refers to the English Lakes. Sells for 2s. 6d.

A GUIDE through the DISTRICT of the LAKES in the NORTH of ENGLAND, with a Description of the Scenery, etc., for the use of Tourists and Residents. Fifth Edition. With considerable additions. By WILLIAM WORDSWORTH. Kendal: published by Hudson and Nicholson; and in London by Longman and Co., Moxon and Whittaker, and Co. 1837. *Foolscap octavo.*

Title as above, and Contents, iv. pp. Directions and Information for the Tourist, xxiv. pp. Description, etc., 139 pp. A Folding Map. Published at 4s. Sells for 2s. 6d.

It has been several times republished. By Whittaker in 1842, 12mo, 5s., with Plates, 7s. 6d. In 1849, edited by Sedgwick, 7s. 6d. In 1853, edited by Hudson, in 12mo, 5s.

The History of the LATE CONSPIRACY against the King and the Nation, with a particular account of the LANCASHIRE PLOT, and all the other attempts and machinations of the disaffected Party since his Majesty's Accession to the Throne. Extracted out of the original Information of the Witnesses, and other authentick Papers. London: Printed for Daniel Brown at the Black Swan and Bible, without the Temple-Bar, and Tho. Barnet, at the Half-Moon, in St. Paul's Churchyard. MDCXCVI. *Octavo.*

Title as above, 1 p. History, 195 pp. Sells for 7s. 6d.
This work, which is in favour of the Pretender, was written by JAMES ABBADIE, Dean of Killaloe, in Ireland.

The LANCASHIRE GAZETTEER, or Alphabetical arranged Account of the Hundreds, Market Towns, Boroughs, Parishes, Townships, Hamlets, Gentlemen's Seats, Rivers, Lakes, Mountains, Moors, Commons, Mosses, Antiquities, etc., in the County Palatine of Lancaster; together with Historical Descriptions of the Chief Places, with the Fairs, Markets, Local and Metropolitan Distances, Charters, Church Livings, Patrons, Population of every Township, etc. The 2d Edition. By

Joseph Aston. London: Published by Longman, Hurst, Rees, Orme, and Brown; and in Manchester by the Author, at the "Exchange Herald" Office. 1822. *Post octavo.*

Title as above, Preface, Introduction, and Ecclesiastical Jurisdiction, xii. pp. The Gazetteer, 176 pp. (not numbered.)

This work contains a folding Map of Lancashire, a Statistical View of the County, and a Table of Distances from Town to Town. Sells for 3s. 6d.

The 1st Edition was published in 1808. The additions in the 2d Edition were—The Population according to the Census of 1821; the notification of Parish to which each Township belongs; and the value of Church Livings.

LANCASHIRE ILLUSTRATED, from Original Drawings by S. Austin, J. Harwood, G. and C. Pyne, etc. etc., with Historical and Topographical Descriptions. [View of Seacome Slip, Liverpool.] London: Henry Fisher, Son, and Peter Jackson. 1832. *Quarto.*

Engraved Title as above, second Title, Preface, and List of Illustrations, vi. pp. Descriptions, 112 pp.

Illustrations.

Abercrombie Square, Liverpool.
Andrew's, St., Scotch Kirk, Rodney Street, Liverpool.
Ashton Hall.
Ashton-under-Lyne.
Baths, New, George Parade.
Ball-room, Town-Hall, Liverpool.
Birch House.
Birkenhead.
Blackrock Fort.
Brunswick Chapel, Liverpool.
Cemetery, St. James', Liverpool.
Chetham Hospital, Manchester.
Childswall Abbey.
Church of the School for the Blind, Liverpool.
Collegiate Church, Manchester.
Conishead Priory.
Cotton Factories, Manchester.
County House of Correction.
Duke's Dock and Warehouses.
Estwaite Water.
Exchange, The, Manchester.
Exchange, Newsroom, Liverpool.
Fairfield, Manchester.
Foxholes.
Friends' Meeting-House, Manchester.
Furness Abbey.
Garrett Hall.
George III., Statue of, Liverpool.
George's, St., Church, Everton.
George's, St., Church, Hulme.
George's, St., Church, Liverpool.

George's, St., Crescent and Castle Street, Liverpool.
Goree Warehouses, The, Liverpool.
Haigh Hall, Wigan.
Hale Hall.
Hall-i'-th'-Wood.
Halton Hall.
Heaton Hall.
Hornby Castle.
Hulme Hall.
Hulton Hall.
Infirmary, etc., Manchester.
Irlam Hall.
Irwell Street Methodist Chapel, Salford.
Knowsley Hall (2 views).
Lancaster.
Liverpool Royal Institution.
Liverpool, 5 views of.
Liverpool, Lord Street, 2 views of.
Low Hill.
Luke's, St., Church, Liverpool (2 views).
Lycæum Newsroom, Liverpool.
Market, St. John's, Liverpool (2 views).
Market Street, Manchester (3 views).
Market Street, Wigan.
Market Place, The Old, Bolton.
Mary's, St., Church, Prescot.
Matthew's, St., Church, Manchester.
Michael, St., Church, Liverpool.
More Street, Liverpool.
Nicholas', St., Church, Liverpool.
New Bailey Prison, etc., Salford.
New Jerusalem Church, Manchester.
Paul's, St., Church, Liverpool.
Philip's, St., Church, Salford.
Preston, from Penwarthan Hill.
Preston Market Place.
Prince's Dock, Liverpool.
Roby Hall.
Roscoe, the House in which he was born.
Royal Amphitheatre, Liverpool.
Scotch Chapel, Liverpool.
Session House, Liverpool.
Speke Hall.
Steam-Engine Manufactory, etc., Bolton.
Storrs, Windermere Lake.
Teviot Dale Chapel, Stockport.
Todmorden Hall.
Town Hall, Liverpool.
Town Hall, Salford.
Tunnel Entrance to Edge Hill.
Turton Tower.
Twist Factory, Manchester.
Unitarian Chapel, Liverpool.
Warrington Church.
Water Street, Liverpool.
Waverline Hall.
Wellington Rooms, Liverpool.
Wesleyan Chapel, Liverpool.
Wigan Market Place.

Published in 1829 at £1 : 18s.; large paper, £2 : 18s. Sells for 12s. Again published in 1831.

The LITERATURE of the LANCASHIRE DIALECT. A Bibliographical Essay. By WILLIAM and A. AXON, F.R.S.L. London: Trübner and Co., 8 and 60 Paternoster Row. 1870.

Title as above, etc., Essay, 23 pp. A valuable handbook.

HISTORY of the COUNTY PALATINE and DUCHY of LANCASTER. By EDWARD BAINES, Esq., M.P. The biographical department by W. R. Whatton, Esq., F.S.A. VOL. I. Fisher, Son, and Co., London, Paris, and New York. MDCCCXXXVI. *Quarto.*

Title as above, Preface, and Contents, xviii. pp. List of Plates, Dedication, and Advertisement, viii. pp., History, 624 pp.

LIST OF PLATES.

Edward Baines, Esq., M.P.	*To face Title.*
Antique Helmet of Bronze found at Ribchester	To face p. 20.
Map of Lancashire according to Domesday Survey	„ 92.
John of Gaunt, Duke of Lancaster	„ 137.
Seals of County Palatine and Duchy of Lancashire	„ 192.
Autographs of Lancashire Lieutenancy in the Reign of Elizabeth	„ 518.

VOL. II.

Title, Contents, vi. pp., History, 3—, 680 pp.

LIST OF PLATES.

Map of Lancashire.	*To face Title.*
Plan of Manchester	P. 149
Roman Antiquities, Plate 1	161
„ „ „ 2	158
„ „ „ 3	158
„ „ „ iv.	160
View of Manchester	192
Exterior of the Collegiate Church, Manchester	193
Interior of the Collegiate Church, Manchester	200
John Bradford	243
Francis Egerton, Duke of Bridgewater	304
Exchange, Manchester	321
Town Hall, „	344
Hulme Hall	352
Humphrey Chetham	365
Messrs. Swainson, Birley, and Co.'s Factory	397
Richard Arkwright	P. 429
Hargrave's Spinning Jenny	432
Spinning Machines, Mule, Jenny and Throstles	442
Carding, Drawing, and Roving	444
Mule Spinning	452
Power-Loom	467
„ „ Weaving	468
Calico-Printing	475
Stockport	483
Patent Machines and Cotton Manufacture	521
Sir Ashton Lever	565
Blue-Coat School, Oldham	578
Bishop Oldham	580
Scaitcliffe, the Seat of John Crossley, Esq.	649
The Right Hon. Sir Robert Peel, Bart.	660
Sir Robert Peel, Bart.	671

Pedigrees.

Ashton of Ashton . .	P. 532	Crossley of Crossley .	P. 649
„ „ Chadderton .	591	Egerton of Heaton House	563
Anderton of Middleton .	596	Eland and Savile . .	620
Barlow of Barlow . .	396	Hopwood of Hopwood .	611
Barons of Manchester .	172-3	Hulme of Hulme . .	394
Birch of Birch . .	531	Lever of Alkrington .	566
Byron of Clayton . .	616-17	Mosley of Ancoats . .	352-3
Chadwick of Chadwick .	655	Prestwick of Hulme .	393
Chetham of Chetham .	395	Radcliffe of Ordsall .	352-3

Vol. III.

Title and Contents, iv. pp. List of Plates and Pedigree, and History, 760 pp.

List of Plates.

James Stanley, 7th Earl of Derby, and Charlotte de la Tremouille . .	*To face Title.*	Stonyhurst College . .	P. 372
Farnworth Paper-Mill .	P. 42	Gillibrand Hall . .	423
Smithell's Hall . .	45	Rufford Old Hall . .	431
Samuel Crompton . .	72	Rufford New Hall . .	432
Hall-i'-th'-Wood, near Bolton	73	Shaw Hall . . .	451
Rivington Pike . .	97	Houghton Towers . .	459
Worsley Hall . .	143	William Roscoe . .	523
Panel Sculpture, originally in Hulme Hall (2 plates)	144-145	The Parish Church of Wigan	537
James Brindley . .	147	Sir Thomas Tyldesley .	610
Whalley Abbey . .	178	Facsimile of Inscription on Winwick Church .	618
Moreton Hall . .	192	Winwick Church . .	623
Clitheroe . . .	205	Warrington Market Place	670
Clitheroe Castle . .	209	Sankey Viaduct . .	682
Wycoller Hall, Christmas, 1650	244	J. P. Kemble, Esq. . .	696
Townley Hall . .	253	Windleshaw Abbey . .	712
Huntroyd Hall . .	309	Bold Hall . . .	717
Fenniscowles . .	310	Monument of Richard Bold, and Anne, his Wife .	723
Walton-le-dale . .	346	Bishop Smith . .	724
Walton Hall . . .	348	Speke Hall . . .	756

PEDIGREES.

Anderton of Euxton and Lostock . . . P. 452-453
Banister of Bank . 406
" of Leven and Whalley 190
Bold of Bold . . 717
Bothe of Boothe or Barton 113, 114
Bradshaw of Haigh . 553
Butler of Bewsey . . 660
Clayton of Clayton-le-Woods 467
Entwistle of Entwistle . 95
Faryngton of Farnyton 446, 447
Gerard of Bryn . . 641
Hesketh of Rufford . 426, 427
Heywood of Little Lever . 85
Hoghton of Hoghton Tower 348
" of Pendleton . 230
Hulton of Hulton . . 40, 41
Hyde of Denton . . 167
Ireland of Hutte . . 753
Johnson and Ormerod of Tildesley . . . 609
Kenyon of Kenyon . P. 634
Lacy, Lords of Clitheroe . 207
Langton, Baron of Newton 642
Lathom of Parbold . 479
Legh of Lyme and Haydock 644
Norreys of Davy Hulme . 128
" of Speke . . 754
Nowell of Reed . . 303
Ormerod of Tildesley . 609
Orrell of Orrell . . 91
Osbaldeston of Osbaldeston 343
Pilkington of Pilkington . 104
" of Rivington . 105
Radclyffe of Radcliffe Tower 6
Rigby of Hartooke . . 481
Sherburne of Stonyhurst 572, 573
Southwork of Samlesbury 354
Standish of Duxbury . 519
Starkie of Huntroyd . 309
Tildesley of Tildesley . 608
Trafford of Trafford 110, 111

VOL. IV.

Title and Contents, iv. pp. List of Plates and Pedigrees, History, Appendix, Additions, and Corrections, and General Index, 876 pp.

LIST OF PLATES.

Liverpool from Toxteth Park. *To face Title.*
Knowsley Hall . . P. 11
Thomas Stanley, 1st Earl of Derby . . . 12
Sir William Stanley, K.G. 19
The Right Hon. E. G. Stanley 20
Croxteth Hall . . 28
Plan of Liverpool and its Environs . . . 55
The Ancient Wishing-Gate, Liverpool . . . P. 68
Liverpool from the Mersey (4 plates) . . . 94, 142
Town-Hall, Liverpool . 144
Right Hon. William Huskisson . . . 147
Blue-Coat School, Liverpool 172
Interior of Exchange Newsroom, Liverpool . . 173

The New Custom-House, Liverpool . . . P. 174
Interior of St. John's Market, Liverpool . . . 175
Interior of Sefton Church 205
Lathom House . . 255
Preston, View of . . 293
Plan of Town of Preston in 1715 . . . 323
N. Grimshaw, Esq. . . 352
H. Fisher, Esq. . . 359
Red Scar . . . 372
Cardinal Allen . . 441
The Vale of Lonsdale . 474
Lancaster, View of . . 482
" Castle, Court-House, and Church . . 516
Quernmore Park . . 547
Dunald Mill Hole . . P. 568
Borwick Hall . . 583
Halton Rectory . . 584
Halton Hall . . . 587
Hornby Castle . . 595
Chapter House, Furness Abbey 627
Furness Abbey . . 633
Lancaster Sands from Lindell 636
Pile of Fouldrey Castle . 666
Coniston Water . . 701
Windermere Lake . . 702
Esthwaite Water . . 703
Cartmel Church . . 715
Newby Bridge . . 717
Holker Hall . . . 733
Bigland Hall . . . 734
Ulverston and Cartmel Sands 736

PEDIGREES.

Bigland of Bigland . . P. 734
Blundell of Crosby . . 218
Booth of Skelmersdale . 247
Booth of Kirkland . . 471
Clifton of Clifton . 404, 405
Dalton of Thurnham . 543
Earls and Dukes of Lancaster 751
Fleetwood of Poulton . 440
Fleming of Aldingham . 648
Harrington of Aldingham and Hornby . . . P. 648
Kings of England . . 751
Langton of Broughton Tower 409
Molineux, Earl of Sefton 216, 217
Plumbe-Tempest of Aughton 230
Preston of Cockerham . 658
Stanley, Earls of Derby . 10, 11
Torbock of Torbock . 616
Wall of Preston . . 375
Westly of Mowbreck . P. 452

Published at £10 : 10s. Large paper, £17 : 10s. Proofs on India paper, £21. Sells for £9. Large paper copies on India paper as high as £18 : 18s.

The original MSS. of Baines are in Dr. Shepherd's Library, Preston. They are bound in 59 volumes.

Edward Baines was born at Walton-le-dale on 5th February 1774, and was apprenticed to a printer in Preston (where his father was then living). He afterwards went to Leeds, where he became the proprietor of the "Leeds Mercury." In 1815 he published "The History of the Wars of the French Revolution," etc., of which 25,000 copies were sold. In 1834 he was elected M.P. for Leeds. He died on the 3d August 1848, and was interred in the Leeds Cemetery.

The HISTORY of the COUNTY PALATINE and DUCHY of LANCASTER. By the late EDWARD BAINES, Esq. The Biographical Department by the late W. R. WHATTON, F.S.A. A new and revised and improved edition. Edited by JOHN HARLAND, F.S.A.

Editor of the Lancashire Lieutenancy, etc.; Ballads and Songs of Lancashire, etc.; Lancashire Lyrics; Mamecestre; Collectanea relating to Manchester and Neighbourhood; Manchester Court Leet Records; House and Farm Accounts of the Shuttleworths of Gawthorpe; Salley Abbey; Charters and Muniments of Clitheroe; Autobiography of William Stout of Lancaster, etc.; Joint Editor of a History of Preston Guild; of Lancashire Folk-Lore, etc. etc.

VOL. I.

London: George Routledge and Sons, The Broadway; Manchester: L. C. Gent. 1868. *Quarto.*

Half-Title, Title as above, Dedication, Introduction, and Contents, xvi. pp. History, Addenda, and Index, 690 pp. Contains Map of Lancashire, from the Ordnance Survey, brought up to 1868.

VOL. II.

Half-Title, Title, To the Memory of John Harland, F.S.A., Introduction, and Contents, xii. pp. History, Appendices, and Index, 729 pp. (Published in 1870.)

Mr. Harland died on the 23d April 1868, and the work of completing this volume fell to the Rev. Brooke Herford.

This edition contains no plates or pedigrees. Published at £3 : 15s. Sells for £2.

HISTORY, DIRECTORY, and GAZETTEER of the COUNTY PALATINE of LANCASTER; with a variety of Commercial and Statistical Information, in two Volumes. Illustrated with Maps and Plans. By EDWARD BAINES. The Directory Department by W. PARSON.

VOL. I.

Liverpool: Published by W. Wales and Co., "Advertiser Office," 68 Castle Street. Sold also by Longman, Hurst, and Co., Paternoster Row, London, and all other Booksellers. 1824. *Octavo.*

Title as above, Contents, and Preface, viii. pp. General History of the County, p. 1 to p. 146. History and Directory, p. 147 to p. 658. Additions and Alterations, 659, 660.

VOL. II.

Title (1825), Advertisement, Contents of Vol. II., History and Directory, General Index, and Index of Places, 744 pp. Sells for 3s. 6d.

LANCASHIRE and CHESHIRE, PAST and PRESENT. A History and a Description of the Palatine Counties of Lancaster and Chester, forming the North-western Division of England. From the earliest ages to the present time. [1867.] By THOMAS BAINES, Member of the Historic Society of Lancashire and Cheshire, and author of "The History of Liverpool." With an account of the Rise and Progress of Manufactures and Commerce, and Civil and Mechanical Engineering in these Districts. By WILLIAM FAIRBAIRN, LL.D., F.R.S., Corresponding Member of the Institute of France; President of the Literary and Philosophical Society of Manchester, etc. etc. With numerous Illustrations from the original Drawings by H. Warren, R.A., and a series of Portraits.

VOL. I.

William Mackenzie, 22 Paternoster Row, London; Liverpool, 14 Great George Street; Manchester, 59 Dale Street; Leeds, 27 Park Square; Carlisle, 3 Earl Street. *Royal quarto.*

Half-Title, Engraved Title (with view of Halton Castle), iv. pp. Title as above, and Address, 4 pp. Lancashire and Cheshire, and Contents, 720 pp.

LIST OF PLATES.

Thomas Baines, F.S.A., *Frontispiece.*

Right Hon. Edward Geoffrey Stanley, Earl of Derby, K.G.

Richard Cobden.

Liverpool.

Beeston Castle.
Worsley Hall.
The Right Hon. W. E. Gladstone.
The Right Hon. Lord Stanley.
Furness Abbey.
Lancaster.
Speke Hall.
Chester.

VOL. II.

Half-Title, Engraved Title, with View of Dutton Viaduct, Title, v. pp. Lancashire and Cheshire, and Contents, 464 pp. The Rise and Progress of Manufactures and Commerce, etc., Title-page, and Introduction, iv. pp. The Rise and Progress, and Contents, cclx. pp.

LIST OF PLATES.

William Fairbairn, LL.D., F.R.S.
John Bright, Esq.
Eaton Hall.
Preston.
Town-Hall, Preston.
Exchange Buildings, Liverpool.
Macclesfield.
Manchester New Town-Hall.
Plan, etc., Manchester Water-Works.
„ „ Liverpool Landing-Stage, George's Pier.
Plan of Barrow Docks.
„ „ Turret-Ship.
„ „ Combing Machine, etc.

Published in four Divisions, £10 : 10s. Sells for £3 : 10s. This work has no Index.

WALKS in SOUTH LANCASHIRE, and on its Borders. With Letters, Descriptions, Narratives, and Observations, current and incidental. By SAMUEL BAMFORD.

Blackley, near Manchester. Published by the Author. 1844. In two vols. Sells for 6s.

The LANCASHIRE and CHESHIRE HISTORICAL COLLECTION. Edited by T. WORTHINGTON BARLOW, F.L.S.

VOL. I.

London: W. Kent and Co.; Manchester: Burge and Perrin, 1853. *Octavo.*

Title as above, and Dedication, iii. pp. Historical Collection and Index, 140 pp. *Frontispiece*, View of Holmes Chapel.

VOL. II.

Title, Historical Collection, and Index, 116 pp. *Frontispiece*, Portrait of Broome, the Cheshire Poet.

Published in monthly parts. Is now scarce. A copy is in the Manchester Free Library.

T. W. Barlow was a barrister, and lived at Holmes Chapel, in Cheshire, of which place he wrote a history. He accepted a Government appointment to the West Coast of Africa, where he died not many years ago.

DOM. BOC. A TRANSLATION of the Record called DOMESDAY, so far as relates to the County of York, including also AMOUNDERNESS, LONSDALE, and FURNESS, in LANCASHIRE; and such parts of Westmoreland and Cumberland as are contained in the Survey. Also the Counties of Derby, Nottingham, Rutland, and Lincoln, with an Introduction, Glossary, and Indexes. By the Rev. WILLIAM BAWDWEN, Vicar of Hooton Pagnell, Yorkshire.

"Neque puto alibi in orbe."—SELDEN.
[And three following lines].

Doncaster: printed by W. Sheardown, High Street, at his office, High Street Buildings; and sold by Messrs. Longman, Hurst, and Rees, Paternoster Row, London. 1809. *Quarto.*

Title as above, Dedication, and List of Subscribers, xviii. pp. Introduction, xxxi. pp. Dom. Boc. Yorkshire, and part of Lancashire, pp. 1 to 286. Derby, etc. pp. 287 to 628, including Half-titles for each County. Glossary and Indexes, 61 pp. List of Errata on last page.

Published at £2 : 2s. Sells for £1 : 1s.

William Bawdwen, the son of William Bawdwen, attorney of Stone Gap, in Craven, Yorkshire, was born 9th March 1762. He took holy orders, and was appointed Vicar of Hooton Pagnell, near Doncaster where he died 14th September 1816.

A LITERAL EXTENSION and TRANSLATION of the portion of DOMESDAY BOOK relating to CHESHIRE and LANCASHIRE, and to part of Flintshire and Denbighshire, Cumberland, Westmoreland,

and Yorkshire; with an Introduction and Notes by WILLIAM BEAMONT, Esquire, to accompany the Facsimile. The original, Photo-Zincographed under the direction of Col. Sir H. James, R.E., and F.R.S. Chester: Marshall and Hughes, publishers and photographers, Eastgate Row, London; Vacher and Sons, 29 Parliament Street. 1863. *Imperial quarto.*

Title as above and Dedication, iv. pp. List of Subscribers and Introduction, xxxii. pp. Domesday Book, 91 pp. The Lancashire portion, pp. 74-91.

Sold to Subscribers only. £1 : 11 : 6.

A DISCOURSE of the WAR in LANCASHIRE. Edited by WILLIAM BEAMONT, Esq. Printed for the Chetham Society. MDCCCLXIV. *Foolscap quarto.*

Chetham Society's Title and List of Council, 2 pp. Title as above, and Preface, xxxiv. pp. List of Illustrations, i. p. A Discourse of the War, Notes, and Index, 164 pp.

ILLUSTRATIONS.

Portrait of James, seventh Earl of Derby, *Frontispiece.*
View of Buckshawe Hall, to face p. 1.

The author of this vivid picture of the Civil War is believed to be Major Edward Robinson of Kirkham, and afterwards of Buckshawe in Leyland.

A REPORT of the State of AGRICULTURE in LANCASHIRE, with observations on the political position and general prospects of the Agricultural Classes, and a Tabular Statement of the prices of corn, and wages of husbandry, etc. at various periods since the Norman Conquest. By GEORGE BEESLEY, land-agent. MDCCCXLIX. Preston: Dobson and Son; J. Walkden, Blackburn, etc. etc. *Octavo.*

Title as above, and Report, 75 pp. Appendix, and a Tabular Statement, vii. pp.

A copy is in the Manchester Free Library.

NOTES on the AGRICULTURE of LANCASHIRE, with Suggestions for its Improvement. By JONATHAN BINNS. Preston: Dobson and Son, 17 Market Place; Simpkin, Marshall, and Co., London. MDCCCLI. *Octavo.*

Title, i. p. Introduction and Notes, 161 pp. Index, 1 p.

BINNS' LANCASHIRE COLLECTION. This consists of thirty folio volumes, which are deposited in the Liverpool Free Public Library. They contain the magnificent collection of Prints, Maps, Portraits, Arms, etc., collected by Thomas Binns of Liverpool, and are arranged as follows:—

Volume 1. Miscellaneous Maps, Plans, etc.
„ 2, 3, and 4. The Hundred of Salford.
„ 5. „ „ „ Amounderness.
„ 6, 7, and 8. „ „ „ Salford.
„ 9, 10, 11, 12, and 13. The Hundred of West Derby.
„ 14 to 20. Portraits.
„ 21 to 23. „ of Monarchs.
„ 24. Statuary and other Antiquities at Ince Blundell.
„ 25 to 27. Appendix.
„ 28 to 29. Engravings, Etchings, etc., in the collection of Henry Blundell, Esq., at Ince.
„ 30. Monandrian Plants of the Order Scitarminæ, chiefly drawn from the Specimens in the Liverpool Botanic Gardens.

There are two smaller volumes containing Indexes to the above.

The BEAUTIES of ENGLAND and WALES, or Original Delineations, TOPOGRAPHICAL, HISTORICAL, and DESCRIPTIVE of EACH COUNTY. Embellished with Engravings. By JOHN BRITTON, F.S.A.

VOL. IX.

[Two verses of Poetry].

London: printed by Thomas Maiden, Sherbourn Lane, for Vernon, Wood, and Sharp, etc. etc. 1807. *Octavo.*

Engraved Title, with Sketch of Roman Altar at Lancaster, and Title as above, iii. pp. Dedication and Introductory Observations, viii. pp. The Beauties, etc., 808 pp. List of Books, Maps, and Prints, etc.

Index (not paged), and corrections to the preceding volume, 31 pp. The Lancashire portion includes p. 1 to p. 312.

PLATES referring to Lancashire.

Lancaster .	*To face* p.	51
Furness Abbey . .	„	85
Ashton Hall . .	„	103
Townley Hall . .	„	144
Liverpool from the Ferry	„	179
The Exchange Building, Liverpool . .	„	199
Allerton Hall . .	„	215
Town Hall, Liverpool	„	201
Hulme Hall .	*To face* p.	285
The College at Manchester . .	„	260
The College Church, view of Choir .	„	264
Heaton House . .	„	287
Newby Bridge . .	„	298
Gilead House . .	„	305
Pooley House . .	„	312

Complete in 18 volumes (generally bound in 26 volumes). Sells for £7 : 7s. Large paper copies fetch a much higher price.

The above volume alone sells for 7s. 6d.

A Compendious HISTORY and DESCRIPTION of the NORTH UNION RAILWAY, comprising an Introductory Sketch, the perspective advantages of the Railway; its statistics; a delineation of the operations which have marked its progress; a detailed reference to all the important features of the route—viz. the Tunnels, Viaducts, Gradients, Localities, etc.; also a List of Fares from Preston to Liverpool or Manchester, and all intermediate places. By E. C. BULLER.

"What cannot art and industry perform,
When Science plans the progress of the Soil."

Preston: printed by Wilcockson and Dobson, "Chronicle" Office. MDCCCXXXVIII. *Duodecimo.*

A STATISTICAL SKETCH of the COUNTY PALATINE of LANCASTER. By EDWIN BUTTERWORTH. London: published by Longman and Co.; Bancks and Co., Manchester; Wareing Webb, Liverpool; D. Evans, Oldham. 1841. *Duodecimo.*

Title as above, Dedication, and Preface, vi. pp. A Statistical Sketch of Lancashire, p. vii. to p. xl. A (second) Statistical Sketch of Lancashire and Index, 168 pp.

Published at 4s. 6d. Sells for 3s. 6d.

Bearing upon this subject are the two following pamphlets by HENRY ASHWORTH, Esq., of Turton, near Bolton—viz. "Statistical Illustrations of the Past and Present State of Lancashire, and more particularly of the Hundred of Salford," from the Journal of the Statistical Society, 1842, and "Historical Data chiefly relating to South Lancashire and the Cotton Manufacture." Manchester. 1866.

Edwin Butterworth commenced a "Concise History of Lancashire," of which the first part was published in 1845. It was never completed.

LANCASHIRE CHARITIES.

ENDOWED CHARITIES. FURTHER RETURN to an Order of the Honourable the House of Commons, dated 26th July 1867, for copies "of the General Digest of Endowed Charities for the Counties and Cities mentioned in the Fourteenth Report of the Charity Commissioners." "And of the Charities vested in the various London Companies in so far as such Digests have been completed, or can be completed, up to the time of publication."

COUNTY OF LANCASTER.

(Lord Robert Montagu).

Ordered by the House of Commons to be printed 19th March 1869. [91-92, price 1s. 4d.] *Folio.*

Title, i. p. (Explanation of Terms on a Slip), Half-title, and General Digest, 117 pp.

III.

FURTHER REPORT of the Commissioners appointed in pursuance of two several Acts of Parliament. The one made and passed in the 58th year of His late Majesty, cap. 91, intituled, "An Act for appointing Commissioners to inquire concerning Charities in England for the Education of the Poor;" and the other made and passed in the 59th year of His late Majesty, cap. 81, intituled, "An Act to Amend an Act of the last Session for appointing Commissioners to inquire concerning Charities in England for the Education of the Poor; and to extend the power thereof to other charities in England and Wales."

Dated 15th January 1820.

No. 5. The Hundred of Lonsdale, p. 181 to p. 229.

XI.

FURTHER REPORT, etc. Dated 25th June 1824.

The Hundred of Amounderness, p. 221 to p. 364.

XV.

FURTHER REPORT, etc. Dated 23d January 1826. No. 383.

Hundreds of Blackburn, Lonsdale, and Leyland, p. 5 to p. 322.

XVI.

FURTHER REPORT, etc.

Hundred of Salford, p. 83 to p. 244.

XIX.

FURTHER REPORT, etc. Dated 26th January 1828. No. 374.

Hundreds of West Derby and Salford, p. 115 to p. 296.

XX.

FURTHER REPORT, etc. Dated 12th July 1828. No. 19.

Hundred of West Derby, p. 83 to p. 231.

XXI.

FURTHER REPORT, etc. Dated 31st January 1829. No. 349.

Hundreds of West Derby, Lonsdale, and Salford, p. 217 to p. 322.

XXXI.

FURTHER REPORT, etc. Dated 4th February 1837.

Parish of Claughton (Crofts' Charity), p. 778.

APPENDIX.

Hundred of Lonsdale (Parish of Coulton and Dalton in-Furness), p. 150 to 160.

An INDEX to the REPORTS of the Commissioners for inquiring concerning Charities, etc. London. 1840.

1 volume. This contains the names of all the Founders of Charities, and the names of the places to which the Charities belong.

The whole of the Reports, 1819 to 1839, and the Index, are in the Manchester Free Library. A few copies (in accordance with a recommendation of the Commission) of the portions relating to Lancashire were bound in one volume, paged in manuscript, and a printed Index added. This volume sells for 21s. It contains 1150 pp. A copy is in the Author's Library.

The NEW LANCASHIRE GAZETTEER, or Topographical Dictionary, containing an accurate description of the several Hundreds, Boroughs, Market Towns, Parishes, Townships, and Hamlets, in the County Palatine of Lancaster, exhibiting—

The bearing and distance of each place from the nearest Post-office town, and the amount of its population according to the census taken in 1821; the valuation and patrons of Ecclesiastical Benefices, and their amount in the king's books; the Monastic Foundations, Antiquities, Grammar Schools, Hospitals, Markets, and Fairs, Corporations, Petty Sessions, and Assizes; Seats of the Nobility and Gentry; with various Local, Historical, Commercial, and Agricultural Information, and Biographical Notices of eminent natives deceased.

Collected from the most Authentic Sources, and alphabetically arranged by STEPHEN REYNOLDS CLARKE, author of "Conversations on the History of England." London: printed for Henry Teesdale and Co., 302 Holborn. 1830. *Octavo.*

Title as above, and Preface, v. pp. Gazetteer, etc., 192 pp.
Published at 10s. Sells for 3s. 6d.

A LIST of the GENTLEMEN who have served the office of HIGH SHERIFF for the COUNTY PALATINE of LANCASTER from the first year of Henry the Second, 1154, to the present year [1830]. Lancaster: printed and sold by C. Clark, Market Place. Price 6d. *Duodecimo.*

Title as above, and List, 17 pp. Scarce.

A similar List up to the year 1819 was prepared by "Tim Bobbin" (J. Collier), and will be found in his collected works.

A TOPOGRAPHICAL and STATISTICAL DESCRIPTION of the COUNTY of LANCASTER, containing an account of its Situation, Extent, Towns, Rivers, Lakes, Mines, Fisheries, Manufactures, Trade, Commerce, Agriculture, Curiosities, Antiquities, Natural History, Civil and Ecclesiastical Jurisdiction, etc. To which are prefixed the direct and principal cross roads, distances of stages, and Noblemen and Gentlemen's Seats; also a list of the Markets and Fairs, and an Index Table, exhibiting at one view the distances of all the towns from London, and of towns from each other. The whole forming a complete County Itinerary. By G. A. Cooke, Esq. Illustrated with a Map of the County. London: printed by assignment from the Executors of the late C. Cooke, for Sherwood, Neely, and Jones, Paternoster Row. Sold by all Booksellers. *Duodecimo.*

Title as above, and Contents, ii. pp. Description of the County, 355 pp. Index, 5 pp.

Published at 4s.; now of little value.

The HISTORY of LANCASHIRE. By J. Corry, Honorary Member of the Philological Society in Manchester.

Vol. I.

London: published by Geo. B. Whittaker. *Quarto.*

Title as above, Dedication, Contents, vi. pp. History, 616 pp.

List of Plates.

Gateway Tower of Lancaster Castle	*To face* p. 152
Collegiate Church Tower, Manchester	" 232
Old Healey Hall	*To face* p. 268
Chadwick Hall	" *Ibid.*
Manchester Exchange	" 276
Braddyl's arms	" 449

Three Plates of Arms at the end of volume, and a view of Ruins of Furness Abbey.

Vol. II.

Title and Contents, iv. pp. History, 726 pp. Appendix, xliv. pp. List of Subscribers, Directions to Binder, etc. iv. pp.

LIST OF PLATES.

Sudell's Arms	*To face* p. 265		View of Healey Hall	*To face* p. 553	
Hargrave's, etc. .	,,	314	Achievement of Chadwicks of Healey, etc.	,,	563
View of Greensnook	,,	330	Illustrative Arms .	,,	586
,, ,, Woodfold Park	,,	346	View of Scaitcliff .	,,	653
Arms of Earl of Stamford, etc. . .	,,	381	Pilkington's Arms, etc.	,,	673
View of Fairfield .	,,	483	View of Church of St. Nicholas . .	,,	683
Egerton's Arms, etc.	,,	496	Walmsley's Arms, etc.	,,	715
Castlemere Hall .	,,	534	Farington's Arms, etc.	,,	722
Crossfield House .	,,	*Ibid.*	View of Hoghton Tower	,,	724
Illustrative Arms .	,,	542			

Royal quarto. Sells for £3.

John Corry was a native of the North of Ireland, and was a self-taught man. He was for some years a writer for a Dublin newspaper, but in 1792 he removed to London, where he supported himself by his pen. The majority of his works were published anonymously. In conjunction with the Rev. John Evan, he wrote a "History of Bristol" (1816). Neither this nor the "History of Lancashire" are of much importance.

MAGNA BRITANNIA et HIBERNIA ANTIQUA et NOVA, or a NEW SURVEY of GREAT BRITAIN. Collected and composed by an impartial hand. London: printed by Eliz. Nutt, and sold by M. Nutt in Exeter Exchange, in the Strand, and J. Moylew, near Stationers' Hall. [1720-31.] *Foolscap quarto.*

This work was compiled by the Rev. THOMAS COX. It is complete in six volumes.

The Lancashire portion is comprised between p. 1272 and p. 1338, which contains a Map of the County by Robert Morden. This part of the work is often advertised as a distinct work. The six volumes were published at £2 : 2s., but fetch a much higher price now. Lancashire alone may be had for 5s. 6d.

A BOOK of RATES for the COUNTY PALLATINE of LANCASTER, wherein are contained divers generale, exact, and true Rules necessary to be observed in the rating and collecting all Taxes and Layes within the said County, very necessary and profitable for all Gentlemen of

Account, Freeholders, and Others, etc. Compiled and published for the general good and benefit of the whole County. By WM. CRABTREE.

[Published after 1650.] Very scarce.

The RACES of LANCASHIRE INDICATED by the LOCAL NAMES and DIALECT of the County. By the Rev. JOHN DAVIES. London: P. G. Taylor and Francis, Red Lion Court, Fleet Street. 1856. Reprinted from the Transactions of the Philological Society. 1855. [No. 13.] *Octavo.*

Title, etc. and Races of Lancashire, 76 pp. Very scarce. Copies have sold for 15s. A copy is in the Manchester Free Library.

GENERAL VIEW of the AGRICULTURE of LANCASHIRE, with Observations on the Means of its Improvement. Drawn up for the consideration of the Board of Agriculture and Internal Improvement. By R. W. DICKSON, Honorary Member of the Board of Agriculture, etc. etc. Revised and prepared for the Press by W. STEVENSON, author of the "Agricultural Report of the County of Surrey." London: 1815. (Price 14s. in boards.)

Title and Contents, xii. pp. General View, with Index, 656 pp., and Map of the County of Lancashire, coloured.

This Volume is a part of the Agricultural Survey of Great Britain and Ireland.

LANCASHIRE WORTHIES. By FRANCIS ESPINASSE.

"Hic manus, ob patriam pugnando vulnera passi."
[And four following lines, with translation from ÆNEID, vi. 660-665.]

London: Simpkin, Marshall, and Co., Stationers' Hall Court; Manchester: Abel Heywood and Son. 1874. *Post octavo.*

Half-Title, Title as above, Contents, v. pp. Lancashire Worthies, 469 pp. Portrait of Humphry Chetham facing Title-page. Published at 7s. 6d. Large paper, 16s.

A valuable addition to Lancashire Biography. A second series is announced.

LANCASHIRE AUTHORS and ORATORS. A series of Literary

Sketches of some of the principal Authors, Divines, Members of Parliament, etc., connected with the County of Lancaster. By JOHN EVANS. London: Houlston and Stoneman. 1850. *Octavo.*

Title as above, Dedication to Sir Elkanah Armitage, Knt., etc. Preface and Index, vii. pp. Authors and Orators, 293 pp. Published at 5s. Sells for 6s.

RURAL HISTORICAL GLEANINGS in SOUTH LANCASHIRE. By JOSEPH FIELDING, Reporter, Middleton.

VOL. I.

Manchester: Abel Heywood, Oldham Street, and John Heywood, Deansgate. MDCCCLII. *Foolscap octavo.*

Title as above, Contents, vii. pp. To the Public, iv. pp. Rural Historical Gleanings, 320 pp.

Contains much of local interest. It was published in five parts, price 6d. each. A copy of this is in the Manchester Free Library.

Joseph Fielding was born at Middleton 14th April 1800. His parents were hand-loom weavers, but his father's ancestor held for some time the farms of Bleakett, Milnrow, and Touchet Hall, near Tandle Hills, in Thornham. In 1806 he became a bobbin-winder, and afterwards a weaver. In 1826 he married, and kept a night-school in Middleton, and subsequently obtained an engagement as Reporter for the "Manchester and Salford Advertiser."

PEDIGREES of the COUNTY FAMILIES of ENGLAND. Compiled by JOSEPH FOSTER, and authenticated by the Members of each Family. The Heraldic Illustrations by J. Forbes-Nixon.

VOL. I.—LANCASHIRE.

London: printed for the Compiler by Heed, Hole, and Co., Farringdon Street, and Paternoster Row. 1873. *Royal quarto.*

Half-Title, Title as above, Plate with Lancashire Arms, List of Pedigrees, xiii. pp. Introduction, 1 p. The whole is unpaged, and contains 107 tabular Pedigrees, exclusive of detailed Descents not so arranged. Besides the Arms on the Pedigree sheets, there are 17 separate Plates. Published at £3 : 3s. small paper. Large paper, £6 : 6s.

Two LECTURES on the LANCASHIRE DIALECT. By the Rev. W. GASKELL, M.A. London: Chapman and Hall, 193 Piccadilly. 1854. *Foolscap octavo.*

Half-Title, Title as above, and Lectures, 31 pp. Sells for 3s. 6d.

PORTFOLIO of FRAGMENTS relating to the HISTORY and ANTIQUITIES, TOPOGRAPHY, and GENEALOGY of the COUNTY PALATINE and DUCHY of LANCASTER. Embellished with numerous Engravings of Views, Seats, Arms, Seals, and Antiquities. By MATTHEW GREGSON, Esq., F.S.A., and Honorary Member of the Society of Antiquaries of Newcastle-upon-Tyne, etc. Third Edition, with Additions and Improvements, containing a Copious Index and a Special Index to the Coats of Arms. Edited by JOHN HARLAND, F.S.A., Editor of Baines's "History of Lancashire," and many works of Lancashire Antiquities. London: George Routledge and Sons, Broadway; Manchester: L. C. Gent. 1869. *Foolscap folio.*

Half-title, 1 p. Title as above, Dedication, Preface to the Third Edition, Contents, and List of Illustrations, xii. pp. Of the County Palatine of Lancaster, 387 pp. Index of Arms, Seals, etc., 389 to 393. General Index, 394 to 426.

LIST OF ILLUSTRATIONS.

The Copperplate and Lithographic Illustrations are printed in italic type.

Portrait of Gregson . *Frontispiece.*
Map of Lancashire, 1598.
Plan of Lancaster Castle P. 1
Liverpool Castle . . 33
Tailpiece . . . 42
King Edward VI. and Edward Prince of Wales . 47
Portrait of Edward III. . 65
Full length Portrait of Edward III. . . . 67
Denbigh Castle . . 88
Portrait of Edward the Black Prince 126
Church of Walton-on-the-Hill 140
Tailpiece 142
Fire Beacon . . . 143
Bank Hall . . . P. 153
St. Michael's Church, Toxteth Park . . . 154
St. Nicholas' Church and the Tower, Water Street, Liverpool 156
Ground Plan of Liverpool Castle . . . 158
Old Custom House, Liverpool 161
Ancient Tower, Garden Gate, Water Street, Liverpool . 164
Tower at Liverpool . . 164
Blue Coat Hospital . . 166
Monument to the Memory of Foster Cunliffe of Liverpool 168
Peel House, near Farnworth 171

Prescot Parish Church . P. 173
Stonyhurst College . . 183
Childwall Church . . 188
Wavertree Church, parish of Childwall . . . 190
Wavertree Well . . 191
Native Bard of Liverpool . 192
Green Bank and Speke Hall 196
Hale Hall. North front . 202
Gatehouse leading to the Hutt in Halewood . . 207
Aughton Church and School 214
Halsall Church and School 215
Melling Chapel . . 217
Lydiate Abbey, parish of Halsall 219
Portrait of Countess of Sefton 221
Monument to the Memory of Henry Blundell, Esq. . 222
Huyton Church . . 228
Portrait of the Earl of Derby 228
Winstanley Hall . . 231
Ince Hall, near Wigan . P. 236
Figure in Ormskirk Church 240
Lathom House . . 245
Hornby Castle, south of the Sands 270
Dalton Castle, near Ulverston 272
Furness Abbey (Chapter House) 276
Gleaston Castle . . 277
Church and Castle of Lancaster 280
Clitheroe Castle . . 287
Cloisters of Whalley Abbey from the south . . . 290
Thomas White, M.D., and Charles White, Esq., F.R.S. 292
Ancoats Hall, Bradshaw Hall, and St. Peter's Church, Manchester 293
Old Church, Manchester . 293
Portrait of Mr. John Byrom, M.A. 294
Wycollar Hall . . . 295
Edward the Black Prince . 307
Tailpiece 336

FOLDING PEDIGREES.

The Genealogies of the Earls and Dukes of Lancaster . *To face* p. 12.
Union of the Houses of York and Lancaster . . " " 46.

And many hundred Woodcuts of Arms, Seals, etc.

Published at £4; large paper, £6 : 6s. Sells for £3; large paper, £3 : 10s.

This Edition is substantially a Reprint of the 2d Edition, with Corrections, Additions, and the much-needed Index.

The 1st Edition of this valuable work appeared in 1817, and the 2d in 1824. The two Editions are thus described in the Preface to the above—" In its original compilation it was literally ' A Portfolio of Fragments.' Its 1st Edition appeared in 1817, but in the course of passing through the press it received various additions from time to time, which were introduced in the form of interpolated pages between those originally printed. These interfering with the pagination, were denoted by the addition of asterisks before and after the number of the page. Thus between the original pages 2 and 7, were introduced 2* 3* 4* 5** and 6*. Then, besides the division of the work into three parts, with separate title-pages and tables of contents, there were introduced, at the end of Part II., thirty-eight pages of Addenda (price 10s. 6d. extra, or 20s. separate). Other additions were called 'More Fragments;' and Part III. was also called the *Appendix*, and its pagination, like that of the Preface, was in Roman numerals, pp. i. to cviii. Such was the second Edition as published; and in Mr. Gregson's 'Advertisement' thereto he announced that after a certain day the price of the volume would be advanced to *Eight Guineas*, and that of the *Additions*, separately, to *Two Guineas and a half.* In this advertisement he announced that he was preparing a Fourth Part, to contain an Index, etc." This Fourth Part was never published.

The 1824 Edition frequently sells for £7.

Matthew Gregson was born in Liverpool in 1749, where he served his apprenticeship to a cabinet-maker, and afterwards was established in the same business, from which he retired in 1814. Mr. Picton, in his "Memorials of Liverpool," stated that his house in St. Anne Street was so noted for hospitality, as to have acquired the name of the "Gregson Hotel." He died in 1824, aged 75, from the effects of a fall whilst reaching down a book in his Library.

LANCASHIRE, its PURITANISM and NONCONFORMITY. By Robert Halley, D.D. In Two Volumes.

Volume I.

Manchester: Tubbs and Brook, 11 Market Street. London: Hodder and Stoughton. MDCCCLXIX. *Octavo.*

Half-title, Title as above, Preface, Contents, and List of Plates, xiii. pp.
Lancashire, its Puritanism, 492 pp.

Plates.

Map of Lancashire	*To face*	*Title.*
Hoghton Tower	"	p. 226
Dukinfield Old Hall Chapel	"	" 294
Manchester and Salford, Plan of, in A.D. 1650	"	" 338
Liverpool, Plan of, in A.D. 1650	"	" 407

VOLUME II.

Half-title, Title, and Contents, viii. pp. Lancashire, its Puritanism, and Index, 525 pp.

PLATES.

Worsley, Major-General	. .	*To face Title.*
Newcome, Rev. Henry, M.A.	.	„ p. 312
Preston, Plan of, A.D. 1715 .	.	„ „ 347

Published at 30s. A cheap Edition, in 1 volume, 10s. 6d.

The CHARTERS of the DUCHY of LANCASTER. Translated and Edited by WILLIAM HARDY, F.S.A., and printed by order of the Chancellor of the Duchy. London, MDCCCXLV. *Octavo.*

Half-title, Title as above, and Preface, xii. pp. Pedigrees of Earls of Chester, Lancaster, etc., and Contents, xx. pp. Charters and Index, 385 pp.

THREE LANCASHIRE DOCUMENTS of the Fourteenth and Fifteenth Centuries. Comprising—

I. The Great de Lacy Inquisition, February 16, 1311.
II. The Survey of 1320-46.
III. Custom Roll and Rental of the Manor of Ashton-under-Lyne, November 11, 1422.

Edited by JOHN HARLAND, F.S.A. Printed for the Chetham Society, MDCCCLXVIII. *Foolscap quarto.*

Chetham Society's Title (Vol. lxxiv.), and List of Council, 3 pp.

Title as above, and Introduction, xii. pp. Contents, 1 p. The De Lacy Inquisition and Index Nominum et Locorum, p. 1 to p. 27. Survey of, 1320-46, and Index Nominum et Locorum, p. 28 to p. 92. Custom Roll of Ashton, and Index Nominum et Locorum, p. 93 to p. 138. Supplemental Index, p. 139 to p. 141. The 24th Report of the Chetham Society, etc., 10 pp.

The LANCASHIRE LIEUTENANCY under the TUDORS and STUARTS. The Civil and Military Government of the Country, as illustrated by a series of Royal and other Letters, orders of the Privy Council, the Lord Lieutenant, and other Authorities, etc. etc. Chiefly derived from the Shuttleworth MSS. at Gawthorpe Hall, Lancashire. Edited by JOHN HARLAND, F.S.A. Printed for the Chetham Society, MDCCCLIX. *Foolscap quarto.*

Chetham Society's Title (Vol. xlix) and List of Council, 3 pp. Title as above, and Introduction and Contents, cxviii. pp. Explanation of Plates, 1 p. Half-title, 1 p. The Lancashire Lieutenancy, 96 pp. The 16th Report of the Society, etc., 10 pp.

ILLUSTRATIONS.

Seven Plates (inserted after page cxviii.) of Arms, etc. etc.

PART II.

Chetham Society's Title-page (Vol. l.), List of Council, and Title-page to Part II., 5 pp. The Lancashire Lieutenancy, and Index to both volumes, p. 97 to p. 333.

OUR COUNTY CHURCHES. By ATTICUS [A. HEWITSON], author of "Preston, its Churches and Chapels;" "Stonyhurst College;" "Past and Present," etc. Preston: A. Hewitson, "Chronicle" Office; London, Simpkin, Marshall, and Co. 1872. *Foolscap octavo.*

Title as above, with a "South-east View of Stydd, the oldest Lancashire Church, founded in the 12th Century."

Second Title, iii. pp. Preface, our County Churches, and Index, 585 pp.

The above was first published in the "Preston Chronicle." Published at 5s.

An ACCOUNT of the EXPENDITURE of the COUNTY PALATINE of LANCASTER for a period of 23 years, commencing 1819, and ending 1842, with remarks by ROBERT HINDLE, Accountant. "There is no system so imperfect as the County Rates, none so much in want of reform." London: Whittaker and Co., Ave Maria Lane; Preston: Walker, Church Street; Liverpool: Smith, Rogerson, and Co.; Manchester: Simms and Dinham. MDCCCXLIII. *Octavo.*

Title as above, Dedication, Preface, and Index, xvi. pp. Account and Appendix, 317 pp. Errata and List of Subscribers, 4 pp.

Sells for 2s. 6d.

General View of the AGRICULTURE of the COUNTY of LANCASTER, with Observations on the Means of its Improvement. Drawn up for the consideration of the Board of Agriculture and Internal Improvement, from the communications of Mr. JOHN HOLT of Walton, near Liverpool. And the additional remarks of several respectable Gentlemen and Farmers of the County. [Here follows 4 lines of Virgil's, and 13 lines of Dyer's.] London: printed for G. Nichol, Pall Mall, bookseller to His Majesty and to the Board of Agriculture, and sold by Messrs. Robinson, Paternoster Row, etc. etc. 1795. *Octavo.*

Title as above, Advertisement, iv. pp. Agricultural Survey and Directions to Binder, 242 pp. Illustrated with a Map of Lancashire, and five Plates of cattle, etc.

This is one of the volumes of the Agricultural Survey of Great Britain and Ireland.

DOOMSDAY BOOK, or the Great Survey of England. By WILLIAM THE CONQUEROR, A.D. MLXXV. Facsimile of the Part relating to Lancashire. [Arms of Lancaster.] Photo-Zincographed by Her Majesty's command at the Ordnance Survey Office, Southampton. Colonel Sir H. JAMES, R.E., F.R.S., etc., Director. MDCCCLXI.

Two Titles, one for Lancashire as above, the other for the Cheshire part, ii. pp. Explanations and Introduction, vi. pp. Facsimile, xiv. pp. and iii. pp.

A magnificent work. The Lancashire and Cheshire portion were published together at 8s. Now sells for 10s. 6d. *See* W. BEAMONT, p. 46.

MISCELLANEOUS PAPERS or SUBJECTS connected with MANUFACTURES of LANCASHIRE. By JOHN KENNEDY. Reprinted from the Memoirs of the Literary and Philosophical Society of Manchester. For Private distribution only. Manchester. MDCCCXLIX. *Post octavo.*

This consists of five Essays, each consisting of about 42 pp. One of these is "A BRIEF MEMOIR of SAMUEL CROMPTON; a Description of his machine called the Mule, and the subsequent improvement of the machine by others."

PHTHISIOLOGIA LANCASTRIENSIS, cui accessit Tentamen philosophicum Mineralibus Aquis in eodem Comitatu observatis. Authore, CAROLO LEIGH, M.D. Londini: Impensis Sam. Smith and Benj. Walford. Soc. Reg. Typograph. and Insignis Principis in Cæmeterio. D. Pauli. 1694. *Duodecimo.*

Title as above, etc., vii. pp. Phthisiologia, 144 pp.

Opposite the Title-page is "Librum hunc cui Titulus phthisiologia, Lancastriensis, Dignum Indicamus qui Imprimatur.

Tho. Burwell, Præses.
Samuel Collins, Fred. Sare, Will. Dawes, Tancred Robinson, } Censores.

Datum in Comitiis Censoriis ex ædibus Collegii nostri. Jan. 5, A.D. 169¾.

This volume formed the basis of the Natural History of Lancashire and Cheshire. It is very scarce. A copy is in Dr. Shepherd's Library, Preston.

The NATURAL HISTORY of LANCASHIRE, CHESHIRE, and the PEAK in DERBYSHIRE, with an account of the British Phœnician, Armenian, Gr. and Rom. Antiquities in those parts. By CHARLES LEIGH, Doctor of Physick. Oxford: printed for the author; and to be had at Mr. George West's and Mr. Henry Clement's, booksellers there; Mr. Edward Evet's, at the Green-Dragon in St. Paul's Churchyard; and Mr. John Nicolson, at the King's Arms in Little Britain, London. MDCC. *Folio.*

Title as above, the Epistle Dedicatory, Epistle to the Reader, Preface, Address to Author by "R. J." List of Subscribers, Advertisement, xxvii. pp. The Natural History, Book I., p. 1 to p. 164. Plates, and 14 pp. unnumbered, explanatory of the Plates. Then follows Vindication of the Author, 2 pp. Book II. Natural History and Errata, 98 pp. Book III. Natural History, Postscript, Errata of the Cuts, Explanation of Cuts, 113 pp. Then follow pages 181 to p. 196 (which is printed 190), and consists of Explanation. Index, 36 pp.

LIST OF ILLUSTRATIONS.

1. Portrait of the author, *Frontispiece.*
2. Map of Lancashire.
3. Coats of Arms of Subscribers.
4. " " "
5. Storm of Hailstones, etc.
6. Instruments.
7. Fossils.
8. "
9. Indian Canoe & other Antiquities dug out of Martinmeer.
10. Head of Stag found at Meales.
11. Sturgeon found at Warrington, etc.
12. Poole's Hole, etc.
13. The horned Cheshire Woman, etc.
14. Birds.
15. Telescope and other Instruments.
16. Trees, etc.
17-26. Ten Plates of Antiquities.

A work of little real value. [See "Phthisiologia Lancastriensis."] It was severely criticised by Dr. Whittaker.

Charles Leigh was born at the Grange, in Kirkham, in 1662, and died about the year 1717. [For notice of him, *see* Fishwick's "History of Kirkham," Chetham Society, vol. xcii. p. 187.] He published a pamphlet, entitled, "A reply to John Colbatch upon his late piece concerning the curing of the biting of a Viper by acids." *Octavo.* London. 1697.

Sells for 17s. 6d. Large paper at 30s.

HISTORY, TOPOGRAPHY, and DIRECTORY of MID-LANCASHIRE, with an ESSAY on GEOLOGY. By MANNEX and Co. [Arms of County.] Preston: printed for the Proprietors, by William Bailey and Henry Thompson. 1854. Price to Subscribers 14s. 6d. in cloth; or 15s. 6d. half-bound in calf or Cape Morocco. *Octavo.*

Title as above, Address, Index, and Seats and Residences, xi. pp. History and Directory, 764 pp. Sells for 4s. 6d.

TRACTS relating to MILITARY PROCEEDINGS in LANCASHIRE during the GREAT CIVIL WAR, commencing with the Removal by Parliament of James, Lord Strange, afterward Earl of Derby, from his Lieutenancy of Lancashire, and terminating with his Execution at Bolton. Edited and Illustrated from Contemporary Documents by GEORGE ORMEROD, D.C.L., F.RS., F.S.A., F.G.S., of Tyldesley and Sedbury, author of "The History of Cheshire." Printed for the Chetham Society. MDCCCXLIV. *Foolscap quarto.*

Chetham Society's Title (Vol. ii.), and List of Council, iv. pp. Title as above, Prefatory Memoir, List of Tracts, etc., Chronological Table, and General Contents, xxxii. pp. Tracts, Biographical Notices, and Index, 371 pp.

George Ormerod, the author of "The History of Cheshire," was born in Manchester 20th October 1785, and was educated at Brazenose College, Oxford. He died at his seat, Sedbury Park, on 9th October 1873.

LANCASHIRE and CHESHIRE WILLS and INVENTORIES. From the Ecclesiastical Court, Chester. The FIRST PORTION. Edited by the Rev. G. J. PICCOPE, M.A., Curate of Brindle. Printed for the Chetham Society. MDCCCLVII. *Foolscap quarto.*

Chetham Society's Title (Vol. xxxiii.), and List of Council, iii. pp. Title as above, Introduction, and Contents, vi. pp. Wills and Inventories, 196 pp.

SECOND PORTION.

Chetham Society's Title (Vol. li.), and List of Council, iii. pp. Title to 2d Portion, and Contents, vi. pp. Wills and Inventories, 283 pp.

THIRD PORTION.

Chetham Society's Title (Vol. liv.), and List of Council, iii. pp. Title to the 3d Portion, and Contents, v. pp. Wills and Inventories, and Index to the three volumes, 271 pp.

The Piccope MSS. are now in the Chetham Library.

George John, the son of the Rev. John Piccope, Incumbent of St. Paul's, Manchester, was born in 1818, educated at the Manchester Free Grammar School, and graduated B.A. and M.A. at Brazenoze College, Oxford. From 1849 to 1864 he was Curate of Brindle, near Leyland, and afterwards Curate in sole charge of Yarwell, in Northamptonshire, where he died, 22d February 1872.

HEALTH OF TOWNS' COMMISSION. REPORT on the STATE of LARGE TOWNS in LANCASHIRE. By Dr. LYON PLAYFAIR, one of Her Majesty's Commissioners for inquiring into the State of Large Towns and Populous Districts in England and Wales. London: printed by W. Clowes and Sons, Stamford Street, for Her Majesty's Stationers' Office. 1845. *Octavo.*

Title as above, and Contents, iv. pp. Report, 136 pp.

POTT'S DISCOVERY of WITCHES in the COUNTY of LANCASTER. Reprinted from the original edition of 1613, with an Introduction and Notes. By JAMES CROSSLEY, Esq. Printed for the Chetham Society. MDCCXLV. (Printer's error—should be MDCCCXLV.)—*Foolscap quarto.*

Chetham Society's Title (Vol. vi.), and List of Council, iii. pp. Title as above, and Introduction, lxxix. pp. Pott's Discovery, 192 pp. (not paged). Notes, 51 pp.

The WONDERFULL DISCOVERIE of WITCHES in the COVNTIE of LANCASTER. With the Arraignement and Trial of Nineteen notorious Witches at the Assizes and general Gaole, deliuerie holden at the Castle of Lancaster upon Munday the seuenteenth of August last, 1612.

Before Sir James Altham and Sir Edward Bromley, Knights, Barons of His Maiestie's Court of Excheqver, and Justices of Assize, Oyer and Terminer, and generall Gaole deliuerie in the circuit of the North Parts. Together with the Arraignement and Triall of Jennet Preston at the Assizes, holden at the Castle of Yorke, the seuen and twentieth day of Julie last past, with her Execution for the Murder of Maister Lister by Witchcraft. Published and set forth by commendment of Her Majestie's Justices of Assizes in the North Parts. London: printed by W. Stansby for John Barnes, dwelling neare Holborn Conduit. 1613.

Half-Title, Title as above, Address, and Epistle Dedicatory, x. pp. Introductory matter, 6 pp. [with a woodcut.] A Particular Declaration, etc., 154 pp. Arraignement of Jennet Preston, etc., 14 pp. [The whole unpaged.] A very rare work. A copy is in the Chetham Library.

NOTITIA CESTRIENSIS, or HISTORICAL NOTICES of the DIOCESE of CHESTER. By the Right Rev. FRANCIS GASTRELL, D.D., Lord Bishop of Chester. Now just printed from the original Manuscript, with Illustrative and Explanatory Notes. By the Rev. F. R. RAINES, M.A., F.S.A., and Rural Dean of Rochdale, Incumbent of Milnrow.

[1] VOL. II. PART I.

Printed for the Chetham Society. MDCCCXLIX. *Foolscap quarto.*

[1] Volume contains Cheshire only.

LANCASHIRE.

Chetham Society's Title (Vol. xix.), and List of Council, iii. pp. (Corrigenda on a slip.) Title as above, and Contents, iv. pp. Notitia Cestriensis, 160 pp. Index, xxviii. pp. The Volume contains the Deanery of Manchester, etc.

VOLUME II. PART II.

Chetham Society's Title (Vol. xxi.), and List of Council, iii. pp. Title, Introduction, and Contents, lxxvi. pp. Corrigenda, 1 p. Notitia Cestriensis, p. 161 to p. 352. Frontispiece. Facsimile of MS. Contains the Deaneries of Warrington, Blackburn, and part of Leyland.

VOLUME II. PART III.

Chetham Society's Title (Vol. xxii.), Title, and List of Council, iii. pp. Title, i. p. Notitia Cestriensis, and Index, p. 353 to p. 621. Contains part of the Deanery of Leyland, and the Deaneries of Amounderness, Lonsdale, Furness, and Cartmel, and Kendal.

A HISTORY of the CHANTRIES within the COUNTY PALATINE of LANCASTER, being the Reports of the Royal Commissioners of Henry VIII., Edward II., and Queen Mary. Edited by the Rev. F. R. RAINES, M.A., F.S.A., Rural Dean, Hon. Canon of Manchester, and Incumbent of Milnrow.

VOL. I.

Printed for the Chetham Society. MDCCCLXII. *Foolscap quarto.*

Chetham Society's Title (Vol. lix.), List of Council, and Title as above (omitting "vol. i."), v. pp. Title as above, Introduction, and Contents, xxxvi. pp. Corrigenda, 1 p. Lancashire Chantries, 168 pp.

VOL. II.

Chetham Society's Title (Vol. lx.), List of Council, and Title, v. pp. Lancashire Chantries, and Index to the two Volumes, p. 169 to p. 323. Nineteenth Report of the Chetham Society, etc., 4 pp.

The "Lancashire Chantries" are two of the most valuable volumes issued by this Society; indeed, to say this, and to say that they are edited by the able and learned Vice-President, is to use a synonyme.

LANCASHIRE FUNERAL CERTIFICATES. Edited by THOMAS WILLIAM KING, F.S.A., "York Herald." With additions by the Rev. F. R. RAINES, M.A., F.S.A., Vice-President of the Chetham Society. Printed for the Chetham Society. MDCCCLXIX. *Foolscap quarto.*

Chetham Society's Title (Vol. lxxv.), and List of Council, iii. pp. Half-Title, Title as above, and Introduction, vi. pp. Contents, i. p. Funeral Certificates and Index, 102 pp. The Twenty-fifth Report of the Society, etc., 10 pp.

The VISITATION of the COUNTY PALATINE of LANCASTER, made in the Year 1567. By WILLIAM FLOWER, Esq., Norroy King of Arms. Edited by the Rev. F. R. RAINES, M.A., F.S.A., Vicar of Milnrow, and Hon. Canon of Manchester. Printed for the Chetham Society. MDCCCLXX. *Foolscap quarto.*

Chetham Society's Title (Vol. lxxxi.), and List of Council, iii. pp. Title as above, and Introduction, xv. pp. Visitation of Lancashire, and Index, 141 pp. The 27th Report of the Society, etc., 10 pp.

The VISITATION of the COUNTY PALATINE of LANCASTER, made in the Year 1613. By RICHARD ST. GEORGE, Esq., Norroy King of Arms. Edited by the Rev. F. R. RAINES, M.A., F.S.A., Vicar of Milnrow, Hon. Canon of Manchester, and Rural Dean. Printed for the Chetham Society. MDCCCLXXI. *Foolscap quarto.*

Chetham Society's Title (Vol. xxxii.), and List of Council, iii. pp. Title as above, and Introduction, xviii. pp. Corrigenda, i. p. Visitation and Index, 142 pp.

The VISITATION of the COUNTY PALATINE of LANCASTER, made in the Year 1664-5. By Sir WILLIAM DUGDALE, Knight, Norroy King of Arms. Edited by the Rev. F. R. RAINES, M.A., F.S.A., Vicar of Milnrow, Hon. Canon of Manchester, and Rural Dean.

PART I.

Printed for the Chetham Society. MDCCCLXXII. *Foolscap quarto.*

Chetham Society's Title (Vol. lxxxiv.), List of Council, and Title as above, v. pp. Second Title omitting (the words Part I.), and Introduction, xiv. pp. One leaf blank on one side, on the other a quotation from Dugdale's Correspondence. Visitation of Lancashire, 104 pp. 28th Report of the Society, etc., 12 pp.

PART II.

Chetham Society's Title (Vol. lxxxv.), List of Council, and Title to Part II., v. pp. Visitation, p. 105 to p. 224.

PART III.

Chetham Society's Title (Vol. lxxxviii.), List of Council, and Title to Part III., v. pp. Life of Sir William Dugdale, 40 pp. Addenda, 1 p. Visitation, and Index to the three Parts, p. 225 to p. 361.

ANCIENT HALLS of LANCASHIRE, from original Drawings. By ALFRED RIMMER, Architect. Liverpool: Deighton and Laughton; London: David Bogue. 1852. *Royal quarto.*

Engraved Title (showing part of Speke Hall), i. p. Title as above, Dedication, and Introductory Preface, ix. pp.

ILLUSTRATIONS.

1. Peel Hall, Inner Court.
2. Peel Hall, Lodge and Stables.
3. Peel Hall, Stables, etc.
4. Wardley Hall.
5. Wardley Hall, Dining-Room.
6. Smithell's Hall, Dining-Room.
7. Turton Hall.
8. Old Hut Hall.
9. Ordsall Hall.
10. Hoghton Tower Courtyard.
11. Salmesbury Hall
12. Salmesbury Hall, Great Hall.
13. Hall-in-the-Wood.
14. Old Hall at Newton.
15. Remains of Old Hall, Bold.
16. Lydiate Hall, Courtyard.
17. Lydiate Hall, Great Hall.
18. Rufford Hall, Banqueting Hall.
19. Speke Hall, Courtyard.

Published at 12s. 6d., and maintains its price. A valuable Lancashire book.

REPORT of the AGRICULTURE of the COUNTY of LANCASTER, with Observations on the means of its Improvement, being a practical detail of the peculiarities of the County, and their advantages or disadvantages duly considered, written for the Royal Agricultural Society of England, 1849. Together with an Appendix containing Reports of Crops, Cultivation, General Improvements, etc. for 1849, and other subsidiary remarks. By WILLIAM ROTHWELL, Winwick, Land-

Agent, Surveyor, and Valuer. London: Groombridge and Sons. Price 2s. 6d. 1850. *Octavo.*

Title as above, Map of County, opposite Title-page, 162 pp. Appendix, 167 pp.

A TOPOGRAPHICAL SURVEY of the COUNTIES of STAFFORD, CHESTER, and LANCASTER, containing a new Engraved Map of each County, with a complete description of the Great, Direct, and Cross Roads; the Situation, Bearing, and Distances of the Seats of the Nobility and Gentry upon or near such Roads, together with elegant Engravings of their Arms, arranged on a new plan by Messrs. Woodman and Mutlow, London.

To which is added the Direction and Survey of the Great Roads, accurately described, the Situation and Distances of Places, adapted to the use of the Gentlemen and Traveller, with an Index explaining the whole. Also the names and Seats of the Nobility and Gentry in each County. Concluding with a Directory of the Principal Merchants and Manufacturers, Market Towns, and days on which their Markets are held, and principal Inns in each Town within the said Counties, etc. etc. By WILLIAM TUNNICLIFFE, Land Surveyor. Nantwich: printed and sold by E. Snelson; sold also by Mr. B. Law, bookseller, and Messrs. Woodman and Co., Engravers, London; and by the principal booksellers in the above Counties. MDCCLXXXVII. *Octavo.*

Title as above, and Dedication, iv. pp. Plates of Arms (Staffordshire), 6 pp. A Survey and Directory of Staffordshire, p. 1 to p. 40 Plates of Arms (Cheshire), 8 pp. Survey and Directory of Cheshire, p. 41 to p. 68. Plates of Arms (Lancashire), 16 pp. Survey and Directory of Lancashire, p. 69 to p. 118. On last page is an advertisement of place wanted (as Steward, etc.) by the author. Sells for 4s.

The MANSIONS of ENGLAND and WALES. Illustrated in a Series of Views of the principal Seats, with Historical and Topographical Descriptions. By EDWARD TWYCROSS, Esq., M.A.

THE COUNTY OF LANCASHIRE.

VOL. I.

Northern Division. The Hundreds of Blackburn and Leyland.

London: published for the Proprietors by Ackermann and Co., Strand. MDCCCXLVII. Entered at Stationers' Hall. *Imperial quarto.*

Title as above, and Contents, iv. pp. List of Illustrations and Introduction, viii. pp. The Mansions, 71 pp.

ILLUSTRATIONS.

Adlington Hall, 2 Plates.
Allspring.
Bank Hall.
Brindle Lodge.
Carr Hall.
Clayton Hall.
Clerk Hill.
Cuerden Hall, 2 Plates.
Downham Hall.
Duxbury Hall, 2 Plates.
Emmot Hall, 2 Plates.
Euxton Hall.
Feniscowles.
Gawthorpe, 2 Plates.
Gillibrand Hall, 2 Plates.
Hollinshead Hall.
Holme.
Howick House, 2 Plates.
Huntroyde, 2 Plates.
Leagram Hall.
Marsden Hall, 2 Plates.
Oaks, The, 2 Plates.
Ormerod House.
Penwortham Hall, 2 Plates.
Penwortham Priory, „
Rufford Hall.
Rufford Old Hall, *Frontispiece.*
Shaw Hill.
Standish Hall.
Towneley.
Walter Lodge.
Witton House.
Woodfold Park, 2 Plates.

VOL. II.

Hundreds of Lonsdale and Amounderness.

Title, Introduction, Contents, and List of Illustrations, xi. pp. The Mansions, 60 pp.

ILLUSTRATIONS.

Aldcliffe Hall.
Ashton Hall.
Ashton Lodge.
Aynsome.
Bigland Hall.
Bleasdale Tower.
Capernwray Hall.
Claughton Hall, 3 plates.
Clifton Hill.
Conishead Priory.
Dalton Hall.
Esthwaite Lodge.
Eller How.
Grassyard Hall.
Grimsargh House.
Haigh House.
Hammershead Hill Villa.
Hermitage, The.

Heysham Hall, 2 Plates.
Heysham Tower, 2 Plates.
Holker Hall.
Holm Island.
Hornby Castle, 2 Plates.
Lark Hill.
Leighton Hall.
Milling Hall.
Millbank.
Quernmore Park.
Raikes Hall.
Red Scar, 2 Plates.
Ribbleton Hall.
Ribby Hall, 2 Plates.
Springfield Hall.
Stalmine Hall.
Summerfield House.
Thornham Hall.
Upland Hall, 2 Plates.
Wennington Hall.
Whittington Hall, 2 Plates.
Wray Castle, 2 Plates.

VOL. III.

The Hundred of West Derby and Salford.

Title, Contents, and List of Illustrations, vi. pp. The Mansions, 99 pp.

ILLUSTRATIONS.

Acresfield.
Allerton Hall, 2 Plates.
Allerton Priory, 2 Plates.
Arley Hall.
Bentcliffe House.
Birch House.
Bold Hall.
Buile Hall.
Calderstone, 2 Plates.
Chaseley.
Childwell Hall.
Claremont, 2 Plates.
Crosby Hall.
Croxteth Park.
Davy Hume Hall, 2 Plates.
Dingle Cottage.
Dovecot House.
Elmswood, 2 Plates.
Green Hill.
Haigh Hall.
Hale Hall.
Halsnead, 2 Plates.
Heaton House.
High Bank.
Highfield House.
Hillside House, 2 Plates.
Hulton Park.
Hurst House, The, 2 Plates.
Ince Blundell Hall.
Knowsley Park.
Lark Hill.
Lathom House.
Moor Hall.
Mydleton Hall.
New Hall.
Norris Green.
Nut Grove House.
Nuttall Hall, 2 Plates.
Otterspool, 2 Plates.
Peel Hall, 3 Plates.

Redgmont.
Roby Hall.
Sherdley Hall.
Smithell's Hall.
Speke Hall.
Springwood, 2 Plates.
Trafford Park, 2 Plates.
West Dingle.
Westwood House.
Winstanley Hall.
Woolton Hayes.
Woolton Wood.
Worsley Hall.
Yewtree.

The above three volumes (all which relate to Lancashire) were published in 1847 at £10 : 10s. They now sell for £4.

DE MOTU PER BRITANNIAM CIVICO ANNIS MDCCXLV. et MDCCXLVI. Liber unicus auctore. T. D. WHITAKERO. [Quotation Lucan. Phars., lib. iv.] Londini : Typis mandabant, J. and J. B. Nichols, R.L.P., Fleet Street. A.D. MDCCCIX. Prostat. venalis apud Longman, etc., xx. *Duodecimo.*

Title as above, and Dedication, iv. pp. De Motu, 145 pp.

This somewhat scarce book contains an account of the Pretender's passage through Lancashire. A copy is in the author's library.

LANCASHIRE, its HISTORY, LEGENDS, and MANUFACTURES. [Engraving of John of Gaunt, Duke of Lancaster, painted by G. Vertue from an ancient glass window in the Library of All Soul's Coll., Oxon., and engraved by S. Freeman.] By the Rev. G. N. WRIGHT, M.A., assisted by residents in various parts of the county. Fisher and Son, London [1842]. *Imperial octavo.*

Engraved Title as above, i. p. Second Title, Preface, Contents, and Lancashire History, etc., 119 pp.

PLATES, ETC.

James Stanley, 7th Earl of Derby, and Charlotte de la Tremouille, *Frontispiece*
Wycollier Hall, Christmas in 1850 . *To face* p. 7
Portrait of Sir Richard Arkwright . . „ 10
Clitheroe . . . „ 16
Calico-Printing . *To face* p. 20
Speke Hall . . „ 32
Carding, Drawing, and Roving . . . „ 36
The New Custom House, Liverpool . „ 40
Hall-i'-th'-Wood, Bolton . . . . „ 42

Interior of the Collegiate Church, Manchester *To face* p. 44
Preston . . . . " 51
Portrait of Humphrey Chetham . . " 57
Stonyhurst College . " 60
Charter House, Furness Abbey . . . . " 62
John Bradford . . " 64
Dunold Mill-hole, near Lancaster . . . " 66
Pile of Fouldrey Castle " 68
Knowsley Hall . . . " 70
Power-loom Weaving . " 74
Sir Thomas Tyldesley . " 76
Whalley Abbey . . " 78
Robert Peel, Sir . . " 82
Sankey Viaduct, Liverpool and Manchester Railroad . . . " 86
The Town-Hall, Manchester . . *To face* p. 88
Scailcliffe . . . . " 90
Lancaster . . . . " 92
The Vale of Lonsdale . " 96
John Philip Kemble, Esq. . . . . " 98
Rufford Hall . . . " 102
Sir William Stanley . " 104
Sefton Church . . " 106
Holker Hall . . . " 110
Bishop Oldham . . " 112
Stockport . . . . " 114
Cartmel Church *To follow the last Plate*
Hoghton Tower *To face* p. 117
Winwick Church . " 118
Warrington Market Place *To follow the last Plate*
Windleshaw Abbey *To face* p. 121.

Plates drawn by G. Pickering, and engraved by J. C. Bentley.
The volume is also illustrated with woodcuts.
Published at £2 : 2s. Sells for 10s. 6d.

Republished in 2 volumes by Peter Jackson, late Fisher, Son, and Co., The Caxton Press, Angel Street, St. Martin's-le-Grand, London.

VOL. I.

Engraved Title, Title, List of Plates, and Letterpress, 136 pp. 70 views.

VOL. II.

Engraved Title, Title, List of Plates, and Contents, vi. pp. Letterpress, p. 137 to p. 236. 75 Views.
This Edition was published at £4 : 4s. Sells for 25s.

CHETHAM MISCELLANIES, VOL. I., containing—

Papers connected with the Affairs of Milton and his Family.
Epistolary Relics of Lancashire and Cheshire Antiquaries.

Calendars of the Names of Families which entered their several Pedigrees in the successive Heraldric Visitations of the County Palatine of Lancaster.

A Fragment, illustrative of Sir William Dugdale's Visitation of Lancashire.

Autobiographical Tracts of Dr. John Dee, Warden of the College of Manchester.

Printed for the Chetham Society. MDCCCLI. *Foolscap quarto.*

Chetham Society's Title-page (Vol. xxiv.) and List of Council, ii. pp. Title as above, and Advertisement, iv. pp. Title to the Milton Papers, i. p. Miscellanies, 83 pp. One page containing Extract of the Entry of Whalley Abbey, from Tong's Visitation, intended for insertion in The Concher Book of Whalley (see *Post*). The 6th, 7th, and 8th Reports of Chetham Society. Contains a Folding Plate of Facsimile of signatures.

VOL. II., containing—

The Rights and Jurisdiction of the County Palatine of Chester, the Earls Palatine, the Chamberlain, and other Officers.

The Scottish Field (a Poem of Flodden).

Examynatyons towcheyne Cokeye More temp. Hen. VIII., in a dispute between the Lords of the Manors of Middleton and Redclyffe.

A History of the Ancient Chapel of Denton, in Manchester Parish.

A Letter from John Bradshawe of Gray's Inn, to Sir Peter Legh of Lyme.

Chetham Society's Title (Vol. xxxvi.), and List of Council, iv. pp. Title and Advertisement, iv. pp. Rights and Jurisdictions, with Title and Introductory Notice, 37 pp. The Scottish Field, Title, and Introduction, xv. pp. Poem, and Notes, and Glossary, 28 pp. Examynatyons towcheyne Cokeye More, including Title, Introductory Observations, and Notes, 30 pp. A History of the Ancient Chapel of Denton. By the Rev. JOHN BOOKER, M.A., F.S.A. Title and Contents, vi. pp. List of Illustrations, 1 p. History, Notes, and Errata, 147 pp. A Letter from John Bradshawe. Title, Introduction, and Letter, 8 pp. Here is inserted a Facsimile of a Deed of Richard Russel, intended as an illustration to Vol. xxx. (Priory of Penwortham).

ILLUSTRATIONS TO THE HISTORY OF DENTON.

Denton Chapel, *Frontispiece* | Denton Hall . . P. 23
Hyde Hall, in Denton P. 35

VOL. III., containing—

I. The South Lancashire Dialect.
II. Rentale de Cokersand; being the Bursar's Rent-Roll of the Abbey of Cokersand for the year 1501.
III. The Names of all the Gentlemen of the best callinge within the Countie of Lancaster. 1588.
IV. Some instructions given by William Booth, Esquire, upon the purchase of Warrington. A.D. MDCXXVIII.
V. Letter from Sir John Seton, Manchester, ye 25 M'ch 1643.
VI. The names of eight hundred inhabitants of Manchester who took the oath of allegiance to Charles II. on April 1679.
VII. The Pole Booke for Manchester, May ye 22d 1690.

Chetham Society's Title (Vol. lvii.), i. p. List of Council, Title, and Advertisement, vi. pp. South Lancashire Dialect, Title, Corrigenda, Dialect, and Index, 84 pp. Rentale de Cokersand, Title and Introductory Notice, xviii. pp. Rentale and Appendix, 46 pp. The Names of Gentlemen of the best Callinge, Title, Introduction, and Names, 9 pp. The Instructions given by W. Boothe, Introductory Remarks, and the Instruction, 8 pp. Letter of Sir John Seton, with Title and Introduction, 15 pp. The Names of 800 Inhabitants, with Title, 8 pp. The Pole Booke, including Title and Remarks, 43 pp., followed by folding sheets containing Analysis of the Pole Book, and a Plan of Manchester, about A.D. 1650.

VOL. IV., containing—

I. Some account of General Robert Venables of Antrobus and Wincham, Cheshire, with the autobiographical memoranda or diary of his widow, Elizabeth Venables.
II. A forme of confession grounded vpon the ancient Catholique and apostolique Faith. Composed by the Honorable Ladie Bridget Egerton. 1636.
III. A Kalender conteyning the names of all such Gents and others as upon Her Maty's Pryve Seales have paid there money to Sir Hugh Cholmondley, Knyghte, collect[r] of Her Hyghnes' Loane with[in] the Countie of Chester.

IV. History of Warrington Friary.

Printed for the Chetham Society. MDCCCLXXII. *Foolscap quarto.*

Chetham Society's Title (Vol. lxxxiii.), List of Council, Title as above, and Advertisement, viii. pp. Title to Account of General Venables, and Introduction, iv. pp. Pedigree of General Venables, 1 p. Account of do., 28 pp. Title to Forme of Confession, and Introduction, Pedigree of Grey de Wilton, Pedigree of Egerton, and Forme of Confession, 31 pp. Title to Kalender, and Introduction, iv. pp. A Kalender, 4 pp. Title to History of Warrington Friary (edited by W. Beamont, Esq.) Preface and List of Illustrations, viii. pp. History of Friary and Index, 80 pp.

LIST OF ILLUSTRATIONS.

Portrait of General Robert Venables . . *Frontispiece,* No. 1.
Facsimile of Title of MS. *of a form of Confession* „ No. 2.
Effigies and Arms from the Friary Windows . „ No. 4.
Coats of Arms (on the Friary Seal) . . . . *Title-Page.*
Effigies and Arms (from the Friary) . . . *To face* p. 18.
Tombstone . „ . . . „ p. 59.
Fragments . „ . . . „ p. 60.

LANCASHIRE MEMORIALS of the REBELLION MDCCXX.

I. Inquiry into the State of Parties in Lancashire preceding the Rebellion.

II. Lancashire during the Rebellion of 1715, comprising a detail of the events of that movement, as collected from the scarce and original documents. *Foolscap quarto.*

Chetham Society's Title-page (Vol. v. 1845), List of Council, and Title as above, 3 pp. 2d Title, State of Parties, etc., Preface, Contents, and Notice signed by the Editor, S. HIBBERT WARE, x. pp. Lancashire Memorials and Index, 292 pp.

An ILLUSTRATED ITINERARY of the COUNTY of LANCASHIRE.

"Time-honoured Lancaster."
SHAKSPEARE.

London: How and Parsons, 132 Fleet Street. MDCCCXLII. *Royal octavo.*

Title as above, Preface, List of Illustrations, vi. pp. Advertisement, 4 pp. Itinerary, 238 pp. Statistical relations of Lancashire, etc. and Index, xlviii. pp.

LIST OF PLATES.

Ulverston Sands (*Frontispiece*).	Hoghton Tower.
Map of Lancashire.	Lancaster.
Liverpool.	Furness Abbey.
Todmorden.	Coniston Water.

and a great number of woodcuts.

This forms one of a series not completed, and intended to have been called "England in the Nineteenth Century." Published at 22s. 6d. Sells for 10s. 6d.

The PICTORIAL HISTORY of the COUNTY of LANCASTER, with One Hundred and Seventy Illustrations, and a Map.

"Time-honoured Lancaster."
SHAKSPEARE.

London: George Routledge, 36 Soho Square. MDCCCXLIV. *Post quarto.*

Title as above, Preface, and List of Illustrations, vi. pp. Pictorial History, 238 pp. Statistical Relations, etc., xlviii. pp.

Sells for 10s. 6d.

FAMOUS HISTORY of the LANCASHIRE WITCHES. Containing the manner of their becoming such, their Enchantments, Spells, Revels, Merry Pranks, raising of Storms and Tempests, Riding on Winds, etc. The Entertainments and Frolicks which have happened among them, with the Loves and Humours of Roger and Dorothy. Also a Treatise on Witches in general, conducive to Mirth and Recreation. The like never before published. Printed and sold in Aldermary Churchyard, Bow Lane, London. 1780. *Duodecimo.*

Title and History, 24 pp. Scarce. A copy is in the British Museum.

PARS PRIMA.

DUCATUS LANCASTRIÆ. CALENDARIUM INQUISITIONEM POST MORTEM etc., Temporibus regum Edw. I., Edw.

III., Ric. II., Hen. V., Hen. VI., Edw. IV., Hen. VII., Hen. VIII., Edw. VI., Regin. Mar., Phil. and Mar., Eliz., Jac. I., Car. I.

PARS SECUNDA.

A CALENDAR to the PLEADINGS, etc., in the Reigns of Hen. VII., Hen. VIII., Edw. VI., Queen Mary, and Phil. and Mary.

Printed by command of His Majesty King George IV. in pursuance of an Address of the House of Commons of Great Britain, 1823. *Folio.*

Title as above, Address, Record Commission, Order, Introduction, and Half-title, x. pp. Calendarium Inquis. Post Mort. 107 pp. Title to Calendar to Pleadings and Calendar, p. 109 to p. 308. Indices Locorum et Nominum to Inquis. Post Mort., p. 309 to p. 342. Indices, Locorum et Nominum to Pleadings, p. 343 to p. 391.

VOL. II.

PARS TERTIA.

CALENDAR to PLEADINGS, DEPOSITIONS, etc., in the reigns of Henry VII., Henry VIII., Edward VI., Queen Mary, and Philip and Mary; and to the Pleadings of the first thirteen years of the reign of Queen Elizabeth. Printed by command, etc. [as in VOL. I.], 1827.

Half-title, Title as above, and Preface, vi. pp. Supplemented Calendar, 404 pp. Indices, Locorum et Nominum, p. 405 to p. 509.

VOL. III.

PARS QUARTO.

CALENDAR to the PLEADINGS, from the 14th year to the end of the Reign of Queen Elizabeth. Printed, etc., 1834.

Half-title, Title, and List of Commissioners, v. pp. Calendar, Indices Locorum et Nominum, 644 pp.

The First and Second Volumes were published at £3 : 5s. The Third at £1 : 10s. The three now sell for £2 : 10s.

OBSERVATIONS in SUPPORT of the TITLE of the KING *jure ducatus* to all ESCHEATS and FORFEITURES arising within the Fees or Liberties of the DUCHY out of the County Palatine, 28th Sept. 1831, and statement of the case of the Bulmer Escheats within the Liberty of the Savoy parcel of the Duchy of Lancaster, 5th April 1832. Privately printed. 1832. *Small folio.*

A copy lately sold for £2 : 2s.

REPORT from the Select Committee on DUCHY of LANCASTER (BERTOLOCCI-PETITION), with the Proceedings of the Committee, Minutes of Evidence, Appendix, and Index. Ordered by the House of Commons to be printed, 29 July 1857. 218. Sess. 2. *Folio.*

Title as above, and Report, xvi. pp. Minute of Evidence, Index, etc., 358 pp.

An HISTORICAL and DESCRIPTIVE ACCOUNT of the TOWN of LANCASTER, collected from the best Authorities. Illustrated with four Engravings. Lancaster: printed and published by C. Clark, Market Place; and sold by T. Ostell, Ave Maria Lane, Ludgate Street, London. 1807. *Octavo.*

Half-title, Title as above, Introduction, Key to Plan of Lancaster Castle, ix. pp. Historical Account, Alterations, and Errata, 120 pp.

ILLUSTRATIONS.

Plan of Lancaster in 1807.
Plan of Lancaster Castle.
Plan of Lancaster, taken by Speed, in the reign of Queen Elizabeth, and woodcut of Roman Pillar.

A work of not much value. Sells for 3s.

A Second Edition was published in 1811. Title and Introduction, viii. pp. History, 128 pp.

The HISTORY and ANTIQUITIES of the Town of LANCASTER, compiled from authentic sources. By the Rev. ROBERT SIMPSON, M.A., of Queen's College, Cambridge, Perpetual Curate of St. Luke's, Skerton,

"Si quid novisti rectius istis candidus imperti;
Si non, his utere mecum."

Lancaster: Published by T. Edmondson, Market Place; London: John Russell Smith, Soho Square, etc. 1852. *Octavo.*

Half-title, Title as above, Dedication, Preface, Contents, and Addenda, xv. pp. The History, 376 pp. List of Subscribers, and Addenda to List, 5 pp.

A View of Lancaster from the Moor forms the Frontispiece.

Published at 8s. Sells for 4s. 6d.

This work still leaves much of the History of "Time-honoured Lancaster" yet to be written.

A GUIDE to LANCASTER and the Neighbourhood. Lancaster: C. Barwick, 75 Market Street. 1843. *Duodecimo.*

Title as above, and Contents, iv. pp. Guide, 84 pp.

Contains neat Views of Lancaster Castle (two), Lancaster Sessions House, and the New Bridge at Lancaster.

Sells for 1s. 6d.

The CHARTER of the BOROUGH of LANCASTER, dated the 7th day of August 1819.

[Arms of Lancaster.]

Lancaster: Printed by Thomas Bell, Market Street. 1819. *Duodecimo.*

Title and Charter, 32 pp. Scarce.

Reprinted from the "Lancaster Gazette."

LANCASTER RECORDS, or Leaves from Local History. Comprising an authentic account of the progress of the Borough of Lancaster during the period of half-a-century. 1801-1850. Lancaster: printed and published by G. C. Clark, "Gazette" Office. 1869. *Post octavo.*

Title as above, Preface, and Introduction, xv. pp. Records and Index, 338 pp.

Facing Title-page, a Plan of Lancaster, taken by Speed in the reign of Queen Elizabeth.

Published at 5s.

This volume contains an immense amount of information, but it has one great defect, it has no *Index.*

LANCASTER CASTLE, its HISTORY and ASSOCIATIONS. By J. HALL.

"After came that Shallow Lone which to old Lancaster his name doth lend."
SPENSER.

"The last abode of crime and folly."

Lancaster: printed and published by W. Ireland; London: Whittaker and Co., Ave Maria Lane. 1843. *Octavo.*

Title as above, Dedication, and Preface, viii. pp. Lancaster Castle, 9-56 pp.
Sells for 2s. 6d.

The NAMES of the MAYOR, RECORDER, ALDERMEN, COUNCIL, and FREE-BURGESSES of the BOROUGH of LANCASTER. [Taken 10th February 1768.] *Small Quarto.*

Title, etc., and the names (printed on one side only), 132 pp.
Scarce. A copy is in the Bodleian Library.

An Alphabetical LIST of the POLL for a MEMBER of PARLIAMENT, in the Room of Fra. Reynolds, Esq. (now Lord Ducie), to represent the BOROUGH of LANCASTER; which commenced on Tuesday the 14th, and closed on Thursday the 30th March 1786, before Miles Mason, Esq., Mayor, Miles Housman, and Thomas Harris, Gentlemen, Bailiffs of the said Borough. The Candidates Sir George Warren, John Lowther, Esq. Together with how each Freemen polled at the Contest in 1784, when the Candidates were Abram Rawlinson, Esq,, Francis Reynolds, Esq., John Lowther, Esq. To which are added a state of each day's poll, and the final close of the poll for 1784. Lancaster: printed and sold by Henry Walmsley. 1786. *Small Quarto.*

Title as above, etc., ii pp. The Poll, 48 pp.
Scarce. A copy of this is in the Bodleian Library.

An Alphabetical LIST of FREEMEN POLLED for two MEMBERS of PARLIAMENT, to represent the BOROUGH of LANCASTER, at the General Election, which commenced on Thursday the 8th July 1802, before James Parkinson, Esquire, Mayor, Thomas Burrow, and W. Housman, Gentlemen, Bailiffs of the said Borough. The Candidates, the Marquis of Douglas, John Dent, Esquire, and J. F. Cawthorne,

Esq. To which is added a state of the poll each day. Lancaster: printed and sold by C. Clark, Market Place. Sold also by H. Walmsley, Lancaster; T. Hurst, Paternoster Row, London; J. Gore and Son, Liverpool; J. Harrop, Manchester; R. Parker, Blackburn; T. Walker and W. Addison, Preston; J. Ware, Whitehaven; M. Branthwaite, Kendal; J. Soulby and G. Ashburner, Ulverston, etc. etc. *Octavo.*

Title, ii pp. List, 42 pp.

Scarce. A copy is in the Bodleian Library.

LANCASTER ELECTIONEERING PAPERS, 1802. The Candidates, the Marquis of Douglas, John Dent, Esquire, and J. Fenton Cawthorne, Esq.

"An election-hall seems to be a Theatre, where every passion is seen without disguise, a school, where fools may readily become worse, and where philosophers may gather wisdom."—GOLDSMITH'S "Citizen of the World."

Lancaster: printed and sold by C. Clark, Market Place. Sold also by T. Hurst, Paternoster Row, London; J. Gore, Liverpool; T. Walker and W. Addison, Preston; M. Branthwaite, Kendal; and G. Ashburner, Ulverston, etc. etc. *Octavo.*

Title as above, ii. pp. Papers, 54 pp.

Scarce. A copy is in the Bodleian Library.

LATHAM SPAW in Lancashire, with some remarkable cases and cures effected by it. London: printed for Rob. Clavel. Anno Dom. 1670. *Post duodecimo.*

Title as above. Dedicatory Epistle to the Earl of Derby (signed E. Borlase), 19 pp. unnumbered. The Spaw, 72 pp.

The above is the First Edition. A second was published in 1672. It is a very scarce book. A copy of the First Edition is in the author's library, and of the Second Edition in the Chetham Library.

Edmund Borlase, M.D., was the son of Sir John Borlase, an eminent physician of Chester, where he died in 1682.

A JOURNAL of the SIEGE of LATHOM HOUSE in LANCASHIRE, defended by Charlotte de la Tremouille, Countess Derby, against Sir Thomas Fairfax, Kt., and other Parliamentary officers. 1644.

"Yt never was sene their Captayne being Stanleye
That Lancashire, Cheshyre, and Wales ran aweye."
MS. Metrical Hist. of the Stanley Family,
By Tho. Stanley, Bp. of Man., Filt. iii. L. 652.

London: printed for Harding, Mavor, and Lepard, Finsbury Square. 1823. *Octavo.*

Title as above, Introduction, and Journal, 78 pp.

A copy of this is in the Manchester Free Library.

This Journal is believed to have been written by Captain EDWARD CHISENHALL.

There are two copies of the Manuscript. The above is from the Harleian MSS. The other copy is in the Ashmolean Museum, Oxford, which was printed in the "European Magazine," vol. xxiii., 1793, and again, with Notes, in the "Kaleidoscope,"[1] a weekly Journal published in Liverpool. The "Journal of Lathom House" commenced in No. 19, November 7, 1820.

See also "The Life of Colonel Hutchinson" (Bohn's Standard Library).

The HISTORY of the PARISH CHURCH of S. MARY'S at LEIGH. By JAMES EDWARDSON WORSLEV, Member of the Chetham Society. Leigh: Josiah Rose, "Chronicle Office;" Manchester, John Heywood. 1870. *Octavo.*

Title as above, Arms of local families (lithographed), Woodcut of the Church, iv. pp. History, 70 pp. Appendix, 6 pp. Index, 6 pp.

LIVERPOOL a few years since. By an Old Stager [the Rev. C. ASPINALL]. London: Whittaker and Co., Ave Maria Lane; Liverpool, Deighton and Laughton, Church Street. 1852. *Post octavo.*

Title, Preface, and Contents, vii. pp. Liverpool, 159 pp.

Sells for 3s. Reprinted in 1869.

The author of the above was the Rev. James Aspinall, M.A., sometime Incumbent of St. Michael's Church, afterwards of St. Luke's, Liverpool, and subsequently Rector of Althorpe in Lincolnshire, where he died in 1861.

[1] The "Kaleidoscope" was continued for several years, and contains some articles of local interest.

HISTORY of the COMMERCE and TOWN of LIVERPOOL, and the rise of Manufacturing Industry in the adjoining counties. By THOMAS BAINES. London: Longman, Brown, Green, and Longmans; Liverpool, published by the author. 1852. *Royal octavo.*

Title as above, Preface, and Contents, xvi. pp. History, 844 pp. Appendix and Index, 13 pp.

Contains Plan of Liverpool, with the ownership of property about 1670. View of Liverpool in 17th century. Facsimile of plan of proposed Royalist Fortifications in 1644. St. George's Church. Blue Coat School. Lyceum Newsroom. New Baths. Exchange Buildings. Interior of Exchange Newsroom. St. Andrew's Scotch Kirk. The Infirmary. St. John's Market. Low Hill Cemetery. The New Custom House. The Wellington Rooms. St. James' Cemetery. Sessions House. Scotch Chapel, Mount Pleasant. Interior of Ball-Room, Town Hall. Liverpool from the Town Hall. The Goree Warehouses, George's Dock. Plan of Docks of Liverpool and Birkenhead.

The whole of these were not originally published with the work, but were inserted by the purchaser of a "remainder."

Published at 26s. Sells for 10s. 6d.

BLACK'S GUIDE to LIVERPOOL. [*See* JAMES STONEHOUSE.]

LIVERPOOL TABLE TALK a HUNDRED YEARS AGO, or a History of Gore's Directory, with anecdotes illustrative of the period of its first publication in 1766 in a letter to the Members of the Historic Society of Lancashire and Cheshire. By JAMES BOARDMAN. To which is added a continuation of the same subject, and a Map of the town in 1650. [Quotation from Smirke.] Liverpool: Henry Young, South Castle Street, and Adam Bowker, Stanley Street. 1871. *Duodecimo.*

Title as above, and Preface to the First Edition, iv. pp. Table-Talk, etc., 54 pp.

The First Edition was published in 1856 in pamphlet form, and is very scarce. This edition, and the one printed in 1872, sell for 2s. 6d. each.

An ACCOUNT of the LIVERPOOL and MANCHESTER Railway, comprising a history of the parliamentary proceedings preparatory to the passing of the Act. A Description of the Railway in an excursion from Liverpool to Manchester, and a popular illustration of the Mechanical principle applicable to Railways; also an abstract of the expenditure from the commencement of the undertaking, with observations on the same. By HENRY BOOTH, Treasurer to the Company. Liverpool: printed by Wales and Baines, and sold by them and the Booksellers in Liverpool; Bancks and Co., Manchester; Cadell and Co., Edinburgh; and Hurst, Chance, and Co., London. *Octavo.*

Title as above, and Account, 104 pp.

Contains a Folding Map of the Railway, Engraving of Entrance to Liverpool Station, and Sections of the Line.

A Second Edition was published in 1831. Sells for 3s. 6d.

SPECULATIONS on the FORMER TOPOGRAPHY of LIVERPOOL and the neighbourhood, being a Paper read before the Liverpool Polytechnic Society, 9th April 1866.

PART I.

By JOSEPH BOULT, F.R., I.B.A., etc. Reprinted from the Society's "Journal" for Private Distribution. Liverpool: G. S. Brakell, Cook Street. 1866.

Title, etc., 20 pp.

PART II.

Title, etc., 30 pp. (Printed 1867.)

PART III.

Title, etc., 30 pp. (Printed 1870.)

PART IV.

Title, etc. 29 pp. (Printed 1873.)

Mr. Boult also published pamphlets on the "Origin of the Liverpool Town Dues, 1857;" "The Former and Recent Topography of Toxteth Park," 1867; and "On the alleged Submarine Forest on the Shores of Liverpool Bay, 1865." *See* also "Transactions of Lancashire and Cheshire Historical Society." *Post.*

LIVERPOOL as it was DURING the LAST QUARTER of the EIGHTEENTH CENTURY, 1755 to 1800. By RICHARD

BROOKE, Esq., F.S.A. Liverpool: J. Mawdsley and Son, Castle Street; London: John Russell Smith, 36 Soho Square. 1853. *Royal octavo.*

Title as above, i. p. Preface, Introduction, History, Appendix, Index, and List of Illustrations, 558 pp.

LIST OF ENGRAVINGS.

View of St. Nicholas' Church and the Old Tavern in the Churchyard.
View of St. George's Church as it appeared in the 18th century.
View of the Exchange as it appeared before the Fire of 1795.
View of the Archery Lodge of the Mersey Bowmen.
View of the Old Theatre in Williamson Square.
View of the old Tower and Water Street as they appeared in the latter part of the 18th century.

Published at 25s. Sells for 7s. 6d.

Mr. Richard Brooke for many years practised as a solicitor in Liverpool. The "Recollections of Liverpool" were chiefly derived from his father, who died 15th June 1852, in his 92d year.

CORNISH'S STRANGERS' GUIDE through LIVERPOOL and its ENVIRONS, with a neatly Engraved Map. Third Edition. London: published by James Cornish, 1 Middle Row; Holborn Bars, 37 Lord Street, Liverpool, and 18 Grafton Street, Dublin. 1845. 18*mo.*

Title and Guide, 60 pp. No Index.

The First Edition was published in 1836. [*See* STONEHOUSE'S GUIDE. *Post.*]

CORNISH'S STRANGER'S GUIDE to LIVERPOOL and MANCHESTER, with the TRAVELLER'S COMPANION on the RAILWAY, and an accurate Engraving of the Line of Road, a Section of the Line, etc. With Woodcut of the Public Baths, Liverpool. London: published by S. Cornish and Co., 126 Newgate Street; J. Cornish, 37 New Street, Birmingham, and 16 Lord Street, Liverpool; J. Banks, Heywood, and Fletcher, Manchester. 1838. 18*mo.*

Title and Guide, 104 pp.

This was edited by Mr. JAMES STONEHOUSE.

Under Sanction of the Right Honourable Lords Commissioners of the Admiralty, SAILING DIRECTIONS from POINT LYNAS to LIVERPOOL, with CHARTS, COAST VIEWS, RIVER SECTIONS, Tidal Courses, and the Guage Table for navigating the DEE and the MERSEY, including the latest alterations. By Commander H. M. DENHAM, R.N., F.R.S. [Sketch of Liverpool from the Rock Lighthouse.] Printed and published, as the Act directs, for H. M. Denham, by J. and J. Rawdesley, Liverpool. 1840. Sold by R. B. Bate, Poultry, London; and J. and A. Walker, Liverpool; and by all Chart Sellers at the Sea Ports of the United Kingdom. *Octavo.*

Title as above, Preface, and Contents, xx. pp. List of Plates and Introductory Remarks, ii. pp. Sailing Directions and Appendix, 169 pp. Published at 21s. Sells for 5s.

An ESSAY towards the HISTORY of LIVERPOOL. Drawn up from Papers left by the late Mr. George Perry, and from other materials since collected. By WILLIAM ENFIELD. With views of the Principal Public Structures, a Chart of the Harbour, and a Map of the Environs.

> "Miratur molem Æneas magalia quondam,
> Miratur portus strepitumque et strata viarum,
> Instant ardentis Tyrii."—VIRGIL.

London: printed by Joseph Johnson, No. 72 St. Paul's Churchyard. 1774. *Foolscap folio.*

Title as above, Preface, List of Subscribers, and Lines by G. Perry, xii. pp. Essay and Appendix, 116 pp.

MAPS, ETC.

Chart of Liverpool Harbour. Map of Environs of Liverpool. The Diagram or series of Triangles by which the most eminent places in the Map of Environs of Liverpool were projected. Plan of Liverpool in 1765.

PLATES.

St. Peter's Church.
St. Nicholas' Church.
St. George's Church.
St. Thomas' Church.
St. Paul's Church.
The Blue Coat Hospital.
North front of the Poor House.
The Exchange.
View of the Custom House.
North View of Sailor's Hospital.

This is the Second Edition of this work. It was published at 10s. 6d. Sells for 15s.

A copy is in the Liverpool Free Public Library.

The first Edition was printed and published at Warrington in 1773.

Title as above (except the date, etc.), List of Subscribers, etc., xii. pp. Essay, 116 pp. Contains nine Plates and two Maps.

A copy of this edition is in the Warrington Public Library.

William Enfield, LL.D., born at Sudbury in 1741, was one of the teachers of the Academy at Warrington. He died at Norwich, 2d November 1796. Dr. Enfield was the author of the "Enfield Speaker," and other works.

FRASER'S GUIDE to LIVERPOOL and BIRKENHEAD, containing History of the Town and River, Eminent Persons, Description of the Docks, Churches, and Chapels, Literary and Scientific Societies, Charitable Institutions, Markets, Principal Streets, Public Buildings, Ferry Boats, Omnibus Times and Routes. River and Country Excursions, etc. etc. etc. Illustrated with Maps, Street Guide, and Ninety Embellishments, by Hugh Gawthrop, Esq., M.C.P. London: W. Kent and Co., Paternoster Row; Liverpool: R. H. Fraser, Cable Street. (Entered at Stationers' Hall. *Duodecimo.* [1855.]

Title as above, Dedication, Index to the Illustrations, Contents, and Preface, xvii. pp. History and Guide, 301 pp.

Published at 3s. 6d., and now sells for about the same price. The author was a Schoolmaster at Birkenhead.

Under the superintendence of the Council of the Natural History Society.

A FLORA of LIVERPOOL, by T. B. HALL. With an Engraved Map and an Appendix, containing Meteorological Tables and Observations for the Year 1838. By WILSON ARMISTEAD. London: Whittaker and Co., Ave Maria Lane; Liverpool: Walmesley, Church Street, and T. Hodgson, Lord Street. Price 6s. Procured of the Members of the Liverpool Natural History Society, 5s. 18*mo.*

Title as above, Abbreviations, Preface, and Essay on Geological Formation of Liverpool, xvii. pp. Flora, and Appendix, 186 pp. Errata, 1 p.

Sells for 2s. 6d.

Wilson Armistead is a native of Leeds, Yorkshire, and the author of several books on slavery, etc. [See Smith's Catalogue of Friends' Books.]

PICTORIAL RELICS of ANCIENT LIVERPOOL, accompanied with Descriptions of the Antique Buildings, etc. Compiled from the original Evidences, private Muniments, and unpublished Collections. By WILLIAM GAWIN HERDMAN, Member of the Liverpool Academy, etc., author of a Folio of Continental Sketches, etc. etc. London: Henry Graves and Company, 6 Pall Mall; Liverpool: William Holden, 13 Ranelagh Street. MDCCCXLIII. *Royal quarto.*

Engraved Title, Title as above, Dedication, Preface, Contents, and List of Plates, xii. pp. Views, etc., 104 pp.

LIST OF PLATES.

Archway, Tower Garden, on Title Page.
Antient View of Liverpool.
Liverpool in 1650.
Old Custom-House and Castle.
Castle and Castle Street.
Tower of Liverpool.
Courtyard of Tower of Liverpool.
Interior of " "
Church Style.
Bank Hall, 2 Plates.
Moore Street, 2 Plates.
Chapel of our Ladye and St. Nicholas.
Walton Church.
Old Exchange.
High Street.
Old St. George's Church.
James Street.
Old Fishmarket.
Red Cross Street.
Lancelot's Hey.
Drury Lane.
Drury Lane and Fenwick Street.
Fenwick Street and Cooper's Row.
Infirmary and Almshouses.
The Mayor's House, Dale Street.
The Tithe Barn.
Union Street, Tithebarn Street.
Liverpool in 1760.
Old Fort.
The Old Baths.
Vandrie's House.
Old Mansion, North Shore.
The Wishing-Gate.
The Folly.
Liverpool in 1715.
The Ferry House.
Old Dock and Custom-House.
Plate xxvii. Fig. 1. White Bear, Dale Street.
" 2. N. Fort.
" 3. Old Drawbridge.
" 4. Spellow House.
" 5. Old Lunatic Asylum.

Plate xxvii. Fig. 6. Town's End Mill.
„ 7. Old Poorhouse.
„ 8. Old Almshouses.
„ 9. Theatre.
St. Stephen's, St. Catherine's, St. Matthew's, Benn's Gardens.
Plate xl. Fig. 1. Mount Quarry.
„ 2. Bowling-green Ho., Mount Pleasant.
„ 3. Roscoe's Birth-place.
Plate xl. Fig. 4. Tall House, South Shore.
„ 5. Spellow Mill.
„ 6. White Chapel.
Interior of Rupert's Cottage.
Rupert's Cottage.
Cross and Beacon, Everton.
Low Hill.
Richmond Fair.
Lord Street.
Mill on the Mount.
Liverpool in 1770.

(*N.B.*—The Plates are not arranged in the order given in the List of Plates.)

Published in 12 Parts, price £3 : 6s. Sells for £1 : 10s. Re-published in 1856. The Plates in this are fine, and the work is one of much interest.

VIEWS of MODERN LIVERPOOL. By WILLIAM HERDMAN. In Chromo-lithograph. By James Orr Marples and the Artist, with an Introduction and Descriptive Letterpress by J. A. PICTON, Esq., F.S.A. Liverpool: printed and published by David Marples. MDCCCLXIV. *Folio.*

Title as above, Dedication, List of Plates, and Introduction, xvii. pp. Descriptive Letterpress, 49 pp. Thirty-seven Plates of the Principal Buildings, etc. in Liverpool. Original price to Subscribers (as published in parts), £3 : 12s.

This is, as far as the Plates are concerned, much inferior to the "Ancient Liverpool." See p. 90.

CONDITION of LIVERPOOL, RELIGIOUS and SOCIAL, including Notices of the State of Education, Morals, Pauperism, and Crime. By the Rev. A. HULME, D.C.L., LL.D., F.S.A., Incumbent of the New Parish of Vauxhall, Liverpool. [Quotations, Isai. xxiii. 7, 8; and Pro. xix. 17.] This Edition is not published. Liverpool: printed by T. Brakell, 7 Cook Street. MDCCCLVIII. *Octavo.*

Title as above, Dedication, and Condition of Liverpool, 38 pp. Map (folding) of Liverpool, "Ecclesiastical and Social, 1858."

The EXPORT COAL TRADE of LIVERPOOL. A Letter to Thomas Littledale, Esq., Chairman of the Liverpool Dock Trust. By WILLIAM LAIRD. Third Edition. Liverpool: printed by Baines and Herbert, Castle Street. 1850. *Royal octavo.*

Title as above, and Preface, iv. pp. Letter, 59 pp.

PLATES.

Frontispiece (folding). Proposed plan of Shipping Coals on the High Level at Liverpool.

Map (folding) of the British Coalfield	*To face* p.	1
River Tyne Coal Drop	„	40
Coal Drops at Hartlepool (folding)	„	42
Ballast Cranes (folding)	„	44
Coal Drops at Cardiff	„	48
Map (folding) showing Railway, proposed connection .	„	54

The GEOLOGY of the COUNTRY AROUND LIVERPOOL. A Lecture to the Liverpool Naturalist's Field Club. November 1861. By GEORGE H. MORTON, F.G.S., Honorary Secretary of the Liverpool Geological Society. Liverpool: printed by Geo. Smith, Watts, and Co. MDCCCLXIII. *Octavo.*

Title as above, and Preface, iv. pp. Geology, etc., 55 pp.

ILLUSTRATIONS.

Views of Sub-marine Forest. | Sections, etc.

Sells for 1s. 6d.

A FAMILIAR MEDICAL SURVEY of LIVERPOOL: addressed to the Inhabitants at Large. Containing Observations on the Situation of the Town; the Qualities and Influence of the Air; the Employments and Manner of Living of the Inhabitants; the Water; and other Natural and Occasional Circumstances whereby the Health of the Inhabitants is liable to be particularly affected. With an Account of the Diseases most peculiar to the Town; and the Rules to be observed for their Prevention and Cure: Including Observations on the Cure of Consumption. The whole rendered perfectly Plain and Familiar. By W. MOSS, Surgeon, Liverpool. Liverpool: printed by H. Hodgson; and sold by T. and W. Lowndes, London. MDCCLXXXIV. *Octavo.*

Title as above, Dedication, Contents, and Errata, x. pp. Medical Survey, 130 pp.

A copy of this is in the Bodleian Library.

The LIVERPOOL GUIDE, including a SKETCH of the ENVIRONS, with a Map of the Town, and Directions for Sea Bathing. By W. Moss. The Third Edition, Enlarged. [Woodcut.] Liverpool: printed by J. M'Creery, for W. Jones, Bookseller, Castle Street; and sold by Vernon and Hood, London. 1799. *Duodecimo.*

Title as above, Dedication, and Contents, iv. pp. Guide, 164 pp. Errata, 1 p. Folding Map and Folding Plate. South-west prospect of Liverpoole.

The First Edition was published in 179—. The Second in 1797. The Third in 1799 as above. A Fourth in 1801 (with Woodcuts by Bewick), and another Edition in 1808.

William Moss was a Surgeon of Liverpool, and was the author of a work on "The Management of Children, etc." London. 1872.

MEMORIALS of LIVERPOOL, Historical and Topographical, including a History of the Dock Estate. By J. A. PICTON, F.S.A. In two volumes.

VOL. I.—HISTORICAL.

London: Longmans, Green, and Co. 1873. All rights reserved. *Octavo.*

Half-title, Title as above, Preface, and Contents, ix. pp. Memorials, 704 pp.

VOL. II.—TOPOGRAPHICAL.

Half-title, Title, Contents, vi. pp. Memorials and Index, 605 pp.

Published at 26s. (to Subscribers). A new Edition of this valuable work is in the Press.

ANCIENT LIVERPOOL in its BUILDINGS and ARCHITECTURE, read before the Liverpool Architectural and Archæological Society, Dec. vi. MDCCCXLVIII. [Arms of Liverpool.] By JAMES A. PICTON. Liverpool: printed (for private distribution only) by D. Marples. MDCCCXLIX. *Octavo.*

Title as above, Introduction, and Ancient Liverpool, 32 pp.

Sells for 3s. 6d.

The COMMERCE of LIVERPOOL. By BRAITHWAITE POOLE, Esq. London: published by Longman and Co.; Liverpool: Thomas Baines, Castle Street. 1854. *Post octavo.*

Title as above, Dedication, Preface, and Letters, viii. pp. Commerce of Liverpool and Index, 208 pp.

Published at 8s. Mr. Poole is the author of "Statistical British Commerce," 1852.

The BOOK of the GRAND JUNCTION RAILWAY, being a HISTORY and DESCRIPTION of the Line from Birmingham to LIVERPOOL and MANCHESTER. With sixteen Engravings and four Maps. By THOMAS ROSCOE, Esq., assisted by the resident Engineers of the Line. London: Orr and Co., Paternoster Row; W. Grapel, Liverpool; George Sims, Manchester; Wrightson and Webb, Birmingham. [1839.] *Octavo.*

Engraved Title (with View of Viaduct at Birmingham), Title as above, and List of Plates, v. pp. The Book, etc., and Index, 157 pp.

LIST OF PLATES.

Map of the Line.
Aston Viaduct.
Aston Hall.
Ascott College.
Newton Road Station.
View near Penkridge.
Stafford, etc.
Whitmore.
Middlewich Canal.
Vale Royal Viaduct.
Excavation near Hartford.
Dutton Viaduct.
Preston Brook, etc.
Warrington Viaduct.
Warrington.
Liverpool Station.
Plan of Liverpool.
Plan of Manchester.
Plan of Birmingham.

Four Drawings by Cox, Bentley, Dodgson, and Radcliffe.
Published at 14s.

PEN and INK SKETCHES of LIVERPOOL TOWN COUNCILLORS. By a local artist [HUGH SHIMMEN]. Reprinted from the "Liverpool Mercury," 1857. Liverpool: Adam Holden, Church Street.

Title as above, Dedication, Contents, and Preface, ix. pp. List of Mayors, 1 p. Sketches, 200 pp. *Foolscap octavo.*

Republished in 1862 at 2s.

Hugh Shimmen was educated in Liverpool, and for some years followed the trade of a bookbinder, and afterwards became editor of the "Porcupine." He published, in 1860, a novelette, entitled, "Harry Birkett, the story of a man who helped himself." *See* also "Rambles in the Lakes," and "John Drayton." *Post.*

Publicity the true cure of Social Evils. LIVERPOOL LIFE, its pleasures, practices, and pastimes, etc. * *

> "'Tis strange, but true: for truth is always strange,
> Stranger than fiction."

Reprinted from the "Liverpool Mercury." Liverpool: Egerton Smith and Co., "Mercury" Office, Lord Street. 1857. 18*mo.*

Title as above, Dedication, Contents, and Liverpool Life, with Appendix, 111 pp.

Written by HUGH SHIMMEN. Sells for 3s.

SMITH'S STRANGER'S GUIDE to LIVERPOOL, its environs, and part of Cheshire, for 1843. By ALEXANDER BROWN, A.M. Liverpool: printed and published by Benjamin Smith, South Castle Street. *Duodecimo.*

Title as above, Preface, List of Illustrations, etc., xv. pp. Guide and Appendix, 257 pp. Plan of Liverpool, and 17 Views.

Sells for 2s. 6d.

LIVERPOOL, its COMMERCE, STATISTICS, and INSTITUTIONS, with a HISTORY of the COTTON TRADE. By HENRY SMITHERS. Liverpool: printed by Thomas Kaye, and sold by T. Kaye, G. Cruickshank, * * * and all other Booksellers. *Octavo.*

Half-title, Title as above, Dedication, and Contents, vii. pp. Prefatory Remarks, viii. pp. Liverpool, 462 pp. Index, 4 pp.

Published at 14s. Sells for 5s. Large paper copies, 8s.

The author of this work was a mathematical teacher in Liverpool.

The STREETS of LIVERPOOL. By JAMES STONEHOUSE, author of "Ye legend of ye pre-historic Manne," "Recollections of a Monogenarian," "Lacy's Handbook," etc. etc. Entered at Stationers' Hall, price 3s. 6d. Liverpool: Hime and Son, Church Street, and all Booksellers. *Post octavo.*

Title, Preface, and Index, iv. pp. Streets of Liverpool, p. 5 to p. 230.

Sells for 3s. 6d. Reprinted in 1871, price 1s.

Mr. James Stonehouse was born at Wandsworth, in Surrey, in August 1809, and settled in Liverpool in 1833, where he was for some years connected with the "Liverpool Standard." He was at one time editor of the "Chester Gazette." Besides several works referring to Liverpool, he has written occasionally for the stage.

Mr. Stonehouse also compiled "Black's Guide to Liverpool."

PICTORIAL LIVERPOOL; its ANNALS, COMMERCE, SHIPPING, INSTITUTIONS, PUBLIC BUILDINGS, Sights, Excursions, etc. A new and complete Handbook for Resident Visitor and Tourist, with a new outline Map and Illustrations. By JAMES STONEHOUSE. Liverpool: To be had of all Booksellers. 1848. [4th Edition.] *Foolscap octavo.*

Title as above, and Handbook, 282 pp.

In 1850 the above was re-issued without the Plates at 2s. 6d. Published by Henry Lacy, Bold Street, Liverpool. The 1st original Edition appeared in 1845.

LIVERPOOL; its HIGHWAYS, BYEWAYS, and THOROUGHFARES by Land and Water, being a Stranger's Guide through Town. By JAMES STONEHOUSE, author of "Lacy's Handbook for Strangers in Liverpool." Twenty-sixth Edition. Published by James Cornish and Sons, 37 Lord Street, and 42 South John Street, Liverpool; 297 High Holborn, London; and 18 Grafton Street, Dublin. 1874. [See "Cornish's Guide," p. 87.] 12*mo.*

Title as above, and Guide, 102 pp. Published at 1s.

RECOLLECTIONS of OLD LIVERPOOL, by a NONAGENARIAN. Liverpool: J. F. Hughes. 1863. Entered at Stationers' Hall. Price 3s. 6d. *Duodecimo.*

Engraved title as above, and Preface, iv. pp. Contents and Recollections, 255 pp. *Frontispiece*, View of Liverpool in 1813.

Originally published in the "Liverpool Compass," the author being Mr. Stonehouse. Published at 1s. 5d. Another Edition was dated 1869.

The STRANGER'S VADE MECUM, or LIVERPOOL DESCRIBED. A Guide to every object of interest in the Town and its Vicinity, together with the Cheshire Coast. By DAVID THOMPSON, M.D., Edin., author of "Introduction to Meteorology," late Hon. Sec. to Literary and Phil. Society, etc. etc. Liverpool: H. Greenwood, 16 Canning Street. London: Ward and Lock. Edinburgh: A. and C. Black. Dublin: J. M'Glashan; and may be had of all the Booksellers, and at the Railway Stations. *Duodecimo.*

Title as above, Dedication, Contents and Preface, xii. pp. The Guide, 196 pp.

Contains a Map of Liverpool, and Engravings of Public Buildings, etc.

LIVERPOOL CHURCHES and CHAPELS; their destruction, removal, or alteration, with Notices of Clergymen, Ministers, and others, in two Parts; to which is added the Scotch Kirks and Congregations of Liverpool, being a brief sketch of their rise and progress. By DAVID THOM, D.D. Jena; and Ph.D. A.M. Heidelberg, one of the Vice-Presidents of the Historic Society of Lancashire and Cheshire.

Read at Meetings of the Historic Society. Printed as portions of the 2d, 4th, and 5th volumes of its Transactions, and now published with the sanction of the Council. With alterations, additions, and improvements. Liverpool: Edward Howell, Church Street. 1854. *Foolscap octavo.*

Title as above, Preface, and Introduction, vi. pp. Liverpool Churches, etc., 154 pp. Sells for 2s. 6d.

A valuable addition to the History of Liverpool. The late Mr. David Thom was minister of the Scotch Church, Rodney Street, Liverpool. He was the author of several works on Divinity, etc.

The HISTORY of LIVERPOOL from the earliest authentic period down to the Present Time. Illustrated with Views of the principal Buildings in the Town and Vicinity. A Map of the Town and one of the Adjacent County. [12 lines from Virgil.] Liverpool: printed and sold by William Robinson, Castle Street. 1810. [By T. TROUGHTON.] *Quarto.*

Title as above, and Contents, viii. pp. Introduction, vi. pp. Half-title, i. p. History, 389 pp.

PLATES.

Plate	Position
View of Liverpool	*Frontispiece*
Prince Rupert's Head Quarters	*To face* p. 56
Liverpool, 1650	„ 66
Ancient Lodge or Gateway leading to "Hut in Hale Wood"	„ 96
The Mount	„ 112
Allerton Hall	„ 144
The Pier Head	„ 160
Burscough Priory	„ 166
Abbey of Birkenhead	„ 168
Formby Hall	„ 177
Ancient Well at Wavertree	„ 192
Gothic Abbey at Lydiate	„ 193
Runcorn	„ 208
Woodside Ferry	„ 224
Knott's Hole	„ 241
North Shore	„ 256
All Saints	*To follow the last*
Liverpool, 1704	*To face* p. 265
Ancient Land Mark	„ 270
Goree Warehouse	„ 274
The Town Hall	„ 284
Infirmary	„ 290
Dispensary	„ 297
School for the Blind (2 Plates)	„ 300
Blue Coat School	„ 306
Workhouse	„ 309
Fever Ward	„ 313

Plate	Position
The Ancient Tower in Bank Street	*To face* p. 317
Almshouse	*To follow the last*
Theatre	*To face* p. 320
Music Hall	„ 326
Exchange Buildings	„ 329
Corn Exchange	„ 335
Custom House	„ 338
King's Tobacco Warehouses	„ 339
Post-Office, Church Street	*To follow the last*
Lyceum and Library	*To face* p. 342
Athenæum	„ 344
Union	„ 345
Free Masons' Hall	„ 352
Corporation Waterworks	„ 362
Entrance to Botanic Gardens (2 Plates)	„ 365
Conservatory in Botanic Gardens	*To follow the last*
St. Nicholas's Church	*To face* p. 370
Peter's the Poor	„ 372
George's	„ 374
Thomas'	„ 376
Paul's	„ 377
Anne's	„ 379
John's	*To follow the last*
Trinity Church	*To face* p. 380
St. Catherine's	„ 381

St. Stephen's .	*To follow the last*	Leeds Street Chapel	*To follow the last*
Christ Church .	*To face* p. 382	Catholic Chapel	*To face* p. 387
St. Michael's .	*To follow the last*	Quakers' Meeting House	„ 389
Andrew's .	*To face* p. 385	St. Mark's Church	*To follow the last*
Scotch Kirk . .	„ 386		

Presbyterian Chapel . . *To follow the last.*

The Plan of Liverpool was published at the same time, but is not bound up with the volume.

The Engravings were many of them done by Nesbit and Branston, who were pupils of Bewick.

Sells for 15s. Though not always to be relied on as to fact, it is a valuable addition to the literature of Liverpool.

In the Liverpool Free Public Library, in addition to the above, is the author's own copy, partly interleaved, and containing a large number of additional Plates, Maps, etc. This is bound in 2 volumes.

Thomas Troughton was a Bookseller in Ranelagh Street, Liverpool. The publication of this work nearly ruined him.

A General and descriptive HISTORY of the antient and present state of the TOWN of LIVERPOOL, comprising a review of its Government, Police, Antiquities, and modern improvements, the progressive increase of Streets, Squares, Public Buildings, and Inhabitants; together with a circumstantial account of the true cause of its extensive African Trade. The whole carefully compiled from original Manuscripts, authentic records, and other warranted authority. Second Edition. Liverpool: printed for and sold by Crane and Jones, Castle Street; and Vernon and Hood, Birchin Lane, London. 1797. *Octavo.*

Title as above, etc., vi. pp. Description, etc., 310 pp.

This was written by J. WALLACE. The First Edition was published in 1795, a copy of which is in the Chetham Library.

An Accurate DESCRIPTION of the LIVERPOOL and MANCHESTER RAIL-WAY; the Tunnel, the bridges, and other works throughout the Line; an account of the opening of the Rail-way, and the melancholy accident which occurred. A Short MEMOIR of the late RIGHT HON. WM. HUSKISSON, and particulars of the Funeral Procession, etc. With a Map of the Line, and a View of the Bridge over Water Street, Manchester. By JAMES SCOTT WALKER.

"Propitious Commerce, hail! thy offspring these,
Thine each gay charm the eye delighted sees."
ROSCOE.

The Second Edition. Liverpool: printed and published by J. F. Cannell, 81 Lord Street, where it may be had, and of the Booksellers in London, etc. etc. MDCCCXXX. *Octavo.*

Title as above, Dedication, and Description, etc., 52 pp.

Sells for 3s. 6d.

James Scott Walker, the son of Mr. W. Walker, was born 25th December 1792, at St. Cyrus, in the County of Kincardine.

Some ACCOUNT of the EPIDEMIC FEVER which prevailed in LIVERPOOL in the latter months of the year 1844. By GEORGE CHURCHILL WATSON, M.D., Edin., Associate Member of the Surgical Society of Ireland. From the "Provincial Medical and Surgical Journal." Deighton and Co., Printers, Worcester. 1846. *Octavo.*

Title as above, and Account, 26 pp. Contains a Map of part of Liverpool.

WHITBY'S GUIDE to LIVERPOOL, containing History and Description of the Town and Docks; eminent Persons; Description of the River, Churches, and Chapels; Literary and Scientific Societies; Charitable Institutions; Markets; Principal Streets; Public Buildings; Ferries; Surrounding Places, etc. etc. With Engravings on Steel and Wood. Liverpool: "Daily Post" Steam Print Works, Cable Street. 1868. *Demy 18mo.*

Title as above, Advertisement, Index to Illustrations, and Contents, xii. pp. Guide, 231 pp. Contains a Folding Map.

The STRANGER in LIVERPOOL, a historical and descriptive View of the Town of Liverpool and its environs. [Quotation from Thompson, 9 lines.] The Eighth Edition, with corrections and additions. Liverpool: printed and sold by T. Kaye, 45 Castle Street; sold also by J. Gore and Son. [A long list of other Booksellers.] 1825. *Duodecimo.*

Title as above, Advertisement, Contents, etc., viii. pp. The Stranger, and Appendix, 352 pp. Contains Folding Plan of Liverpool, and a number of views of principal Buildings.

The following Editions were published:—The First in 1807; Second in 1810; Third in 1812; Fourth in 1814; Fifth in 1816; Sixth in 1820 (this is the First Edition with the Appendix of the Journal of Edward Moore); the Seventh in 1823 (the plan of the work being re-arranged, and the number of Illustrations at the end); the Eighth in 1825 (an Import and Export Chart added); the Ninth in 1829 (an Appendix for the Ancient Town Records added); the Tenth in 1833; the Eleventh in 1836; the Twelfth in 1839, which was reprinted in 1840, 1841, 1848, and 1850.

The ROYAL PICTURESQUE HAND-BOOK of LIVERPOOL: a Manual for Residents and Visitors, with a day at Birkenhead, and a series of pleasure Excursions in the Environs. Embellished with a Map of the Town and numerous Engravings. Eighth Edition. Liverpool: Edward Howell, Church Street; Chapman and Hall, London, and sold by all the Booksellers in Liverpool and Manchester. 1852. *Duodecimo.*

Title as above, Dedication (signed H. M. Addey), Advertisement, etc., List of Illustrations, Hand-Book, and Index, 157 pp.

Sells for 2s. 6d.

A GENERAL and DESCRIPTIVE HISTORY of the ANCIENT and present state of the TOWN of LIVERPOOL, comprising a review of its Government, Police, Antiquities, and modern improvements; the progressive increase of Streets, Squares, Public Buildings, and Inhabitants, together with a circumstantial account of the true causes of its extensive African Trade. The whole carefully compiled from original manuscripts, authentic records, and other warranted authorities. Liverpool: printed by J. M'Creery, Houghton Street; and sold by all Booksellers. *Octavo.*

Title as above, Dedication, and Introduction, vi. pp. History, 301 pp. Errata, 1 p. Folding Map of Liverpool.

Published in 1795. A duplicate of this Edition was printed in the same year by R. Phillips. The Second Edition was printed for and sold by Crane and Jones, Castle Street, Liverpool, and Vernon and Hood, Birchin Lane, London.

Title and Introduction, iv. pp. History, 302 pp.

A copy of the First Edition is in the Liverpool Free Public Library, and of the Second in the Bodleian Library.

Sells for 5s.

New practical GUIDE to the TOWN of LIVERPOOL, or LIVERPOOL AS IT IS IN 1865, forming a guide to the stranger, and a companion for the resident. With a tour through Birkenhead and the country round. Illustrated with nearly 50 woodcut engravings, and a reference map of the town and suburbs. Liverpool: Edward Howell, Church Street, "Temple of the Muses." MDCCCLXV. *Foolscap octavo.*

Title as above, Dedication, and Preface, v. pp. Guide and Index, 178 pp. Folding Map and Woodcuts at head of chapters.

A Lecture on the RISE and PROGRESS of LIVERPOOL. By JAMES M. WALTHEW. Liverpool: Gilbert G. Walmsley, 50 Lord Street. 1865. *Octavo.*

Title as above, Preface, and Lecture, 57 pp. Contains a Plan of "Site of Liverpool."

Sells for 1s. 6d.

The PICTURE of LIVERPOOL, or STRANGER'S GUIDE. Liverpool: W. Jones and C. Woodward. 1805. *Duodecimo.*

A second Edition was published in 1808, and other editions in 1834 and 1838.

Sells for 2s.

Sepherah Shelosh. [The same words in Hebrew.] Three LETTERS, sent to some DISPERSED, but well-advised JEWS, now resident at LIVERPOOL, in Lancashire. Proving the true Advent of their Messias, from the Annals of sacred Scripture, and by the Science of the Stars; without the help of Prophane History. In which the Gospel is freed from all Rabbinical Aspersion, and Jewish Infamy. By J. WILLME.

φιλαλεθὴς, 2 Cor. 13, 8, and Jo. 17, 17.
Atq.; Αρότης, Eccles. 5, 9, and Is. 28, 23-29.

London: printed for the Author, in the Year MDCCLVI. *Sm. quarto.*

Title as above, Carnal Counsil, Contents, and Explanation, 14 pp. The First or Rabbi's Letter, p. 15 to p. 68. The Second Letter to the Jews, p. 69 to p. 122. The Third Letter, p. 123 to p. 150. The Postscript, p. 151 to p. 195. The Epilogue, p. 196 to p. 235. General Index, p. 236 to p. 240.

A copy of this extremely rare work is in the Library of Dr. Kendrick, Warrington.

The author of the above was of the family of Willme of Martin's Croft, near Warrington, from which place the Letters above named are dated.

A Correct TRANSLATION of the CHARTER granted to the BURGESSES of LIVERPOOL by KING WILLIAM the THIRD, with remarks and explanatory Notes. To which are added the Charter granted by King George the Second. The order of the Common Council, and the Petition for obtaining that Charter, with the Report of the Attorney and Solicitor-General thereon. Liverpool: printed by J. Johnson in Fenwick Street. MDCCLXXXIII. *Octavo.*

Title as above, and Preface, viii. pp. Translation, 48 pp. By Philodemus [Joseph Clegg]. First published in 1757.

Sells for 3s. 6d.

The CHARTERS granted to the Burgesses of LIVERPOOL by William III., with notes and explanatory remarks on the same. Also the Charter of George II., the order of Common Council, and the petition for obtaining that Charter, with the Report of the Attorney and Solicitor-General thereon. Opinion of Counsel respecting the Power of making Bye-laws, and an Extract from the Act of 2 George III. To which is added a Summary of the Proceedings of the Burgesses and Common Council from the reign of Elizabeth to the present time, with an Epitome of the two Trials at Lancaster between the Corporation and the Common Council. Liverpool: printed for the Editor by Egerton Smith and Co., and sold by them and by W. Robinson, Castle Street, and the rest of the Booksellers. 1810. *Octavo.*

Title as above, Dedication, and Preface, 8 pp. The Charters, 9-128 pp.

Sells for 3s. 6d.

BOROUGH of LIVERPOOL PROCEEDINGS of the COUNCIL, 1862-63.

[Arms of Liverpool.]

Printed for the Corporation of Liverpool by George M'Corquodale and Co. 1863. *Octavo.*

Title as above, and Introduction, xxii. pp. Proceedings, 263 pp. (Followed by Financial Statements, etc.)

This is the first volume since 1863. The proceedings have been regularly published.

PROCEEDINGS in an ACTION at LAW brought by the MAYOR, Bailiffs, and Burgesses of the Borough of LIVERPOOL, for the recovery of a penalty under a Bye-law made there in Common Hall assembled, containing the argument of the Counsel as well at Nisi Prius as upon the motion of a New Trial in the Court of Queen's Bench. The Proceedings of the second Trial at Lancaster, and on a motion in the Court of King's Bench for a Third Trial, with the reasons at large of the Hon. the Justices of the said Court for granting the same. Taken in Shorthand by Mr. GURNEY. Liverpool: printed and sold by J. M'CREERY. Sold also by Crane and Jones and W. Robinson, Liverpool; and by M. Poole and Son, Chester. 1796. *Octavo.*

Title as above, and Introduction, xiii. pp. Report, 404 pp. Errata, 1 p. Sells for 5s. 6d.

A copy is in the Liverpool Free Public Library.

A copious REPORT of the INQUIRY into the AFFAIRS of the CORPORATION of LIVERPOOL, before Her Majesty's Commissioners, George Hutton Wilkinson and Thomas Jefferson Hogg, Esqs. Commenced on the 4th, and ended on the 30th November 1833, in the Sessions-House, Chapel Street. [Arms of Liverpool.] Liverpool: printed and published by Egerton Smith and Co., "Mercury" Office, 68 Lord Street. 1833. *Quarto.*

Title as above, and Report, 76 pp.

A copy is in the Liverpool Free Public Library.

LIVERPOOL CLERGY. REPORT of the PROCEEDINGS in the COURT of CHANCERY, before the Right Hon. the Master of the Rolls, upon an Information filed on the 13th November 1835 by His Majesty's Attorney-General, at the relation of Thomas Bolton and Timothy Jevons, against the Mayor, Bailiffs, and Burgesses of the Town of Liverpool, in the County of Lancaster, touching the Endowment of the Rectors and Curates of the Parish, and of certain of the Clergy of some of the Churches in Liverpool (as taken in shorthand), with an Appendix, containing copies of the Information and Affidavits. London: published by Saunders and Benning, 43 Fleet Street; and Thomas Kaye, Castle Street, Liverpool. 1835. *Octavo.*

Title as above, Report, and Appendix, 257 pp.

A copy is in the Liverpool Free Public Library.

TOWN-HALL LIVERPOOL OATH BOOK. List of Oaths. [The Mayor's and 15 others.] Printed by J. Gore and Son, Lithographers, Liverpool. 1824. *Folio.*

Title, i. p. Oaths, 34 pp. (Printed on one side only.)

A copy is in the Liverpool Free Public Library.

The FLORA of LIVERPOOL. A List of the Indigenous Flowering Plants and Ferns growing within fifteen miles of the Liverpool Exchange, and two miles of Southport. Published by the Liverpool Naturalists' Field Club, and sold at their Depository by Mr. R. P. Ker, 6 Basnet Street, and at the Honorary Treasurer's, Mr. John Abraham, 87 Bond Street. Liverpool: printed by W. Fearnall, 12 Old Post-Office Place, Church Street. 1872. *Octavo.*

Title as above (Errata on a slip), and Preface, vi. pp. Flora, 178 pp. Index, 4 pp.

The basis of this work is T. B. Hall's "Flora of Liverpool." [See p. 89.]

LIVERPOOL 18TH CENTURY DIRECTORIES.

The LIVERPOOL DIRECTORY for the year 1766, containing an Alphabetical List of the Merchants, Tradesmen, and Principal Inhabitants of the Town of Liverpool, with their respective Addresses; also separate Lists of the Worshipful the Mayor and Common Council; Officers of the Customs and Excise; Commissioners of the Docks, Light-Houses, Watch, Lamp, and Scavengers; Stage-Coaches, Waggons, and Carriers, with the times of coming in and going out; Vessels trading to London, Manchester, Bankey, Northwich, Winsford, Chester, Preston, and Lancaster, with their Agents. Liverpool: printed by J. Gore, Bookseller, near the Exchange. 1766. *Foolscap octavo.*

Title as above, and Directory, 28 pp.

GORE'S LIVERPOOL DIRECTORY for 1769. Title as in the 1st Edition, except that "Bristol" was added to the List of Trade Places. (Printed by William Nevett and Co. in Prince's Street, Liverpool.)

Title and Directory, 53 pp.

In 1773 J. Gore published another Liverpool Directory. Title and Directory, 62 pp., in which he states that "the very small sale of the former editions of this work had well nigh prevented any further attempt of the same kind; but the publisher, anxious to contribute his mite to the service of the community, has determined *once more* to solicit its countenance and support."

GORE'S LIVERPOOL DIRECTORY for 1774. Printed for John Gore, No. 1 Castle Street. *Foolscap octavo.*

Title and Directory, 80 pp.

In addition to the Addresses of the Inhabitants, the numbers as affixed to their houses are added.

GORE'S LIVERPOOL DIRECTORY for 1777. Printed for John Gore (as above). *Foolscap octavo.*

Title and Directory, 123 pp.

GORE'S LIVERPOOL DIRECTORY for 1781. *Post octavo.*

Title and Directory, 136 pp.

LIVERPOOL DIRECTORY for 1783. This Directory was published by William Bailey, Liverpool. We have not seen a copy of it.

GORE'S LIVERPOOL DIRECTORY for 1790. *Octavo.*

Title and Directory, 256 pp.

GORE'S LIVERPOOL DIRECTORY for 1796. *Octavo.*

Title and Directory, 272 pp.

A complete set of Gore's Directories is preserved by Messrs. J. Mawdsley and Son of Castle Street, Liverpool.

The LIVERPOOL DIRECTORY for the Year 1790, etc.[1] By CHARLES WOSENCROFT, Printer. Printed and sold by the Author at his Office in Cook Street; also sold by most of the Booksellers. *Royal* 18*mo.*

Title, Dedication, and Directory, 152 pp.

A copy is in the Liverpool Free Public Library.

LIVERPOOL ELECTIONS.

A true and impartial ACCOUNT of the ELECTION of the Representatives in Parliament for the Corporation and Borough of LEVERPOOL. October the 16th, 1710. London. [No printer's name.]

Title, etc., 31 pp.

A copy of this very rare work is in the Library of J. A. Picton, Esq., F.S.A. of Liverpool. It affords important evidence as to the early existence of a Liverpool newspaper. The editor, alluding to the votes recorded, states —"I cannot give the exact account the *newspaper* returned them, etc."

A GENUINE COLLECTION of all the PAPERS, ADDRESSES, SONGS, EPIGRAMS, and ACROSTICKS. Printed by all Parties during the late CONTEST for REPRESENTATIVE in the ensuing Parliament for the Borough of LIVERPOOL. Which began on Tuesday, March 31, and ended April 6th. With some curious Manuscripts, to which is added an Alphabetical List of the Poll. Liverpool: printed by R. Williamson, near the Exchange. MDCCLXI. *Octavo.*

Title as above, and Papers, etc., 148 pp. List of Poll, 60 pp.

A copy of this is in the Manchester Free Public Library.

An entire and impartial COLLECTION of all the PAPERS, etc., published on both sides concerning the late ELECTION in LIVERPOOL, for Members to serve in Parliament. (A List of the Poll and of Members since 1660 added.)

Published May 12, 1761, by John Sibbald, Castle Street, Liverpool.

A COLLECTION of PAPERS, ADDRESSES, SONGS, etc. Printed on all sides, during the CONTEST for REPRESENTATIVES

[1] Not quoted in full.

in PARLIAMENT for the BOROUGH of LIVERPOOL, between Bamber Gascoyne jun., Richard Pennant, and Henry Rawlinson, Esquires. Which began on Tuesday, September 12, and ended September the 16th, 1780. To which is annexed an Alphabetical List of the Poll; as also the Names of the Gentlemen who have represented this Corporation in Parliament. From the year 1660 to the present time. Liverpool: printed by T. Johnson, near the Exchange. MDCCLXXX. *Octavo.*

Title as above, xi. pp. Collection, 128 pp.
Very scarce. A copy is in the Bodleian Library.

An Alphabetical LIST of the FREEMEN who voted at the contested ELECTION for MEMBERS of PARLIAMENT to represent the BOROUGH of LIVERPOOL; between Bamber Gascoyne Jun., Esquire, Colonel Tarleton, the Right Hon. Lord Penryhn, and Sir William Meredith, Baronet. Which began on Saturday, the 3d of APRIL 1784, and closed on the Saturday following, before the Worshipful William Hesketh, Esq., Mayor; Charles Pole and Edmond Rigby, Gentlemen Bailiffs. Liverpool: printed by Thomas Johnson, No. 10 Castle Street. MDCCLXXXIV. *Octavo.*

Title as above, etc., ii. pp. List, etc., 50 pp.
A copy is in the Bodleian Library.

In Mr. Mott's List of Books, published in Liverpool (Lanc. and Ches. His. Soc.) is included "The Poll for the Election of M.P.'s for the Borough and Corporation of Liverpool." [1754.] We have not seen a copy of this.

The POLL for the ELECTION of MEMBERS of PARLIAMENT for the BOROUGH of LIVERPOOL, taken between Colonel Tarleton, Bamber Gascoyne Jun., Esq., the Right Hon. Richard, Lord Penrhyn, and Thomas Townley Parker, Esq., which begun at the Exchange on Monday the 21st June 1790, and ended the Monday evening following, before the Worshipful Thomas Smyth, Esq., Mayor, Henry Blundell, and John Shaw, Esquires, Bailiffs. Also the ADDRESSES, SONGS, SQUIBS, etc., with the list of the Members who have represented this Borough since the year 1660. Liverpool: Printed by T. Johnson, Castle Street. *Octavo.*

Title, Addresses, etc., and Poll List, 116 pp.
A copy is in the Liverpool Free Public Library.

The POLL for the ELECTION of MEMBERS of PARLIAMENT for the BOROUGH of LIVERPOOL, taken between General Tarleton, Colonel Gascoyne, and John Tarleton, Esq., which begun at the Hustings on Saturday the 28th May of 1796, and ended on Wednesday the 1st of June, before the Worshipful Thomas Naylor, Esq., Mayor, Spencer Steers, and Peter W. Brancker, Esquires, Bailiffs. Also the ADDRESSES, SONGS, SQUIBS, etc., with the list of those Members who have represented the Borough since the year 1660. Liverpool: printed and sold by H. Hodgson, No. 51 Ranelagh Street. *Octavo.*

Title as above, Addresses, etc., and Poll List, 108 pp.

A copy is in the Liverpool Free Public Library.

The POLL for the ELECTION of MEMBERS of PARLIAMENT for the BOROUGH of LIVERPOOL, taken between Lieutenant-General Tarleton, Major-General Gascoyne, Mr. Joseph Birch, and Mr. Francis Chalmer, Merchants, which began at the Exchange on Tuesday the 6th of July 1802, and ended the Friday following, before the Worshipful Peter Whitfield Brancker, Mayor, Thomas Hinde, and John Bridge Aspinall, Esqs., Bailiffs. Also the ADDRESSES, SONGS, SQUIBS, etc., with a list of the Members who have represented Liverpool since 1660. Liverpool: printed by Ferguson, Mackey, and Co., at the General Printing Office, near the top of Lord Street. 1802. *Octavo.*

Title as above, Addresses, and List, etc., 80 pp.

A copy is in the Liverpool Free Public Library.

HISTORY of the ELECTION for MEMBERS of PARLIAMENT for the BOROUGH of LIVERPOOL, 1806, containing the Addresses of the different Candidates, with a list of the Freemen's names who voted. To which are prefixed observations on the importance of the Representative system, with hints on the necessity of a Reform in that branch of the constitution.

"On virtue can alone this kingdom stand."
[10 following lines.]
THOMSON'S "Liberty."

Liverpool: printed by Jones and Wright, "Chronicle" Office, and sold by W. Jones, 56 Castle Street. Price 3s. 6d. *Octavo.*

Title as above, Preface, etc., x. pp. Addresses, etc., 46 pp. Poll, 56 pp.

A copy is in the Bodleian Library.

An IMPARTIAL COLLECTION of the ADDRESSES, SONGS, SQUIBS, etc., that were published at LIVERPOOL during the ELECTION of MEMBERS of PARLIAMENT in November 1806.

CANDIDATES.

Lieut.-Gen. Ban. Tarleton. | Major-General Isaac Gascoyne.
and Wm. Roscoe, Esq.

Dublin: printed by John Adams, Franklin Street. Price Two Shillings, British. *Foolscap octavo.*

Title as above, and Collection, 88 pp.

Very scarce. The copy in the author's library has all names (originally left blank) written on the margin in red ink.

The POLL for the ELECTION of MEMBERS of PARLIAMENT for the BOROUGH and CORPORATION of LIVERPOOL, taken between Lieut.-Gen. Banastre-Tarleton, Major-Gen. Isaac Gascoyne, William Roscoe, Esq., and William Joseph Denison, Esq., begun and held on the Hustings, fronting the Town Hall of the said Borough, on Thursday the 7th, and ended on Thursday the 14th day of May 1807, before the Worshipful Thomas Molyneux, Esq., Mayor, Wm. Rigg, and John Clarke, Esqs., Bailiffs. Liverpool: printed by J. Gore, Castle Street. Price One Shilling and Sixpence. *Duodecimo.*

Title as above, and Poll, 51 pp.

A copy is in the Liverpool Free Public Library.

A COLLECTION of ADDRESSES, SONGS, SQUIBS, etc., published at LIVERPOOL during the ELECTION for MEMBERS of PARLIAMENT in May 1807.

CANDIDATES.

Lieut.-Gen. B. Tarleton. | W. Roscoe, Esq.,
Major-Gen. J. Gascoyne. | J. W. Denison, Esq.,
and Mr. George Dyke.

Isleman: printed by John Herring. 1807. *Duodecimo.*

Title as above, and a Collection, 165 pp.

A copy of this is in the Liverpool Free Public Library.

The POLL for the ELECTION of MEMBERS of PARLIAMENT for the BOROUGH and CORPORATION of LIVERPOOL, taken between the Right Hon. George Canning, Lieut.-Gen. Isaac Gascoyne, Henry Brougham, Esq., Thomas Creevey, Esq., and Gen. Banastre Tarleton, Begun and held in the Hustings, in front of the Town-Hall, on Thursday the 8th, and ended on Friday the 16th day of October 1812. Before the Worshipful John Bourne, Esq., Mayor; Edward Pearson and Thos. Corrie, Esqs., Bailiffs. Liverpool: printed by J. Gore, Castle Street. Price Two Shillings. *Duodecimo.*

Title and work, 68 pp.

A copy of this is in the Liverpool Free Public Library.

An impartial COLLECTION of ADDRESSES, SONGS, SQUIBS, etc., published during the Election of MEMBERS of PARLIAMENT for the borough of LIVERPOOL, October 1812.

CANDIDATES.

Right Hon. George Canning.
Lieutenant-General Isaac Gascoyne.
Henry Brougham, Esq.
Thomas Creevey, Esq.
And General Banastre Tarleton.

Isleman: printed by Timothy Herring. 1812. *Duodecimo.*

Title as above, and Collection, etc., 134 pp.

A copy of this is in the Liverpool Free Public Library.

The SQUIB BOOK, being a collection of the Addresses, Songs, Squibs, and other Papers issued during the contested election at Liverpool in June 1818.

CANDIDATES.

Right Hon. George Canning.
General Gascoyne.
Lord Sefton.

Liverpool: printed and published by W. Bethell, Marshall Street. 1818. *Octavo.*

Title, Addresses, etc., 64 pp.

A copy is in the Liverpool Free Public Library.

The SQUIB BOOK, being an impartial account of the Liverpool Election, March 1820, containing the Addresses, Songs, Squibs, and Speeches of each party during the Contest, to which is prefixed the Law of Elections.

CANDIDATES.

Right Hon. George Canning.
General Gascoyne.
Dr. Crompton.
Thomas Leyland, Esq.

Liverpool: printed and sold by Taylor and Willmer, Ranelagh Street; sold also by all the Booksellers. 1820. *Duodecimo.*

Title as above, and Account of Election, xiv. pp. Squib Book, 134 pp. Addenda, 16 pp.

A copy is in the Liverpool Free Public Library.

The POLL for the ELECTION of a MEMBER of PARLIAMENT for the Borough of LIVERPOOL, taken between

William Ewart, Esq.,
And John Evelyn Dennison, Esq.,

in Front of the Town Hall, from Tuesday, November 23d to Tuesday November 30th, 1830. Before Thomas Brancker, Esq., Mayor, Anthony Molyneux, and Thomas Fisher, Esqs., Bailiffs. To which are added a History of the Election, Lists of the unpolled Freemen, etc. Liverpool: printed by J. Gore and Son, Castle Street. 1830.

Title as above and Election, lx. pp. List of Freemen, 92 pp.

The copy of this in the Liverpool Free Public Library has in MS. the amount paid to a large number of the voters [Freemen !]

LIVERPOOL ELECTION, MAY 2d, 1831.

CANDIDATES.

William Ewart, Esq.
John Evelyn Denison, Esq.
General Gascoyne.

The SQUIB BOOK, containing the SONGS, SQUIBS, ADDRESSES,

etc., issued during the Election. Printed and sold by E. Metcalfe, Lord Street. *Octavo.*

Title as above and Squibs Book, 18 pp.

A copy is in the Liverpool Free Public Library.

The POLL for the ELECTION of MEMBERS of PARLIAMENT for the BOROUGH of LIVERPOOL taken between William Ewart, Esq., Lord Viscount Sandon, Thomas Thorneley, Esq., and Major-General Sir Howard Douglas, Bart., at the Polling Booths on Wednesday the 12th of December and Thursday the 13th December 1832, to which is added a brief History of the Election, being the first Election of Members for the Borough of Liverpool under the Reform Bill.

The Worshipful Charles Horsfall, Esq., Mayor; James Aspinall and Robertson Gladstone, Esqs., Bailiffs. Liverpool: printed by J. and J. Mawdsley (successors to J. Gore and Son), Castle Street. *Royal 18mo.*

Title as above and History of Election, xii. pp. The Poll, etc., 204 pp.

A copy is in the Liverpool Free Public Library.

The POLL for the ELECTION of MEMBERS of PARLIAMENT for the BOROUGH of LIVERPOOL taken between William Ewart, Esq., Lord Viscount Sandon, Thomas Thorneley, Esq., and Major-General Sir Howard Douglas, Bart., at the Polling Booths on Wednesday the 12th December and Thursday the 13th December 1832. To which is affixed a brief History of the Election, being the first Election of Members for the Borough under the Reform Bill.

The worshipful Charles Horsfall, Esq., Mayor; James Aspinall and Robertson Gladstone, Esqs., Bailiffs. Liverpool: printed by J. and J. Mawdsley (successors to J. Gore and Son), Castle Street. 1833. *Duodecimo.*

Title as above and Introductory pages, xii. pp. The Poll, etc., 162 pp.

A copy of this is in the Liverpool Free Public Library.

The POLL for the ELECTION of MEMBERS of PARLIAMENT for the BOROUGH of LIVERPOOL taken between Lord Viscount Sandon, Cresswell Cresswell, Esq., William Ewart, Esq., and Howard Elphinstone, Esq., in the Sixteen Wards on Tuesday the 25th July 1837.

The Worshipful William Earle Jun., Esq., Mayor. Liverpool: printed by J. and J. Mawdsley, Castle Street. 1837. *Duodecimo.*

Title as above and Poll, 176 pp.

A copy of this is in the Liverpool Free Public Library.

The POLL for the ELECTION of MEMBERS of PARLIAMENT for the BOROUGH of LIVERPOOL taken between Lord Viscount Sandon, Cresswell Cresswell, Esq., Lord Viscount Palmerston, and Sir Joshua Walmsley, Knt., in the Sixteen Wards on Wednesday the 30th June 1841. The Worshipful Thomas Bolton, Esq., Mayor. Liverpool: printed by J. Mawdsley, Castle Street. 1841. *Duodecimo.*

Title as above and Poll, etc., 204 pp.

A copy is in the Liverpool Free Public Library.

Account of the TRIAL of CHARLES ANGUS, Esq., on an Indictment for the murder (by attempted abortion) of Margaret Burns, at Lancaster Assizes, 2d September 1808. Liverpool. 1808. *Octavo.*

Title and Trial, 288 pp.

Sells for 5s.

LIVERPOOL in 1825, a SATIRE. See Part III.

MOUNT PLEASANT, A DESCRIPTIVE POEM. By W. Roscoe. See Part III.

LETTER written from LIVERPOOL, Chester, etc. By S. Derrick. See Part IV.

A TOUR from LIVERPOOL to LONDON. By Ephraim Wood. See Part IV.

TOPOGRAPHY and DIRECTORY of the NORTH and SOUTH LONSDALE, AMOUNDERNESS, LEYLAND, and the TOWN of SOUTHPORT, with a History of FURNESS ABBEY and the Religious Orders, and an Essay on the GEOLOGY of the LAKE DIS-

TRICT, and their Approaches. By P. MANNEX and Co. Preston: printed for the Proprietors, Oxford Street, by J. Hackness, 121 Church Street. 1866. Price to non-subscribers, 12s. 6d. *Octavo.*

Title as above, Contents, etc., viii. pp. Topography, etc., 612 pp.

HISTORY, TOPOGRAPHY, and DIRECTORY of Westmoreland, and of the HUNDREDS of LONSDALE and AMOUNDERNESS, in LANCASHIRE, together with a Description and Geological View of the whole of the LAKE DISTRICT. Illustrated by a Map of each County. By MANNEX and Co. Printed for the Authors by W. H. Johnson Beverley. 1851. *Octavo.*

Title as above, and Preface, iv. pp. History, etc., 719 pp.
Price to Subscribers, 17s. 6d. Sells for 3s. 6d.

HISTORY of NORTH LANCASHIRE, or the HUNDRED of LONSDALE North of the Sands, from the History of Cumberland and Westmoreland. By THOMAS WRIGHT, F.S.A., Rev. J. G. CUMMING, F.G.S., and HARRIET MARTINEAU. Edited by WILLIAM WHELLAN. Only ten copies detached. Manchester. MDCCCLX. *Quarto.*

Title as above, i. p. History of Lonsdale, p. 897 to p. 944.
One of these ten is in the Rochdale Free Public Library, and another is in the Author's Library.

HISTORY of LYTHAM, in the Hundred of Amounderness, County Palatine of Lancaster.

The Editor of the "York Lynx" states that "Lytham possesses many pretty scenes and delightful walks, and is well calculated for the restoration of health to the valetudinarian—L'été est la plus agreable de toutes les saisons."

Latham and Baines' Account of the Marine Village are included, and a Descriptive History is also given from a Yorkshire publication, entitled the "Babbler." A cento is added, consisting of Tales in prose and poetry, and other analectæ, or the Phenomena of the Ocean and its Inhabitants. Dedicated to those who visit the saline shores of Lytham. Authorities: Leigh, Carlisle, Ashton, Baines, Latham, Gregson, and others. [By P. WHITTLE.] *Octavo.*

Title as above, Preface, and History, 88 pp. Frontispiece is a View of Lytham.
This forms one of the Histories in Whittle's "Marina." See p. 7.

A CURSORY DESCRIPTION of LYTHAM and its adjacencies.

"Ye who, amid this feverish world, would wear."
[And nine other lines.] ARMSTRONG.

Preston: printed by A. Walker, and sold by Hugh Holmes.
Lytham.
* *
*
1813. *Foolscap octavo.*

Half-title, Title as above, and Description, 23 pp. Scarce.

A History of Lytham was written by Captain WILLIAM LATHAM, and published at Preston in 1799.

HISTORICAL NOTICES of the TOWN and PARISH of MIDDLETON, in the County Palatine of Lancaster. By EDWIN BUTTERWORTH. Middleton: printed and sold by William Horsman. 1840. *Post octavo.*

Title as above, Introduction, Addendum, Notices, and Index, 62 pp.

Contains little original matter. Scarce. A copy is in the Author's Library.

The VILLAGE of MILNROW, and the COTTAGE of TIM BOBBIN, near Rochdale. By EDWIN WAUGH. Manchester: printed by John J. Sale, 1 Spring Gardens. 1850. *Octavo.*

Title as above, and Village of Milnrow, etc., 12 pp.

Although only a Tract, this is of sufficient interest to warrant its insertion here.

MYTTON. See Stonyhurst (*Post*).

MEOLS, NORTH. See Southport (*Post*).

A Description of the Country from thirty to forty Miles round MANCHESTER. Containing its Geography, Natural and Civil; principal productions; river and canal navigations; a particular account of its towns and chief villages; their history, population, commerce, and manufactures; buildings, government, etc. The materials arranged, and the work composed, by J. AIKIN, M.D. Embellished with seventy-three plates.

> "The echoing hills repeat
> The stroke of ax and hammer; scaffolds rise," etc. etc.
> [5 more lines from DYER'S "Fleece."]

London: printed for John Stockdale. *Quarto.*

Half-title, Title as above, Prefatory Advertisement, List of Plates, and Contents, xvi. pp. List of Subscribers, 8 pp. (not paged). Introduction, Description, and Index, 624 pp.

LIST OF PLATES.

1. *Frontispiece.*
2. *Title, with Vignette.*
3. Index, Map to Canals . . . P. 1
4. Map of Lancashire . . . 9
5. „ Cheshire . . . 39
6. „ Derbyshire . . . 64
7. „ Yorkshire (West Riding) . . . 89
8. Map of Staffordshire . . . 98
9. Plan of Canal from Manchester to Runcorn . . . 112
10. View of the Aqueduct at Barton Bridge . . . 113
11. Plan of the Canal from the Trent to Mersey . . . 116
12. Plan of the Leeds and Liverpool Canal . . . 123
13. Plan of the Rochdale Canal 130
14. „ Huddersfield Canal to Ashton . . . 131
15. Plan of the Lancaster Canal . . . 133
16. Plan of the Ellesmere Canal . . . 135
17. Plan of a Lock for a Canal . . . 137
18. Plan of an Aqueduct for a Canal . . . *ib.*
19. Plan of a Bridge for a Canal . . . 138
20. Plan of an Accommodation Bridge . . . *ib.*
21. Plan of Melandra Castle, *ib.*; for description, see page . . . 618
22. View of Christ Church, Manchester . . . 149
23. View of Ancoats Hall . . . 211
24. „ Hartshead Pike, *ibid.*; for a description, see page . . . 221
25. View of Manchester . . . 212
26. „ Jailors' Chapel 226
27. „ two supposed Dungeons . . . *ib.*
28. View of Old Wall . . . *ib.*
29. „ Ashton . . . 227
30. „ Staleybridge . . . 230
31. „ Stanley Hall . . . *ib.*
32. „ Scout Mill . . . 231
33. „ Fairfield . . . 233
34. „ Heaton House 236
35. „ Royton Hall . . . 239
36. „ Chadderton Hall 241
37. Plan of Castlecroft . . . 269
38. „ Castlesteads . . . *ib.*

39. Plan of Liverpool . 331
40. „ „ from Everton . . . 376
41. Plan of Liverpool from the Cheshire shore . 383
42. Plan of Chester . . 384
43. View of Tatton Hall . 423
44. „ Booth Hall . 424
45. „ Dunham Massey 426
46. „ Macclesfield . 439
47. „ Lime Hall . 440
48. „ Poynton . 441
49. „ Stockport . 447
50. „ Harden Hall . 449
51. „ Hyde Hall . 451
52. „ Dunfield Hall 452
53. „ Bridge, *ibid.*; for description, see page 453
54. View of Lodge . . *ib.*
55. Portrait of the Rev. Mr. La Trobe . . 455
56. Map of the Environs of Mottram . . . 457
57. View of Mottram Church 458
58. View of the Monument of Ralph Stealey and his Wife . . . 459
59. View of Cottage at Roecross, *ibid.*; see page 464
60. View of Mottram . *ib.*
61. „ Broadbottom Bridge *ib.*
62. „ Cat Torr . 465
63. Plan of Bucton Castle 471
64. „ Castle Shaw, *ibid.*; for a description see page 559
65. View of Buxton . . 491
66. „ Chatsworth . 494
67. „ Castleton . 498
68. „ Ashbourn . 503
69. „ Matlock . 508
70. „ Smithfield . 517
71. „ Leek . . 538
72. Large two-sheet Maps of the environs of Manchester . . . 624
73. Large two-sheet Plan of Manchester to follow the Map.

The large Maps (72 and 73) are often wanting in second-hand copies. Published at £2 : 2s. Large paper, £3 : 13 : 6. Selling price, 15s. to 25s. Large paper, 30s. to £2.

A portion of this work was reprinted and published under the title of "A Survey of the Counties of Lancashire, Cheshire, Derbyshire, West-Riding of Yorkshire, and the Northern part of Staffordshire, etc. London: printed for John Stockdale, Piccadilly, and sold by Messrs. Clarkes, Manchester; J. Gore, Liverpool; and J. Reddish, Stockport. 1797. *Octavo.*

Title and Contents, xv. pp. Survey, 216 pp. This contains several of the maps of the original work on a reduced scale.

Published at 4s. 6d. Sells for 3s. An earlier edition printed in 1796.

John Aikin, M.D., was the son of the Rev. J. Aikin, LL.D., and brother to Anne Letitia Aikin, afterwards Mrs. Barbauld. He was born at Kilworth in Leicestershire in 1747, and was educated at the Dissenters'

Academy at Warrington. He died at Stoke-Newington 1822. A List of his works will be found in Watt's "Bib. Brit.," vol. i.

HISTORY and DESCRIPTION of the COLLEGIATE CHURCH of CHRIST, MANCHESTER. By JOSEPH ASTON. [View of Church.] Manchester: printed by Joseph Aston at the "Exchange Herald" Office, St. Anne's Street, and sold by all Booksellers. *Duodecimo.*

Title as above, Address to Reader, and History, 36 pp.

A PICTURE of MANCHESTER. By JOSEPH ASTON. Manchester: printed and published by the Author at the "Exchange Herald" Office, St. Anne's Street, and sold in London by Messrs. Longman, Hurst, Rees, Orme, and Co., Paternoster Row. *Post octavo.*

Title as above, i. p. Preface, iv. pp. A Picture and Index, 234 pp. Map of Manchester (folding), and a few Woodcuts.

This is the 1st Edition, published in 1816. The 3d Edition was issued in 1826. Sells for 3s. 6d.

Joseph Aston (born 1762), the author of several Manchester books, was the son of William Aston, gunsmith of Deansgate, in Manchester, and was the editor or publisher of the "Manchester Mail," and afterwards of the "Exchange Herald." In addition to his topographical works, he wrote several pieces for the stage, one of which, "Conscience," was acted at the Theatre Royal, Manchester, in 1815. He for some time resided in Rochdale, where he started a paper called the "Rochdale Recorder," a copy of which is in the Rochdale Free Public Library. He died at Chadderton 19th October 1844. For a further notice of him, see Procter's "Memorials of Manchester Street."

METRICAL RECORDS of MANCHESTER, in which its HISTORY is traced (currente calamo) from the days of the Ancient Britons to the present time. By the Editor of the "Manchester Herald." London: sold by Longman, Hurst, Orme, and Co., Paternoster Row; in Manchester, by J. Aston; and all other Booksellers. 1822. *Octavo.*

Title as above, and Advertisement, iv. pp. Metrical Records, p. 5 to p. 105. Index, 3 pp.

Reprinted from the "Exchange Herald." Sells for 3s.

The RED BASIL BOOK, or Parish Register of Arrears for the maintenance of the unfortunate offspring of illicit amours, with a further development of most shameful and unprecedented acts of abuse in the Town of Manchester. Part First. By THOMAS BATTYE.

> "Fie on't! O fie! 'tis an unweeded garden
> That grows to seed; things rank and gross . . .
> Possess it merely."
>
> SHAKSPEARE.

Sold by J. Hopper and Son; W. Graham, Market Street Lane; Cowdroy and Boden, St. Mary's Gate, and J. Reddish, Market Place. Price Two Shillings and Sixpence. *Post octavo.*

Title as above, and Introduction, vii. pp. Exact Account of Arrears of Bastardy, and Development of Abuse, 146 pp. An error in the pages—40 to 70 appear twice over.

A copy of this is in the Manchester Free Library.

Thomas Battye was the son of William Battye of Manchester, and grandson of James Battye.

A DISCLOSURE of PAROCHIAL ABUSE, ARTIFICE, and PECULATION in the TOWN of MANCHESTER, which have been the means of burthening the Inhabitants with the present enormous parish Rates, with other existing Impositions of office in a variety of Facts exhibiting the Cruel and Inhuman Conduct of the Hireling Officers of the Town towards the Poor. To which is added a BOOK of COUNTY RATES, showing the exact proportion of every Hundred in this County, and of every Township in the Hundred of Salford. By THOMAS BATTYE. Second Edition. Manchester. 1796. *Octavo.*

A copy is in the Manchester Free Library.

AN ADDRESS to the INHABITANTS of MANCHESTER, particularly to those Gentlemen who were present at the reading of the Constables' accounts at the Collegiate Church, explaining certain Facts, etc., misrepresented at that meeting. By THOMAS BATTYE. Manchester: printed by Mark Wardle, No. 48 Spinning Field, Deansgate. 1802. *Post octavo.*

Half-title, Title as above, and Address, 40 pp.

The above and several other Tracts by the same author are in the Manchester Free Library.

The JACOBITE TRIALS at MANCHESTER in 1694, from an unpublished manuscript. Edited by WILLIAM BEAMONT, Esq. Printed for the Chetham Society. MDCCCLIII. *Foolscap quarto.*

Chetham Society's Title (Vol. xxviii.), List of Council, iv. pp, Title as above, and Introduction, xc. pp. Second Title, i. p. Trials and Index, 132 pp.

TRÉSORS D'ART exposés à Manchester en 1857 et provenant des Collections Royales des Collections publiques et des Collections particulières de La Grande-Bretagne, per W. BURGER. Paris : Ve Jules Renouard, Libraire-Editeur 6 Rue de Tournon. A Londres chez Barthês et Lowell, Marlbrough Street, 14. 1857.

Droit de traduction reservé. *Post duodecimo.*

Half-title, Title as above, and Preface, viii. pp. Trésors et Table, 460 pp. Published at 3s. 6d.

A copy of this is in the Manchester Free Library.

VIEWS on the MANCHESTER and LEEDS RAILWAY, drawn from Nature and on Stone by A. F. TAIT. With a Descriptive History by EDWIN BUTTERWORTH. Published for A. F. Tait by Bradshaw and Blacklock, 59 Fleet Street, London, and 27 Brown Street, Manchester, publishers of the "Railway and Steam Navigation Guide," etc. etc. 1845. *Folio.*

Title as above, Dedication, and Description, 34 pp.

LIST OF PLATES.

1. Additional Title. Views on the Manchester and Leeds Railway, drawn from Nature and on Stone by A. F. Tait. Published by A. F. Tait, 59 Islington, Liverpool; Day and Haghe, Lithographers to the Queen; with Vignette, "East Entrance to Elland Tunnel."
2. Manchester. Bridge over the Irwell, Victoria Station.
3. Manchester. Victoria Station, Hunt's Bank. Interior.
4. ,, ,, Exterior.
5. Rochdale Station.
6. Littleborough and Rochdale.
7. Todmorden Valley.
8. Summit Tunnel, West Entrance.
9. Gawksholme Viaduct and Bridge.
10. Todmorden from the North.
11. ,, Viaduct and Bridge.

12. Whiteley's Viaduct. Charleston Curves.
13. Hebden Bridge Station.
14. Sowerby Bridge from King's Cross.
15. Halifax.
16. Rastrick Terrace and Viaduct.
17. Brighouse.
19. Wakefield.
20. Normanton Station.

Sells for 10s.

BIOGRAPHY of EMINENT NATIVES resident and benefactors of the Town of MANCHESTER. By EDWIN BUTTERWORTH of Oldham. J. Bradshaw, Printer, 31 Church Street, Manchester. 1829. *Duodecimo.* Title as above, Biographies, and Appendix, 33 pp. Scarce.

The ANTIQUITIES of the TOWN, and a Complete HISTORY of the TRADE of MANCHESTER, with a DESCRIPTION of MANCHESTER and SALFORD. To which is added an Account of the late Improvements in the Town, etc. By JAMES BUTTERWORTH.

> . . . . I'll walk quite clear of party,
> Follow the undaunted steps of faithful history
> On the broad and beaten road of independence.—EGO.

Manchester: printed for the Author by C. W. Leake, St. Mary's Gate. 1822. *Foolscap octavo.*

Title as above, Dedications, viii. pp. Preface, v. pp. The Antiquities, etc., 302 [no Index]. List of Subscribers, and Errata, xiv. pp.

PLATES.

Frontispiece. View of Collegiate Church, Manchester.
Manchester Tokens in the possession of W. Yates, Esq.
(And 2 Woodcuts.)

Sells for 5s. 6d.

This was afterwards re-published (or more probably the remaining stock was sold with a new title), as

A COMPLETE HISTORY of the COTTON TRADE, including also that of the Silk, Calico-Printing, and Steel Manufactories. With remarks on their Progress in Bolton, Bury, Stockport, Blackburn, and Wigan. To which is added an account of the Chief Mart of these Goods, the TOWN of MANCHESTER. By a Person concerned in Trade, C. W. Leake, Printer, St. Mary's Gate, Manchester. 1823.

TABULA MANCUNIENSIS, or a CHRONOLOGICAL TABLE of Events, comprising within the compass of a few pages the HISTORY of the TOWN and NEIGHBOURHOOD of MANCHESTER from the remotest period to the present time, or a concise statement of every remarkable event which has occurred in Manchester and its vicinity, whether regarding its antiquities, churches, chapels, public buildings, extensive trade, or history. Highly useful as a pocket companion or Reference Book. By JAMES BUTTERWORTH, author of various miscellaneous works. Manchester, printed by J. Bradshaw, 34 Church Street. 1829. *Octavo.*

Title as above, and Tabula, 16 pp.

Second and Third Editions, by Edwin Butterworth, were published in 1832 and 1834. See Timperley (*post*).

A BOTANICAL GUIDE to the FLOWERING PLANTS, FERNS, MOSSES, and ALGÆ, found indigenous within sixteen miles of MANCHESTER, with some information as to the Agricultural, Medicinal, and other uses. By RICHARD BUXTON. Together with a sketch of the Author's Life, and remarks on the Geology of the District. London: Longman and Co., Paternoster Row; Manchester: Abel Heywood, 58 Oldham Road; and all Booksellers. 1849. Price 6s. *Duodecimo.*

Title as above, Memoir, and Geology, xxi. pp. List of Abbreviations, Botanical Guide, Index, and Appendix, 168 pp.

Richard Buxton was born at Sedgeley, near Manchester, in 1796. His father was at one time a farmer, but afterwards a day labourer, and consequently unable to give his son any education, who at sixteen years old was unable even to read. Throughout his life he continued to be poor, but by perseverance and industry he became an educated man and a good botanist. He died in Ancoats not many years ago.

The PICTORIAL HISTORY of MANCHESTER, by GEORGE R. CATT. Reprinted from "The Pictorial Times," with additions and corrections. Office, 135 Fleet Street. Sold by all Booksellers. *Quarto.*

Engraved Title as above, Advertisement, Contents, and Address to Manchester by John Bolton Rogers, 4 pp. History, 40 pp.

ILLUSTRATIONS.

View of Manchester, *Frontispiece*, and 46 Woodcuts.

Sells for 4s. 6d.

The COLLEGIATE CHURCH of MANCHESTER, from its foundation in 1422 to the present time, with Observations on the proposed Bill for the Sub-division of the Parish of Manchester, and for the appropriation of the Revenue of the Chapter. By G. C. CLIFTON, M.A., Canon of Manchester, and Registrar of the Chapter. Manchester: T. Sowler, St. Anne's Square. 1850. *Octavo.*

Title as above, Dedication, and Epistle, vi. pp. The Collegiate Church, 63 pp.

CURIOUS REMARKS on the HISTORY of MANCHESTER.

"With a judicious Incredulity of Spirit let us inquire and think for ourselves."—Preface to the "History of Manchester."

By MUSCIPULA Sen. London: printed for and sold by the Booksellers in Town and County. 1771. Price 1s. *Octavo.*

Title as above, Address, "To all whom it may concern, and Remarks on the Preface, ix. pp. Remarks on the History, 65 pp.

Reprint by John Heywood, 143 Deansgate, Manchester. [1864.] In *Foolscap octavo.*

Title-page, "To whom it may concern," and Remarks on the Preface, x. pp. Remarks on the History of Manchester, 77 pp.

The author of this was JOHN COLLIER (Tim Bobbin), or, perhaps, as the author of the "Manchester School Register" puts it—"Tim Bobbin supplied the jokes, and his neighbour, Colonel Townley of Bellfield Hall, the learning."

MORE FRUITS from the SAME PANNIER, or ADDITIONAL REMARKS on the HISTORY of MANCHESTER. [Two quotations from History of Manchester.] London: printed for and sold by the Booksellers in Town and County. 1781. *Octavo.*

Title as above, i. p. Preface, iv. pp. Additional Remarks, 73 pp. Dated "Milnrow, Jan. 1773." Index, viii. pp.

Written by JOHN COLLIER ("Tim Bobbin").

CORNISH'S STRANGERS' GUIDE to LIVERPOOL and MANCHESTER. [See p. 87.]

The STRANGERS' GUIDE to MANCHESTER, containing information on every subject interesting to Residents or Strangers, Chronological, Historical, and Descriptive, derived from the most authentic sources. Illustrated with Engravings and a Map of Town and its Vicinity. By H. G. DUFFIELD. Manchester: C. Duffield, Bury New Road. London: Simpkin and Marshall; and sold by all the Booksellers. Entered at Stationers' Hall. Second Thousand. [1844.] Reprinted 1851. 16*mo.*

Title as above, Preface, and Contents, viii. pp. Guide, 204 pp.

Illustrated with numerous Views of Buildings, etc. in Manchester Sells for 2s. 6d.

The LAND and FRESH WATER SHELLS of the District around MANCHESTER, with their particular Localities; to which are added Instructions to Collectors. By DAVID DYSON. Manchester: John Harrison, Abraham's Court, Market Street. 1850. *Duodecimo.*

Title as above, Preface, and Instructions, xi. pp. Measurement of Shells, with Plate, not paged. Land and Fresh Water Shells, with Appendix, 95 pp.

MANCHESTER and the MANCHESTER PEOPLE, with a Sketch of BOLTON, STOCKPORT, ROCHDALE, and OLDHAM, and their Inhabitants. By a CITIZEN OF THE WORLD. [John Easby.] Manchester: Literary Agency Office, 47 Princess Street. 1834. *Post octavo.*

Title as above, and Description, 33 pp.

Published at 6d.

MANCHESTER WORTHIES, and their Foundations, or Six Chapters of Local History, with an Epilogue, by way of Moral. By EDWARD EDWARDS. Manchester: James Galt and Co., Ducie Street, Exchange. 1855. *Octavo.*

Title as above, Contents, and Preface, vii. pp. Worthies, etc., 88 pp. Sells for 3s. 6d.

Refers to the Founders of the Manchester Charities.

WESLEYAN METHODISM in MANCHESTER and its Vicinity. By JAMES EVERETT.

"Thou shalt remember all the ways that the Lord led thee these forty years in the wilderness."—MOSES.

VOL. I.

Manchester: printed by the Executors of S. Russell, Deansgate; sold by James Everett, 10 Market Street, Manchester; John Stephens, 16 City Road; J. Kershaw, 14 City Road, and 66 Paternoster Row, London. 1827. *Octavo.*

Frontispiece, Portrait of Richard Bradley, aged 90. Title, Dedication, Contents, and Preface, xv. pp. Methodism, 190 pp.

A copy of this is in the Manchester Free Library.

James Everett was born at Alnwick, in Northumberland, 16th May 1784. For some years he was a Wesleyan Methodist Minister, and afterwards a Bookseller and Stationer in Sheffield and Manchester. He died 10th May 1872. He was the author of "Methodism as it is;" the "Village Blacksmith," etc. etc. "A Biography of James Everett," by the Rev. Richard Chew, has just been published (London, 1875).

PANORAMA of MANCHESTER, and RAILWAY COMPANION.

"... dives pictai vestis et auri."—VIRGIL.

Manchester: published by J. Everett, Market Street; also by Hamilton, Adams, and Co., Paternoster Row, London. 1834. *Post octavo.*

Title as above, Preface, and Contents, viii. pp. Panorama, 258 pp.

PLATES.

Plate	Page	Plate	Page
Manchester from Kersal Moor . . .	*Frontispiece*	Entrance to Royal Infirmary across Walker Street .	197
Plan of Manchester (A.D. 800)	P. 14	Excavation of Olive Mount	199
Plan of Manchester (A.D. 1650)	30	View on Railway near Liverpool . . .	199
Collegiate Church . .	58	Town Hall, Manchester .	214
Royal Infirmary (A.D. 1832)	44		199
Entrance to Royal Infirmary	104	The Exchange, Manchester	217

Royal Institution, Manchester 220

James Everett was the author as well as publisher.

OBSERVATIONS on IMPROVEMENTS of the TOWN of MANCHESTER, particularly as regards the importance of blending in those improvements the Chaste and Beautiful with the Ornamental and Useful. By WILLIAM FAIRBAIRN. Manchester: printed by Robert Robinson, St. Ann's Place. 1836. *Quarto.*

Title as above, and Explanatory Address, x. pp. Improvement, 44 pp.

PLATES.

(*Folding*)	Perspective View of Bridgewater Crescent, Piccadilly, Manchester	*Frontispiece*
	Plan showing the proposed Improvements .	*To face* p. 25
	Designs for a New Exchange and Quadrant .	„ 31
	Sketches of an elegant style of Steam-Engine Chimney	„ 39

Scarce.

MANCHESTER in 1844: its present condition and future prospects. By M. LEON FAUCHER. Translated from the French, with copious Notes appended by a Member of the Manchester Athenæum.

"There is no portion of Society which strives with greater avidity for a better future."—P. 122.

London: Simpkin, Marshall, and Co., Stationers' Hall Court, Manchester; Abel Heywood, 38 Oldham Street. 1845. *Duodecimo.*

Title as above, Dedication, and Preface, xv. pp. Manchester in 1844, 152 pp.

Published at 3s.

This book forms the translation of two articles, published in the "Revue des deux Mondes" under the title of "Studies upon England."

I.

ABBOTT'S JOURNAL.

II.

THE TRIALS at MANCHESTER in 1694. Edited by Right Rev. ALEXANDER GOSS, D.D. Printed for the Chetham Society. MDCCCLXIV. *Foolscap quarto.*

Chetham Society's Title (Vol. lxi.), List of Council, Title, and Title to

Abbott's Narrative, vii. pp. Introduction, xix. pp. Abbot's Journal, 32 pp.

Title to "Tryalls at Manchester," and Introduction, xxi. pp. Trials, 42 pp. Index to the volume, 5 pp.

The 20th and 21st Reports of the Society, viii. pp.

GIMCRACKIANA, or Fugitive Pieces on MANCHESTER MEN AND MANNERS Ten Years Ago. [Small view of bottom of Market Street.]

> "The hallowed season and the joyful time,
> In which I used to greet you all with rhyme,
> Is now return'd."—"Oxford Sausage."

Manchester: printed by Wilmot Henry Jones, Market Street; sold by the author and Thomas Richardson, Derby. 1833. *Post octavo.*

Half-title, Title as above, Dedication, Contents, Fugitive Pieces, and List of Illustrations, 196 pp.

This work contains 7 small Engravings and a Frontispiece. Sells for 5s. 6d.

A work of considerable local interest. Its author was John Stanley Gregson, who was for some years a Manchester Bookseller.

MANCHESTER WALKS and WILD FLOWERS. An Introduction to the Botany and Rural Beauty of the District, with Biographical Notices of the Lancashire Botanists, and an Account of their Societies; select Lists of the Birds and other living creatures of the neighbourhood, etc. By LEO GRINDON, Lecturer on Botany at the Royal School, Manchester, author of "The Manchester Flora," "Life, its nature, varieties, and phenomena," etc. etc. 2d Edition. London: Whittaker and Co.; Manchester: All Booksellers. *Duodecimo.*

Engraved Half-title, Title as above, Preface, and Contents, ix. pp. Walks and Wild Flowers, and Index, 172 pp.

Published at 2s. 6d. The 1st Edition was published in 1859.

The MANCHESTER FLORA. A Descriptive List of the Plants growing wild within eighteen miles of Manchester, with Names of the Plants commonly cultivated in Gardens. Preceded by an Introduction to Botany. By LEO HARTLEY GRINDON, Lecturer on Botany at the Royal School of Medicine, Manchester, author of "Manchester Walks and Wild

Flowers," "Life, its nature, varieties, and phenomena," "Emblems," etc. With numerous Woodcut illustrations.

"Consider the lilies of the field."

London: William White, 36 Bloomsbury; Manchester: All the Booksellers. 1859. *Post octavo.*

Half-title, Engraved Title, Title as above, vi. pp. Dedication, Contents, and Preface, viii. pp. Introduction, Manchester Flora, General Index, and Additions and Corrections, 575 pp.

Published at 12s. 6d.

A VOLUME of COURT LEET RECORDS of the MANOR of MANCHESTER in the SIXTEENTH CENTURY. Compiled and edited by JOHN HARLAND, F.S.A. Printed for the Chetham Society. MDCCCLXIV. *Foolscap quarto.*

Chetham Society's Title (Vol. lxiii.) and List of Council, iii. pp. Title as above, and Introduction, xix. pp. Court Leet Records, Appendices, and Index, 208 pp.

Frontispiece—Plan of Manchester and Salford in 1650.

VOL. II.

Chetham Society's Title (Vol. lxv.) and List of Council, iii. pp. Title and Introduction, viii. pp. Corrigenda on a slip. Court Leet (continued) Appendix, and Index, 128 pp. The Twenty-Second Report of the Society, etc., 4 pp.

MAMESCESTRE, being chapters from the early recorded History of the Barony, the Lordship or Manor, the Vill, Borough, or Town of MANCHESTER. Edited by JOHN HARLAND, F.S.A.

VOL. I.

Printed for the Chetham Society. MDCCCLXI. *Foolscap quarto.*

Chetham Society's Title (Vol. liii.) and List of Council, iii. pp. Title and Contents, iii. pp. Slip referring to Charter. Mamescestre, 206 pp.

Frontispiece, Facsimile of Charter.

VOL. II.

Chetham Society's Title (Vol. lvi.) and List of Council, iii. pp. Title and Contents, iii. pp. Mamescestre, p. 209 to p. 431.

VOL. III.

Chetham Society's Title (Vol. lviii.) and List of Council, iii. pp. Title, Introduction, and Contents, xxxiii. pp. Errata et Corrigenda, p. xxxv. to p. xl. Mamescestre, and Index, p. 431 to p. 627.

COLLECTANEA relating to MANCHESTER and its neighbourhood at various periods. Compiled, arranged, and edited by JOHN HARLAND, F.S.A. Printed for the Chetham Society. MDCCCLXVI. *Foolscap quarto.*

Chetham Society's Title (Vol. lxviii.) and List of Council, ii. pp. Title as above, Introduction, and Contents, vi. pp. Half-title, i. p. Collectanea, 258 pp.

VOL. II.

Chetham Society's Title (Vol. lxxii.) and List of Council, iii. pp. Title, Introduction, and Contents, viii. pp. Collectanea, 252 pp. Title to Vol. I., 1 p.

The MANNER and SOLEMNITIE of the CORONATION of the Most Gracious Majestie KING CHARLES the SECOND at MANCHESTER, in the Countie Palatine of Lancaster, on the 23d day of April 1661. By WILLIAM HEAWOOD, Gentleman.

Also the celebration of the CORONATION of the Most Gracious King GEORGE III. and QUEEN CHARLOTTE at MANCHESTER on the 22d September 1761, with Biographical Notices of the principal Persons taking part in each celebration. John Camden Hotten, London, Piccadilly. 1863. *Quarto.*

Title as above, and the Manner, etc., 23 pp.

4 Copies were printed on vellum, 49 copies on small, and 23 copies on large paper.

Printed for private circulation only. Sells for 5s. 6d.

Part of this is a reprint of a scarce Tract; see PART V.

MANCUNIENSIS, or an HISTORY of the TOWNE of MAN-

CHESTER, and what is most concerning it. By R. HOLLINGWORTH. Manchester: published by William Willis, Hanging Ditch; and sold by Joseph Lilly and Edward Lumley, London. MDCCCXXXIX. *Foolscap octavo.*

Engraved Title, Title as above, Dedication, Description of the Engraved Title-page, and Prefatory Notice, 10 pp. Mancuniensis, 126 pp.

Sells for 5s. A few copies were printed on large paper.

Richard Hollingworth, who was a Fellow of Christ College, Manchester (see PART VI.), died in 1656, and the above work is from his unfinished MS., which is in the Chetham Library.

HISTORY of the CHOLERA in MANCHESTER, in 1849, as reported to the Registrar-General of Births, Deaths, etc. By JOHN LEIGH, M.R.C.S. of England, and Mr. GARDINER, Superintendent Registrar of Manchester. London: Simpkin, Marshall, and Co.; Manchester, Simms and Dinham. 1850. *Octavo.*

Title as above, and History, 35 pp., with a Map showing where the disease was most fatal.

The HAND-BOOK of MANCHESTER, containing statistical and general information on the trade, social condition, and institutions of the Metropolis of Manufactures, being a second and enlarged edition of "Manchester as it is." By B. LOVE, Member of the Literary and Philosophical Society of Manchester. *Duodecimo.*

Title as above, Dedication, Preface, Contents, and List of Plates, viii. pp. Hand-book and Index, 296 pp.

ILLUSTRATIONS.

Frontispiece, The Collegiate Church.
Bridgewater Foundry.
Royal Infirmary.
Royal Institution.
Blind Asylum.
Female Penitentiary.
Chetham College.
Athenæum.
Union Club House.
Portrait of Dr. Dalton.
Natural History Society's Hall.
Corn Exchange.
Exchange.
Portico.
Town Hall, Chorlton-upon-Medlock.
Town Hall, Salford.
Town Hall, Manchester.
Concert Hall.

Plan of Streets and Railways in Manchester.

Published in 1842 at 4s. 6d.

"MANCHESTER AS IT IS" was published in 1839.

Benjamin Love also wrote "A FEW PAGES ABOUT MANCHESTER," with Engravings. *Octavo*, 32 pp.

SOME ACCOUNT of the BLUE COAT HOSPITAL and PUBLIC LIBRARY in the COLLEGE, MANCHESTER, founded by Humphrey Chetham, Esq., in the year 1651. Incorporated by King Charles the Second, 1665.

[Arms of Chetham.]

Manchester: printed by Joseph Pratt, Bridge Street. 1843. *Duodecimo.*

Frontispiece, View of College. Title as above, and the Account, 21 pp.

Compiled by WILLIAM MULLIS, and originally published in 1819. Printed by J. Leach, Wright's Court, Market Street, Manchester.

William Mullis, at the time he wrote this, was employed as deputy Librarian and Bookbinder to Chetham's Library.

HANDBOOK to the CATHEDRALS of ENGLAND, NORTHERN DIVISION.

PART II.

Durham, Chester, MANCHESTER. With Illustrations. London: John Murray, Albemarle Street. 1869. *Post octavo.*

Title as above, and List of Illustrations, iv. pp. Plan and References to Plan of Durham Cathedral, etc., 4 pp. Durham and Chester Cathedral, p. 231 to p. 416. Manchester Cathedral, p. 417 to p. 435.

PLATES to Manchester Portion.

South-East View of Manchester Cathedral.
The Choir of Manchester Cathedral.
Entrance to Chapter House, Manchester Cathedral.
Interior of Chapter House, Manchester Cathedral.

Published at 18s.

Six Months' OBSERVATIONS in the COLLEGIATE CHURCH of MANCHESTER, on the Dark Ages of the Nineteenth Century. By JOHN NEAL, Late Deputy Parish Clerk of the Collegiate Church.

" Ex fumo dare Lucem."—[Prob. xxii. 22, 23.]

Manchester: printed for the author; and sold at No. 12 Fennel Street, near the old Church. M. Kiernan, printer, 83 King Street, Salford. *Octavo.*

Title as above, Address, and Preface, vii. pp. Observations, etc., 48 pp.

A copy of this is in the Manchester Free Library.

A DESCRIPTION of MANCHESTER, giving an Historical Account of those limits in which the Town was formerly included; some observations upon its public edifices, present extent, and late alterations; with a succinct history of its former original manufactories, and their gradual advancement to the present state of perfection at which they are arrived. By a NATIVE OF THE TOWN. [James Ogden.] Printed by C. Wheeler, for M. Falkner, in the Market Place; S. Falkner, Corner of Old Mill-gate and Hanging Ditch; and Richardson and Urquhart, Royal Exchange, London. MDCCLXXXIII. *Post octavo.*

Title as above, and Description, 94 pp. Sells for 3s. 6d.

This work was reprinted by John Heywood, 143 Deansgate, Manchester, in 1849. This Edition contained two Views of Market Street in 1820. It comprised 58 pp. It was again reprinted in 1862 and 1864.

James Ogden was born in Manchester in 1718, and was by trade a fustian shearer, and afterwards a schoolmaster. In 1762 he published a poem entitled "The British Lion roused," and subsequently "The Revolution, an Epic Poem," and other poetic effusions. He died in August 1802. He is said to have collected much of the material used by Dr. Aikin in his "History of Manchester."

MANUAL of LOCAL ACTS affecting the TOWNSHIPS comprised in the BOROUGH of MANCHESTER. By G. WAREING ORMEROD, Solicitor. Manchester: T. Fowler, St. Ann's Square. 1838. *Royal octavo.*

Title as above, Preface, Contents, and Index, xii. pp. The Manual, 98 pp.

The HISTORY of the SIEGE of MANCHESTER by the King's Forces, under the command of Lord Strange. 1642. By JOHN PALMER,

Architect; to which is added the Complaint of Lieutenant-Colonel John Rosworm, against the Inhabitants of Manchester, relative to that event.

> "Unnatural wars! when in the field,"
> [Three more lines.]
>
> WARD, *Canto* IV.

Manchester: printed for the Author by John Leigh, Market Street, and sold by Longman and Co., London; Clarke, 14 Market Place. [List of other Booksellers.] 1822. *Royal octavo.*

Title as above, and Dedication, iv. pp. Preface, iii. pp. History of the Siege, etc., 107 pp. Plan of Manchester.
Sells for 5s.

The MANCHESTER HAND-BOOK, or Authentic Account of the Place and its People. By JOSEPH PERRIN, Member of the Historic Society of Lancashire and Cheshire. With Illustrations on Wood by George Measom, and a Map. Manchester: Hale and Roworth, 45 King Street; London: Whittaker and Co. *Post octavo.*

Title, Preface, and List of Cuts, vi. pp. Hand-Book and Index, 180 pp.
First Edition, 1857. Second Edition, 1859. Published at 2s. 6d.

An EXPOSURE of the CALUMNIES circulated by the Enemies of Social Order, reiterated by their Abettors, AGAINST the MAGISTRATES and the YEOMAN CAVALRY of MANCHESTER and SALFORD. By FRANCIS PHILIPS. [Latin quotation.] The second Edition. London: published by Longman, Hurst, Rees, Orme, and Brown, Paternoster Row, etc. 1819. *Octavo.*

Title as above, Dedication, Preface, and Documents referred to, xxvi. pp. Exposure, 61 pp. Appendix, xxix. pp.

HISTORICAL SKETCH and PERSONAL RECOLLECTIONS of MANCHESTER. Intended to illustrate the Progress of Public Opinion from 1792 to 1832. By ARCHIBALD PRENTICE. London: Charles Gilpin, Bishopgate Street, Without; Manchester: J. T. Parkes, Market Street. MDCCCLI. *Octavo.*

Title as above, Dedication, Contents, and Errata, xii. pp. Sketch, 432 pp.
The Second Edition was published in 1852 at 6s. Sells for 4s. 6d.

MEMORIALS of MANCHESTER STREETS. (View of Residence of the Head Master of the Grammar School.) By RICHARD WRIGHT PROCTER. Manchester: Thomas Sutcliffe, Market Place. 1874.

Half-title, Title as above, Dedication, Preface, Contents, and Descriptive List of Illustrations, xxii. pp. List of Subscribers to the Large Paper Impression, p. 1 to p. 32. Memorials of Manchester Streets, 296 pp. Appendix (containing Articles on "The Chetham Library," by James Crossley, Esq., F.S.A.; and "Old Manchester and its Worthies," by James Croston, Esq., F.S.A.), and Index, p. 297 to p. 388.

PLATES.

(Photograph) Rural Sport, or a Peep at a Lancashire Rushcart. *Frontispiece.*
Seal of Old Manchester . . . . P. 1
House of Correction, Hunt's Bank, about 1766 13
Strangeways Hall, 1746 18
Residence of the High Master of the Grammar School . . 25
View near the Old Apple Market 26
Ancient Houses in Long Millgate 28
College, Old Gate, and Grammar School 34
The "Red Rover" Stage Coach 75
The Infirmary, 1815 79
The Queen's Visit to Manchester, 1851 85
Remains of the Roman Wall in Castle Field, 1873 100
Outlet of the River Tib at Gaythorn, 1873 109
Emblematic Carving on a Church Boss 120
Statuette of Jupiter Stator, found in Camp Field 128
The Key (Quay), 1746 133
The Liverseege Memorial 152
The Market Place 194
Printing Office of Harrop's "Mercury," 1752 199
South-west Prospect of Manchester, 1728 204
Old Coffee-House and Shops about 1774 220
St. Ann's Square, 1746 256
Tombstone of Thomas de Quincey 263
The First Exchange, 1729-1792 268
North-west View of Chetham's Hospital and Library, 1797 . . 299
Crumpsall College 341
Crumpsall Hall 352

Published at 12s. 6d. Large Paper, 21s.

MANCHESTER in HOLIDAY DRESS. By RICHARD WRIGHT PROCTER, author of "The Barber's Shop," "Literary Reminiscences," and "Our Turf, Stage, and Ring."

"Play's the thing."—HAMLET.

London: Simpkin, Marshall, and Co.; Manchester: Abel Heywood and Son. 1866. *Post octavo.*

Half-title, Title as above, and Contents, viii. pp. Manchester in Holiday Dress, 179 pp.

Published at 3s. 6d.

Mr. Procter also edited "Gems of Thought, and Flowers of Fancy," 1855, which contains many extracts from the works of the Lancaster Poets.

OUR TURF, our STAGE, our RING. By RICHARD WRIGHT PROCTER, author of "The Barber's Shop" and "Literary Reminiscences." With Illustrations by William Morton.

"Perchance 'twill help to banish care,
To know hereafter such things were."

Manchester: Dinham and Co., 7 Corporation Street; London, Simpkin, Marshall, and Co. 1862. *Post octavo.*

Half-title, Title as above, Contents, Illustrations, and Errata, vii. pp. The Turf, etc., 91 pp. Notices of the Press, p. 92 to p. 100.

Frontispiece, View of Kersal Moor Races.

Published at 1s. 6d.

The HISTORY of MANCHESTER. By JOHN REILLY, author of the "History and Topography of Cumberland and Westmoreland," etc. etc.

VOL. I.

Manchester: John Gray Bell, Oxford Street; James Galt and Co., Ducie Street, Exchange; Reilly and Co., 376 Rochdale Road; London, John Russell Smith, Soho Square. 1861. *Royal octavo.*

Title as above, Contents, and List of Illustrations, v. pp. History of Manchester, and Appendix, 560 pp.

LIST OF ILLUSTRATIONS.

Ancient Charter of Manchester, *Frontispiece.*
Map of Manchester and Salford about 1650.
Salford Cross.
Old Market Place.
Old Blackfriars' Bridge.
Southerly View of Market Street in 1820.

This volume is all that appeared. Published at £1. Sells for 10s.

The ADMISSION REGISTER of the MANCHESTER SCHOOL, with some notices of the more distinguished Scholars. Edited by the Rev. JEREMIAH FINCH SMITH, M.A., Rector of Aldridge, Staffordshire, and Rural Dean.

VOL. I.

From A.D. 1730 to A.D. 1775.

Printed for the Chetham Society. MDCCCLXVI. *Foolscap quarto.*

Chetham Society's Title (Vol. lxix.) and List of Council, iii. pp. Title as above, and Introduction, viii. pp. Corrigenda, 1 p. Manchester School Register, and Index, 253 pp.

VOL. II.

From A.D. 1776 to A.D. 1807.

Chetham Society's Title (Vol. lxxiii.) and List of Council, iii. pp. Title and Introduction, v. pp. Corrigenda, 1 p. School Register Addenda, Addenda to Vol. I., and Index, 302 pp.

VOL. III.—PART I.

From May A.D. 1807 to September A.D. 1837.

Chetham Society's Title (Vol. xciii.), List of Council, and Title, v. pp. 2d Title, and Introduction to Vol. III., vi. pp. Corrigenda, 1 p. School Register, 176 pp. The 31st Report of the Society, etc., 12 pp.

VOL. III.—PART II.

From May A.D. 1807 to September A.D. 1837.

Chetham Society's Title (Vol. xciv.), List of Council, and Title, v. pp. School Register, Addenda, Addenda to Vol. I. and Vol. II., List of Portraits, etc., and Index (note on slip), p. 177 to p. 367.

LIST OF ILLUSTRATIONS.

1.	Bishop Oldham . .	*Frontispiece* to Vol. I.
2.	Bishop Oldham's Tomb .	„ „ II.
3.	Dr. Smith	„ „ III.
4.	Charles Lawson . .	*To face* p. 121, Vol. I.
5.	Residential House . .	„ 1, Vol. III.

Nos. 1 and 2 were issued with the last volume, the remainder with Vol. III., Part I.

A small number of copies of Vols. I. and.II. were sold to the public at 10s. 6d. each to original subscribers, and 12s. 6d. to non-subscribers. The price of the third volume (of which there was a similar issue) was 12s. 6d. and 15s.

The Manchester School Register contains a perfect store of facts relating to Lancashire families.

GEOLOGICAL ESSAYS and Sketch of the Geology of MANCHESTER and the neighbourhood. By JOHN TAYLOR, Member of the Council of the Manchester Geological Society, etc., author of "Coal Measures of Great Britain," etc. etc.

"The very stones prate of my whereabouts."—MACBETH.

London: Simpkin, Marshall, and Co., Stationers' Hall Court; Manchester, Alexander Ireland and Co. 1864. *Octavo.*

Half-title, i. p. Title as above, Preface, and Contents, ix. pp. Geological Essays, 282 pp.

A few woodcuts of Fossils. Published at 1s.

ANNALS of MANCHESTER, Biographical, Historical, Ecclesiastical and Commercial, from the earliest Period to the close of the year 1839. By C. H. TIMPERLEY.[1] Manchester: Bancks and Co., Exchange Street. 1839. 32*mo.*

Title as above, Introduction, Annals, Addenda, and Itinerary, 108 pp.

Frontispiece, Statue of John Dalton. Sells for 3s.

This work, the basis of which was Butterworth's "Tabula Mancuniensis" (see p. 123), was republished, with additions, in 1845, by a

[1] The original MSS. of some of Timperley's works are in Owen's College Library, Manchester.

"Native of the Town" [W. FORD], under the title of the "Manchester Recorder." It contained Title and Preface, iv. pp. Recorder, with Addenda, 156 pp. *Frontispiece,* Lady Lever's House (now the White Bear), Piccadilly. Another Edition, edited by E. WAUGH and T. FAWCETT, was published in 1851.

Title and Introduction, vi. pp. Recorder, 174 pp.

It has recently been republished as follows :—

The MANCHESTER HISTORICAL RECORDER, being an analysis of the MUNICIPAL, ECCLESIASTICAL, BIOGRAPHICAL, COMMERCIAL and STATISTICAL HISTORY of MANCHESTER from the earliest Period. Chronologically arranged. Revised and corrected to the present time. Manchester: John Heywood, 141 and 148 Deansgate; London, Simpkin and Marshall and Co.

Title as above, Introduction, and Historical Recorder, 196 pp.

Without date or Index, but published in 1874.

Frontispiece, Old Watchman about 1754.

Published at 2s. 6d.

If the above was printed in good type, and with a copious Index, it would be of much greater value.

Dr. Spencer T. Hall, in an article in the "Reliquary" (Vol. xiv., p. 143), writes, "More than forty years since a stranger, lame from being before wounded in a battle, limped in the gloom of a winter evening into Nottingham. A load of coals had been put down. * * * Our wayfarer asked if he might be employed in 'getting in' the said coals, and cheered by an affirmative answer, did the work well. * * * A few days afterwards he was working by my side in the "Nottingham Mercury" Office * * * His name was CHARLES H. TIMPERLEY."

He is known best as the author of the "History of Printing."

The whole Proceedings of the TRIAL of an Indictment against THOMAS WALKER of MANCHESTER, Merchant, William Paul, Samuel Jackson, James Chetham, Oliver Pearsall, Benjamin Booth, and Joseph Collier, for a Conspiracy to overthrow the Constitution and Government, and to aid and assist the French (being the King's Enemies), in case they should invade this Kingdom. Tried at Lancaster, April 2,

1794. Before the Hon. Mr. Justice Heath, one of the Judges of His Majesty's Court of Common Pleas. Taken in Shorthand by Joseph Gurney. Printed for T. Boden, Manchester; J. Johnson, No. 72 St. Paul's Churchyard; and J. Debrett, opposite Burlington House, Piccadilly, London. 1794. *Octavo.*

Half-title, Title as above, Advertisement, Contents, and Copy of Indictment, etc., xvi. pp. Trial and Appendix, 134 pp. Errata, 1 p.

Sells for 5s. 6d.

A REVIEW of some of the POLITICAL EVENTS which have occurred in MANCHESTER during the LAST FIVE YEARS, being a sequel to the trial of Thomas Walker and others for a conspiracy to overthrow the constitution and Government of this Country, and to aid and assist the French, being the King's enemies. By THOMAS WALKER. London: printed by J. Johnson in St. Paul's Churchyard. 1794. *Octavo.*

Title as above, Preface, and Contents, xiv. pp. A Review and Appendix, 161 pp.

Sells for 4s. 6d. A few copies on large paper were printed.

The ANCIENT PARISH CHURCH of MANCHESTER, and why it was collegiated. By SAMUEL HIBBERT WARE, M.D., F.R.S., Honorary Member of the Antiquarian Society of Scotland, Member of the Royal Society of Northern Antiquaries of Copenhagen, of the Literary Society of Heidelberg, of the Geological Societies of London and France. Manchester: Thomas Agnew's Repository of Arts. MDCCCXLVIII. *Quarto.*

Title as above, Dedication, Advertisement, Preface, and Contents, xvi. pp. The ancient Parish Church, and Index, 206 pp.

ILLUSTRATIONS.

Woden's Cave at Ordshal as it existed in the last century.

Fragments of the Seal and obverse of Henry V. attached to the Royal License of Foundation, and several small woodcuts.

Samuel Hibbert was the son of Titus Hibbert of Manchester. He was born in St. Ann's Square, Manchester, 24th April 1784. He was Vice-President of the Antiquarian Society of Scotland, author of the "Philosophy of Apparitions," and other works, and died at Hall Barns, Cheshire, 30th December 1848, and was buried at Ardwick Cemetery. He assumed the name of Ware in addition to his own patronymic.

The CATHEDRAL CHURCH of MANCHESTER. Illustrated with six highly finished plates, from Drawings made expressly for this work, with Historical and Descriptive Account, forming the completion of "Winkles'" English Cathedrals. London: David Bogue, 86 Fleet Street. Price 2s. 6d. *Royal octavo.*

Title, etc., p. 161 to p. 176.

R. B. Winkles' "English Cathedrals" was published in 1835-42, in 3 Vols., 178 Plates. £3 : 3s.; reduced to £2 : 5s. Published in parts.

OBSERVATIONS on the ARMORIAL BEARINGS of the TOWN of MANCHESTER, and on the Descent of the Baronial Family of Grelley. By WILLIAM ROBERT WHATTON, F.A.S., Member of the Royal College of Surgeons of London, and of the Literary and Philosophical Society of Manchester. Manchester: printed for the Author. MDCCCXXIV. *Post quarto.*

Half-title, Title as above, and Notice, Observations, and Appendix, 32 pp.

Between p. 26 and p. 27 is Pedigree of Grelley Family.

Frontispiece, Arms of Grelley Family.

Very scarce. Originally a Paper read before the Literary and Philosophical Society of Manchester, 20th February 1824.

HISTORY of the FOUNDATIONS in MANCHESTER, of CHRIST'S COLLEGE, CHETHAM HOSPITAL, and the FREE GRAMMAR SCHOOL. [Woodcut of Seals.]

VOLUME THE FIRST.

Manchester: Thomas Agnew and Joseph Taneth, Repository of Arts. MDCCCXXX. *Quarto.*

Title as above, and Dedication, iii. pp. Preface, Title to Part I., Title to History of Collegiate Church,[1] Preface to Part II., and Contents, xvi. pp. History of the Collegiate Church, Appendix, and Addenda, 418 pp.

PLATES.

Collegiate Church, *Frontispiece.*
Effigy of the Rev. J. Huntingdon, Baculaureus in Decretis (the first Warden) . . . . . . *To face* p. 46
View of the Chapel of St. Nicholas . . ,, ,, p. 60
View of the Chantry of St. Mary. *To follow the last Plate.*
Portrait of Dr. Chaderton . . . *To face* p. 101

1 This portion of the work was written by S. Hibbert, M.D., F.R.S.E., etc.

VOLUME THE SECOND.

Title, Half-title, and Advertisement, vi. pp. Continuation of History of the Collegiate Church, and Appendix, 184 pp.

Title to Part II. An Architectural Description of the Collegiate Church and College of Manchester. By JOHN PALMER, Architect.

Reference to Ground Plan, Appendix, and Index, p. 185 to p. 368.

PLATES.

Collegiate Church from the South-East, *Frontispiece.*		
Portrait of Nicholas Stratford, D.D., Bishop of Chester	*To face* p.	5
Portrait of Samuel Peploe, D.D., Bishop of Chester	„	56
Portrait of Samuel Peploe, LL.D.	„	82
Portrait of the Rev. Thomas Calvert, D.D. . .	„	172
Collegiate Church, Entrance to the Chapter House	„	208
„ „ View of the North Door before the alteration in 1818 . .	„	214
„ „ Derby Chapel	„	215
„ „ Ground of the	„	221
„ „ Interior of	„	250
„ „ Interior of the Nave, looking East	„	275
„ „ Curious Sculpture on Wood .	„	276
„ „ The Choir. *To follow the last Plate.*		
„ „ Monumental Brass Plate commemorating the Ordsall Family .	„	288
„ „ Monumental Plate, commemorating the Ordsall Family . .	„	298
„ „ Effigy of Warden Stanley .	„	327
„ „ Ground Plan of	„	343

These two volumes are often sold with the "History of the Manchester School," etc.

The HISTORY of MANCHESTER SCHOOL, comprising the foundation, the original charters and Statutes, and the revenues and expenditure. Also an account of the Exhibitions and Scholarships, with List of those persons who have enjoyed the various allowances to the Universities, and the nomination of the Feoffees and High Masters. Illustrated by numerous Biographical and Explanatory Notes, and a

Memoir of the Life of the Founder. By WILLIAM ROBERT WHATTON, F.A.S., London and Edinburgh, and Member and Librarian of the Literary and Philosophical Society of Manchester, etc. Published by Agnew and Zanetti, Repository of Arts, Exchange Street, Manchester; and W. H. Ainsworth, Old Bond Street, London. 1828. *Quarto.*

Title as above, and Advertisement, iv. pp. History of the Manchester School, 124 pp. 2d Title, "A HISTORY of the CHETHAM HOSPITAL and LIBRARY, with a genealogical account of the Founder and the Family of Chetham. To which is added an Appendix containing Letters and Papers from the Privy Council and Lieutenancy relating to the office of High Sheriff and Treasurer of the County of Lancaster, etc. etc. By WILLIAM ROBERT WHATTON, F.A.S., etc. etc." Published (as above) in 1833.

Title as above, and Advertisement, and Reference to the Ground Plan of Chetham Hospital, 5 pp. History of Chetham Hospital, etc., p. 125 to p. 242. Appendices, p. 243 to p. 294.

PLATES.

Portrait of Hugh Oldham, D.D., Bishop of Chester. *Frontispiece.*
Monument of „ „ „ *To face page* 6
Portrait of Charles Lawson, M.A. . . . „ 111
„ Jeremiah Smith, D.D. . . . „ 114
„ Humphrey Chetham, Esq. *Frontispiece* to the "History of the Chetham Hospital."
Ground Plan of the College. *To face the References.*
View of College Gateway after it was rebuilt in 1816 „ 179
South-West View of Chetham's College . . . „ 180
North „ „ „ *To follow the last Plate.*
Interior View of the Refectory „ „
„ ancient Dining Room „
Ancient Sculpture on the Ceiling of Audit Room „
Interior View of the Feoffees Room „
Ancient Reading Desk and Chair „
Two Boys of the Hospital in Costume „ 182
South-East View of Chetham College . . . . „ 225

The three last volumes, together with Ware's "Ancient Parish Church" (see p. 140), are often sold together under the Title of the "Manchester Foundations."

The four vols. sell for from £3 to £4 : 10s. (ordinary copies). Large paper, with proof impressions of the plates on India paper, are worth about £7 : 10s. (*i.e.* without Ware's "Ancient Church.") The three volumes were published at £7 : 7s. Large paper, £12 : 12s. India paper and proofs, £18 : 18s.

The three volumes above alluded to were written from the materials left by the Rev. J. Greswell of Manchester, which Dr. Hibbert-Ware undertook to remodel, and which were finally completed by W. R. Whatton, who was one of the Surgeons of the Royal Infirmary, Manchester. He died at Portland Place on the 5th December 1835. He wrote the Biographical portion of Baines' "History of Lancashire."

MANCHESTER, its POLITICAL, SOCIAL, and COMMERCIAL HISTORY, Ancient and Modern. By JAMES WHEELER.

"Quæ regio in terris nostri non plena laboris."—VIRGIL.

Manchester: Simms and Dinham, Exchange Street; London, Simpkin, Marshall, and Co. 1836. *Post octavo.*

Title as above, Preface, Contents, and Errata, xii. pp. Manchester, etc., and Supplement, 538 pp.

The Appendix contains a map of 10 miles round Manchester, and a folding sheet showing distances of Market Towns from Manchester.

Sells for 4s. 6d.

It was reprinted in 1842, price 4s.

James Wheeler, son of James Wheeler of Manchester, and grandson of Charles Wheeler, who was the publisher of the "Manchester Chronicle," which first appeared in 1781.

The FOUNDATION CHARTER of CHRIST COLLEGE, MANCHESTER, granted by King Charles the First, and Dated 2d October 1635. Translated by THOMAS WHEELER, Esq., S.C.L., Barrister-at-Law. Cave and Lever, 18 St. Ann's Street, Manchester. 1847. *Octavo.*

Half-title, Title, and Preface, vii. pp. The Charter, 43 pp.

A copy is in the Manchester Free Library.

The HISTORY of MANCHESTER. By the Rev. Mr. WHITAKER. London: printed for Joseph Johnson, No. 72 in St. Paul's Church Yard and J. Murray, No. 32 Fleet Street, opposite St. Dunstan's Church. MDCCLXXV. *Quarto.*

VOL. I.

Title as above, Mem., Advertisement, Title to the first Book, Preface, and Order of the Plates, x. pp. The History of Manchester, 469 pp. Additions and Corrections, the Conclusion, Appendices, and Index, lxxiii. pp.

PLATES.

British Battle-axes	*To face* p. 16
British Mancenion	„ 26
Roman Mancunium	„ 38
Roman Inscriptions found at Manchester .	„ 46
Roman Remains found at Manchester .	„ 50
Roman Remains found at Cambodunum .	„ 89
The Ground-plan of the Summer Station .	„ 186
The Map of the original Town of Manchester about A.D. 300	„ 355

VOL. II.

Half-title and Advertisement, vii. pp. The History of Manchester and Appendix, 594 pp. Index and Errata, 24 pp.

PLATES (exclusive of those on the letterpress).

A Plan of the original Town of Manchester about A.D. 446	*Frontispiece.*
Ancient Inscription	*To face* p. 67
Original Plan of Manchester and its Castle	„ 404
A Ground-plan of Manchester about the year 800	„ 498

Sells for £2 : 10s.

The First Volume was originally published in 1771, and the Second Volume in 1775.

The so-called Second Edition is reprint in 2 Volumes Octavo of the first Quarto Volume. It was never completed, and now sells for about 5s. 6d.

John Whitaker, the son of James Whitaker, Innkeeper of Manchester, was born in 1735. He was educated at the Manchester Grammar School, and afterwards went to Brazenose College, Oxford, where he took the degrees of B.A., M.A., and B.D.

In 1777 he became Rector of Ruan, Lanyhorne, near Tregony, Cornwall. He died 30th October 1808.

He married a Miss Tregenna, and had issue three daughters, of whom the last surviving one was the widow of Dr. Taunton of Truro, who died in 1864.

John Whitaker was a voluminous writer. A life of him is in Polwhele's "Reminiscences in Prose and Verse," London, 1836, and in the Supplement to the "Encyclopædia Britannica."

The CHARTERS of MANCHESTER translated, with explanations and remarks by the Rev. JOHN WHITAKER. 1787. Manchester: Clarke and Co., Printers, Market Place. 1838. *Octavo.*

Title, Introduction, etc., x. pp. The Charters, 28 pp.

FLORA MANCUNIENSIS, or a Catalogue of the flowering plants, the ferns and their allies, found (indigenous) within fifteen miles of Manchester. Arranged according to the Linnæan system. By JOHN WOOD, M.D., assisted by Messrs. Grindon, Buxton, Crozier, and others. Halifax: Leyland and Son, Printers. 1840. *Octavo.*

Half-title, Title as above, Preface, and Subscribers' names, ix. pp. Flora and Index, 81 pp.

This volume is said to have been mostly the work of Richard Buxton [see p. 123] and James Crowther.

MANCHESTER 18TH CENTURY DIRECTORIES.

MANCHESTER DIRECTORY for the year 1772. Containing an alphabetical list of the Merchants, Tradesmen, and principal inhabitants in the Town of Manchester, with the situation of their warehouses and places of abode. Also separate lists of the City Tradesmen and their warehouses in Manchester. The Officers of the Infirmary and Lunatic Hospital. The Officers of the Excise. The principal Whitsters, Stage Coaches, Waggons, and Carriers, with their days of coming in and going out. The Vessels to and from Liverpool upon the Old Navigation and Duke of Bridgewater's Canal, and their agents. Manchester Bank and Insurance Office. His Majesty's Justices of the Peace in and near Manchester; and the Committee for the detection and prosecution of Felons and Receivers of Stolen or embezzled goods. London: printed for the author; and sold by R. Baldwin, No. 47 Paternoster Row, and by the author at Manchester. *Octavo.*

The above Title is printed on the outside cover of the Directory. On the inside is an address to the public, signed ELIZABETH RAFFALD. The Directory itself occupies 46 pp., and the other matter 14 pp.

A copy of this rare volume is in the library of James Crossley, Esq., F.S.A., of Manchester.

For a notice of Mrs. Raffald, see "Manchester Collectanea," Vol. II., p. 157. A description of her Directories is given in Vol. I. of the same work.

Mrs. Raffald published a second Directory of Manchester in 1773. This was in 12mo. "Printed for and sold by the author; and J. Harrop, opposite the Exchange."

It is contained in 78 pp.

Mr. Crossley also possesses a copy of this.

A third Directory was published by Mrs. Raffald in 1781 (12mo, 105 pp).

A DIRECTORY for the TOWNS of MANCHESTER and SALFORD for the year 1788. Manchester: printed by J. Radford in Miller's Street, for the author [EDMOND HOLME]. *Post octavo.*

Title as above, Second Title, Address, and Directory, 131 pp.

A copy of this is in the Chetham Library, where is preserved a complete series of Manchester Directories from 1788 to 1865, 46 Volumes.

SCHOLES'S MANCHESTER and SALFORD DIRECTORY, etc. * * * Manchester: printed by Sowler and Russell. 1794. *Duodecimo.*

Title, etc., and Directory, 200 pp.

This contains a "Short Sketch of the History of Manchester, first published in the Encyclopædia Britannica."

SCHOLES'S MANCHESTER and SALFORD DIRECTORY, an Alphabetical List of the Merchants, Manufacturers, and Principal Inhabitants, with numbers as affixed to their Houses. Also an Alphabetical List of County Manufacturers, Bleachers, etc.; an Alphabetical List of the Streets, Squares, Lanes, and Passages; a List of Carriers by

Land and by Water, with the Days of their arrival and return; an account of Stage Coaches going out from the different Inns; the Situation of the Assurance Offices, and the names of the agents; the Situations of the Fire Plugs and Engine Houses, with the names of the Conductors and Firemen; with other matters of useful Information. Second Edition. Manchester: printed by Sowler and Russell, Deansgate. 1797.

Title as above, Address, and Contents, iv. pp. Directory, 197 pp.

A copy is in the Chetham Library.

BANCKS'S MANCHESTER and SALFORD DIRECTORY, or alphabetical list of Merchants, manufacturers, and principal inhabitants, with the number affixed to their houses, etc. * * Manchester: printed and sold by G. Bancks, corner of St. Ann's Square. 1800. 12*mo.*

Title, etc., and Directory, 248 pp.

A copy is in the Chetham Library.

For a detailed description of these and the Manchester Directories of the early part of this century, *see* "Manchester Collectanea," Vol. I.

The ELECTORS' GUIDE, containing a List of names of those Electors of the BOROUGH of MANCHESTER who voted at the FIRST ELECTION held on the 12th, 13th, and 14th days of December 1832, with their residences and qualifications, and the names of the Candidates for whom they voted. Carefully compiled from the Poll Books, and alphabetically arranged. Manchester: printed by George Cave, Pool Fold, corner of Chapel Walks. 1833. *Octavo.*

Title as above and Guide, 102 pp.

A copy is in the Manchester Free Library.

No Squib Book referring to the Election was published, but a weekly paper called "The Squib, being a Satire on passing Events in Lancashire," was printed by J. A. Robinson, Star Street, Deansgate, Manchester. It was published at 2d. The first part appeared on 28th July 1832.

A nearly complete set is in the author's library.

The "Bullock Smithy Gazette," of which No. 1 was published 17th June 1832, also contains "Squibs," etc., referring to the Election.

MANCHESTER REPRESENTED or MISREPRESENTED. [7 lines from Hen. IV., Act v. Sc. 1.] Edinburgh: printed for William

Blackwood, Edinburgh; and for W. and W. Clarke, Manchester. 1820. *Octavo.*

Title as above, etc., 46 pp.

A copy in the Manchester Free Library.

[Arms.]

BOROUGH of MANCHESTER [Copy], PROCEEDINGS of the COUNCIL, to which is prefixed a copy of the CHARTER of INCORPORATION from October 1838 to November 1839. Manchester: printed by Cave and Sever, 18 St. Ann's Street. *Royal octavo.*

Title as above, Charter, and Index, xxi. pp. The Proceedings (each part paged separately).

A copy of this and the subsequently published Volume of "Proceedings" are in the Manchester Free Library.

A VINDICATION of "MANCHESTER and the MANCHESTER PEOPLE" from the foul calumnies and aspersions of "A citizen of the World" (see p. 115). By a FOREIGNER.

"Nimis uncis
Naribus indulges."
[And Quotation from Shakspeare.]

Manchester: B. Wheeler, Exchange Street. Printed by P. Grant, 1 Pall Mall, Market Street. 1843. *Duodecimo.*

Title as above, and A Vindication, 32 pp.

CHARACTERISTIC STRICTURES, or REMARKS on upwards of one Hundred Portraits of the most eminent Persons in the Counties of LANCASTER and Chester, particularly in the TOWN and NEIGHBOURHOOD of MANCHESTER. Now supposed to be on exhibition. Addressed to John Astley, Esq., of Duckinfield Lodge. In imitation of an ingenious Publication entitled "Sketches from Nature." Interspersed with Critical and Explanatory Notes. London: printed by J. Millidge, in Maiden Lane, Covent Garden; and to be had of the Booksellers in Chester, Manchester, Warrington, and Liverpool, 1779. Price 2s. 6d. *Quarto.*

Title as above, Dedication, and a List of the Artists, vi. pp. Strictures, 40 pp. Errata, etc., 1 p.

A copy of this work, which is now seldom to be purchased, is in the Manchester Free Library.

CATALOGUE of the ART TREASURES of the United Kingdom collected at MANCHESTER in 1857. [Provisional.] Second Edition. Price 1s. *Post octavo.*

Half-title, Title as above, Provisional Advertisement, and Contents, p. i. to p. vii. Catalogue, p. 9 to p. 208.

The following works, though not all strictly speaking "Lancashire Books," will not be out of place under the heading of the "Manchester Art Treasures:"—

ART TREASURES of the UNITED KINGDOM, consisting of Examples from the MANCHESTER ART TREASURES EXHIBITION of 1857, with Descriptive Essays by Owen James, Digby Wyatt, Scharf, etc. Edited by J. R. WARING. London, 1857. Illustrated with 100 Plates in Chromo-Lithography, mostly in gold and colours. *Royal folio.*

Published, London, 1858, at £22. Only 750 copies printed. Sells for £8 : 10s.

ART TREASURES EXHIBITION at MANCHESTER, containing Engravings after Hogarth, Wilkie, Landseer, Gainsborough, etc.

Published in *Octavo* by John Cassell. London. Sells for 5s.

ART TREASURES EXHIBITION at MANCHESTER, being examples of Metal Work, Jewellery, Decorative Furniture, Sculpture, Pottery, Glass and Enamel, and Porcelain, Weaving, Embroidery, etc. Edited by J. B. Waring. Chromo-lithographed. The Woodcuts by R. C. Dudley. London: n. d. In 6 volumes folio.

Published at £21. Sells for £12.

EXHIBITION of ART TREASURES of the United Kingdom,

held at MANCHESTER in 1857. REPORT of the EXECUTIVE COMMITTEE. Manchester: George Simms, St. Ann's Square; London: Longman, Brown, Green, Longmans, and Roberts. 1859. *Royal octavo.*

Title as above, List of Patrons and Council, etc., vii. pp. Report, 48 pp. Appendices, lvi. pp.

PLATES.

Ground-plan of Exhibition. *To face* p. 40.
Diagram, showing the fluctuation in the number of Visitors. *To face* p. i. Appendix (folding).
Plan showing the water arrangements. *To face* p. xxxii. Appendix.
Ground-plan of the Central Hall (folding). *To face* p. xxxvi. Appendix.

Published at 5s. Cloth, 6s. Sells for 4s. 6d.

THE ARTS TREASURES EXAMINER. A Pictorial, Critical, and Historical Record of the Art Treasures Exhibition at Manchester. 1857. Illustrated by upwards of 150 Engravings on Wood, by W. J. Linton, H. Linton, F. G. Smythe, R. Langton, W. Morton, T. S. Jewsbury, M. Carbonneau, M. Facnion, etc. etc. Alexander Ireland and Co., 22 Market Street, Manchester; W. H. Smith and Son, 186 Strand, London. [1857.] *Folio.*

Title as above, Preface, List of Illustrations, and Index, viii. pp. Preliminary Number, viii. pp. Arts Treasures Examiner, 300 pp.

Frontispiece—Exterior of Arts Treasures Palace.
Facing do. Interior " " "

Illustrated with 148 Woodcuts.
Published at 12s. Sells for 7s. 6d.
A considerable number of Guide-books to the Arts Treasures Exhibition were published, many of them in cheap pamphlet form.

MANCHESTER VINDICATED. Being a Compleat Collection of the Papers lately published in defence of that Town in the "Chester Courant." Together with all those on the other side of the question, printed in the "Manchester Magazine," or elsewhere, which are answered in the said "Chester Courant."

"Inclyta Brundusium cui jam convicia solæ
Ignavos homines ingeminare juvat."
[And six following lines.]
ANONYM. AUTHOR, ex vel. Cod. MS.

Chester: printed by and for Elij. Adams. MDCCXLIX. *Duodecimo.*

Title as above, Preface, and a Table, xii. pp. Manchester Vindicated, 324 pp.

Scarce. Sells for 10s. 6d.

A copy is in the Manchester Free Library.

These papers were extracted from the "Journal and Remains of John Byrom."

A CATALOGUE of the COLLECTION of TRACTS for and against POPERY (published in or about the reign of James II.) in the Manchester Library founded by Humphrey Chetham, in which is incorporated, with large additions and biographical notes, the whole of Peck's List of the Tracts in the controversy, with his references. Edited by THOMAS JONES, B.A., Librarian of the Chetham Library. *Foolscap Quarto.*

PART I.

Printed for the Chetham Society. MDCCCLIX. Chetham Society's Title (Vol. xlviii.) and List of Council, 3 pp. Title as above, Preface, and Contents, xii. pp. A Catalogue, etc., 256 pp.

PART II.

Chetham Society's Title-page (Vol. lxiv.) and List of Council, 2 pp. Title to Part II., and Preface to Part II., and Contents, x. pp. Catalogue, etc., Supplement, Index to Titles, Addenda et Corrigenda, 525 pp. Reprint of Charles Dodd's "Certamen utriusque Ecclesiæ," etc., 18 pp, including Half-title and Title.

An ACCOUNT of the WARDENS of CHRIST'S COLLEGE CHURCH, MANCHESTER, since the Foundation in 1422 to the present time. Illustrated with elegant view of Christ Church. London. Printed by W. E., and sold by A. and J. Clarke, Booksellers, at the Bible and Crown, Market Place, Manchester. MDCCLXXIII. *Octavo.*

Title as above, and Account, 16 pp.

A copy is in the Chetham Library.

The CHARTERS of the COLLEGIATE CHURCH, the FREE GRAMMAR SCHOOL, the BLUE-COAT HOSPITAL, and the Last Will and Testament of the late Catherine Richards, and other Ancient Curiosities. Manchester: printed by T. Harper, in Smity Door, MDCCXCI., and sold by M. Falkner, Stationer, in the Market Place; and J. Dawson, in Newton Lane. Price 2s. *Octavo.*

Title as above, Charters, etc., 160 pp. Folding Plate of Christ Church, Manchester.

Sells for 5s. 6d.

A DESCRIPTIVE ACCOUNT of MANCHESTER EXCHANGE. [Arms.] Printed and Sold by Joseph Aston, at the "Exchange Herald" Office, and sold by the Porter to the Institution. 1810. 16*mo.*

Frontispiece [View of the Exchange.] Title, Preface, and Description, 20 pp.

The NEW GUIDE, or useful Pocket Companion, containing a brief HISTORICAL ACCOUNT of MANCHESTER and SALFORD. From the earliest period to the present time, with comprehensive descriptions of the Public Edifices, Places of Amusement, etc. etc. * * *

A New Edition. Embellished with a Map for 1815, a Ground Plan of the Town as it appeared in the year 800, and with Views of the Principal Buildings. Manchester: printed and sold by J. Leech, 3 Wright's Court, Market Street, and sold also by all the Booksellers. *Duodecimo.*

Title as above, Dedication, and Contents, ii. pp. Guide, 204 pp.

Scarce.

The MANCHESTER GUIDE. A brief Historical Description of the Towns of Manchester and Salford, the Public Buildings, and the Charitable and Literary Institutions. Illustrated by a Map, exhibiting the Improvements and Additions made since the year 1770. Manchester: printed and sold by Joseph Aston, No. 84 Deansgate. Sold also by all the Booksellers in Manchester; and R. Bickerstaff, Bookseller, Strand, London. 1804. 8*vo.*

Title as above, Dedication to the Inhabitants of Manchester and Salford, Preface, and Contents, 8 pp. (not numbered). The Guide, 290 pp. Additions, Corrections, and Errata, 2 pp. Sells for 3s. 6d.

A 2d Edition was published in 1815, and a 3d (with plates) in 1826.

The whole PROCEEDINGS on the TRIAL of an ACTION brought by THOMAS WALKER against WILLIAM ROBERTS, Barrister at Law, for Libel. Tried by Special Jury at the Assizes at Lancaster, March 28, 1791. Before the Hon. Sir Alexander Thompson, Knight, one of the Barons of Her Majesty's Court of Exchequer. Taken in Shorthand by Joseph Gurney. Manchester: printed by Charles Wheeler. Sold by Messrs. Falkner and Birch, Stationers, in the Market Place; and by all the Booksellers in Manchester. * * * MDCCXCI. *Octavo.*

Title as above, List of Counsel, Contents, and Trial, 206 pp. [See p. 139.]

A copy in the Chetham Library.

An EXAMINATION of the LATE DREADFUL OCCURRENCE at the MEETING on AUGUST 16, 1819. Being a clear statement and review of its object, circumstances, and results. Newcastle-on-Tyne: printed by William Andrew Mitchell, St. Nicholas' Churchyard. *Octavo.*

Title as above, and Examination, 27 pp.

DISTURBANCES at MANCHESTER, or dreadful effects of the dispersion of the Reform Meeting by the Yeomanry Cavalry, being a full Account of the Proceedings that took place on that dreadful day, prior to and succeeding the apprehension of Henry Hunt, Esq., and a number of other persons who were assembled at St. Peter's Place; also an Account of the persons killed and wounded; with an exact and full Description of the Triumphal Entry of Mr. Hunt into London on Monday 13th September 1819; with all the particulars of the Procession that accompanied him on that memorable day. London: printed and published by J. Bailey, 116 Chancery Lane. Price 6d. *Duodecimo.*

Title and Account, 26 pp. Return of killed and wounded, 2 pp. *Frontispiece*, Coloured plate of the Peterloo Riot. Scarce.

A copy of this is in the Manchester Free Library.

The whole PROCEEDINGS before the CORONER'S INQUEST at OLDHAM, etc., on the body of JOHN LEES, who died of Sabre Wounds at MANCHESTER, August 16, 1819. Being the fullest and only authentic information concerning the transactions of that fatal day. Detailing the evidence on both sides upon oath; the legal arguments before the coroner; his various decisions; the applications to the Court of King's Bench for a mandamus to him to proceed; the affidavits thereon; and the petition of the Father of the deceased to Parliament, with the references to the cases on the subject, and a copious analytical Index. Taken in shorthand and edited by JOSEPH AUGUSTUS DOWLING, Esq. With an accurate Plan of St. Peter's Field [Folding]. London: printed for William Stone, Ludgate Hill. 1820. *Octavo.*

Title as above, Address, and references to the Plan, 5 pp. Coroner's Inquest, 580 pp. Court of Queen's Bench, etc., 37 pp. Index, and Errata, 16 pp. (not paged).

This was reprinted in 1823. Either of the editions now sell for 7s. 6d.

This Coroner's Inquest extended to ten days.

MANCHESTER MEETING, sixteenth of August 1819. A REPORT of the TRIAL REDFORD against BIRLEY and OTHERS for an Assault on the sixteenth of August 1819, before Mr. Justice Holroyd and a special Jury, at the Lancaster Assizes, 1822. Taken in Court expressly by the Publisher. Manchester: printed by James Harrop Junr., at the "Mercury and British Volunteer" Office, and sold by all the Booksellers. 1822. *Octavo.*

Title as above, and Trial, 64 pp.

The TRIAL of HENRY HUNT, Esq., Jno. Knight, Jos. Johnson Jno. Thacker Saxton, Samuel Bamford, Jos. Healey, James Moorhouse, Robert Jones, Geo. Swift, and Robert Wylde, for an alledged conspiracy to overturn the Government, etc., by threats and force of arms. Before Mr. Justice Bayley and a Special Jury, at the York Lent Assizes, 1820. [Here follows 36 lines of quotations from the Bible.] London: printed by T. Dolby, 299 Strand, and may be had of all Booksellers. 1820. *Octavo.*

Title as above, Index to Witnesses, iv. pp. Preface, viii. pp. The Trial, p. 3 to p. 309.

Sells for 4s. 6d.

THIRD EDITION.

WHO KILLED COCK ROBIN? A satirical Tragedy or Hierogryphic Prophecy on the MANCHESTER BLOT!!!

"Read, Mark, Learn, and inwardly Digest,
If the Cap fits ye! wear it as your Best."

London: printed and published by John Cahuac, 53 Blackman Street, Southwark. 1819. *Octavo.*

Title as above, and satirical Tragedy, 23 pp.

This is another of the Peterloo pieces of Literature. It is illustrated with five woodcuts, and is scarce.

A copy is in the Manchester Free Library.

Amongst other Pamphlets which were published on this occasion, were—

Letter to Earl Fitzwilliam on the late Transactions at Manchester. 1819. *Octavo.* 100 pp.

Exposure of the Calumnies circulated by the Enemies of Social Order against the Magistrates and Yeomanry Cavalry of Manchester and Salford, by Fran. Phillips. 1819. *Octavo.*

Essay on the necessity of a Parliamentary Enquiry into the Transactions at Manchester. 1819. *Octavo.*

MEMOIRS of the LITERARY and PHILOSOPHICAL SOCIETY of MANCHESTER.

VOL. I.

Warrington: printed by W. Eyres for T. Cadel, in the Strand, London. MDCCLXXXV. *Octavo.*

Afterwards published in Manchester. The volumes have been regularly published up to the present time, and contain many articles referring to Lancashire.

The TRANSACTIONS of the MANCHESTER GEOLOGICAL SOCIETY.

VOLUME I.

London: Simpkin, Marshall, and Co.; Simms and Dinham, Manchester. 1841. *Octavo.*

Title as above, List of Officers, and Contents, vi. pp. Transactions, 236 pp. Plates and Maps.

This Society has published 12 volumes (1841-1874), in which are many articles referring to the Geology of Lancashire.

A GUIDE to HEAVEN from the WORD, good counsel how to close savingly with Christ; serious questions for morning and evening; rules for the due observance of the Lord's Day. Manchester: printed at Smithy Door. 1664. 32*mo.*

This is extracted from Ford's Catalogue for 1832. It is inserted here as perhaps the earliest example of the Manchester Press.

A HISTORY of OLDHAM in LANCASHIRE. By EDWIN BUTTERWORTH. London: Chapman and Hall, 186 Strand. Price 1s. 6d. *Duodecimo.*

Title as above, Preface, History, and Index, 62 pp. The Preface is dated Busk, near Oldham, 1832. Scarce.

A copy is in the Author's Library.

HISTORICAL SKETCHES of OLDHAM. By the late EDWIN BUTTERWORTH. With an Appendix containing the History of the Town to the Present Time. *Duodecimo.*

Title and Preface, iv. pp. Sketches, 256 pp., and 9 unnumbered. *Frontispiece*—Oldham Lyceum. Published in 1856.

Sells for 3s. 6d.

An HISTORICAL and DESCRIPTIVE ACCOUNT of the PAROCHIAL CHAPELRY of OLDHAM, in the County of Lancaster, including some biographical sketches of remarkable persons, natives or residents thereof; together with a DIRECTORY, etc. By J. BUTTERWORTH. Oldham: printed and sold by J. Clarke, Market Place; sold also by Baldwin, Cradock, and Joy, 47 Paternoster Row, London; Messrs. Clarke, Manchester; J. Hartley, Rochdale; J. Lomax, Stockport; Howarth, Bury; W. Cunningham, Ashton-under-Lyne; J. Brook, Delph; and by the Author. 1817. *Post octavo.*

Title as above, Dedication, and Preface, xii. pp. History, Directory, and Errata, 212 pp. (1 page announcing other works by the same Author.) Contains folding Pedigrees of Cudworth of Wernith and Radcliffe of Radcliffe Tower.

Published at 5s. Sells for about its published price.

A second Edition appeared in 1826.

ANTIQUITATES BREMETONACENSES, or the ROMAN ANTIQUITIES of OVERBOROUGH. By the Rev. RICHARD RAUTHMEL. Reprinted from the original Edition of 1746, with additions.

Quibus rebus multæ civitates quæ in illum diem ex æquo egerant; datis obsidibus iram posuere et præsidiis CASTELLISQUE circumdate.—TACITUS.

Kirkby Lonsdale: printed by and for Arthur Foster. 1824. *Octavo.*

Title as above, Dedication, and Contents, vi. pp. Roman Antiquities and Appendix, 139 pp.

PLATES.

Burrow Hall, *Frontispiece.* | Plan of Fortress.
Roman Road. | Map of Garrisons.
Roman Remains, 2 plates.

The original Edition (1746) sells for 7s. 6d.; but fine copies sell for as much as 15s. It is now scarce. The Reprint sells for 4s. 6d.

This work contains a short biographical notice of Thomas West, the author of "The Antiquities of Furness," etc.

Richard Rauthmel, the son of Arthur Rauthmel, husbandman, was born at Laas, in Yorkshire. He took the degree of B.A. at St. John's College, Cambridge, in 1713, and afterwards was Perpetual Curate of Whitewell, in Bowland. He held this cure until his death. He was buried at Chipping.

A CORRECT REPORT of the TRIAL of WILLIAM HOLDEN, JAMES ASHCROFT the elder, James Ashcroft the younger, David Ashcroft, and John Robinson, for the MURDER of MARGARET MARSDEN and HARRIET PENNINGTON, and for Robbery in the Dwelling-house of Mr. Thomas Littlewood at PENDLETON. Before Sir Richard Richards, etc., at the Lancaster Assizes, on Friday the 5th of September 1817. Taken in shorthand by GEORGE TAYLOR, Solicitor, Manchester. With a view of Mr. Littlewood's House and adjoining premises, Ground-plan, and Plan of the Roads and principal Station. Manchester: printed and published by J. Pratt, 23 St. Mary's Gate, and sold by all the Booksellers in town and country. *Octavo.*

Title as above, List of Jury, Report, and Appendix, 56 pp.

A second Edition followed within the year.

Another Edition, dated 1817, was published by J. and J. Harrop, Manchester. This also contained View of Littlewood's House, etc.

DOCUMENTS relating to the PRIORY of PENWORTHAM and other possessions in Lancashire of the ABBEY of EVESHAM. Edited by W. A. HULTON, Esq. Printed for the Chetham Society. MDCCCLIII. *Foolscap quarto.*

Chetham Society's Title (Vol. xxx.), and List of Council, 4 pp. Title as above, Introduction, and Contents, lxxvii. pp. Half-title, 1 p. De Prioratu de Penwortham, etc., and Index nominum et Locorum, 136 pp.

Frontispiece—Plate of Seals.

A DESCRIPTION of ST. MARY'S CISTERCIAN CHURCH at PENWORTHAM, near Preston in Lancashire. By P. WHITTLE, F.S.A., author of the "History of Preston," "Marina," "Sunbeams of Catholicity," etc. [Ten lines of poetry.] Preston: P. Whittle, Fishergate. *Demy 18mo.*

Title as above and Description, 33 pp.

POULTON-LE-FYLDE. See Blackpool, p. 5.

HISTORY of METHODISM in PRESTON and its VICINITY, with Notices of its Introduction into East Lancashire and the Fylde. By RICHARD ALLEN, Wesleyan Minister. Preston: Toulmin, Printer, "Guardian" Office, Cannon Street. Sold also at 66 Paternoster Row, London. MDCCCLXVI. *Post octavo.*

Title and Preface, 11 pp. History, 62 pp.

HISTORY of the BOROUGH of PRESTON, and its ENVIRONS, in the County of Lancashire. By CHARLES HARDWICK, Member of and Contributor to the Lancashire and Cheshire Historic Society; Author of "Friendly Societies, their History and Financial Prospects, etc."

"Nothing extenuate, nor set down aught in Malice."—SHAKSPEARE.
"The just object of History is Truth."—LAMARTINE.

Preston: Worthington and Co., Town-Hall Corner; London: Simpkin, Marshall, and Co. MDCCCLVII. *Royal octavo.*

Title as above, Dedication, Advertisement, Preface, Contents, List of Plates, Errata, and Addenda, xvii. pp. History, Chronological Table, and Index, 687 pp.

This volume contains a Map of the County, a Map of Preston, and 50 engraved plates, illustrative of the subject. It is the best History of Preston which has appeared.

Published at 27s. 6d. Is somewhat scarce, and sells for 12s.

The HISTORY, TOPOGRAPHY, and DIRECTORY of the BOROUGH of PRESTON, with the TOWN and PARISH of CHORLEY. By MANNEX and Co. Beverley: printed for the Authors by W. B. Johnson, Market Place. Price to Subscribers, with a Map of the County, 5s. 6d., neatly bound. 1851. *Post octavo.*

Half-title, Title as above, Address, and Index, viii. pp. History, etc., 181 pp.

Of no value except as a Directory of that date. Sells for 2s. 6d.

A BRIEF DESCRIPTION of the BURROUGH and TOWN of PRESTON, and its Government and Guild. Originally composed between the years 1682 and 1686. With occasional Notes by JOHN TAYLOR. Preston: printed and sold by J. Wilcockson, Market Place; sold also by the other booksellers in Preston; and by Baldwin, Cradock, and Joy, Paternoster Row, London. 1818. *Octavo.*

Half-title, Title as above, Dedication, and Advertisement, viii. pp. Table of Contents and Description, 94 pp. Addenda, A List of Mayors, Bailiffs, etc., 6 pp.

Published at 4s. 6d. in boards. Now very scarce.

John Taylor, Agriculturalist and Seedsman, was for many years a member of the Old Corporation of Preston. He died in Liverpool, 7th January 1867, and was buried at Ainfield Cemetery.

A TOPOGRAPHICAL, STATISTICAL, and HISTORICAL ACCOUNT of the BOROUGH of PRESTON in the Hundred of Amounderness, County Palatine of Lancaster. Its antiquities and modern Improvements, including a correct copy of the Charter granted in the reign of Charles II. Biographical Sketches of Eminent Men. An extensive Chronology brought down to the present time, with a description of its Environs, the origin of the Guild Merchants' Fête held here every twentieth year, with much information not generally known. A list of Mayors, Bailiffs, Recorders, and Representatives in Parliament who have served the Borough. A Directory for 1821, with a list of the Streets,

Courts, etc., compiled from the most authentic sources, and published purposely for the use of those Ladies and Gentlemen resorting to Preston Guild, which will be celebrated in the year 1822. By MARMADUKE TULKET, O.S.B. [*i.e.*, PETER WHITTLE].

"I present not my Topography to the Reader as if I had chosen the best method of ensuring his approbation, but as using the only means I possessed of engaging his attention."

"It is our business to collect the valuable and scattered remains."

Preston: printed for and sold by P. Whittle; sold by J. Wilcockson, Mrs. Walker, W. Addison, and L. Clarke, Preston,[1] etc. etc. 1821. *Duodecimo.*

Title as above, i. p. Dedication, Contents, and Advertisement, viii. pp. History, Address to Reader (on pp. 323-324), and Directory, 347 pp.

PLATES.

Market Place.	Trinity Church.
The Town and Guild Hall.	The National School.
The Parish Church.	The Catholic School in Fox Street.

This volume was published at 6s., and sells for 5s.

The Second Volume did not appear until 1837, and was entitled The HISTORY of the BOROUGH of PRESTON in the County Palatine of Lancaster.

"Preston may well be proud! when she has cradled an Arkwright of Cromford, and adopted as her son a Horrocks of Edgeworth! The commercial part of civilised Europe will remember Preston in the Annals of History to the latest posterity."

By P. WHITTLE, F.A.S., author of "Marina, or a History of Southport, Lytham, and Blackpool," etc.

VOL. II.

Preston: printed and sold by P. and H. Whittle, 25 Fishgate; and sold by all other Booksellers in Lancashire. MDCCCXXXVII.

Title and Address, vi. pp. History, p. 8 to p. 395. Contents, iii. pp.

The two volumes sell for 7s. 6d.

---

[1] A long list of local booksellers follows.

Peter Whittle was born, 9th July 1789, at Inglewhite, and received his early education at the Goosnargh Free Grammar School. He began business in Preston as a bookseller, etc., in 1810, where in 1827 he married Matilda Henrietta Armstrong (daughter of Major Armstrong of the 7th Rifles).

He died at Liverpool on 7th January 1867, and was there buried.

PRESTON GUILDS.

The GUILD MERCHANT of PRESTON; or Preston Guild Companion. Being an exact Representation on nineteen Copper Plates, curiously drawn and engraved, of that ancient procession, with a Letter-Press explanation. The whole laid down so easy and expressive as to render it proper help to those gentlemen and ladies resorting to Preston. Manchester. 1762. *Octavo.*

Very Scarce. *See* GUILD, 1822.

The GUILD MERCHANT of PRESTON, with an extract of the original Charter granted for holding the same. An account of the Processions and public Entertainments, an authentic List of the Nobility and Gentry who dined with the Mayor and his Lady, also separate Lists of the Subscribers to the Ladies and Trade Assemblies. Publish'd at the request of the Nobility, etc., by permission of the Mayor.

——" Then Music, Sports, and Play,
Give time yet quicker wings to fly away,
Beguiled the Night and hurried on the Day."

Manchester: printed and sold by T. Harrop and Mr. Newton, Booksellers; Mr. Marshall, Bookseller in St. Clement's Churchyard: and at the Pamphlet Shops in London. Likewise by Mr. Smalley and Mr. Abbot in Preston; by the Booksellers in Town and Country; and by all News Carriers. [1762.] *Octavo.*

Title as above, Dedication, Advertisement, Contents, Guild Merchants, Lists, and Address to the Reader, 40 pp.

Sells for 5s.

An ACCOUNT of the GUILD MERCHANT of PRESTON, with a List of the Nobility and Gentry who appeared at the Balls and Assemblies at Preston Guild, Sept. 1762. Printed for WILLIAM STUART, Bookseller in Preston; and sold by Z. Stuart, at the Lamb in Paternoster Row, London. Price 1s. *Octavo.*

Title as above, and Account, 18 pp.

A copy of this is in the British Museum.

AUTHENTIC RECORDS of the GUILD MERCHANT of PRESTON, in the County Palatine of Lancaster, in the year 1822. With an Introduction containing an Historical dissertation on the origin of Guilds; and a relation of all the different celebrations of the Guilda Mercatoria of Preston of which any records remain. Carefully compiled and arranged as a work of reference and authority. By I. Wilcockson. Embellished with a Portrait of N. Grimshaw, Esq., Guild Mayor in 1802 and 1822, and a print of the Procession of trades.

[Arms of Preston.]

Preston: printed and published by I. Wilcockson, "Chronicle" Office, Market Place. Sold also by C. Clarke, Lancaster; T. Kaye, Liverpool; T. Sowler, Manchester; T. Rogerson, Blackburn; J. Ogle, Bolton; J. Brown, Wigan; and all other Booksellers in Lancashire; and by R. Ackermann, 101 Strand, London. *Octavo.*

Title as above, Contents, Introduction, 40 pp. Records, p. 41 to p. 128.
Published at 5s. Sells for 3s. 6d.

Isaac Wilcockson was a native of Preston, and a Bookseller there in 1812. He was the proprietor of the "Preston Chronicle."

The HISTORY of PRESTON in Lancashire, together with the GUILD MERCHANT, and some account of the Duchy and County Palatine of Lancaster. With eighteen Plates. London: printed for Edward Jeffrey and Son, Pall Mall; and sold also by J. Wilcockson, Preston. 1822. *Quarto.*

Title as above, and Contents, iv. pp. Preston, etc., 156 pp.

Plates.

(*Frontispiece.*) 1. The Corporation.
2. The Standard of Preston and Mayor's Mace.
3, 4, and 5. Ensign's Armorial.
6. The Marshall.
7. Cordwainers' Company.
8. Tanners' Company.
9. Woolcombers' Company.
10. Masons' Company.
11. Weavers' Company.

12. Carpenters' Company.
13. Butchers' Company.
14. Vintners' Company.
15. Clergy, Ladies, and Gentlemen.
16. Skinners and Glovers.
17. Smiths, etc.
18. Mercers' Company.

These plates were originally published in 1762. See p. 162.

Published at £1 : 4s. Sells for 10s. A work of considerable local interest.

A full and detailed ACCOUNT of the GUILD MERCHANT of PRESTON, in the county Palatine of Lancaster, as celebrated in the year 1842. Illustrated with a view of the Procession of Trades, the Mayoress's Public Breakfast, the Grand Costume Ball, and a View of Preston and the Race-Course. Preston: published by W. Pollard, 25 Church Street. Sold also by S. Kaye, Castle Street, Liverpool; Simms and Denham, Manchester; S. Barwick, Lancaster; J. Walkden, Blackburn; C. S. Simms, Wigan; and J. Ogle, Bolton. *Post octavo.*

Frontispiece (View of Preston). Title as above, Contents, and Preface, viii. pp. Introduction, and Account, 52 pp.

Sells for 3s.

The GUILD GUIDE and HAND BOOK of PRESTON, with a concise History of the Guilds, and the Arrangements for the Festival of 1862. Together with an Historic account of the Borough, also particulars of all the objects and places of interest in the town and neighbourhood, and a full Chronology of Local Events. By R. CLARKSON and JOS. DEARDEN. Price 6d. Preston: Toulmin, Steam-Printing Office, Cannon Street. 1862. 12*mo.*

Title as above, Preface, and Hand Book, 76 pp. Illustrated with a Map, "shewing principal streets in Preston."

An ACCOUNT of the celebration of PRESTON GUILD in 1862. Compiled by William Dobson.[1] Preston: W. and J. Dobson; London: Simpkin, Marshall, and Co.; Manchester: E. Slater; and all Booksellers. 12*mo.*

[1] Mr. Dobson also wrote "Preston in the Olden Time, or Illustrations of Manners and Customs in Preston in the 17th and 18th Centuries." Preston, 1857. Price 2d.

Title as above (with woodcut of the Arms of Preston), Advertisement, and the Guild, 96 pp.
Published at 6d.

A HISTORY of PRESTON GUILD, the Ordinances of various Guilds Merchant, the Custumal of Preston, the Charters to the Borough, the Incorporated Companies, List of Mayors from 1327, etc. etc. By WILLIAM DOBSON and JOHN HARLAND, F.S.A. Second Edition. Preston: W. and J. Dobson, Fishergate; London: Simpkin, Marshall, and Co.; Manchester: E. Slater, and all Booksellers. *12mo.*

Published at 1s. The first Edition issued in 1862, and was followed by two other Editions.

Title as above, Introduction, History, and Index, 116 pp. An Appendix (published afterwards), 15 pp.

The Carnivals of a Century; or the GUILDS of PRESTON for a HUNDRED YEARS: being an ACCOUNT of the GUILD MERCHANT held in PRESTON from 1742 to 1842. Those of 1822 and 1842 fully detailed, with the names of all who took a part in them. Also some observations as to the Guild Mayor, and on the holding of the Guild in 1862. Preston: printed and published by Edw. Ambler, Stanley Buildings. *Octavo.*

Title as above and Preface, iv. pp. The Guilds, 48 pp.

The CHARTERS granted by different Sovereigns to the Burgesses of PRESTON in the County Palatine of Lancaster. Printed from attested copies. The English translations by the Rev. JOHN LINGARD, D.D., LL.D. Preston: published and sold by J. Wilcockson, "Chronicle" Office, Market Place. 1821. *Octavo.*

Title as above and Preface, iv. pp. Charters, etc., 94 pp. Sells for 5s. 6d.

John Lingard, D.D., LL.D., was born 5th February 1771, and died 13th July 1851. He was a native of Winchester, and for forty years he was the Roman Catholic priest of the chapel at Hornby in Lancashire.

His chief work was "A History of England from the first Invasion by the Romans to the year 1688."

HISTORY of the PARLIAMENTARY REPRESENTATION of PRESTON during the last Hundred Years. By WILLIAM DOBSON. Preston: Dobson and Son, Fishergate; London: Simpkin, Marshall, and Co. 1856. *12mo.*

Title as above, Advertisement, History, and Appendix, 75 pp. Originally published in the "Preston Chronicle."

An ENTIRE and IMPARTIAL COLLECTION of all the PAPERS, SQUIBS, and SONGS, published on both sides, concerning the late ELECTION at PRESTON for Members to serve in Parliament, with a State of the Poll for each day. Preston: printed by R. Law, Market Place. 1796. (Price 1s.) *Octavo.*

Title as above, and Collection, 40 pp. Scarce. A copy is in the Library of Dr. Kendrick, Warrington.

A Complete COLLECTION of the ADDRESSES and PAPERS (on both sides) which were published within the BOROUGH of PRESTON during the Canvass for a MEMBER to serve in PARLIAMENT in the room of the late John Horrocks, Esquire. Preston: printed by T. Walker. Price 6d. [1804.] *Octavo.*

Title and Dedication, 11 pp. Collection, 19 pp.

A Complete COLLECTION of ADDRESSES, SQUIBS, SONGS, and other Papers, published at the time of the late contested Election for the BOROUGH of PRESTON (which commenced Wednesday, May 6th, 1807, and ended the 19th following). With a State of the Poll for each day. The Candidates were Lord Stanley, S. Horrocks, Esq., and J. Harrison, Esq. Preston: printed by Thomas Walker, Bookseller. *Octavo.*

Title as above, and Collection, 40 pp. A copy of this is in the Manchester Free Library.

A Complete COLLECTION of ADDRESSES, SQUIBS, SONGS. etc., published during the late Contested Election for the BOROUGH of PRESTON (which commenced Wednesday, October 8th, 1812, and ended on the 15th following). With a State of the Poll, etc. etc. Preston: printed for Mrs. Walker, Corner of the old Shambles. *Octavo.*

Title and Collection, 20 pp.

A Complete COLLECTION of ADDRESSES, SQUIBS, SONGS, etc., published during the late Contested Election for the BOROUGH of PRESTON (which commenced June 18th, and ended June 25th, 1818), the proceedings on the day of Nomination, etc. etc. Preston: printed for L. Clarke, 143 Church Street, and J. Wilcockson, "Chronicle" Office, Market Place. *Octavo.*

Title and Collection, 32 pp.

A COLLECTION of ADDRESSES, SQUIBS, SONGS, etc., published during the late contested ELECTION for the BOROUGH of PRESTON, which commenced March 7th, and ended March 22d, 1820. Also proceedings on the day of nomination, and Speeches of the several Gentlemen who addressed the Electors at the opening of the Election, etc. etc. Preston: printed for and sold by J. Wilcockson, L. Clarke, and Mrs. Walker. *Octavo.*

Title and Collection, 46 pp.

A COLLECTION of ADDRESSES, SQUIBS, SONGS, etc., together with the Political Mountebank (showing the changeable opinion of Mr. Cobbett), published during the contested ELECTION for the BOROUGH of PRESTON, which commenced June 9, and ended June 26, 1826. Also proceedings on the day of the nomination, and speeches of the several Gentlemen who addressed the Electors at the opening and close of the Election, with a state of each day's poll. The Candidates were—Hon. E. G. Stanley, John Wood, Esq., Captain Barrie, C.B., R.N., William Cobbett, Esq. Preston: sold by the Booksellers; sold also by T. Rogerson, Blackburn, etc. etc. *Octavo.*

Title as above, and Address, etc., 127 pp. A copy is in the Manchester Free Library.

ADDRESSES, SQUIBS, SPEECHES, SONGS, etc., at the PRESTON Election, July 1837. Candidates—Peter Hesketh Fleetwood, Esq., Robert

Townley Parker, Esq., John Crawford, Esq., and Fergus O'Connor. Preston: printed by George Bateman, 13 Fishergate, and may be had of all Booksellers in Preston. 1837. *Octavo.*

Title, Addresses, etc., 58 pp.

*** Some of the Squib Books of Preston are, strictly speaking, Pamphlets; but, to render the subject complete, it has been thought advisable to insert the whole.

BOROUGH of PRESTON. PROCEEDINGS of the COUNCIL. Thomas Miller, Esquire, Mayor, 1836.

[Arms of the Borough.]

Preston: printed by L. Clarke, 143 Church Street. *Small quarto.*

Title and Proceedings, 98 pp. Financial Statement, 19 pp.

This is the first printed volume of the Council's Proceedings. They have been published regularly from 1836 to the present time. A copy of the whole series is in Dr. Shepherd's Library, Preston.

PRESTON TOWN-COUNCIL; or PORTRAITS of LOCAL LEGISLATORS, together with a List of all the Mayors, Aldermen, and Councillors Elected for the Borough of Preston between 1835 and 1870. By "Atticus" (A. HEWITSON). Reprinted from the "Preston Chronicle."

"Speak of me as I am; nothing extenuate, nor set down aught in malice."
SHAKSPEARE.

Price 1s. Preston: printed at the "Chronicle" Office. 1870. *Foolscap octavo.*

Title as above, Index, and Portraits, etc., 133 pp.

The PRESTON SONGSTER, or the New Roundelay. A Select Collection of the newest and most admired Songs; to which is added a Collection of Toast and Sentiment. Preston: printed by G. Sergent. 1789. *Duodecimo.*

Title as above, and Songs, etc., 256 pp. Index, viii. pp.

Scarce. A copy is in the library of Richard Wood, Esq., Manchester. Contains a few local songs not to be found elsewhere.

OUR CHURCHES and CHAPELS, their Parsons, Priests, and Congregations, being a Critical and Historical Account of every place of Worship in PRESTON. By ATTICUS [A. Hewitson.]

> "'Tis pleasant through the loopholes of retreat
> To peep at such a world."—COWPER.

Reprinted from the "Preston Chronicle," Preston. Printed at the "Chronicle" Office, Fishergate. *Post 12mo.*

Title as above, Address to the Reader, Index, and Our Churches, 214 pp.

Published at 2s. 6d.

PRESTONIAD, a Poem. *See* PART III.

MEMORIALS of the CHURCH of PRESTWICH, being a contribution towards the history of the Parent Church of the Parish, including notices of the local families; their pedigrees, etc.; extracts from the Parish Registers and Records, illustrating the descent of families adjacent and remote; constituting in a certain degree the history of the place, derived chiefly from unpublished and authentic sources. By JOHN BOOKER, B.A. of Magdalene College, Cambridge, Curate of Prestwich. Manchester: Simms and Dunham, St. Ann's Square. 1852. *Foolscap quarto.*

(Uniform in size, etc., with the Chetham Society's publications.)
Title as above, Dedication to the Right Hon. Thomas Egerton, Earl of Wilton, and Preface, vii. pp. Memorials and Appendix, 250 pp. Errata on Slip.

LIST OF ILLUSTRATIONS.

Prestwich Church . . . *Frontispiece*
Ground-plan of Prestwich Church . . P. 54
Heaton House . . P. 78
Deyne Hall . . 88
Agecroft Hall . . 198
Tonge Hall . . . P. 200.

This is a valuable local work, and is very scarce.

RAMBLES by THE RIBBLE. First Series. By WILLIAM DOBSON, author of "History of the Parliamentary Representation of Preston," "Preston in the olden Time," etc.

> "'Tis that loveliest stream,
> I've learned by heart its sweet and devious course
> By frequent tracing."—ALEXANDER SMITH.

Preston: printed by W. and J. Dobson, "Chronicle" Office; London: Simpkin, Marshall, and Co. 1864. *Foolscap octavo.*

Title as above, and Introduction, iv. pp. Rambles, and Index, 144 pp.

Published at 1s. 6d. A Second Edition followed.
The above first appeared in the "Preston Chronicle."

The STATUTES and CHARTERS of RIVINGTON SCHOOL, in the County of Lancaster, with a MEMOIR of the Founder, the right reverend JAMES PILKINGTON, B.D., Lord Bishop of Durham. By the Rev. J. W. WHITAKER, M.A., Head Master of the School. (Engraved copy of the School Seal.) London: Whittaker, Treacher, and Co.; Bancks and Co., Manchester, and J. Brown, Wigan. 1837. *Octavo.*

Title as above, and Contents, v. pp. Memoir, 139 pp. Half-title, Statutes, etc., p. 143 to p. 244.

Sells for 5s. 6d.
The Rev. J. W. Whitaker was incumbent of Rivington.

An HISTORICAL and TOPOGRAPHICAL ACCOUNT of the TOWN and PARISH of ROCHDALE, in Lancashire, and also of the Parochial Chapelry of Saddleworth, in the County of York. By JAMES BUTTERWORTH, author of "Histories of Oldham, Ashton-under-Lyne, Manchester, Stockport," etc. Manchester: printed by W. D. Varey, 3 Red Lion Street, St. Ann's Square. 1828. *Octavo.*

Title as above, Second Title, Dedication, and Preface, vi. pp. Supplement or Appendix, List of Subscribers, Contents, Index, and History of Rochdale, 206 pp. Errata, 1 p.
Title to History of Saddleworth, "A History and Description of the Parochial Chapelry of Saddleworth, in the County of York (6 lines of verse.) By James Butterworth. Manchester: printed by W.

D. Verey, etc. 1828." Dedication, History of Saddleworth, Addenda, and Index, 86 pp.

Sells for 7s. 6d.

ROCHDALE in 1745 and 1746. By an old Inhabitant (Mr. SAMUEL BRIERLEY). Rochdale: printed by John Turner, Drake Street. 1874. *Octavo.*

Title as above, and Rochdale in 1745 and 1746, 22 pp.

Price 6d. This is an interesting episode in the History of Rochdale.

ROCHDALE PAST and PRESENT; a HISTORY and GUIDE. By WILLIAM ROBERTSON, Reporter. [Quotation 4 lines.] Rochdale: printed and published by Schofield and Hoblyn. 1875. [All rights of reproduction are reserved.] *Foolscap octavo.*

Title as above, Preface, and Contents, viii. pp. Introduction and Guide, 352 pp.

ILLUSTRATIONS (tinted).

The Town Hall . *Frontispiece.*
The Park.
Grammar and Sparrow Hill Schools.
The Cemetery.
The Residence of the Right. Hon. John Bright.
Hollingworth Lake.
Hollingworth Lake by Moonlight.

Published at 3s.

MEMORIALS of ROCHDALE GRAMMAR SCHOOL. By the Rev. F. R. RAINES, F.S.A., Incumbent of Milnrow, and Editor of Bishop Gastrell's "Notitia Cestriensis" for the Chetham Society; the Report of the Ladies' Committee of the Bazaar for the re-building of the Grammar School; a General Statement of the Proceedings connected with the building of the Parish Church, Sunday and Infant School, and the re-building of the Grammar School. London: J. G. F. and J. Rivington, St. Paul's Churchyard, and Waterloo Place, Pall Mall: Manchester, T. Sowler, and Sims and Dinham; Rochdale, T. Holden. *Octavo.*

Title as above, Dedication, Memorials, etc., 47 pp.

Published in 1845; the profit to go to the Grammar School. Price 1s.

A copy is in the Rochdale Free Public Library.

A Treatise on CANALS and RESERVOIRS, and the best mode of designing and executing them, with observations on the ROCHDALE, LEEDS, AND LIVERPOOL, and Huddersfield Canals, etc. etc.[1] By JOHN SUTCLIFFE, Civil Engineer. Rochdale: printed for the author by J. Hartley, and sold by him; also by Law and Whitaker, Ave Maria Lane, London; and by the principal Booksellers in York, Leeds, Bradford, Huddersfield, Halifax, etc. 1816. *Octavo.*

Title as above, Dedication to Sir Robert Peel, Baronet, Preface, and Contents, xiv. pp. Treatise, 413 pp. Errata on last page.

A rather scarce book. A copy is in the Rochdale Free Public Library.

PAPERS PUBLISHED in favour of the intended ROCHDALE CANAL, in the applications made to parliament in the Sessions of 1791, 1792, and 1793. Chester: printed by J. Fletcher. *Octavo.*

Title as above, ii. pp. Papers, 80 pp.

PLATES.

The Track of the Intended Rochdale Canal through Manchester, p. 68.
Plan of the Intended Rochdale Canal, p. 70.

A copy of this is in the Bodleian Library.

ROCHDALE, a Fragment. By W. NUTTALL. *See* PART III.

ROCHER VALE, a poem. By JAMES BUTTERWORTH. *See* PART III.

HISTORY of the FOREST of ROSSENDALE. By THOMAS NEWBIGGING, Member of the Historic Society of Lancashire and Cheshire. With a Chapter on the Geology of Rossendale by Captain Aitken, J.P., Vice-President of the Manchester Geological Society; and Observations on the Botany of the District by Abraham Stansfield, President of the Todmorden Botanical Society. London: Simpkin, Marshall, and Co.; Bacup: T. Brown. 1868. *Octavo.*

Engraved Title, with View of Hareholme Mill. Title as above, Dedica-

[1] Full title not quoted.

tion, Preface, and Contents, xx. pp. History of Rossendale, and Index, 337 pp.

Frontispiece, View of Newchurch, Rossendale.

Published at 10s. 6d. Large paper copies, 21s.

An ACCOUNT and MEASUREMENT of the PUBLIC BRIDGES within the HUNDRED of SALFORD, in the County Palatine of Lancaster. By EDMOND HOLME, Bridge Master. Manchester: printed in the year MDCCLXXXII. *Octavo.*

Title as above, and Dedication, iii. pp. Account, 74 pp.

A copy of this is in the Manchester Free Library.

The MEMORIAL STATUES and ROYAL FREE MUSEUM and LIBRARY, Peel Park, SALFORD.

No. —— Presented to ————

———— Chairman.

Photographed by A. Brothers, Manchester. Letterpress by John Plant, Curator, Royal Museum and Library. Done at the expense of the Cobden Memorial Fund. Printed by W. F. Jackson, Salford. 1868. *Quarto.*

Title as above, i. pp. Letterpress, 17 pp.

PHOTOGRAPHS.

1. The Royal Museum and Library.
2. Statue of the Queen.
3. Statue of the Prince Consort.
4. Statue of Sir Robert Peel.
5. Statue of Joseph Brotherton.
6. Statue of Richard Cobden.

A SHORT HISTORY of the SALFORD CHARITIES. 1858. Salford: printed and published by W. F. Jackson and Son, New Bailey Street. 1858. *Octavo.*

Title as above, Index, and History, 52 pp., exclusive of 5 folding plans of land belonging to various Charities.

Published at 2s. 6d.

A Description of Manchester and SALFORD (by J. BUTTERWORTH). *See* p. 122.

SALFORD DIRECTORIES, 18th Century. *See* p. 147.

A Description of Manchester and SALFORD (ASTON'S). *See* p. 153.

"THE FEAST of FOLLY," a Poem. *See* PART III.

A HISTORY of the ANCIENT HALL of SAMLESBURY, with an account of its earlier possessors, and particulars relating to the more recent descent of the Manor, derived chiefly from unpublished and authentic sources. By JAMES CROSTON, Member of the Architectural, Archæological, and historic society of Chester; Member of the Council of the Holbein Society, etc. London: printed by Whittingham and Wilkins at the Chiswick Press. 1871. *Folio.*

Half-title, Title as above, Dedication, and Preface, x. pp. List of Illustrations, History, and Index, Nominum, 274 pp.

LIST OF ILLUSTRATIONS.

Gothic Window formerly at Whalley Abbey . . . . . P. 12
Piscina 12
Samlesbury Hall 14
Southworth Hall 39
Samlesbury Church 42
Helmet and Shield in Samlesbury Church 43
The Lower Hall, Samlesbury 103
Facsimile of Indenture conveying Samlesbury Hall and Manor from Southworth to Braddyll 152
Samlesbury Hall—the Great Hall 202
Corbel under the Window, Samlesbury Hall 256
Samlesbury Hall, Ground-plan 256

PEDIGREES.

Holand of Up Holland . . . . P. 32-33
Southworth of Southworth and Samlesbury 160-1
Braddyll of Braddyll Samlesbury, etc. 200-1

Only 200 printed for private circulation. Will always be a valuable Lancashire Book.

A copy is in the Manchester Free Public Library.
Copies have sold for £8 : 8s.

TOPOGRAPHICAL ACCOUNT of the HIGHER HALL in SAMLESBURY, formerly the seat of the Knightly family of the SOUTHWORTHS, now converted into an inn called the "Braddyll's Arms."

"Historia est temporum," etc.

Preston: Peter Whittle, Fishergate. *Demy* 18*mo.*

Title as above, and Account, 16 pp.

SEFTON CHURCH, with part of the interior decorations. London: published Feb. 7, 1822. By R. BRIDGENS.

Engraved Title as above, i. p. Account of Sefton Church and Dedication, vi. pp.

The Plates, including the Title, are numbered from i. to xxxi.
Sells for 15s.

India Proofs, *Royal folio*, published at £3 : 13 : 6. Sells for £1 : 10s.

A BRIEF ACCOUNT of SEFTON CHURCH. By THOMAS ASCROFT. Was published in 1819.

A DESCRIPTION of SMITHELL'S-HALL near BOLTON, with an account of the print of a Foot; and a relation of other Particulars respecting the Place.

To which is added—

MEMOIRS of SIR ANDREW BARTON.

"Adde tot egregias operumque laborem."—VIRG. GEORG.

Bolton: printed and sold by B. Jackson; and S. Falkner, Manchester. 1787. *Octavo.*

Title as above, and Description, etc., 19 pp.

A very scarce book. *See* PART II. (George Marshe).
A copy of this is in Dr. Shepherd's Library, Preston.

A GUIDE to SOUTHPORT, NORTH MEOLS, in the County of Lancaster, with an account of the Places in its immediate neighbourhood. By THOMAS KIRKLAND GLAZEBROOK, F.L.S., etc. Second Edition; revised and corrected, and considerably enlarged.

"Unus erat toto naturæ vultus in orbe."
[Four more lines.]

London: printed for C. and J. Rivington, Longman, Rees, Orme, Brown, and Green, etc. etc. 1826. *Octavo.*

Title as above, Dedication, Introduction, and Preface, xiii. pp. List of Books quoted, Guide, and Index, p. 15 to p. 176.

ILLUSTRATIONS.

Christ Church, Southport.
Ormskirk Church.
Ruins of Lydiate Abbey,
Hornby Hall, and two Plates of Coats of Arms.

Sells for 3s. 6d.

The First Edition was printed at Warrington in 1809.

Thomas Kirkland Glazebrook, the son of the Rev. James Glazebrook, and afterwards Vicar of Bolton, in Leicestershire, Incumbent of St. James', Latchford, was born at Ashby-de-la-Zouch on the 4th June 1780. He is one of the Warrington worthies whose profiles Dr. Kendrich has preserved for us (see *post.*)

Mr. Glazebrook lived in Warrington from his infancy until 1835, when he removed to Southport, where he died 17th January 1855. Whilst at Warrington he was engaged as a manufacturer of flint-glass, and in 1803 was captain in the local volunteer corps. He was the author of "Lissa," a poem; "A Chronological List of Trades," and a poetical translation of "The First Eclogue of Virgil."

HANDBOOK for SOUTHPORT, Medical and General, with copious notices of the Natural History of the District. By DAVID H. M'NICOLL, M.D., Fellow of the Ethnological Society; Physician to the Southport Sea-bathing Infirmary. [View of Lord Street.] London: Arthur Hall and Co.; Liverpool, Edward Howell; Southport, R. Johnson. 1859. *Octavo.*

Title as above, Preface, and Half-Title, vii. pp. Handbook, Tables of Temperature, etc., 175 pp.

Illustrated with 3 Coloured Plates of Flowers, Birds, and Reptiles.
A Second Edition was published in 1861, price 3s. 6d.

HISTORY of SOUTHPORT, situated in North Meols, in the County of Lancaster; much frequented by the Nobility and gentry as a Watering-Place. Southport is beautified with Cottages Ornées, situated amid Sand Hills, holden together by the Sea Matweed. The Beach is firm; the Sea is only to be approached at the flux; after which it retires from the Strand at least half a mile.

"And oft conducted by historic truth,
We tread the long extent of backward time."

(Dedicated to those who visit the saline shores of Southport.)

The following authorities have been used:—Ptolemy, Tanner, Cambden, O'Connor, Carlisle, Aston, Whitaker, Baines, Leigh, Aikin, Crosby, Holt, Gregson, Shuttleworth, Nathantiquarii, and others. Printed by P. and H. Whittle, at the Marine Press, Fishergate Street, Preston. *Octavo.*

Title as above, Preface, and History, 160 pp. Map of Southport in 1830.
This work was republished in 1831 under the general title of "Marina, or an Historical and Descriptive Account of Southport, Lytham, and Blackpool, situate on the Western Coast of Lancashire." By P. WHITTLE, F.S.A., —R., etc. etc. The three Histories are separately paged. *See* Blackpool, p. 7, and Lytham, p. 115.

A CONCISE HISTORY and DESCRIPTION of SOUTHPORT, a fashionable Watering-place, situated in North Meols, in the County Palatine of Lancashire, together with a Tide-Table and Directory. [Four lines of poetry.] Southport: printed and sold by William Alsop, 5 Grovis Terrace. *Duodecimo.*

Title as above, Dedication, and Preface, x. pp. History, etc., and Index, 118 pp.
Plan of Southport Assembly Rooms as *Frontispiece.*

The New ILLUSTRATED GUIDE to SOUTHPORT and the NEIGHBOURHOOD, to which is appended a Guide to Bathing. Southport: printed and published by Wm. L. Lang at the "Southport News" Office, 13 Nevill Street. [1874.]

Title as above, Index, iv. pp., and Guide, 97 pp. Guide to Sea-bathing, 56 pp.

Folding Map and Views. Published at 6d.

The appearance of the book is spoiled by the introduction of advertisements between the pages.

SOUTHPORT TOWN, *see* p. 114.

An INQUIRY into the probability of a Tradition connected with the Library and Furniture of James IV. of Scotland, and of their having been carried off after the Battle of Flodden and set up at SPEKE HALL, in the County of Lancaster. By WILLIAM ROBERT WHATTON, Esq., F.S.A., Member of the Royal College of Surgeons of London, etc. etc. In a letter to the Secretary of the Society of Antiquaries of Scotland [read 28th January 1828]. *Quarto.*

Inquiry, 14 pp.

PLATES.

I. View of Speke Hall.
II. Folding View of Oak Carvings on the Great Hall of Speke.
III. Folding View of Oak Carvings in the Dinning (*sic*) Room of Speke.
IV. Back Entrance to Speke Hall.

Sketched by G. Nicholson, and etched by W. Penny.

LEGEND of SPEKE HALL. *See* PART III.

STONYHURST COLLEGE, its PAST and PRESENT. An account of its History, Architecture, Treasures, Curiosities, etc. By A. HEWITSON. Illustrated by Dalziel Brothers. [Woodcut.] Preston: printed and published at the "Chronicle" Office. 1870. *Octavo.*

Half-title, Title as above, Dedication, and Preface, viii. pp. Stonyhurst College, and Index, 132 pp.

PLATES.

Stonyhurst College, *To face* p. 18.
Facsimile of MS. Gospel of St. John of the 7th century, 2 Plates between p. 60 and p. 61.
Facsimile of MS. Prayer Book of Queen Mary, 2 Plates between p. 76 and p. 77.

Interior of Stonyhurst College Church, *To face* p. 102.
Also several Cuts on the letterpress.

Published at 5s. and 7s. 6d.

NOTITIÆ SAXOSYLVENSES.

A TOPOGRAPHICAL HISTORY of STONYHURST and MYTTON, situated in a portion of the Township of Aighton, Bailey, and Chaighley, and in the parish of Mytton, County of Lancaster.

The princely fabric of the Knightly Sherburnes is now converted into a noble College, under the superintendence of a Society of Catholic Clergymen, for the Education of Youth.

The ancient Church of "All Hallows" at Mytton contains within its walls the Funeral Monuments of the Sherburnes, which will be noticed at considerable length, with other rare and curious matter connected with the notorious Johannes Styphantes (*alias* Webster), the celebrated Wise Man of Mytton. By an OLD ANTIQUARIAN. [Peter Whittle.]

"Forsan et hæc olim Meminisse Juvabit;
Durate et rebus vosmet servate secundis."

Preston: Whittle, 10 Fox Street. *Foolscap octavo.*

Title as above, Introductory Remarks and History, 65 pp. A great portion of the above is made up of Extracts from William Howitt's "Visits to Remarkable Places." P. 58, *et seq.*, contains a reprint from the "Manchester Guardian," of "Inventory of Whalley Abbey, taken at the time of the Dissolution."

The HISTORY of STYDD CHAPEL and PRECEPTORY, near Ribchester, Lancashire. Illustrated by GEORGE LATHAM, Architect. London: published by Atchley and Co., Great Russell Street, Bedford Square. 1853. *Post folio.*

Title as above, and Dedication, 111 pp. History, 16 pp. Second Title Page, and the following Plates:—

1. Stydd Chapel. North-East View.
2. Interior View restored.
3. Ground Plan.
4. Ground Plan restored.
5. South Elevation.
6. East Elevation.
7. West Elevation.
8. Cross section.
9. Cross section restored.

10. Doorway. South Side.
11. Window. South Side, etc.
12. Font, etc.
13. Grave Stones.
14. Elevation of Pulpit, etc.

The design and execution of these plates are admirable. Published at 21s. Scarce. A copy is in the Author's Library.

SWARTHMOOR HALL and its ASSOCIATIONS. By HENRY BARBER, M.D.

[Quotation from Macaulay's "Essay on Milton."]

London: F. B. Kitto, 5 Bishopsgate Street; Ulverston: D. Atkinson, King Street. *Foolscap octavo.*

Title as above, Dedication, and Swarthmoor Hall, 56 pp. *Frontispiece,* Swarthmoor Hall, Woodcut of Arms, and on p. 28 and p. 29 Pedigree of the Fells of Swarthmoor.

A RECORD of the Commencement and Progress of the Erection and Building at "GOOSE COAT HILL," or the TOWNSHIP of TURTON, known by the name of "THE TURTON WORKHOUSE," and also particulars of THE BEQUEST of the late HUMPHREY CHETHAM, Esq. (of Turton Tower), of Goose Coat Hill Farm, and other charities. Bolton: J. Tillotson, Printer, Mealhouse. 1855. *Octavo.*

Title and Record, 28 pp.

BIBLIOGRAPHICAL NOTICES of the CHURCH LIBRARIES at TURTON and GORTON, bequeathed by Humphrey Chetham.

[Engraving of the Turton Book Case.]

Printed for the Chetham Society. 1855. *Foolscap quarto.*

Chetham Society's Title (vol. xxxviii.), List of Council, Title-page as above printed in colours, and Contents, 7 pp. Second Title as follows, "A Catalogue (with the Title-pages in full and illustrative extracts) of Books chained to an old oak case deposited in the Church of St. Ann's, Turton, being the gift of Humphrey Chetham, Esq., 1655. Rebound and repaired by Subscription 1855. Edited by GILBERT J. FRENCH, corresponding Member of the Society of Antiquaries of Scotland." Introduction and Catalogue, 103 pp. Third Title as follows, "A Catalogue (with the Title-pages in full and illustrative extracts), of Books from the collection bequeathed by Humphrey Chetham to the Chapel of St. Thomas, Gorton, 1655." Addendum, and Index, 199 pp.

TURTON FAIR. See Part III.

The WALTON-LE-DALE MOCK CORPORATION. The Corporation not a Jacobite Institution; the "Moot Hall"; the Regalia; List of Mayors; the Jacobite Rebellions of 1715 and 1745; the Manuscript Records; curious Titles of the Corporate Officers; the Freemen and Revels of the Corporation; the Effusions of the Poets Laureate, etc. By HENRY H. BARKER. Blackburn: H. H. Barker, 47 King William Street; Preston: W. Dobson, 23 Fishergate; Manchester; John Heywood, 141 and 143 Deansgate. 1874. Price 3d. *Duodecimo.*

Title as above, and Mock Corporation, 22 pp.

WARRINGTON in MCCCCLXV., as described in a contemporary Rent Roll of the Legh Family in the possession of Thomas Legh, Esquire, of Lyme Park. Edited by WILLIAM BEAMONT, Esq. Printed for the Chetham Society. MDCCCXLIX. *Foolscap Quarto.*

Chetham Society's Title, List of Council, iv. pp. Title as above, and Introduction, lxxviii. pp. Warrington in 1465. Half-title, i. p. Extractum and Translation, and Index, 151 pp.

Frontispiece, Folding Map of Part of Warrington from the Legh MSS. Facsimile of Legh MSS., *to face* p. lxxviii.

William Beamont, Esq., of Orford Hall, may correctly be styled the "Historian of Warrington." Besides the Lancashire Books enumerated in the work, he is the author of the "History of the Castle of Halton and Abbey of Norton." "A Lecture on Warrington in the Thirteenth Century." 1856. (17 pp.) Etc. etc.

ANNALS of THE LORDS of WARRINGTON for the first five centuries after the conquest. With historical notices of the place and neighbourhood. By WILLIAM BEAMONT, Esq.

"Where by the Mersey's willow margent peers
Walinturn's forded town and manor seat."
[And 7 following lines.]
"Alfred," a poem, by John Fitchett, Esq., B. 44.

PART I.

Printed for the Chetham Society. MDCCCLXXII. *Foolscap quarto.*

Chetham Society's Title (Vol. lxxxvi.), List of Council, and Title as above, v. pp. Second Title, omitting the words "Part I.," Introduction, and List of Illustrations, xxvii. pp. Annals of Warrington, 262 pp.

ILLUSTRATIONS.

Bewsey Hall	*Frontispiece*
Seals of Pincera and Ferrars .	*To face* p. 34
General Seals	„ 149
End of Tomb	„ 263
North side of Tomb . .	„ 297
South side of Tomb . .	„ 300

PART II.

Chetham Society's Title (Vol. lxxxvii.), List of Council, and Title, v. pp. Annals of Warrington, and Index to the two volumes, p. 263 to p. 535. Twenty-ninth Report of the Society, etc., 12 pp.

ANNALS of the LORDS of WARRINGTON and BEWSEY from 1587 to 1833, when Warrington became a Parliamentary Borough. In two parts. PART I.—Warrington. PART II.—Bewsey. With notices of historical and local events. By WILLIAM BEAMONT, Esq. Manchester: Charles Simms and Co.; Warrington: Percival Pearse. MDCCCLXXIII. *Foolscap quarto.*

Title as above and Preface, xxiv. pp. Title to Part I., 1 p. Annals of Warrington, 124 pp. Title to Part II., the Lords of Bewsey, and Index, p. 124 to p. 165. Published at 10s. 6d.

A GLANCE at the LOCAL HISTORY of WARRINGTON. By an INHABITANT. Warrington: printed by H. Wood, Corporation Street. No date. *Duodecimo.*

Title as above and History, 22 pp.

Second Edition. Price 6s.

PROFILES of WARRINGTON WORTHIES. Collected and arranged by JAMES KENDRICK, M.D., Warrington. Longman, Brown, Green, and Longman, London; Haddock and Son, Warrington. 1854. *Royal quarto.*

Engraved title as above, Introduction, and Warrington Worthies, 11 pp. Five plates of Profiles.

The first Edition was published in 1853. Both are now scarce, and sell for published price.

Dr. Kendrick of Warrington has been a considerable contributor to our county literature. See "Lancashire and Cheshire Historical Society, etc," *Post.*

The SQUIB-BOOK, containing the whole of the ADDRESSES, SONGS, SQUIBS, etc. etc., previously to and during the late contested WARRINGTON ELECTION, December 13, 1832. Candidates, John Ireland Blackburne, Esq.; Edmund George Hornby, Esq. Printed and published by C. Malley, Horse Market, Warrington. *Octavo.*

Title as above, and Squib Book, 34 pp. A copy is in Dr. Kendrick's Library.

The COUCHER BOOK, or CHARTULARY of WHALLEY ABBEY. Edited by W. A. HULTON, Esq.

VOL. I.

Printed for the Chetham Society. MDCCCXLVII. *Foolscap quarto.*

Chetham Society's Title (Vol. x.), and List of Council, iii. pp. Title as above, Introduction, and Contents, xxxix. pp. The Coucher Book, 338 pp. *Frontispiece,* Facsimile of MSS.

VOL. II.

Chetham Society's Title (Vol. xi.) and List of Council, iii. pp. Title, i. p. The Coucher Book, p. 339 to p. 636.

VOL. III.

Chetham Society's Title (Vol. xii.) and List of Council, iii. pp. Title and Contents, p. xl. to p. liii. The Coucher Book, p. 637 to p. 936. The Fifth Report of the Society, etc., 4 pp.

VOL. IV.

Chetham Society's Title (Vol. xx.) and List of Council, iii. pp. Title and Contents, p. liv. to p. lxiii. The Coucher Book and Appendix, Glossary, Index Locorum et Index Nominum, p. 937 to p. 1314.

The HISTORY of the original PARISH of WHALLEY and HONOR of CLITHEROE, in the Counties of Lancaster and York. By THOMAS DUNHAM WHITAKER, LL.D., F.S.A. The Second Edition, with additions, and eight new Engravings. London: printed by J. Nichols and Son, Red Lion Passage, Fleet Street; and sold by T. Payne, Castle Street, St. Martin's; J. White, Fleet Street, Hatchard, Piccadilly; Longman and Co., Paternoster Row; and Edwards, Halifax. 1806. *Royal quarto.*

Title as above, Advertisement, Table of Contents, and Directions to the Binder, iii. pp. List of Plates and Pedigrees on loose sheets, 1 p. The History of Whalley, 408 pp. Additional Corrections, Addenda, and Corrigenda, 8 pp. (not paged). The History of Whalley continued, p. 411 to p. 483. Additional Corrections, Addenda, et Corrigenda, Appendix No. I. and II., general Additions and Corrections (not paged), 9 pp. Index, 4 pp.

Errors of paging—p. 31 is repeated; pp. 35 and 36 are omitted; p. 110 ends with the catch-word "may;" pp. 111 and 112 have an asterisk, and p. 113 is generally pasted over with a blank sheet; pp. 113 to 124, 127, 128, 325, 328, 353, 354, 355, and 356 are repeated with asterisks; pp. 223 and 224 are omitted; pp. 428 and 429 are repeated, containing letters, and follow p. 428.

LIST OF PLATES.

1. A Folding Map . . . . *To face Title-page*
2. Roman Fragments found at Ribchester . . . P. 22
3. Roman Fragments found at Ribchester, from the Museum of Charles Townley, Esq. 22
4. Various Ancient Crosses (numbered Plate IV.) . . 31
5. The Remains of Whalley Abbey (Plate VI.) . . 48
6. The Cloisters of Whalley Abbey (Plate VII.) . . 70
7. Ground-plan of Whalley Abbey, with the Shields of Henry de Lacy, Earl of Lincoln, and John of Gaunt, Duke of Lancaster, King of Castile and Leon (Plate IX.) . 104

8. Remains of Whalley Abbey (Plate VIII.) . . *P. 124
9. Seals of Whalley Abbey (Plate III.) . . . 114
10. Seals of the Lords of Blackburnshire (Plate X.) . . 142
11. View of Clitheroe off Eadsford Bridge . . . 151
12. View of Browsholme (Plate XII.) . . . 208
13. *View of Whitewell and the Keeper's Lodge in the Forest of Bowland 211
14. *Portrait of Edward Parker, Esq., in the costume of Bow-bearer of Bowland, circa 1690; Legionary stone from Ribchester; ancient Dog-guage of the Forest; ancient Wooden Tankard, Seals, etc. 212
15. *Portrait of Henry Tilson, Painter 212
16. Portrait of Sir Richard Beaumont of Whitley Hall, Knight and Baronet 236
17. *Another Portrait of Sir Richard Beaumont . . 236
18. *Portrait of Sir Thomas Beaumont of Whitley Hall, Knight and Deputy-Governor of Sheffield Castle . . 237
19. *Another Portrait of Sir Thomas Beaumont of Whitley Hall, Knight 237
20. *View of Read Hall as it appeared in 1750 . . 224
21. Huntroyd, the Seat of Legendre Piers Starkie, Esq. . 250
22. View of Gawthorp 320
23. *View of Townley Hall and Park 321
24. View of Townley Hall 322
25. The Hall of Radcliffe Tower, with the Seal of Rodulph de Radclif, and Monumental Figures of James de Radcliffe and Family 402
26. View of Stoneyhurst 445
27. The Hall of Little Mitton 447
28. The Sherburne Chapel in Mitton Church . . 448

PEDIGREES ON LOOSE SHEETS.

1. Pedigree of Parker of Browsholme 210
2. Pedigree of Parker of Braddyll 219-220
3. Pedigree of Assheton 220-221
4. Pedigree of Whalley, Gardiner, and Smythe . . 233-234
5. Pedigree of Nowell of Read, with the Seal of Laurence Nowell 245-246
6. Pedigree of Radcliffe 279-280
7. Pedigree of Townley of Townley . . . 325-328

8. Pedigree of Whitaker . . . . . P. 337-338
9. Pedigree of Lawrence Townley . . . 377-378
10. Pedigree of Radcliffe of Radcliffe Tower . . 397-400
11. Pedigree of Holden 409-410

PLATES ON THE LETTERPRESS.

1. Seal of John de Lasey, mounted on . . . . „ 48
2. „ John de Topcliff „ . . „ 126
3. „ Alice de Lasey „ . . . „ 148
4. „ for Approbation of Ministers . . „ 210
5. A Mysterious Diagram . . . „ 272
6. Inscription on the Font at Chipping . . . „ 446

The First Edition of this work was published in 1801 (Blackburn).

A copy of it is in the Library of the Rochdale Equitable Pioneers Society.

The above edition is a reprint of the same, with a new Title-page and the addition of the Plates and Letterpress, which are marked with an asterisk, and the corrections at the end of the volume. The First Edition contains a Preface and List of Subscribers which are omitted in the Second Edition.

Published at £6 : 6s. Sells for £4.

Large paper copies published at £12 : 12s.

An HISTORY of the original PARISH of WHALLEY and HONOR of CLITHEROE, in the Counties of Lancaster and York. To which is subjoined an Account of the Parish of Cartmell. By THOMAS DUNHAM WHITAKER, LL.D., F.S.A., Vicar of Whalley. The Third Edition, revised and enlarged, with additional Engravings. London: printed by and for Nichols, Son, and Bentley, Red Lion Passage, Fleet Street; and Thomas Edwards, Bookseller, Halifax. 1818. *Royal quarto.*

Title as above, Dedication, Advertisement, Contents, and List of Plates, viii. pp. History of Whalley and Cartmel, and Index, 568 pp.

Six additional pages, numbered 523 to 528, are marked with an asterisk.

LIST OF PLATES.

Those marked with * are not in the previous Editions.

1. * Portrait of the Author . . . *Facing Title-page*

2. Folding Map of the Parish . . . . . P. 1
3, 4. Roman Antiquities (Plates I. and XI.) . . 28
5. Crosses (Plate IV.) 50
6. Remains of Whalley Abbey (Plate VI.) . . . 61
7. Cloisters of Whalley Abbey (Plate VII.) . . . 80
8. Plan of Whalley Abbey (Plate IX.) . . . 110
9. Remains of Whalley Abbey (Plate VIII.) . . 111
10. Seals of Whalley Abbey (Plate III.) . . . 143
11. Seals of Lords of Blackburnshire (Plate X.) . . 178
12. Clitheroe (Plate XI.) 184
13. Whitewell and the Keeper's Lodge . . . 235
14. *Whitewell Chapel 236
15. Browsholme (Plate XII.) 237
16. *Browsholme, another view 237
17. *Interior of Browsholme Hall 238
18. Portrait of Edward Parker, and Miscellaneous Plates . 238
19. *Interior of Whalley Church 247
20. Hall of Mitton 256
21. Portrait of Sir Richard Beaumont, Bart. . . . 256
22. Portrait of Sir Thomas Beaumont 256
23. Portrait of Sir Thomas Beaumont at Whitely Hall . . 256
24. *Portrait of Sarah, daughter of Sir Thomas Beaumont . 256
25. Read Hall 263
26. Huntroyd 266
27. *Bay-window at Little Merley Hall . . . 293
28. Gawthorp 338
29. Townley (Plate V.) 340
30. Townley Hall and Park 341
31. *Holme 353
32. Hall of Radcliffe Tower 413
33. *Chamber at Samlesbury Hall 431
34. Stoneyhurst 464
35. Sherburne Chapel 467
36. *Waddington Hall 473
37. *Waddington Parsonage 473
38. *Portrait of Dr. Alexander Nowell 480
39. *Autographs of John Townley, Esq., Bishop Jewell, Dr. A. Nowell, Dr. Lawrence Nowell, and Dr. Whitaker . 480
40. *Dr. A. Nowell's Monument in old St. Paul's . . 482
41. *Remains of his Bust 482

42. *Portrait of Charles Townley, Esq. . . . P. 484
43. *Portrait of John Townley, Esq. 488
44. *Portrait of Dr. William Whitaker . 493
45. *North-East View of Cartmell Church . . 555
46. *Choir of Cartmell Church 555
47. *Monument of Harrington Family at Cartmell Church . 556

PEDIGREES, ETC., ON LOOSE SHEETS.

Pedigree of Parker of Browsholme 239
Pedigree of Assheton Family 244
Arms in the painted Window in Whalley Church (2 Plates) 246
Pedigrees of Whalley, Gardiner, Smythe . . . 252
Pedigree of Nowell of Read 264
Pedigree of Radcliffe of Todmorden and Merley . . 292
Pedigree of Townley of Townley 344
Pedigree of Ormerod 364
Pedigrees of De Radcliffe (two Pedigrees) . . . 413

The Plates printed on the Letterpress are the same as the Second Edition.

Published at £6 : 6s. Copies rarely now are offered for sale.

Large paper copies in *Imperial quarto* were published at £12 : 12s., and now fetch a very high price. Copies have been sold for £20.

It is said that only 100 small paper, and 25 large paper, copies were issued of this edition.

A copy of Whitaker's History of Whalley, with the author's MS. notes and additions, is now in the possession of Richard H. Wood, Esq., F.S.A., the Hon. Secretary of the Chetham Society.

An HISTORY of the ORIGINAL PARISH of WHALLEY and the HONOR of CLITHEROE, to which is subjoined an ACCOUNT of the PARISH of CARTMELL. By THOMAS DUNHAM WHITAKER, LL.D., F.S.A., Vicar of Whalley. The Fourth Edition, revised and enlarged, by JOHN GOUGH NICHOLS, F.S.A., and the Rev. PONSONBY A. LYONS, B.A.

VOL. I.

[Quotation from Lord Bacon.]

London: George Routledge and Sons, The Broadway, Ludgate; Manchester, L. C. Gent. 1872. *Royal quarto.*

Half-title, Title as above, Contents, Preface, Biographical Memoir of Thomas Dunham Whitaker, Dedication, Preface to the First Edition, Subscribers to the History of Whalley, 1802-1806, Advertisement to the Second Edition, and Advertisement to the Third Edition, lxvi. pp. History of Whalley, 362 pp.

LIST OF PLATES.

Portrait of the Author	*To face the Title*
Map of the ancient Parish of Whalley	P. 1
Roman Antiquities. 2 Plates	32-34
Distant View of Whalley Abbey	83
Whalley Abbey from the River	135
Whalley Abbey from the Cloister Court	139
Plan of Whalley Abbey	140
Seals attached to Whalley Abbey Charters	200
Seals of the ancient Lords of Blackburnshire	252
View of Clitheroe from Eadisford Bridge	255
Whitewell and the Keeper's Lodge	333
Browsholme. 2 Views	336-337
Portrait of Edward Parker	338
Pedigree of Parker of Browsholme	*To follow* p. 340

Woodcuts in the Letterpress of Seals, Inscriptions, etc.
The Second Volume of this Edition is now in the Press.

WIGAN, the Mayor of. A Tale by Hillary Butler. *See* PART III.

PART II.

BIOGRAPHY AND FAMILY HISTORY.

MEMOIRS, MISCELLANIES, and LETTERS of the late LUCY AIKIN, including those addressed to the Rev. Dr. Channing from 1826 to 1842. Edited by PHILIP HEMERY LE BRETON of the Inner Temple. London: Longmans, Green, Longman, Roberts, and Green. 1864. *Post octavo.*

Half-title, Title as above, Preface, Contents, and Memoirs, xxviii. pp. Miscellanies, 440 pp.

Published at 8s. 6d.

ISAAC AMBROSE, Memoir of. *See* PART VI.

The Temperance and other POEMS of the late HENRY ANDERTON of WALTON-LE-DALE, near Preston, with a SKETCH of his LIFE. By his friend and fellow-labourer EDWARD GUBB. Preston: printed by W. and J. Dobson. 1863. *Post octavo.*

Title as above, Dedication, Preface, Life, and Index, xxxii. pp. Poems, 136 pp.

LIFE and POEMS of HENRY ANDERTON of WALTON-LE-DALE. London: W. Tweedie, 337 Strand; Preston, Ferguson, Cannon Street. MDCCCLXVIII. *Duodecimo.*

Title as above, Preface, and Contents, xii. pp. Life, etc., 25 pp. Poems etc., 171 pp.

Narrative of the HOLY LIFE AND HAPPY DEATH of that Reverend, Faithful, and Zealous Man of God, and Minister of the Gospel of Jesus Christ, Mr. JOHN ANGIER, many years pastor of the Church of Christ at Denton, near Manchester, in Lancashire. Wherein are related many passages that concern his Birth, Education, his entrance into the ministry, discharge of his trust therein, and his death.

Phil. iii. 17.—Brethren, be followers together of me, and mark them which walk so, as ye have us for an ensample.

London: printed by Thomas Parkhurst, at the Bible and Three Crowns, at the lower end of Cheapside, near Mercer's Chapel. 1685. *Foolscap 12mo.*

Title as above, and Preface, v. pp., not numbered. Life, 227 pp., and 3 pages containing list of books printed and sold by Thomas Parkhurst.

This is a very scarce book (unknown to Lowndes and other Bibliographists).

J. Angier was born in 1605. He was twice married, first, in 1628, to Ellen Winstanley of Wigan, in Lancashire, and second, to "Margaret Moseley of Ancots, in Manchester, in the heat of the Wars." He died 3d September 1667, and was buried in Denton Chapel, in "the alley before the pulpit."

For notice of his works, *see* Part vi.

This Memoir is believed to have been written by Oliver Heywood.

A copy is in the Chetham Library.

The TRIAL of a cause instituted by Richard Peppar Arden, Esq., his Majesty's Attorney-General, by Writ of Scire Facias, to repeal a Patent granted on the Sixteenth of December 1775, to Mr. Richard Arkwright. For an invention of certain Instruments and Machines for preparing Silks, Cotton, Flax, and Wool for Spinning. Before the Honourable Francis Buller, one of the Judges of his Majesty's Court of King's Bench, at the Westminster Hall, on Saturday, the 25th of June 1785. London: printed for Hughes and Walsh, Inner Temple-Lane. MDCCLXXXV. *Folio.*

Title as above, and the Trial, 191 pp.

Frontispiece, Folding Plan of the Machine for Spinning.

A copy is in the Chetham Library.

Richard Arkwright was born in Preston, 23d December 1732, and was apprenticed to a barber in that town. In 1786 he was knighted, and died 3d August 1792.

A True and Exact RELATION of the DEATH of Two CATHOLICS who suffered for their Religion at the Summer Assizes, held at Lancaster in the year 1628. Republished with additions on account of a wonderful cure wrought by the Intercession of one of them, F. EDMUND ARROWSMITH, a Priest of the Society of Jesus, in the person of Thomas Hawarden, son of Caryl Hawarden of Appleton, within Widness, in Lancashire. The death of the generous Lay-man, RICHARD HERST, was not to be omitted; that the happy cause which united them in their sufferings may jointly preserve their memories. London: printed in the year MDCCXXXVII. *Octavo.*

Title as above, to the Reader, etc., vi. pp. A True Relation, 68 pp. 2 Plates. *Frontispiece*, "P. Edmundus Arrowsmith, Soc. Jesu fidei odio Suspensus et Dissectus Lancastriæ, An. Domi. 1628." Facing p. 33, "Ricardus Herst Fidei odio suspensus Lancastriæ, 19 Augusti An. Dom. 1628."

Sells for 5s. 6d.

The Memoirs of Missionary Priests and other Catholics of both sexes from 1577 to 1684. By Bishop Challoner, V.A.L. (2 vols., 8vo, Manchester, 1803), contains the Lives of the above and other Lancashire priests.

PEDIGREE of the FAMILY of ASHBURNER, Co. Lancaster. (Arms of Ashburner Family). Privately printed. London: Taylor and Co., Printers, Little Queen Street, W.C. 1872. *Quarto.*

Pedigree, 8 pp. Sells for 10s. 6d.

A copy is in the author's library.

The JOURNAL of NICHOLAS ASSHETON of DOWNHAM, in the County of Lancaster, Esq., for part of the year 1617, and part of the year following. Interspersed with Notes from the life of his contemporary John Bruen, of Bruen, Stapelford, in the County of Chester, Esq. Edited by the Rev. F. R. RAINES, M.A., F.S.A., Rural Dean of Rochdale, and Incumbent of Milnrow. Printed for the Chetham Society. MDCCCXLVIII. *Foolscap quarto.*

Chetham Society's Title (Vol. xiv.) and List of Council, iii. pp. Title as above (Corrigenda on a Slip), and Introduction, xxx. pp. Second Title, i. p., the Journal, and Index, 163 pp. The Fourth Report of the Society, etc., 5 pp.

The Christian indeed and faithful Pastor; represented in the LIFE and WORKS of W. ASSHETON. London. 1714. *Octavo.*

Scarce.

The Rev. William Assheton, D.D., was the son of the Rev. William Assheton, Rector of Middleton, in Lancashire. Born 1641, died 1711. (*See* Sermons).

A short ACCOUNT of MRS. ELIZA ATMORE, who departed this life August 22, 1794. To which are subjoined some of her letters. By C. ATMORE, Minister of the Gospel. [Text of Scripture.] York: printed by Wilson, Spence, and Mawman. 1794. *Duodecimo.*

Title as above, Memoir, and Letters, 36 pp.

Scarce. A copy is in the author's library.

Charles Atmore was a Wesleyan Methodist Minister stationed at Colne in 1785. His wife, whose Memoir (as above) he wrote, was a sister of Roger Crane, one of the Founders of Wesleyanism in Preston.

The LIFE of EDWARD BAINES, late M.P. for the Borough of Leeds, by his son EDWARD BAINES, author of the "History of the Cotton Manufacture," etc. London: Longman, Brown, Green, and Longmans. 1851. *Octavo.*

Title as above, and Contents, ix. pp. Introduction and Life, 372 pp.

Frontispiece, Portrait of Edward Baines.

Published at 9s.

A cheap reissue in 1859, *12mo*, at 2s. 6d., which also contains a Photograph of Edward Baines.

PASSAGES in the LIFE of a RADICAL. By SAMUEL BAMFORD.

VOL. I.

London: Simpkin, Marshall, and Co. 1844. *Foolscap octavo.*

Title as above, i. p. Introduction, Passages, and Table of Contents, 288 pp.

VOL. II.

Title, i. p. Life of Bamford, and Contents, 282 pp.

Published at 8s. Sells for 4s. 6d. A Second Edition was published by J. Heywood, of Heywood, in 2 volumes.

A work which bears the impress of reality in every line.

Samuel Bamford was born in Middleton, in Lancashire, in the year 1788, and was buried there 20th April 1872.

EARLY DAYS of SAMUEL BAMFORD, author of "Passages in the life of a Radical," "Walks in South Lancashire," "Poems," etc. Second Edition, revised and corrected by the author.

"Is there for honest poverty," etc. etc.

Manchester: John Heywood 143 Deansgate and 3 Brazenose Street; London, Simpkin, Marshall, and Co. 1859. *Duodecimo.*

Title as above, Advertisement. Preface, and Index, viii. pp. Early Days, 312 pp.

This First Edition was published in 1849 at 4s. *See* PART III.

LIVES of the ARCHBISHOPS of CANTERBURY by WALTER FARQUHAR HOOK, D.D., F.R.S., Dean of Chichester.

VOL. V.

New Series, Reformation Period. [Quotation.] London: Richard Bentley and Son, New Burlington Street, Publishers in ordinary to Her Majesty. 1875. The right of Translation is reserved. *Octavo.*

Half-title, and Title as above, iii. pp. Second Title, Third Title, Advertisement, and Contents, xviii. pp. Lives of the Archbishops, 307 pp.

Published at 12s.

The Life of RICHARD BANCROFT, a native of Farnworth, in Lancashire, is contained in p. 177 to p. 221.

A Memoir of HENRY VINCENT BAYLEY, D.D. Printed for private circulation. 1846. *Octavo.*

Title as above, i. p. Memoir and Appendix, 66 pp.

Henry Vincent Bayley was the son of T. B. Bayley, of Hope Hall, near Manchester, Esq.

Sells for 3s. 6d. A copy is in the Manchester Free Library.

A charge delivered to the Clergy of the Archdeaconry of Stow at the Visitation, May 1826, by Dr. Bayley, is often bound up with the above book.

BIOGRAPHICAL MEMOIRS of the late THOMAS BUTTERWORTH BAYLEY, Esq., F.R.S., etc. etc., of Hope Hall, near Manchester.

—— "by all aprov'd,
Prais'd, wept, and honour'd by the friend he lov'd."

Manchester: printed by W. Shelmerdine and Co. 1802.[1] *Post quarto.*

Title as above, and Memoir, 12 pp.

The author was Thomas Percival, M.D. The subject of it was the founder of the Manchester New Bayley Prison, which was pulled down in 1873.

GENEALOGICAL and BIOGRAPHICAL ACCOUNT of the FAMILY of BOLTON in ENGLAND and AMERICA, deduced from an early period, and continued down to the present time. Collected chiefly from original Papers and Records; with an Appendix. By ROBERT BOLTON, A.M., author of the "History of West Chester County," also "History of the Protestant Episcopal Church and the County of West Chester," "Guide to New Rochelle," a Member of the Protestant Episcopal Society, and of the New York and General Historical Societies. [Monogram and Rebus of Bolton.] New York: John A. Gray, Printer, Stereotyper, and Binder, Fire-Proof Buildings, corner of Frankfort and Jacob Streets. 1862. *Demy octavo.*

Title as above, and Genealogical, etc., Account, 224 pp. Contains folding pedigree of "Boltons of Bolton and Blackburn, in Lancashire, Wales, in Yorkshire, Philadelphia, Penn., and of Savannah, Georgia;" also Sketch-map of Brookhouse estate, Blackburn. Woodcuts—Brookhouse, Blackburn, Rev. Robert Bolton's Monument in St. Andrew's Church, Broughton; Seal on Will of Dr. Samuel Bolton (1669); and residences, autographs, and arms of several Boltons of America.

Memoirs of the Life of BARTON BOOTH, Esq., with his character. To which are added several Poetical pieces written by himself, viz.—Translations from Horace, Songs, Odes, etc. To which is likewise annexed The CASE of MR. BOOTH'S last Illness, and what was ob-

[1] The Shelmerdines were established as Booksellers in Manchester in 1611.

serv'd (particularly with regard to the Quick-Silver found in his Intestines) upon opening of his Body, in the presence of Sir Hans Sloan by Mr. Alexander Small, Surgeon. Published by an intimate acquaintance of Mr. Booth by the consent of his widow.

—— "Quæ doctus Roscius egit."—HOR.

London: printed for John Watts at the Printing Office in Wild-Court, near Lincoln's-Inn Fields. 1733. [Price 1s. 6d.] *Octavo.*

Title as above, Memoirs, etc., 58 pp.

Frontispiece, Portrait of Barton Booth.

Now sells for 5s.
The author was Mr. Victor.

Another Life of BARTON BOOTH, giving an account of Education, etc., was published in the same year as the above, and sells for about the same price. Notices of him will also be found in "Biographia Britannica," Chetwood's "General History of the Stage," Epinasse's "Lancashire Worthies," etc. etc.

Barton Booth was the third son of John Booth of Barton, Esq., and was born in 1681.

All the EXAMINATIONS of the constante MARTIR of GOD, MR. JOHN BRADFORDE, before the Lorde Chauncellour, B. of Winchester, the B. of London (and other comissioners), whereunto are annexed his private talk and conflectes in prison after his condemnacion with the Archbishop of York, the B. of Chichester, Alfonus, and King Philip's confessour, two Spanish freers, and sundry others. 18*mo.*

"With his modest, learned, and godly answeres."
Anno Domini 1561.
"Cum privilegio ad imprimendum solum."

Title as above, Life, and Examinations, 223 pp. [not paged].

A copy of this very scarce Black Letter volume is in the Chetham Library.

The HISTORY of the worthy martyr, JOHN BRADFORD (who was born in Manchester), with a particular account of his Life—acts, various conflicts with his adversaries, imprisonment, condemnation, and suffering martyrdom for the Testimony of Christ and his Truth. With various Letters to his Friends.

ALSO,

The LIFE of the REV. RICH. ROTHWELL (who was born in Bolton-le-moors), with an account of his conversation, ministry, sickness, and a particular Recital of his contest with the devil in a possessed man, near Nottingham.

Likewise The LIFE and MARTYRDOM of GEORGE MARSHE, (who was born in the Parish of Dean), containing a full account of his troubles, examinations, imprisonments, and condemnation for preaching the Gospel of Christ. Written chiefly by himself. With various Letters to his friends, composed during his Imprisonment.

Also the Particulars respecting The Print of a Foot on the Flag, shewn at SMITHILL'S HALL, near BOLTON. To which is added an ancient and curious writing, called the Testament of the Twelve Patriarchs, the sons of Jacob. To the credit whereof an ancient Greek copy, written on parchment, is kept in the University Library of Cambridge. Bolton: Printed by B. Jackson. *Octavo.*

Title as above, and Life of J. Bradford, 166 pp. Life of R. Rothwell p. 167 to p. 183. An account of the Spanish Inquisition p. 184 to p. 220. Life of G. Marshe p. 221 to p. 296. A Description of Smithill's Hall, with an account of the Print of a Foot p. 297 to p. 312. The Testament, etc., p. 313 to p. 434. *Frontispiece*, "A Representation of the Burning of George Marshe at West Chester, April 24th, 1555. Published as the Act directs October 2d, 1787, by B. Jackson, printer, Bolton. Scarce.

A copy is in the Author's library, another is in the Bolton Free Library. The Description of Smithill's Hall is an exact copy of the one published in 1787 (see page 175) as a distinct work.

MARTYROLOGICAL BIOGRAPHY.

MEMOIR of the LIFE and MARTYRDOM of JOHN BRADFORD, M.A., Fellow of Pembroke Hall, Cambridge; with the Examination Letters, etc., arranged in chronological order.

Together with a Translation of Bishop Gardiner's Book, "De vera obedientia" and Bonner's Preparatory Letter." [Latin quotation.] By

WILLIAM STEVENS. London: Printed by R. Fenn, Horner's Head, Charing Cross, and T. Stevenson, Cambridge. MDCCCXXXII. *Octavo.*

Title, i. p., a page of Extracts, Dedication, Preface and Contents, xxv. pp. Memoir, etc., 410 pp. Appendix clxxviii. pp. Plates, Frontispiece, Portrait of John Bradford. (Exterior View of the Consistory Court of S. Saviour's Church, Southwark), to face page clxxviii. Published 16s.

The WRITINGS of JOHN BRADFORD, M.A., Fellow of Pembroke Hall, Cambridge, and Prebendary of St. Paul's. Martyr, 1555. Containing Sermons, Meditations, Examinations, etc. Edited for the Parker Society by AUBREY TOWNSEND, B.D. of Trinity College, Dublin, Curate of St. Michael's, Bath. Cambridge: printed at the University Press. MDCCCXLVIII.

Half-title, Title as above, Preface, and Contents, xi. pp. Writings, etc., 592 pp. *Octavo.*

VOL. II.

Half-title, Title, Contents, Preface, and BIOGRAPHICAL NOTICE of JOHN BRADFORD, xlviii. pp. Letters, etc., and Index, 432 pp.

The Letters of Maister JOHN BRADFORDE, a faythfull Minister and synguler piller of Christe's Church, etc. *Small quarto.*

Black Letter. No Title. Letters from p. 251 to p. 490.

A copy of this scarce book is in the Chetham Library. It is a portion of Bishop Coverdale's "Letters of the Martyrs," printed by Daye, London, 1564.

WILL of the DUKE of BRIDGEWATER. London: printed by Stewart and Co., 15 Old Bailey. 1836.

Title as above, Will, and Index, 82 pp.

Sells for 2s. 6d.

The PRIVATE JOURNAL and LITERARY REMAINS of JOHN BYROM. Edited by RICHARD PARKINSON, D.D., F.S.A., Principal of Saint Bees College, and Canon of Manchester.

VOL. I.—PART I.

Printed for the Chetham Society. MDCCCLIV. *Foolscap quarto.*

Chetham Society's Title (Vol. xxxii.), and List of Council, iii. pp. Title as above, and Introduction, x. pp. Corrigenda on a Slip. Remains, 320 pp.

Frontispiece, Portrait of John Byron.

VOL. I.—PART II.

Chetham Society's Title (Vol. xxxiv.), and List of Council iii. pp. Title, and Addenda, and Corrigenda, iii. pp. Remains, p. 321 to p. 639.

VOL. II.—PART I.

Society's Title (Vol. xl.), and List of Council, iii. pp. Title, i. p. Remains and Index to Notes in Vol. i., 646 pp. Index to Notes in Vol. ii., Part I., v. pp.

VOL. II.—PART II.

Society's Title (Vol. xliv.), List of Council and Title, v. pp. (Corrigenda on a slip.) Remains, p. 327 to p. 654.

The Byrom Pedigrees. 1. Byrom of Byrom. 2. Byrom of Salford. 3. Byrom of Manchester, with Illustrative Note by Rev. F. R. Raines, M.A. Title and Notes, 41 pp. 3. Folding Pedigree. Index to Notes in Vol. ii. Part II. v. pp.

The JOURNAL of ELIZABETH BYROM in 1745. Edited by RICHARD PARKINSON, D.D., F.S.A., Principal of S. Bee's College, and Canon of Manchester. Reprinted from Vol. ii., Part ii., of the Remains of John Byrom. Published by the Chetham Society. Manchester, 1857. *Quarto.*

Title and Journal, 32 pp. Only 38 copies printed. Sells for 15s.

The BYROM PEDIGREES—

1. Byrom of Byrom.
2. „ „ Salford.
3. „ „ Manchester.

With Illustrative Notes by the Rev. F. R. RAINES, M.A., F.S.A.. *Quarto.*

Title as above. Introduction and Notes, 41 pp., exclusive of three folding pedigrees. Only 25 copies printed. Sells for 10s. 6d.

An Authentic HISTORY of the LIFE and CHARACTER of THOMAS CAPPOCH (the Rebel Bishop of Carlisle), who was Executed for High-Treason at Carlisle, in the County of Cumberland, on Saturday the 18th of October 1746 (with Eight other Traitors), for adhering to his Majesty's Enemies, and levying a cruel and destructive War in these Kingdoms.

CONTAINING

I. His Birth, and Education at a Free-School at Manchester, from whence he was sent for by his Uncle to Oxford; and the Method he took to get Ordained, by forging the Hand of a Right Rev. Bishop.

II. His Trial at large; with his Speech before the Court, and Defence he made to prove he was forced into the Rebellion by the Testimony of Miss Humphreys, a very great Favourite of his.

III. His Conviction, after a long Trial; and the vile expressions he us'd in Court before the Jury, after they had found him Guilty.

IV. His Behaviour whilst under Sentence, and at the Place of Execution.

V. Also a short account of John MacNaughton (who murdered the gallant Col. Gardener at the Battle of Preston-Pans), and the other Traitors who were executed at Carlisle with the Rebel Bishop.

This Account is taken by a GENTLEMAN who attended the Prisoners at Carlisle, both before and after their Condemnation. London [MDCCCXXXIX.]: printed and sold by J. Thomson, opposite the Sessions-House in the Old-Baily; and sold at all the Pamphlet-shops in London and Westminster, and by the News-sellers. *Octavo.*

Half-title, Title as above, Preface, etc., vi. pp. The Trial and Life, 31 pp.

This is the Second Edition, of which there were two impressions, one printed in April 1839, and the other in December in the same year. They were both printed in Carlisle, and are very scarce.

The First Edition was published without date, but probably printed about the year 1746.

VITA LAURENTII CHADERTONI, S. T. P. & COLLEGII EMMANUELIS apud CANTABRIGIENSES MAGISTRI PRIMI una cum Vita Jacobi Usserii Archiepiscopi Armachani, etc. * * *

Auctore WILHELMO DILLINGHAM, S.T.P., accesserunt etiam ejusdem conciones, altera pro gradu Baccalaureatûs in SSia. Theologia pro Doctoratus gradu altera. Cantabrigiæ: Typis Academeus. Prostant Venales apud Tho. Dawson, Bishop. Cantab. necnon Sam. Smith et Benj. Walford, Bibliopolas ad insignia, Principis in Coemeter. D. Pauli, Londini. MDCC. *Octavo.*

Title and Preface, iv. pp. Life, etc., 140 pp.

A copy of this very scarce work is in the British Museum.

Laurence Chaderton, son of Thomas Chaderton of Lees Hall, Oldham, was born 14th September 1536. He was the first Master of Emmanuel College, Cambridge, and for fifty years was the minister of St. Clement's Church there. He died 16th November 1640, aged 103 years. He was the author of "De Justificatione coram Dei, etc." and several Sermons, etc. etc.

The last WILL of HUMPHRY CHETHAM, of Clayton in the county of Lancaster, Esq. Dated December 16, 1651. Whereby he founded and endowed a Hospital and Library in Manchester. Also the Charter of King Charles II., dated November 10, 1665, for making the Trustees under Mr. Chetham's Will a Body-corporate. Manchester: printed by J. Harrop, opposite the Exchange. *Quarto.*

Title as above, 1 p. Will and Charter, 5 pp.

A scarce book. Sells for from 10s. to 15s.

MEMORIALS of the CLAYTON FAMILY. With unpublished Correspondence of the Countess of Huntingdon, Lady Glenorchy, the Revs. John Newton, A. Toplady, etc. etc. etc. By the Rev. THOMAS W. AVELING. London: Jackson, Walford, and Hodder, 27 Paternoster Row. 1867. *Octavo.*

Half-title, Title as above, Preface, and Contents, xii. pp. Memorials, 516 pp. *Frontispiece,* Portraits of the Clayton Family.

The Rev. John Clayton, the principal subject of the above Memoir, was one of the Claytons of Adlington, and was educated at the Leyland Grammar School.

The LIFE and TIMES of SAMUEL CROMPTON, Inventor of the

Spinning Machine called the Mule. Being the substance of Two Papers read to the Members of the Bolton Mechanics' Institution. By GILBERT FRENCH. London: Simpkin, Marshall, and Co.; Manchester, Thomas Dinham and Co.; Bolton, J. Cunliff, Oxford Street, Henry Bradbury, Deansgate, and the Committee and Librarian of the Bolton Mechanics' Institution. 1859. *Post octavo.*

Title as above, Preface, and Contents, xix. pp. Life and Appendix, 293 pp. List of Subscribers, v. pp.

PLATES.

Portrait of Samuel Compton, *Frontispiece.*	
Carved Panel in Crompton's Room, Hall-in-the-Wood	p. xx.
View of Hall-i'-th'-Wood	49
Facsimile of Writing of Crompton . (misprint for 85)	82
View of Oldhams in Sharples	90
Facsimile of Music composed by Crompton . .	138
„ „ Writing of Lewis Paul	250
„ „ „ „ Dr. Johnson	270

Published at 5s. 100 Copies on Large Paper were also issued.

The LIFE and TIMES of SAMUEL CROMPTON of Hall-in-the-Wood, Inventor of the Spinning Machine called the Mule. By GILBERT J. FRENCH, F.S.A., Corr. Mem. S. Ant. Scot., etc. Third Edition. Manchester: Charles Simms and Co. 1862. *Foolscap octavo.*

Title as above, Dedication, Preface, and Contents, x. pp. Life of Crompton and Index, 164 pp.

ILLUSTRATIONS.

Portrait of Samuel Crompton.
Cottage at Lower-Wood.
Birthplace of Samuel Crompton.
Hall-in-the-Wood.
Carved Panel in Crompton's Room, Hall-in-the-Wood.
Entrance Porch, Hall-in-the-Wood.
Oldhams in Sharples.
The house in which Crompton died.
Tomb of Crompton.

The Second Edition was published in 1860; the last, or People's Edition, in 1862, at 1s., stiff cover.

Gilbert James French was born in Edinburgh in 1804, in which city his father, James French, was a shawl manufacturer. He was educated and passed his early life there. About 1829 he came to Bolton in Lancashire, where he was first a draper and afterwards a church furnisher. He died 4th May 1866, and was buried at Walmsley Church near Bolton. He edited for the Chetham Society "Notices of the Church Libraries of Turton and Gorton." *See* p. 180.

The BASIS of MR. SAMUEL CROMPTON'S CLAIMS to a Second Remuneration from Parliament for his Discovery of the Mule Spinning Machine. Reprinted verbatim from the original pamphlet by Mr. J. Brown, which appeared circa 1825. Manchester: printed by Charles Simms and Co. 1868. *Quarto.*

Title as above, and the Basis, etc., 42 pp.

See Brown's "History of Bolton," p. 8.

MEMOIR of the LIFE, WRITINGS, and CORRESPONDENCE of JAMES CURRIE, M.D., F.R.S., of LIVERPOOL, Fellow of the Royal College of Physicians, Edinburgh; London Medical Society, etc. Edited by his Son, WILLIAM WALLACE CURRIE. In Two Volumes.

VOL. I.

London: Printed for Longman, Rees, Orme, Brown, and Green, Paternoster Row. 1831.

Title as above. Dedication and Contents, xv. pp. Memoir and Appendix, 524 pp. *Frontispiece,* Portrait of Dr. Currie.

VOL. II.

Title and Contents, xii. pp. Letter to Dr. James Currie, and Memoir, 503 pp. Published 24s. Sells at 5s. 6d.

A Short ACCOUNT of the LIFE and DEATH of ANN CUTLER, commonly known by the name of "PRAYING NANNY." By the Rev. WILLIAM BRAMWELL. With an account of Elizabeth Dickinson Frances. Leeds, 1798. *Duodecimo.*

Ann Cutler was born at Thornley, near Longridge, in 1759, and died 1794. She was buried at Christ Church, Macclesfield. William Bramwell was born at Elswick, in the Parish of St. Michael-le-Wyre, and was in 1788 a Wesleyan minister stationed at Blackburn.

CONFESSIONS of an ENGLISH OPIUM EATER. By THOMAS DE QUINCEY. Carefully revised by the author, and greatly enlarged.

> "To weep afresh a long since cancell'd woe,
> And moan the expense of many a vanish'd sight."—
> SHAKSPEARE'S SONNETS.

Edinburgh: Adam and Charles Black. MDCCCLXII. The right of translation is reserved. *Post octavo.*

Half-title, Title as above. Advertisement, Preface to the works, xviii. pp. Original Preface to "The Confessions" in 1821, and prefatory Notice of the New Edition, xv. pp. Confessions and Appendix, 290 pp. *Frontispiece,* Portrait of Thomas de Quincey.

This forms Vol. i. of the Author's Edition of De Quincey's Works, and was published at 4s. 6d. As a separate work it was first published in 1821, and went through many editions. A Portrait of De Quincey forms the frontispiece of Vol. iv. of "Noctes Ambrosianæ," by Professor Wilson. (Edinburgh, 1864.)

The FARINGTON PAPERS. The Shrievalty of William Ffarington, Esq., A.D. 1636. Documents relating to the Civil War, and an Appendix containing a collection of Letters taken from the Ffarington correspondence, between the years 1547 and 1688. Selected from the original manuscripts at Worden, and edited by SUSAN MARIA FFARINGTON. Printed for the Chetham Society MDCCCLVI. *Foolscap quarto.*

Chetham Society's Title (Vol. xxxix.), List of Council, Title as above, Introductory Notice and Contents, xiv. pp. 2d Title-page, The Ffarington Papers, etc., 179 pp. The 13th Report of the Society, etc., 5 pp.

ILLUSTRATIONS.

Frontispiece, Facsimile Signatures, (Royalists).
(2 sheets), Facsimile Signatures (Royalists) to face page 56.
(2 sheets), Facsimile Signatures (Parliamentary) to face page 118.

A BRIEF ACCOUNT of THOMAS FELL, of SWARTHMORE HALL. By THOMAS MOUNSEY. Manchester: William Irwin, 39 Oldham Street. London: Charles Gilpin, 5 Bishopsgate Street. 1846. *Foolscap octavo.*

Title as above, and Account, 20 pp. The Second Edition, printed in 1847, has a Frontispiece of the Hall where the Friends met for Divine Worship.

The FELLS of SWARTHMOOR HALL and their Friends. With an account of their descent. A Portraiture of Religion and Family Life in the 17th century. Compiled chiefly from original Letters and other Documents, never before published. By MARIA WEBB. [Daniel xii. 3.] London : Alfred W. Bennet, 5 Bishopsgate Without. Dublin : J. Robinson, 3 Grafton Street. 1865. *Octavo.*

Title as above. Preface, Contents, and List of Illustrations, xi. pp. The Fells, etc., and Appendix, 434 pp.

PLATES.

Swarthmoor Hall, *Frontispiece.*
Marsh Grange.
Swarthmoor Meeting House.
Tomb of Thomas Lawson, and Facsimile of Autograph.

Published at 7s. 6d.

The FELLS of SWARTHMOOR HALL and their Friends, with an account of their ancestor ANNE ASKEW, the Martyr. A Portraiture of religion and early life in the seventeenth century, compiled chiefly from the original Letters and other documents never before published. By MARIA WEBB, author of "The Penns and Penningtons," "Annotations on Dr. D'Aubigne's Sketch of the Early Christian Church." [Daniel xii. 3.] Second Edition. London : F. Bowyer Kitto, 5 Bishopsgate Without. MDCCCLXVII. *Foolscap octavo.*

Half-title, Title as above, Preface, and Contents, xvi. pp. The Fells, and Appendix, 382 pp.

Frontispiece, Marsh Grange, the Ancient Residence of the Askew Family in Furness.

Published at 3s. 6d.
See Works of Margaret Fell, Part VI.

A BRIEF COLLECTION of REMARKABLE PASSAGES and OCCURRENCES relating to the BIRTH, EDUCATION, LIFE, Conversion, Travels, Services, and Deep Sufferings of that Ancient, Eminent, and Faithful Servant of the Lord, MARGARET FELL, by her second marriage MARGARET FOX. Together with the Epistles, Books, and Christian Testimonies to Friends and others, and also to those in Superior

Authority in the several late Revolutions of Government. [Matth. v. 16; Luke xviii. 7.] London: printed and sold by S. and J. Sowle, in White-Hart-Court, in Gracious Street. 1710. *Octavo.*

Title as above, and Testimonies from her children, etc., xiv. pp. A Collection, etc., 535 pp. Index, 3 pp.

Scarce. Sells for 15s.

MEMOIR of GEORGE FISHWICK, Esq. of Springfield, SCORTIN. By the Rev. PETER M'OWEN. Extracted from the "Wesleyan Methodist Magazine" [January 1856]. *Octavo.*

Title as above, and Memoir, 16 pp.

Printed for private circulation.

MEMORIALS of MISS MARY FISHWICK of Springfield, near Garstang, containing selections from her correspondence, etc., with an Introduction. By the Rev. PETER M'OWEN.

> "For those who throng the eternal throne,
> Lost are the tears we shed,
> They are the living, they alone,
> Whom thus we call the dead."

London: published and sold by Hamilton, Adams, and Co., Paternoster Row; sold also by John Mason, 14 City Road, and at 66 Paternoster Row. 1840. *Foolscap octavo.*

Title as above, Contents, viii. pp. Introduction, and Memorials, 282 pp.

Published at 2s. 6d.

Friendship's Tribute to the Memory of the Late MRS. FISHWICK, of Springfield, near Garstang, with selections from her correspondence.

> "The righteous shall be had in everlasting remembrance."

Lancaster: printed by A. Milner, Church Street. 1852. *Post octavo.*

Title as above, Dedication, and Memoir, 200 pp.

Portrait of Mrs. Fishwick facing Title-page.

Published for private circulation.

Memoirs of MRS. FISHWICK, late of Southport. By the Rev. WILLIAM A. POPE. Southport: James Ingham, "Caxton" Works, Lord Street. 1872. *Post octavo.*

Title as above, and Memoir, 18 pp.

Frontispiece, Photograph of Mrs. Fishwick.

Privately printed.

MEMOIRS of the LIFE and GOSPEL LABOURS of SAMUEL FOTHERGILL, with Selections from his correspondence; also an account of the LIFE and TRAVELS of his Father, JOHN FOTHERGILL, and notices of some of his descendants. Liverpool: printed and published by D. Marples; London, Charles Gilpin. 1843. *Octavo.*

Title as above, Memoirs, etc., 548 pp.

Frontispiece, View of Carr End.

The Second Edition (12*mo*) was published in 1857.

GEORGE CROSSFIELD, the author of the above, was the son of George and Ann Crossfield, of Warrington, and was born there in 1785. A profile of him is amongst Dr. Kendrick's "Warrington Worthies." He was the writer of "The Calendar of Flora for the year 1809," etc. Samuel Fothergill was the author of several Friends' Books, Sermons, etc.; he died 15th June 1772 at Warrington.[1]

The LIFE of MARGARET FOX, WIFE of GEORGE FOX, compiled from her own narrative, and other sources, with a selection from her Epistles, etc. etc. etc. Philadelphia: published by the Association of Friends for the diffusion of Religious and Useful Knowledge, 109 North Tenth Street. 1859. 12*mo.*

See p. 205.

For Private Circulation only.

MEMORANDA of the GREENHALGH FAMILY. By JOSEPH DODSON GREENHALGH. 1869. Bolton: printed at T. Abbatt's Machine Printing Works. *Small octavo.*

Title as above, Dedication, Preface, and Memoranda, etc., 236 pp. Errata, i. p.

[1] "Smith's Cat. of Friends' Books."

Frontispiece, Photograph of the author. (Portrait) Photograph of John Greenhalgh of Brandlesome.

Only 50 copies of this were printed.

WILLIAM GRIMSHAW, Incumbent of Haworth, 1742-63. By R. SPENCE HARDY, Hon. M.R.A.S. Second Edition. London: published by John Mason, City Road, sold at 66 Paternoster Row. 1861. *Foolscap octavo.*

Title as above, Preface, and Contents, vii. pp. Life, 287 pp.

William Grimshaw was born at Brindle, 3d September 1708.

The LIFE and WRITINGS of the late WILLIAM GRIMSHAW. By WILLIAM MYLES, etc. * * Newcastle-on-Tyne. 1806. *Duodecimo.*

Title, etc., 199 pp.

William Myles was a Methodist Minister, a native of Limerick, and author of "A Short Chronological History of the Methodists."

A Short SKETCH or MEMOIR of the late JOSEPH HANSON, Esq., of STRANGEWAYS HALL, near MANCHESTER.

"Men's evil deeds we write on brass,
Their good ones in water."
SHAKSPEARE.

Salford: printed by Cowdroy and Slack, Bury Street. 1811. *Octavo.*

Title as above, Dedication, and Short Sketch, 24 pp.

Frontispiece, Portrait of Joseph Hanson, Esq. Died September 7, 1811, aged 37.

Now very scarce. A copy of this is in Peel Park Library, Salford.

Amongst the pamphlets which appeared at this period is one, a copy of which is in the Peel Park Library, entitled "Remarks on Slander and Envy, inscribed to F. D. Astley, Esq., and the Friends of Joseph Hanson, Esq. To which are added Mr. Hanson's address, etc. Manchester." This contains several poems by L. W. Praizer, and has a portrait of J. Hanson.

The Whole PROCEEDINGS on the TRIAL of an INDICTMENT

against JOSEPH HANSON, Esq., for a Conspiracy to aid the WEAVERS of MANCHESTER in raising their Wages. Before Mr. Justice Le Blanc, one of the Justices of his Majesty's Court of Queen's Bench, and a Special Jury, at the Lancaster Spring Assizes, 1809. Taken in shorthand by Mr. Jones, Liverpool. London: printed and published by T. Gillet, Crown Court, Fleet Street, C. Chapple, Pall Mall, and Sherwood, Neely, and Jones, Paternoster Row; may be had also of Thompson and Son, etc. [a list of local booksellers follows]. 1809. *Octavo.*

Title as above, and the Defendant's Preface, xiv. pp. List of Counsel, 1 p. The Trial, 116 pp. Folding Plan of part of Manchester.

Scarce. A copy is in the Manchester Free Library.

Statement of the Officers of the late First Regiment of Manchester and Salford Volunteers, commanded by Lieut.-Col. J. L. Philips. Manchester. 1804. *Octavo.*

Brief Remarks on the Present Volunteer Establishment. By JOSEPH HANSON, Lieutenant-Colonel Commandant of the Manchester, Salford, etc., Independent Rifle Regiment. Salford. n. d. [1805.] *Octavo.*

A Letter to Lieut.-Col. Joseph Hanson, containing concise observations on his Brief Remarks, etc. By a VOLUNTEER. Manchester. n. d. [1805.] *Octavo.*

Cursory Strictures on the Concise Observations of a Volunteer. Being a Defence of Col. Hanson's Remarks, etc. etc. Salford. n. d. [1805.] *Octavo.*

A Letter to Colonel Hanson by an ENGLISHMAN. Manchester. 1806. *Octavo.*

A COLLECTION of the CHRISTIAN WRITINGS, LABOURS, TRAVELS, and SUFFERINGS of that FAITHFUL and APPROVED MINISTER of Jesus Christ, ROGER HAYDOCK. To which is added an ACCOUNT of his DEATH and Burial. [Dan. xii. 3.] London: printed and sold by T. Sowle in White-Hart Court in Gracious Street. 1700. *Foolscap octavo.*

Title as above, Address, and Contents, viii. pp. The Testimony of

Eleanor Haydock and others (containing the signatures of 98 Friends), 60 pp. (unpaged). A Brief Account, 223 pp. A List of Books sold by T. Sowle, x. pp.

Amongst these Lancashire Quakers who gave testimony to Haydock's worth were Isaac Ashton senior of Ormskirk.

Sells for 5s. 6d.

Roger Haydock was born in Coppul in the Parish of Standish in Lancashire. He was the author of two well-known Friend's Books—viz. the "Skirmisher Confounded," which was a reply to JOHN CHEYNEY, who styled himself the author of "The Skirmish upon Quakerism;" and "A Hypocrite unvailed and a Blasphemer made manifest. Being an examination of John Cheyney's False Relation of his dispute with the Quakers at Arley Hall in Cheshire." John Cheyney was an Episcopal priest of Warrington.

MEMORIALS of Mrs. HEMANS. With Illustrations of her Literary Character, from her private correspondence. By HENRY F. CHORLEY. In Two Volumes.

VOL. I.

London: Saunders and Otley, Conduit Street. 1836.

Half-title i. p. Title as above, Dedication, Advertisement, and Contents, xiv. pp. Memorials, 309 pp. *Frontispiece*, Portrait of Mrs. Hemans, from a miniature by Edward Robertson.

VOL. II.

Title and Contents, viii. pp. Memorials, 358 pp. *Frontispiece*, View of Rhyllon, near St. Asaph.

Published at 21s. Sells for 5s.

EARLY BLOSSOMS: A COLLECTION of POEMS written between eight and fifteen years of age. By FELICIA DOROTHEA BROWNE, afterwards Mrs. HEMANS. With a LIFE of the AUTHORESS. London: T. Allman, 42 Holborn Hill. 1839. 32*mo*.

Engraved Title, i. p. Title as above, Dedication, and Life, lx. pp. Poems, 146 pp. Engraved Frontispiece.

Originally printed at Liverpool, and published 1808.

The WORKS of Mrs. HEMANS. With a MEMOIR by her Sister. In Seven Volumes.

Vol. I.

William Blackwood and Sons, Edinburgh and London. MDCCCXLI. *Foolscap octavo.*

1st Title, "Memoir of Mrs. Hemans [Vignette]. Edinburgh: William Blackwood and Sons. MDCCCXL." 2d Title as above. Dedication, Contents, 3d Title, ix. pp. Memoir p. 1 to p. 315. Poems, p. 317 to p. 352. Portrait by West.

The other six volumes contains Mrs. Hemans' Poems, etc. Published at 5s. The First Volume is sometimes advertised as a Memoir in one volume.

This Memoir was again published by Blackwood, 1857. *12mo.* 5s.

The Poetical Works, with Life, were published in seven volumes (as above) in 1839, at 35s.; and in six volumes, *16mo*, in 1850, at 4s. each volume. Felicia Dorothea Browne was born in Liverpool in 1794. In 1812 she married Captain Hemans, of the 4th Regiment, and died in 1835. Her Poems (which are not of a local character) were also published in 1848, at 21s.; 1851 and 1861 at 12s. 6d.

A BIOGRAPHICAL ACCOUNT of the late Dr. HENRY. By William Charles Henry, M.D., F.R.S., S.G.S. Manchester: Printed by F. Looney, Oak Street, Swan Street. 1837.

Title as above, and Biographical Account, 45 pp. *Octavo.*

Dr. Henry was a native of Manchester.

The LIFE of the Rev. OLIVER HEYWOOD. With HISTORICAL SKETCHES of the Times in which he lived, and Anecdotes of some other eminent Ministers in Yorkshire, Lancashire, etc. By J. Fawcett, A.M. [Quotation 2 lines.] Printed and sold at Wood Hall, near Halifax. 1796. *Duodecimo.*

Title as above. Preface and Life, 212 pp. Index, 4 pp.

A copy is in the British Museum.

The Rise of the Old Dissent exemplified in the LIFE of OLIVER HEYWOOD, one of the Founders of the Presbyterian Congregations in the County of York, 1630-1702. By the Rev. JOSEPH HUNTER, F.S.A. London : Longman, Brown, and Green and Longmans. 1842. *Octavo.*

Title as above. Preface and Contents, xix. pp. Life and Index, 463 pp.

Republished in 1862 at 14s.

Oliver Heywood was the son of Richard and Alice Heywood, of Little Lever, in the Parish of Bolton. He was born in 1629. His collected works were first published in 1827. (*See* also "Nonconformist Remains.")

SELECT NONCONFORMISTS' REMAINS, being original Sermons of OLIVER HEYWOOD, THOMAS JOLLIE, HENRY NEWCOME, and HENRY PENDLEBURY, selected from manuscripts. With MEMOIRS of the Authors, compiled mostly from their private papers. By RICHARD SLATE. [Quotations, Jer. vi. 16, and Heb. xiii. 7-9.] London : Printed for Longman, Hurst, Rees, Orme, and Browne, Paternoster Row, and B. Crompton, Bury, Lancashire. 1814. *Octavo.*

Title as above, Preface and Contents, xii. pp. Memoirs and Sermons, 389 pp. Errata, 1 p.

Sells for 7s. 6d.

The whole WORKS of the REV. OLIVER HEYWOOD, B.A. Now first collected, revised, and arranged, including some Tracts extremely scarce, and others from unpublished manuscripts. With a MEMOIR of his LIFE. In Five Volumes. Containing Life of Mr. O. Heywood. Extracts from his Diary, Soliloquies, Letters, etc. Life of Mr. N. Heywood. Life of Mr. Angier. Lives of Mr. O. Heywood's Relations. Idle : Printed by John Vint for the Editor, etc. 1827.

Title as above. List of subscribers and Contents, x. pp. Memoirs, 608 pp.

PLATES.

Portrait of Oliver Heywood, *Frontispiece.*
Facsimile of Diary, page 374.
Facsimile of Presentation, page 444.

VOL. II.

Title, Contents, and Preface, xvii. pp. Heart Treasure, etc., 500 pp. *Frontispiece*, Facsimile of Presentation.

VOL. III.

Title and Contents, vi. pp. Closet Prayers, etc., 523 pp.

VOL. IV.

Title and Contents, v. pp. Baptismal Bonds Renewed, etc., 568 pp. *Frontispiece,* Facsimile of Letter from Oliver Heywood to Rev. Thomas Jollie

VOL. V.

Title, Contents, and Preface, ix. pp. A New Creature, etc., 603 pp.

Sells for 21s.

The LIFE and MEMOIR of the Late REV. JOHN HIRST, Forty-Two Years Pastor of the Baptist Church, BACUP. Also an Appendix containing a sketch of the rise of that Church and of the Churches at Clough Fold, Rodhillend, Rawden, Salendine Nook, Accrington, Blackburn, Cowling-Hill, Goodshaw, and a short account of several Ministers, particularly Messrs. Mitchel, Crosley, Moore, Piccop, Lord, Turner, Holden, Mitchell, Ashworth, etc. By JAMES HARGREAVES. Rochdale: printed and sold by Joseph Littlewood. 1816. *Foolscap octavo.*

Title as above, Dedication, Preface, and Contents, xii. pp. Memoir, p. 13 to p. 300. Appendix, p. 301 to p. 419. Sells for 5s. 6d.

The subject of this Memoir was born in Blackwater Street, Rochdale, in 1736.

James Hargreaves was the Baptist Minister at Ogden, near Rochdale.

INCIDENTS in the LIFE of DAVID HOLT, including a SKETCH of some of the PHILANTHROPIC INSTITUTIONS of MANCHESTER during a period of forty years. Written by himself. Manchester: John Harrison, Printer, Market Street. 1843. *Foolscap octavo.*

Title as above, Dedication, and Incidents, 49 pp.

Memoir of the Life and Labors of the REV. JEREMIAH HORROX, Curate of Hoole, near Preston, to which is appended a translation of his celebrated discourse upon the Transit of Venus across the Sun. By the Rev. ARUNDELL BLOUNT WHATTON, LL.B. London: Westheim, Macintosh, and Hunt, 24 Paternoster Row, and 23 Holles Street, Cavendish Square. MDCCCLIX. *Foolscap octavo.*

Title as above, "In Memoriam Patris delectissimi Gul. Rob. Whatton, F.R.S., F.S.A.," etc. etc., Contents, and Preface, xvi. pp. Memoir, 216 pp.

Diagram of Transit of Venus, facing p. 122.

Published at 3s. 6d. Sells for about the original price.

In 1869 this was republished with a new Title, "The Transit of Venus across the Sun; a Translation, etc., and Memoir." The Rev. A. B. Whatton is the son of the late W. R. Whatton.

In 1673 was printed in London for J. Martyn, "Jeremiæ Horocci, Liverpoliensis Angli, ex Palitinatu Lancastriæ opera posthuma—viz. Astronomia Kepleriana, defensa et promota. Excerpta ex Epistolis ad Crabtræum suum. Observationum Cœlestium Catalogus. Lunæ Theoria nova; accedunt Gulielmi Crabtræi Mancestriensis, observationes Cœlestes; in calce adjiciunter Joannis Flamstedii de temporis Equatione diatriba, numeri ad lunæ Theoriam Horoccianam."

Published at 9s.

The LIFE of PETER HOUGHTON, B.A., late Assistant Curate, WALTON-LE-DALE. By ROGER CARUS WILSON, M.A., Vicar of Preston, Lancashire. [Greek Quotation.] London: Hatchard and Son, 187 Piccadilly. 1832. *Duodecimo.*

Title as above, and Preface, xi. pp. The Life, 141 pp.

Peter Houghton was the son of Thomas and Jane Houghton of Preston, where he was born 17th May 1802.

Sells for 2s. 6d.

The LIFE and REMAINS of the REV. ROBERT HOUSMAN, A.B., the Founder, and for above forty years the Incumbent Minister of St. Anne's, Lancaster, and formerly curate to the Rev. T. Robinson, M.A., of Leicester. By ROBERT FLETCHER HOUSMAN, Esq. London: Simpkin, Marshall, and Co.; Hatchard and Son; James Nisbet and Co.; and L. and G. Seeley. 1841. *Octavo.*

Title as above, Advertisement, Preface, Contents, and Errata, viii. pp. Memoir, p. ix. to p. ccclxxx. Sermons (including Half-title), 276 pp.

Frontispiece, Portrait of the Rev. Robert Housman.

Published at 10s. 6d.

From the Eleventh Vol. of Memoirs of the Literary and Philosophical Society of Manchester, Sessions 1852-3,

MEMOIR of the late Mr. JOHN JUST of Bury. By Mr. Jno. Harland. Manchester: Cave and Sever, Printers, Palatine Buildings, Hunt's Bank. 1854. *Duodecimo.*

Title, i. p. Memoirs, p. 91 to p. 121.

JOLLIE, THOMAS, Rev. *See* p. 212.

A TESTIMONIAL in behalf of MERIT NEGLECTED and GENIUS UNREWARDED, and RECORD of the Services and Sufferings of one of England's greatest Benefactors. By a Desendant [sic] of John Kay of Bury.

"Facts are chiels that winna ding,
And douna be disputed."—Burns.

[Lithographic sketch, and quotation from Wheeler's History of Manchester.] London: Published by the Author. [1847.] *Quarto.*

Title as above, i. p., and Introduction, iv. pp. Record, etc., 32 pp. Address to Merchants and Manufacturers of Great Britain, 2 pp.

Contains a folding sheet, containing a large number of names of manufacturers and others who are "convinced of the justice of the claims preferred by the descendant of Mr. Kay to public remuneration." The descendant was Thomas Sutcliffe.

The KEMBLES: an ACCOUNT of the KEMBLE FAMILY, including the LIVES of Mrs. SIDDONS and her brother JOHN PHILIP KEMBLE. By Percy Fitzgerald, M.A., F.S.A., author of "The Life of Garrick," "Principles of Comedy," etc. In Two Volumes.

Vol. I.

London: Tinsley Brothers, 18 Catherine Street, Strand.
(All rights of Translation and Reproduction are reserved.) [1871.]

Half-title, Title as above. Dedication, Preface, Contents, and List of Illustrations, xxiii. pp. The Kembles, and Appendix, 352 pp. *Octavo.*

Plates.

Mrs. Siddons, *Frontispiece.*

Roger Kemble	P. 12
Mrs. Roger Kemble	24
Caricature of Mrs. Siddons as "Melpomine" .	176
Mrs. Siddons as "Lady Macbeth" . . .	242
Mrs. Siddons at the age of thirty . . .	256
Drawing of J. P. Kemble after Laurence . .	298
Autographs of the Kemble family . . .	330

VOL. II.

Half-title, Title and Contents, vi. pp. The Kembles, and Index, 414 pp.

PLATES.

J. P. Kemble	*Frontispiece.*
J. P. Kemble as "Penruddock" . . .	P. 4
Facsimile of Letter	30
Charles Kemble	78
Stephen Kemble	108
Caricature of the Kemble family . . .	114
Ticket for the Farewell Dinner to J. P. Kemble .	263

Published at 30s. Sells for 9s. 6d.

MEMOIRS of the LIFE of JOHN PHILIP KEMBLE, Esq. Including a History of the Stage from the time of Garrick to the present period. By JAMES BOADEN, Esq. [Two Latin quotations.] In Two Volumes.

VOL. I.

London: Printed for Longman, Hurst, Rees, Orme, Brown, and Green, Paternoster Row. 1825. *Octavo.*

Title as above. Dedication, Introduction, and Contents, xl. pp. Life of Kemble, 477 pp. *Frontispiece,* Portrait of J. P. Kemble.

VOL. II.

Half-title and Title, 3 pp. Life of Kemble, 595 pp.

Published at £1 : 8s. Sells for 7s. 6d.

MEMOIRS of JOHN PHILIP KEMBLE. With an Original Critique on his Performance. By JOHN AMBROSE WILLIAMS, Author of

Metrical Essays. [Quotations from Collins and Dr. Johnson.] London: Printed for John Bowley Wood, Leather Lane, Holborn. 1817. *Octavo.*

Title as above, Sonnet, and Memoirs, 80 pp. *Frontispiece*, Portrait of Kemble.

Sells for 5s.

REPORT of the TRIAL (in ejectment) Doe Dem. GIBSON and Others *v.* HARGRAVE and Others. Lancaster Assizes, March 23, 1837. From Notes taken by Mr. ALEXANDER FRASER, Shorthand Writer. Preston: printed by Addison, Church Street. MDCCCXXXVIII. *Octavo.*

Title as above, List of Jurors, Report, Pedigrees, and Appendix, 108 pp. Index to the Appendix, 1 p.

This trial was respecting the lawful heirs of ALEXANDER KERSHAW, who died in 1788, seized of Heskin Hall, near Wigan, and other Estates. Scarce.

A copy of this is in the Author's Library.

Memorials of the Mercies of a Covenant God while travelling through the Wilderness. Being The AUTOBIOGRAPHY of JOHN KERSHAW of Rochdale. To which is added an account of his last days by his Widow. [Ps. cvii. 43.] Second Edition. London: Gadsby, 18 Bouverie Street. 1871. Price, 3s. cloth; and 4s. 6d. half calf; 7s. full calf, marble edges. *Post octavo.*

Title as above, Preface, Epistle, and Contents, viii. pp. Autobiography, etc., 404 pp. *Frontispiece*, Portrait of John Kershaw.

John Kershaw was born at Lower Fold, Healey, in the Parish of Rochdale, 25th August 1792. He was for fifty-three years minister of "Hope Chapel," Rochdale, and died 11th January 1870.

Considerations on the Theory of Religion. BY EDMUND LAW, D.D., late Bishop of Carlisle. To which is added a LIFE of the AUTHOR by the late W. B. PALEY, D.D. A New Edition. By GEORGE HENRY LAW, D.D., Lord Bishop of Chester. London: Printed by Rodwell and Martin, New Bond Street, and Messrs. Rivington, St. Paul's Churchyard. 1820. *Octavo.*

The First Edition was printed in 1800. The Life of Edmund Law is contained in 16 pp. of the above. The Second Edition (as above) is in the British Museum. Bishop Law was born in 1703 at Cartmel in Lancashire.

LIFE and TIMES of the late ALDERMAN T. LIVESEY. By Miss N. R. LAHEE. Manchester: Abel Heywood and Son, Printers, Oldham Street. London: Simpkin, Marshall, and Co., Stationers' Hall Court. *Post octavo.*

Title as above, i. p. Preface, Contents, and Life and Times, 156 pp. *Frontispiece*, photograph of Alderman Livesey.

A SHORT ACCOUNT of JOHN MARRIOTT, including extracts from some of his Letters. To which are added some of his Poetical Productions. Doncaster: printed and sold by D. Boys. And sold in London by W. Phillips, George-Yard, Lombard Street, and Darton and Harvey, No. 55 Grace-Church Street; also by W. Leicester, Warrington; H. Earnshaw Coln; W. Bleckley, York, etc. etc. 1803. *Duodecimo.*

Half-title, Title as above, and Contents, 7 pp. Short Account, Poetical Pieces, and Errata, 196 pp.

John Marriott was a native of Edgend, near Coln.

Sells for 2s. 6d.

TROUBLES and MARTYRDOM of the Rev. GEORGE MARSH, Protestant Martyr, of the Parish of Dean, near Bolton, Lancashire, who suffered Martyrdom April 24, A.D. 1555; his Letters, and an Introduction by the Reverend ALFRED HEWLETT, M.A., Incumbent of Astley. London: Hamilton, Adams, and Co.; Manchester: Whitmore; all booksellers, and the Author. MDCCCXLIV. *Small octavo.*

Title, Preface, etc., xli. pp. Troubles and Martyrdom, 102 pp.

[*See* p. 197.]

The LIFE of ADAM MARTINDALE. Written by himself, and now first printed from the original manuscript in the British Museum. Edited by the Rev. RICHARD PARKINSON, B.D., Canon of Manchester. Printed for the Chetham Society. MDCCCXLV. *Foolscap quarto.*

Chetham Society's Title (Vol. iv.), and List of Council, iii. pp. Title as above, Preface, and Contents, xv. pp. Life of Adam Martindale, and Index, 245 pp.

Adam Martindale was a native of Prescot, where he was born in September 1623. The Rev. Richard Parkinson, B.D., formerly a Fellow of St. John's College, and Hulsean Lecturer, Cambridge, was the Principal of St. Bees College, Cumberland, Perpetual Curate of St. Bees, and

Canon of Manchester. He died 28th January 1858. He edited several volumes for the Chetham Society, and was the author of "The Old Church Clock." [*See* PART III.]

The MOORE RENTAL. Edited by THOMAS HEYWOOD, Esq., F.S.A. Printed for the Chetham Society. MDCCCXLVII. *Foolscap quarto.*

Title of Chetham Society (Vol. xii.), List of Council, and Title as above, vi. pp. Contents and Introduction, lii. pp. The Moore Rental and Index, 158 pp.

Frontispiece, a Plan of Liverpool, and the Pool as it appeared about the year 1650. Copied from the original drawing in the court of the Duchy of Lancaster, etc., for the Stranger in Liverpool. Published by Thos. Kaye. 1829. (*See* p. 101.)

FAMILY MEMOIRS of SIR OSWALD MOSLEY, Bart. Printed for private circulation. 1849. *Quarto.*

Title as above, i. p. Dedication, iv. pp. Memoirs, 78 pp. Appendix, xxviii.

LIST OF PLATES.

Portrait of Sir Oswald Mosley, Bart.	*Frontispiece.*
Vignette containing arms	(After the Dedication.)
Mansion at Hough End	P. 7
Mural Monuments in Didsbury Church (coloured)	10
Old Ancoats Hall	22
Monumental Brasses in the Collegiate Church, Manchester	25
Rolleston Church in Staffordshire	49
Facsimile of grant of arms to Nicholas Mosley in 1592,	p. xii. Appendix.
Monument of Sir Edward Mosley in south aisle of Rolleston Church	p. xxi. Appendix.

The DIARY of the Rev. HENRY NEWCOME, from September 30, 1661 to September 29, 1663. Edited by THOMAS HEYWOOD, Esq., F.S.A. Printed for the Chetham Society. MDCCCXLIX. *Foolscap quarto.*

Chetham Society's Title (Vol. xviii.), List of Council, and Title as above, iii. pp. Introduction, xl. pp. Diary and Index, 242 pp.

Thomas Heywood was the son of Nathaniel Heywood, Esq., Banker, of Manchester. Was born 3d September 1797, and died at Hope End, near Ledbury, Herefordshire, 20th November 1866. (*See* "Manchester

School Register," Vol. iii., Part I.) He contributed several volumes to the Chetham Society.

The AUTOBIOGRAPHY of HENRY NEWCOME, M.A. Edited by RICHARD PARKINSON, D.D., F.S.A., Principal of Saint Bees College, and Canon of Manchester. Printed for the Chetham Society. MDCCCLII. *Foolscap quarto.*

Chetham Society's Title (Vol. xxvi.), List of Council, and Title as above, vi. pp. Title as above, with the words added "In Two Volumes. Vol. I." and Introduction, xxv. pp. Autobiography, 184 pp.

This volume contains the Autobiography A.D. 1627 to 1670.

VOL. II.

Chetham Society's Title, List of Council, and Title to 2d Vol., vi. pp. Autobiography, Letters, etc., and Index, 185 to 390 pp.

The NORRIS PAPERS. Edited by THOMAS HEYWOOD, Esq., F.S.A. Printed for the Chetham Society. MDCCCXLVI. *Foolscap quarto.*

Chetham Society's Title (Vol. ix.), and List of Council, 3 pp. Title as above, Introduction, Contents, and Errata, xxxiv. pp. The Norris Papers and Index, 190 pp.

The LIFE of ALEXANDER NOWELL, Dean of St. Paul's. Chiefly compiled from Registers, Letters, and other authentic evidence. By RALPH CHURTON, M.A., Rector of Middleton Cheney, Northamptonshire, Archdeacon of St. David's, and late Fellow of Brazenose College.

"Such persons who served God by holy living, industrious preaching, and religious dying, ought to have their names preserved in honour, and their holy doctrines and lives published and imitated."—JEREMY TAYLOR.

Oxford: at the University Press for the Author. Sold by F. C. and J. Rivington and J. White, London; J. Parker, Oxford; and Ford, Manchester. 1809. *Octavo.*

Title as above, Dedication, Preface, and Contents, xxix. pp. Life of A. Nowell, Appendix, and Index, 448 pp.

PLATES.

Portrait of Alexander Nowell, *Frontispiece.*
Read Hall.
Remains of the Bust of Dean Nowell.
John Towneley of Towneley.
William Whitaker.
View of Holme.
Mrs. Joyce Frankland.
Facsimile of Autographs.
Nowell's Monument.

Folding Pedigree of Nowell Family.

Sells for 6s. Large paper copies (only 25 printed) fetch a much higher price.

HISTORICAL SKETCH of THE LIFE of the late MR. JOSIAH NUTTALL of HEYWOOD, Ornithologist and Taxidermist. [Facsimile of signature.] Heywood: printed and sold by V. Cook, Market Place. 1849. *Octavo.*

Title as above, and Historical Sketch, etc., 12 pp.

Some ACCOUNT of the late AMOS OGDEN of MIDDLETON. 1853. Printed and published by W. Horsman, Middleton; sold also by Abel Heywood, Oldham Street; John Heywood, Deansgate, Manchester; and by all booksellers. *Small octavo.*

Title as above, and Account, 17 pp., including Title.

This was written by SAMUEL BAMFORD, and is dated "London, January 27th, 1853." Ogden was a native of Middleton, and took an active part in the Reform movements prior to 1819. The Account chiefly relates to some mis-statements in Fielding's "Rural Gleanings."

A copy of this is in the Library of William Harrison, Esq., of St. John's, Isle of Man.

HUGH OLDHAM. *See* "Oldham's Tenement," p. 12.

MEMOIRS of the late HENRY PARK, Esq., Surgeon, of LIVERPOOL. William Grapel, Church Street; D. Marples, Lord Street. 1848. *Octavo.*

Title as above, and Memoirs, 38 pp., with an Engraved Portrait and autograph of H. Park.

SIR ROBERT PEEL, an HISTORICAL SKETCH. By HENRY, LORD DALLING and BULWER, Author of "Historical Characters," etc. London: Richard Bentley and Son, New Burlington Street, Publishers in ordinary to Her Majesty. 1874. [The right of Translation is reserved.] *Octavo.*

Half-title, Title as above, Prefatory Note, and Preface, viii. pp. Half-title, and Sketch, 147 pp.

Published at 7s. 6d.

The POLITICAL LIFE of the RIGHT HONOURABLE SIR ROBERT PEEL, BART. An analytical Biography. By THOMAS DOUBLEDAY, author of "The true law of Population;" "Financial History of England;" "Essay on Mundane Moral Government," etc.

"The people cannot see, but they can feel."
JAMES WARRINGTON'S "Political Aphorism."

In two Volumes.

VOL. I.

London: Smith, Elder, and Co., 65 Cornhill. 1856. *Octavo.*

Title as above, Preface, and Contents, xii. pp. The Political Life, 510 pp.

VOL. II.

Title and Contents, viii. pp. The Political Life and Index, 530 pp.

Published at 30s., reduced to 18s.; now sell for 7s. 6d.

The Late SIR ROBERT PEEL, Bart. A CRITICAL BIOGRAPHY. By GEORGE HENRY FRANCIS. Reprinted, with additions, from "Fraser's Magazine." London: John W. Parker and Son, West Strand. MDCCCLII. 16*mo.*

Title and Biography, 119 pp.

Published at 1s. Sells for 2s. 6d.

MEMOIR of SIR ROBERT PEEL. By M. GUIZOT. London: Richard Bentley, New Burlington Street, Publisher in Ordinary to Her Majesty the Queen. MDCCCLVII. *Octavo.*

Title as above and Contents, vii. pp. Memoir and Appendix, 398 pp.

Published at 14s.

The LIFE of the RIGHT HONOURABLE SIR ROBERT PEEL, as Subject and Citizen, as Legislator and Minister, and as a Patron of Learning and the Arts. With a Portrait. By WILLIAM HARVEY. A new Edition, with numerous alterations and additions. London: George Routledge and Co., Soho Square. 1850. *Duodecimo.*

Title as above and Contents, iv. pp. Introduction and the Life, 220 pp.

A SKETCH of the LIFE and CHARACTER of SIR ROBERT PEEL. By Sir LAURENCE PEEL. London. 1860. *Post octavo.*

Sells for 3s.

A Life of Sir Robert Peel was also published by Routledge and Co. in 1850. *12mo.* Price 1s.

MEMOIRS of the RIGHT HONOURABLE SIR ROBERT PEEL, Bart., M.P., etc. Published by the Trustees of his Papers, Lord Mahon (now Earl Stanhope) and the Right Hon. Edward Cardwell, M.P. PART I. The Roman Catholic Question, 1828-9. London: John Murray, Albemarle Street. 1856. The right of translation is reserved. *Post octavo.*

Title as above, Preface, and Codicil, xii. pp. Memoirs, 366 pp.

VOL. II. [1857.]

PART II. The new Government, 1834-5.
" III. Repeal of the Corn Law, 1845-6.

Title and Preface, iv. pp. Half-title, i. p. Memoirs, 357 pp.

Published at 15s.

Also have been published—"Sir R. Peel's Speeches during his Administration," 1835; "Sir R. Peel's Speeches in the House of Commons," 1853; "Sir Robert Peel as a Type of Statesmanship," by Symons, 1856; and "Sir Robert Peel and his Era," 1843.

LIFE and TIMES of SIR ROBERT PEEL. By W. COOKE TAYLOR, LL.D. of Trinity College, Dublin, author of "The Natural History of Society," "Revolutions of Europe," "The Factory System," etc.

Vol. I.

Peter Jackson, late Fisher, Son, and Co., Angel Street, St. Martin's-le-Grand, London. *Octavo.*

Title as above, Preface and Contents, and List of Plates, viii. pp. Life and Times, 524 pp. The Volume contains 18 Plates.[1]

[1] The List of Plates is not given, because only a small number of them refer to the County.

VOL. II.

Title, Contents, and List of Plates, iv. pp. Life and Times, 452 pp. Contains 12 Plates.

VOL. III.

Title, Contents, and List of Plates, iv. pp. Life and Times, 618 pp. Contains 11 Plates.

Published in Twelve Divisions in 1850. Sells for 10s. 6d.

A fourth volume, by C. Mackay, was published in 1851. The first three volumes were published at 12s. each; but afterwards reduced to 10/6; the 4th volume at 14s. The set, £3 : 3s.; but now sells for much less.

The WORKS of JAMES PILKINGTON, B.D., Lord Bishop of Durham. Edited for the Parker Society, by the Rev. JAMES SCHOLEFIELD, A.M., Regius Professor of Greek, Cambridge. Cambridge: Printed at the University Press. MDCCCXLII.

Half-title, Title as above, and BIOGRAPHICAL NOTES of JAMES PILKINGTON, xvi. pp. Works and Index, 703 pp. *Octavo.*

James Pilkington was born at Rivington in Lancashire in 1520, and was the third son of Richard Pilkington of Rivington Pike, Esq. (*See* p. 170.)

JOHN CRITCHLEY PRINCE. *See* PART III.

LITERARY REMINISCENCES and GLEANINGS. By RICHARD WRIGHT PROCTOR, author of "The Barber's Shop. With Illustrations by James Stephenson and William Morton.

"Time honoured Lancaster."—SHAKSPEARE.

Manchester: Thomas Dinham and Co. London: Simpkin, Marshall and Co. 1860. *Post octavo.*

Title as above, Dedication, Contents, Embellishments, vii. pp. Reminiscences, 162 pp.

ILLUSTRATIONS.

View of Kersall Cell. *Frontispiece.*
Portrait and Autograph facsimile of John Bolton Rogerson.
Portrait of John Byrom.
Town Residence of John Byrom.
Portrait of John Collier.
View of John Collier's birthplace.
View of Ancient School at Urmston.

Tim Bobbin's Chair.
A Mite from Milnrow.
View of Tim's Cottage.
View of Rochdale Church.
Monument and Autograph Facsimile of William Roscoe.
Autograph Facsimile of Henry Liverseege.
The Poets' Corner in 1858.
Autograph Facsimile of Robert Story.
View of Northenden Church and Ferry.
Sun-dial in Northenden Churchyard.
Portrait and Autograph Facsimile of John Critchley Prince.
Middleton Church.
Cottage near Boggart-ho-Clough.

Published at 4s.

JOHN ROBY: "Sketch of his Literary Life." *See* Poetry, etc. (*Post.*)

The LIFE OF GEO. ROMNEY, Esq.

"He was famous, etc."—SHAKSPEARE.

[Ayara vita di Mengo, etc.] By WILLIAM BAYLEY, Esq. Chichester: Printed by W. Mason for T. Payne, Pall Mall, London. 1809. *Quarto.*

Introduction, Preface, and Contents, x. pp. The Life, 416 pp.

LIST OF PLATES.

1.	Portrait of Romney.	
2.	The Introduction of Dr. Hop into the parlour of Mr. Shandy	P. 31
3.	Sketch	84
4.	Head of Sensibility	121
5.	Study for head of Miranda	141
6.	Portrait of Madam de Genlis	170
7.	Cassandra	172
8.	Head of our Saviour	231
9.	Infant Shakespeare	304
10.	Newton with the Prism	314
11.	Portrait, 1795	Last page
12.	Portrait of Romney Robinson	335

The LIFE of WILLIAM ROSCOE. By his son, HENRY ROSCOE. In two volumes.

Vol. I.

London: printed for T. Cadel, Strand, and W. Blackwood, Edinburgh. 1833. *Octavo.*

Title as above, Preface, and Contents, xv. pp. Life of William Roscoe, 501 pp.

Portrait of Roscoe, ætat. 38, *Frontispicce.*

Vol. II.

Half-title, Title, and Contents, xii. pp. Life, 491 pp.

Published at 30s. Sells for 7s. 6d.

A MEMOIR of WILLIAM ROSCOE was also written by Dr. T. S. Traill. Liverpool. 1853. *Post octavo.*

ROTHWELL, Rev. RICHARD. *See* p. 197.

MEMOIR of the LIFE, TRAVELS, and RELIGIOUS EXPERIENCE of MARTHA ROUTH, written by herself, or compiled from her own narrative. York: printed and published by W. Alexander and Son; sold also by Harvey and Darton, etc. etc. etc. 1832. *Duodecimo.*

Title, etc., and Memoir, 106 pp.

Reprinted, Second Edition, 1842.

RUSHTON, EDWARD, of Liverpool. Life of the Rev. WILLIAM SHEPHERD. *See* Part III.

Earl of Sefton *v.* Hopwood.

A REPORT of the HOPWOOD WILL CASE, tried at the South Lancashire Spring Assizes, 1855, before Mr. Justice Cresswell and a special Jury. Taken from the Notes of Messrs. Snell and Counsell, Shorthand Writers, Chancery Lane, London. Manchester: George Simms, 16 St. Ann's Square; London, Simpkin, Marshall, and Co., and sold by all Booksellers. 1855. *Quarto.*

Title as above, List of Jury, and Contents, viii. pp. Report, 534 pp.

A copy is in the Manchester Free Library.

The HOUSE and FARM ACCOUNTS of the SHUTTLEWORTHS, of Gawthorpe Hall, in the County of Lancaster, at Smithells and Gawthorpe from September 1582 to October 1621. Edited by JOHN HARLAND, F.S.A.

PART I.

Printed for the Chetham Society. MDCCCLVI. *Foolscap quarto.*

Chetham Society's Title (Vol. xxxv.), List of Council, and Title as above, iii. pp. The House and Farm Accounts, 232 pp.

Frontispiece, Gawthorpe Hall.

PART II.

Chetham Society's Title[1] (Vol. xli.), List of Council, and Title to the Second Part, v. pp. House and Farm Accounts, p. 233 to p. 258. Appendix I., p. 259 to p. 333. Appendix II., and Notes, p. 334 to p. 472.

Frontispiece, Portrait of Lawrence Shuttleworthe.

PART III.

Chetham Society's Title (Vol. xliii.), and List of Council, iii. pp. Title to the Third Part, and Introduction, x. pp. Notes (continued), p. 473 to p. 776.

PART IV.

Chetham Society's Title (Vol. xlvi.), List of Council, Title to the Fourth Part, and General Title, vii. pp. Notes (continued), and Index to the whole, p. 777 to p. 1171. The Fifteenth Report of the Society, etc., 5 pp. List of Members, 4 pp.

The LIVES of WILLIAM SMITH, BISHOP of LINCOLN, and Sir Richard Sutton, Knight, Founders of Brazenose College, Oxford. 1800. *Octavo.*

Title, Dedication, Preface, Contents, Lives, and Index, 602 pp.

ILLUSTRATIONS.

Portrait of Bishop Smith . . .	P. 1
St. John's Hospital, Litchfield . . .	86

[1] In this, and many other volumes of this Society, a List of its publications precedes the Title-page.

Collegium Aenei Nasi . . . . P. 310
Portrait of Sir Richard Sutton . . . 405
Pedigree of Smith (two sheets) . . . 483
Pedigree of Sutton 533

Sells for 15s.

William Smith, the fourth son of Robert Smith, of Peel House, in Widness, was born about 1460.

HISTORICAL SKETCHES of the HOUSE of STANLEY, and Biography of EDWARD GEOFFREY, 14th EARL of DERBY, comprising numerous brilliant adventures, thrilling incidents, and interesting speeches and debates. By THOMAS ASPDEN. Published by Messrs. Fiske and Co., London; Mr. John Heywood, Manchester; "Herald" Newspaper Company, Preston and Blackburn. Preston: printed at the "Herald" Office, 120 Fishergate. [1873.] *Post quarto.*

Title as above, Dedication, and Preface, iv. pp. Sketches, 95 pp.

The GREAT STANLEY, or James, viith Earl of Derby, and his noble Countess, Charlotte de la Tremouillé, in their Land of Man. A Narrative to the xvii. Century, interspersed with Notices of Manx Manners, Customs, Laws, Legends, and Fairy Tales. Copiously illustrated from Manx Scenery and Antiquities. [Seal.] By the Rev. J. G. CUMMING, F.G.S., Incumbent of St. John's, Bethnal Green, London, late Warder of Queen's College, Birmingham, and formerly vice-principal of King William's College, Isle of Man. London: William Macintosh, 24 Paternoster Row, E.C. 1867. *Post octavo.*

Title as above, Dedication, and Preface, viii. pp. The Great Stanley, and Notes, 279 pp.

Published at 7s. 6d.

The HISTORY of the HOUSE of STANLEY, including the Sieges of Lathom House, with Notices of the Relative and Cotemporary Incidents, etc. By PETER DRAPER, of "Ormskirk Advertiser." Ormskirk: published by S. Hutton, Church Street. MDCCCLXIV. *Octavo.*

Title as above, and Preface, iv. pp. History and Index, 342 pp.

STEEL ENGRAVINGS.

Old Lathom House.	Portrait of James, 7th Earl of Derby.
Ruins of Burscough Priory.	Charlotte de la Trëmoille.

The STANLEY PAPERS. Part I. Printed for the Chetham Society. MDCCCLIII. *Foolscap quarto.*

Chetham Society's Title (Vol. xxix.), List of Council, Title as above, vi. pp. Second Title as follows, "The EARLS of DERBY and the Verse Writers and Poets of the Sixteenth and Seventeenth Centuries. By THOMAS HEYWOOD, Esq., F.S.A. (Quotation from 'Le Paneygyric de Messire Loys de la Tremouille.') Printed for the Chetham Society, MDCCCLIII." The Earls of Derby, etc., and Index, 63 pp. The Ninth and Tenth Report of the Chetham Society, etc., 5 pp.

PART II.

The DERBY HOUSEHOLD BOOKS. Comprising an Account of the Household Regulations and Expenses of Edward and Henry, Third and Fourth Earls of Derby. Together with a DIARY containing the NAMES of the GUESTS who VISITED the LATTER EARL at his Houses in Lancashire. By WILLIAM FFARINGTON, Esquire, the Comptroller. Edited by the Rev. F. R. RAINES, M.A., F.S.A., Hon. Canon of Manchester, Rural Dean of Rochdale, and Incumbent of Milnrow. Printed for the Chetham Society. MDCCCLIII.

Chetham Society's Title (Vol. xxxi.), List of Council, and Title to 2d Part, v. pp. Title as above, and Introduction, xcviii. pp. Household Expenses, etc., Notes, and Index, 247 pp.

ILLUSTRATIONS.

Frontispiece, Portrait of Edward, Earl of Derby, 1568.
" " Henry, Earl of Derby, 1569.
" " Ferdinand, Earl of Derby, 1590, *facing* p. lxv.
(All with *facsimile* signatures.)

PART III.[1] (VOL. I.)

PRIVATE DEVOTIONS and MISCELLANIES of JAMES, SEVENTH of DERBY, K.G. With a Prefatory MEMOIR and an

[1] The two previous Parts were issued as two volumes of the Chetham Series.

Appendix of Documents. Edited by the Rev. F. R. RAINES, M.A., F.S.A., Honorary Canon of Manchester, Vicar of Milnrow, and Rural Dean.

VOL. I.

Printed for the Chetham Society. MDCCCLXVII.

Chetham Society's Title (Vol. lxvi.), List of Council, Title to 3d Part, and Title as above, vii. pp. Notice, Contents, and List of Plates, xii. pp. (*Corrigenda* slip.) Memoirs of James, seventh Earl, ccviii. pp.

LIST OF PLATES.

Portrait of James, seventh Earl of Derby, *Frontispiece.*
Facsimile of a letter by the Earl . . . . . *To face* p. lxxi.
" " " Countess . . . . " " lxxvi.
The House at Knowsley in the time of Charles the eighth Earl " clx.

PART III. (VOL. II.)

Chetham Society's Title (Vol. lxvii.), List of Council, Title to 3d Part, and Title to Vol. II., 7 pp. Memoirs, ccix. to cccxi. pp. Appendix, ccciii. to cccxcv. pp.

LIST OF ILLUSTRATIONS.

Portrait of the Widowed Countess, *Frontispiece.*
The Derby Chapel in Ormskirk Church . . . *To face* p. ccxl.
The Old Parish Church at Bolton . . . . . " " ccl.
The Chair at which the Earl knelt in prayer on the Scaffold " " ccliii.

PART III. (VOL. III.)

Chetham Society's Title (Vol. lxx.), List of Council, Title to Part III., and Title as above (to Vol. I. Part III.), 8 pp. The Private Devotions, Diary, etc., and Index to the Three Parts, 65 pp.

Frontispiece, Portrait of the Right Revd. Samuel Rutter, D.D., Lord Bishop of Sodor and Man.

The STANLEYS of KNOWSLEY, a HISTORY of that NOBLE FAMILY, including Sketch of the Political and Public Lives of the Right Hon. the Earl of Derby, K.G., and the Right Hon. Lord Stanley, M.P. By WILLIAM POLLARD. Liverpool: Edward Howell, 26 Church Street. 1868. *Post octavo.*

Half-title, Title as above, and Contents, viii. pp. A History, 239 pp.

Frontispiece, Photograph of the Earl of Derby.

Published at 3s. 6d.

SKETCH of the HISTORY of THE HOUSE OF STANLEY and THE HOUSE OF SEFTON. By DAVID ROSS, of the "Liverpool Chronicle." London: W. S. Orr and Co., Paternoster Row. 1848 *Foolscap octavo.*

Title as above, 1 p. Sketch of House of Stanley, 61 pp. Appendix, xviii. pp. Sketch of House of Sefton, 12 pp. Appendix, vi. pp.
Published at 1s.

MEMOIRS; containing a GENEALOGICAL and HISTORICAL ACCOUNT of the Antient and Honourable HOUSE OF STANLEY, from the Conquest to the death of James, late Earl of Derby, in the year 1735; as also a full DESCRIPTION of the ISLE of MAN, etc. By JOHN SEACOME of Liverpool, Gent. Liverpool: printed by A. Sadler. *Post quarto.*

Title as above, Dedication to James, Duke of Athol, and Epistle to the Reader, 6 pp. (unnumbered). Historical Account, 203 pp.

HISTORY OF ISLE OF MAN, Title-page, Introduction, and History, 54 pp. Illustrated with woodcuts of Arms, etc.

This, the 1st Edition of this work, was printed in 1741, and is interesting as being one of the early specimens of the Liverpool Press. Very scarce. Sells for 21s.

A copy is in the Author's Library, which bears the following inscription—"Henry Hatten, his Book, 1741." It was republished without Author's name, Dedication, or Preface, in 1767.

John Seacome, Gentleman, was for several years household steward to the ninth Earl of Derby. The late George Ormerod, author of the "History of Cheshire," says of this author—"His opinions on all points, excepting those of the Civil War, or others subsequent to it, are beneath notice," but that "much is due to him for preserving what he has given, and he disarms criticism by describing his education as narrow and scanty" (*See* "Civil War Tracts").

Seacome's "House of Stanley" has frequently been reprinted, and it has formed the basis of other works on the same subject. The reprints are as follows:—

MANCHESTER: printed by J. Harrop, opposite the Exchange. 1768. *Quarto.*

Title, i. p. Memoirs, 187 pp. Isle of Man, p. 189 to p. 238.

Sells for 12s. It was again issued in 1783.

PRESTON: printed by E. Sergent, in the Market Place. 1793. *Octavo.*

Title, 1 p. Memoirs, etc., 614 pp. Portrait of Edward, Earl of Derby.
Sells for 10s. 6d.

The HISTORY of the HOUSE OF STANLEY, from the Conquest to the death of the Right Honourable Edward, late Earl of Derby, in 1776, containing a Genealogical and Historical Account of that Illustrious House; to which is added a description of the Isle of Man, with a comparative view of the past and present state of Society and Manners, containing also Anecdotes of eminent persons connected with that Island. Manchester: printed and published by J. Gleave, No. 191 Deansgate, and sold by T. Tallis, 16 Warwick Square, London. 1821. *Octavo.*

Title as above, i. p. Contents and History, etc., 209 pp. Appendix, p. 211 to p. 260.

Frontispiece, Portrait of James, Earl of Derby.

Sells for 7s. 6d.

A LIVERPOOL Edition was printed in 1830.

The HISTORY of the Noble HOUSE of STANLEY, from the Conquest to the present time (with considerable additions), containing a Genealogical and Historical Account of that Illustrious House. To which is added a Description of the Isle of Man. Manchester: published and sold by William Willis, at his Wholesale Warehouse, Hanging Ditch and Old Churchyard. 1840. 16*mo.*

Title as above, and Preface, iv. pp. Genealogia, p. v. to p. xii. History of the House, etc., p. 13 to p. 320.

On the last page are "Valedictory Remarks," signed J. Lee, Hulme, Manchester. Sells for 3s. 6d.

An Account of the STANLEY FAMILY will also be found in Peck's "Desiderata Curiosa."

The EARLS of DERBY and the VERSE WRITERS and Poets of the 16th and 17th Centuries. See PART III.

A notice of JAMES, EARL of DERBY, is contained in "ENGLAND'S BLACK TRIBUNAL, set forth in the Trial of King Charles I.," the 1st Edition of which was published in London 1660.

The LADY of LATHAM, being the Life and Original Letters of CHARLOTTE DE LA TRÉMOILLE, Countess of Derby. By WILLIAM GUIZOT DE WITT. With a Portrait. London: Smith, Elder, and Co., 15 Waterloo Place. 1869. The right of Translation reserved. *Octavo.*

Title as above, Contents, and Preface, vii. pp. The Lady of Latham, 299 pp.

Sells for 10s. 6d.

The STANLEY LEGEND, a GENEALOGICAL MEMOIR, illustrative of the early Traditional connection of Boteler of Amounderness, Fitz-Ailward, Lathom, and Stanley. Westminster: printed by J. B. Nichols and Son, 25 Parliament Street. MDCCCXXXIX. *Octavo.*

Title as above, and, on the next page, "The following Memoir, illustrative of some obscure points in Lancashire Genealogy, was written as a contribution to the seventh volume of the Collectanea Topographica et Genealogica. A few copies have been printed in this form for presents to the friends of the author, Geo. Ormerod." 24 pp., including Title.

A very scarce book.

MEMOIRS of the present COUNTESS of DERBY (late Miss Farren), including Anecdotes of several distinguished Persons, particularly the Right Hon. C. J. F——, R. B. S——n, Esq., the Earl of D——y, Lord St—nl—y, the late General Burgoyne, Lord M—t—wn, the late Mr. Parsons, the Duke of R—m—d, Mr. King the actor, Mr. Farren her Ladyship's father, Mrs. Farren her Ladyship's mother, Mrs. Knight her Ladyship's sister, Captain Farren her Ladyship's uncle, George Colman the elder, the late Earl of Chesterfield, Mr. J. Palmer the actor, Mr. Dignum the Shoreditch Prophet, the late Mr. Younger, etc. etc. With a Postscript Extraordinary. By PETRONIUS ARBITER, Esq.

"—— ridenten dicere verum,
Quid vetat?"

London: published by H. D. Symonds, No. 20 Paternoster Row, and to be had of all the Booksellers. [Price 1s. 6d.] *Foolscap quarto.*

Half-title, Title as above, and Dedication, vi. pp. Memoirs, etc., p. 7 to p. 31.

This is the 5th Edition, "with considerable Additions" (a copy of which is in the Author's Library). It was published in or about 1797, and called forth several pamphlets in reply.

The TESTIMONY of TRUTH to exalted Merit, or a BIOGRAPHICAL SKETCH of the RIGHT HONOURABLE The COUNTESS of DERBY, in refutation of a false and scandalous Libel. Third Edition. London: printed and published by George Cawthorn, British Library, No. 132 Strand. 1797. *Quarto.*

Half-title, 1 p. Title as above, and Biographical Sketch, 37 pp.

Frontispiece, Engraved Portrait of the Countess of Derby.

A copy of this Edition is in the Author's Library, and in the Manchester Free Library is a copy of the 2d Edition, published in 1791. We have not met with the 1st Edition. All the Editions are scarce.

The MEMOIRS of the present COUNTESS of DERBY rescued by truth from the assassinating pen of Petronius Arbiter; and proving the stage, from the patronage of the most exalted personages, to have been always considered as a school for morality. The K—, the Q—, Louis XII., Louis XIII., Earl D—y, Lord Ch—n—r, Lord St—y, Molière, the Christ. Missionaries, Julius Cæsar, Empress of Russia, Dutchess D—, Scipio Africanus, Duke of P—r—a, Sophocles, Euripides, Plato, Mr. W—d—d, Augustus Cæsar, Dionysius, Prince Dei—h—n, Bishop Tr—i—no, Cardinal B—ma, Cardinal M—s—n, Cardinal R—l—u, Corneille, An Edict in France, etc. By SCRIPTOR VERITATIS.

"If thou dost marry, I'll give thee this plague for thy dowry. Be thou as chaste as ice, as pure as snow, thou shalt not escape calumny."—HAMLET.

London: printed for the author; and sold by Lee and Hirst, Paternoster Row. 1797. *Octavo.*

Half-title and Title, iv. pp. Memoirs, 80 pp.

A copy is in the Library of J. F. Marsh, Esq., Chepstow.

MEMOIRS of the present COUNTESS of DERBY (Miss Farren) RESCUED by TRUTH from the ASSASSINATING PEN of PETRONIUS ARBITER, and proving the Stage, from the patronage of exalted personages, to have been always considered as a School of Morality. Manchester [n. d.] *Octavo.*

Title, etc., and Memoirs, 84 pp.

An ACCOUNT ot the CHARITIES of the late WILLIAM STRATFORD, LL.D., Commissary of the Archdeaconry of Richmond. Kendal: printed by James Ashburner. MDCCLXVI. *Octavo.*

15 pp.

Dr. Stratford died 7th September 1752, and was buried in St. Mary's Church, Lancaster, where a monument records that it was "his delight to do good, and to distribute."

A SHORT ACCOUNT of MISS MARY TITHERINGTON of Liverpool, with Extracts from her Journal, and a Preface. York. 1819. *Duodecimo.*

Title, etc., 135 pp.

The Rev. Henry Moore (the biographer and executor of the Rev. John Wesley) was the writer of the above. He was born near Dublin in 1751, and died 27th April 1844.

LETTERS of the late JOHN THORP of MANCHESTER, a Minister of the Gospel in the Society of Friends; to which is prefixed a MEMOIR of the LIFE of the WRITER. [Edited by JOHN BRADSHAW.] Liverpool: printed by James and Jonathan Smith for John Bradshaw, Deansgate, Manchester. 1820. *Octavo.*

Title, Letters, and Memoir, 244 pp.

Sells for 3s. 6d.

The Second Edition, with additions, printed in Manchester by Henry Smith for John Bradshaw. *Duodecimo*, 1828.

Reprinted at New York 1821.

John Thorp was not a native of Lancashire (born at Wilmslow, in Cheshire, 1742), but he was long a resident in Manchester, and his Letters contain much of local interest.

The TRIAL and EXECUTION of. COLONEL TOWNLEY, Governor of the City of Carlisle, who was executed for High Treason July 30, 1746. [Arms of Carlisle.] Carlisle: Samuel Jefferson, 34 Scotch Street; and sold by E. Charnley, Newcastle. MDCCCXXXIX. *Crown octavo.*

Title-page as above, and Trial, etc., 31 pp.

Francis Townley was born near Wigan, and was Colonel of the Regiment known as the "Manchester Regiment."

Previously he had served abroad, and held a Colonel's commission from the King of France. He joined the Pretender at Carlisle, and was present at Manchester, Preston, etc. A ballad called "Townley's Ghost" is amongst the "Ballads and Songs of Lancashire," collected by John Harland.

The TYLDESLEY DIARY. Personal Records of THOMAS TYLDESLEY (Grandson of Sir Thomas Tyldesley the Royalist) during the years 1712-13-14, with Introduction, Notes, and Index. By JOSEPH GILLOW and ANTHONY HEWITSON. Illustrated.

> *Hal.* "What hast thou found?
> *Poins.* Nothing but papers, my lord.
> *Hal.* Let's see what they be: read them."

Preston: A. Hewitson, Printer and Publisher, "Chronicle" Office. 1873. *Post quarto.*

Half-title, i. p. Title as above, Map of Lancashire, Introduction, Diary, and Index, 192 pp. Selection from the List of Subscribers, 3 pp.

ILLUSTRATIONS.

Folding Plate of Facsimile of a Page of the Diary.
Foxhall 50 years ago.
Stone in the Wall at Myerscough Lodge, etc.
Carved Chimney-piece at Myerscough Lodge.
Sir Thomas Tyldesley.
Monument to Sir Thomas Tyldesley at Wigan Lane.
Sir Thomas Tyldesley's Sword, etc.
Myerscough Lodge.
Original Entrance to Myerscough Lodge.
Myerscough Lodge (Back View).

Published at 12s. 6d.

EXTRACTS from the DIARY of the REV. PETER WALKDEN, NONCONFORMIST MINISTER, for the years 1725-1729 and 1730, with notes. By WILLIAM DOBSON, Author of "Rambles by the Ribble," "History of the Parliamentary Representation of Preston," etc. Preston: W. and J. Dobson; London, Simpkin, Marshall, and Co. 1866. *Duodecimo.*

Title as above, and Introduction, viii. pp. Extracts, 118 pp.
An interesting bit of local biography.

GVILIELMI WHITAKERI Anglobritanni Lancastriensis, Sacræ Theologiæ Doctoris ac Professoris Regii, celeberrimi Collegii D. Johannis Euangelistæ in Cantebrigiensi Academia prudentissimi Præfecti. Opera Theologica Dvobvs tomis nunc primum collecta. Svbivncta est ad primi Tomi finem de AUCTORIS VITA & MORTE DESCRIPTIO. * * * Tomvs Primvs. Genevæ: Svmptibvs samvelis Crispini. MDCX. *Folio.*

VOL. I.

Title as above, Præfatio, et Index, xxx. pp. Opera et Vita, 714 pp.

VOL. II.

Title and Præfatio, xii. pp. Opera, 805 pp. Index, xvii. pp.
A copy of this rare book is in the Chetham Library.
A short sketch of the LIFE of Dr. W. WHITAKER, taken from the above, is contained in "A REMEMBRANCER of EXCELLENT MEN." London: printed for John Martyn, at the Bell, without Temple Bar. 1670.

DOCUMENTS relating to THE WINKLEY FAMILY, collected by WILLIAM WINKLEY JUN., F.S.A. Printed at the Harrow Press. *Octavo.*

Title as above, and Winkley Family, 10 pp. Copies of Wills, 44 pp., only printed on one side of each leaf, and 7 Pedigrees. One folding Pedigree printed separate as an Addendum.

The DIARY and CORRESPONDENCE of Dr. JOHN WORTHINGTON, Master of Jesus College, Cambridge, Vice-Chancellor of the University of Cambridge, etc. etc. From the Baker MSS. in the British Museum and the Cambridge University Library, and other Sources. Edited by JAMES CROSSLEY, Esq.

VOL. I.

Printed for the Chetham Society. MDCCCXLVII. *Foolscap quarto.*

Chetham Society's Title (Vol. xiii.), and List of Council, 3 pp. Title as above, and Preface, viii. pp. Diary and Correspondence and Index, 398 pp.

VOL. II. PART I.

Chetham Society's Title (Vol. xxxvi.), and List of Council, 3 pp. Title, i. p. Additions and Errata, on a slip. Diary and Correspondence 248 pp.

The 11th and 12th Reports of the Society, etc., 8 pp.

Where there's a Will there's a Way; or Science in the Cottage. An account of the LABOURS of NATURALISTS in HUMBLE LIFE. By JAMES CASH. London: Robert Hardwicke, 192 Piccadilly. 1873. *Duodecimo.*

Title as above, Preface, and Contents, vi. pp. Where there's a Will, etc., 224 pp.

Published at 3s. 6d.

Contains notices of the following Lancashire Botanists, viz.—John Dewhurst; George Caley; Edward Hobson; John Horsefield of Prestwich; John Crowther of Manchester; John Mellor of Royton; Richard Baxter of Manchester; John Martin of Tyldesley; George Crozier; Thomas Townley of Manchester; John Just and William Wilson.

For Notices of distinguished Lancashire Roman Catholics, see Dodd's "Church History of England. Brussels, 1737." "History of the English Priests of Doway from 1568-1713." "Concertatio Ecclesiæ Catholicæ. By JOAN AQUEPONTANUS." [Bridgewater]. Treves, 1588-1594. Challoner's "Memoirs of Missionary Priests and other Catholics of both Sexes that have suffered Death in England on religious accounts for the years 1577 to 1684." The latter contains a Plate of the Leading to Execution of Arrowsmith from Lancaster Castle.

PART III.

POETRY, FICTION, AND MISCELLANY.[1]

The LANCASHIRE WITCHES, a ROMANCE of PENDLE FOREST. By WILLIAM HARRISON AINSWORTH.

Sir Jeffery —"Is there a justice in Lancashire has so much skill in witches as I have? Nay, I'll speak a proud word, you shall turn me loose against any Witchfinder in Europe. I'd make an ass of Hopkins if he were alive."—SHADWELL.

In three Volumes.

VOL. I.

The author reserves to himself the right of issuing a German Translation in Prussia. London: Henry Colburn, Publisher, Great Marlborough Street. 1849. *Post octavo.*

Title as above, i. p. Half-title and Contents, iv. pp. The Lancashire Witches, 320 pp.

VOL. II.

Title, i. p. Half-title and Contents, iv. pp. The Lancashire Witches, 318 pp.

VOL. III.

Title, i. p. Half-title and Contents, iv. pp. The Lancashire Witches, 359 pp.

First published in 1848 at 31s. 6d. Has been several times re-issued. An *octavo* Edition at 2s., and an illustrated *octavo* at 6s.

The GOOD OLD TIMES: the STORY of the MANCHESTER REBELS of '45. By WILLIAM HARRISON AINSWORTH, Author of

[1] Books written by Lancashire men, but which in no way refer to the County, are not included in our list.

"Boscobel," "Tower of London," etc. etc. [Quotation 4 lines from Shenstone.] In three Volumes.

VOL. I.

London: Tinsley Brothers, 18 Catherine Street, Strand. 1873. (Right of Translation reserved by the Author.) *Post octavo.*

Title as above, Dedication, and Contents, viii. pp. Title to Book I., and The Good Old Times, 287 pp.

VOL. II.

Title and Contents, vi. pp. Title to Book II., and The Good Old Times, 288 pp.

VOL. III.

Title and Contents, vi. pp. Title to Book III., and The Good Old Times, 275 pp.

Published at 31s. 6d.

Republished in 1874 in one Volume, *post octavo,* by Tinsley Brothers, under the Title of "The MANCHESTER REBELS of the FATAL '45."

ALEXIS; or the Worthy Unfortunate. Being a TRUE NARRATIVE of the Affecting Case of a YOUNG GENTLEMAN whose Ruin was occasioned by the late REBELLION. [Quotation 2 lines VIRG. ÆN.] London: printed for J. Cobham, New St. Pauls. MDCCXLVII. *Octavo.*

Title as above, and Alexis, 114 pp.

This scarce volume refers to the passing of the Pretender through Lancashire. It is written in the form of Letters from "Mr. J—n L—r—nce at Manchester to Mr. H—n—y L—r—nce in London." The first is dated Manchester, 1745.

A copy is in the British Museum.

IRWELL, and other POEMS. By A. Dedicated to Charles Swain. London: Longman and Co.; Manchester: T. Sowler, Simms and Denham. 1843. *Duodecimo.*

Title as above, Dedication, and Preface, vi. pp. Half-title, i. p. Irwell, etc., 58 pp.

The above scarce poem was written by Joseph Anthony, who then lived in King Street, Salford.

This work is in the Manchester Free Library.

STRANGE TALES from HUMBLE LIFE.

"The poor ye have always with you."

First and Second Series. Manchester: Tubbs and Brook, 11 Market Street; London, Simpkin, Marshall, and Co., Hamilton, Adams, and Co., and Fred. Pitman. (All rights reserved.) *Foolscap octavo.*

Title as above, Preface, and Contents, iv. pp. Tales, 360 pp.

Published in 1865 at 3s. and 4s. Queen's Edition (with Plates), 6s. and 9s. 6d.

THE THIRD AND FOURTH SERIES.

Title, etc., iv. pp. Strange Tales, 344 pp.

Published in 1867 at the same price as above.

THE FIFTH SERIES.

Title, etc., iv. pp. Strange Tales, 172 pp. Published in 1874 at 1s. 6d.

Several of these Tales have been published in Swedish, German, and French. The Tales for the most part refer to Lancashire people. A very large number of these in the tract form have been sold.

SIMPLE RECORDS by JOHN ASHWORTH, Author of "Strange Tales," "Walks in Canaan," etc. First and Second Series, 10,000. Manchester: Tubbs and Brook, 11 Market Street; London, Simpkin, Marshall, and Co., etc. *Foolscap octavo.*

Title as above, Preface, and Contents, iv. pp. Records, 328 pp.

Frontispiece, "Edward's Grave."

Published at 3s. and 4s.

The above only in part refers to Lancashire.

John Ashworth was born on the 8th July 1813 at Cutgate, Rochdale. His parents were hand-loom woollen weavers, and he for some years followed the same occupation. He subsequently learned the trade of a house-painter, and continued in that business until about 1866, when he devoted himself entirely to Missionary labour amongst the poor. In 1858 he established in Rochdale a "Chapel for the Destitute," where he ministered until 1874, when his health failed him. He died at Rochdale 26th January 1875.

The FOLK SONG and FOLK SPEECH of LANCASHIRE on the Ballad and Songs of the County Palatine, with Notes on the Dialect in which many of them are written, and an Appendix on Lancashire Folk Lore. By WILLIAM E. A. AXON, F.R.S.L., Author of "The Literature of the Lancashire Dialect, a Bibliographical Essay," "The Black Knight of Ashton," etc. Manchester: Tubbs and Brook, 11 Market Street. *Duodecimo.*

Half-title, List of Works by the same author, Title as above, Dedication, and Preface, vii. pp. Folk Song, p. 9 to p. 94. Index, 2 pp.

The UPLAND HALL; or, a Tale of other Times. By R. R. B. Rochdale: Aldis and Pearson, Printers, 96 Yorkshire Street. [186–.]

Title as above, and Preface, v. pp. Upland Hall, 57 pp.
This is a Rochdale tale.

MISCELLANEOUS POETRY. By SAMUEL BAMFORD, Weaver ot Middleton, Lancashire, lately imprisoned in the Castle of Lincoln.

"Even late in prison did I write
(This is the fifth in which I've lain)
Not for infringing any right;
No person's property I've ta'en,
Ask you the reason then—'tis plain
I did escape upon that day
When many of my friends were slain,
And many sorely wounded lay
Gasping in their strong agony."

London: printed and published by T. Dolby at the Britannia Press, 299 Strand. Price 2s. 6d., extra Boards. *Post octavo.*

Title as above, Preface, and Contents, vi. pp. Poems, 102 pp.
Amongst other local poems are "The Lancashire Hymn, "Oldham Local," "Touch Him" and "Ode to a Plotting Parson." On the cover of this book, which is very scarce, is an emblematical woodcut by G. Cruikshank.
A copy is in the Author's Library. The Preface is dated 1821.

HOURS in the BOWERS. Poems, etc. By SAMUEL BAMFORD. Manchester: printed for the Author by J. P. Jennings and H. Cowdroy, Market Place. 1834. *Octavo.*

Title as above, Preface, Poems, and Contents, 96 pp.

Contains several local poems.

Another Edition, with slightly altered Title, appeared in 1843.

HOMELY RHYMES. Poems and Reminiscences of SAMUEL BAMFORD. Revised and Enlarged Edition. London: Simpkin, Marshall, and Co.; Manchester, A. Ireland and Co. 1864. *Post octavo.*

Title as above, Notice, and Contents, viii. pp. Reminiscences, Poems, and Glossary, 248 pp.

Frontispiece, Portrait of Author.

This is a reprint (with additions) of the Edition of 1843.

POETIC TALES and Miscellanies.

> "'Tis best sometimes your censure to restrain
> And charitably let the dull be vain."—POPE.

Liverpool: printed by James Smith; sold by William Robinson, Castle Street; also by Longman, Hurst, Rees, Orme, and Brown, London. 1812. *Octavo.*

Title as above and Contents, iv. pp. Introductory Lines (signed MARY BISHOP, Liverpool, February 1812), and Poems, 151 pp. Note, 1 p.

One of the miscellaneous poems is entitled "The Ribble," and the book is sometimes sold as "Poetic Tales of the Ribble."

Sells for 2s. 6d.

GREENFIELD, a Poem. Saddleworth, near Manchester. *Duodecimo.*

Engraved Title. *Frontispiece.* Title as above, and Advertisement, vi. pp. Poem, p. 3 to p. 21. Historical Sketch of Saddleworth, p. 23 to p. 64. Illustrated with views of Greenfield. Eight steel engravings.

Written by Mr. Bottomley of Saddleworth. A copy is in the Manchester Free Library.

The TWO LANCASHIRE LOVERS; or the Excellent History of Philocles and Doricles. Expressing the faithful constancy and mutual fidelity of two loyall lovers, stored with no lesse variety of discourse to delight the generous, than of serious advice to instruct the amorous. Pereo si taceo. By MUSÆUS PALATINUS [R. Braithwait]. London: printed by Edward Griffin, for R. B., or his Assignes. 1640. *Octavo.*

Title, Dedication, Argument, and the Two Lancashire, etc., 268 pp. Contains an Engraved Title and a print at p. 246. The Dedication is to "My truly generous and Iudiciovs Friend Alexander Rigby, Esq., Clarke of the Crowne for the Co. Palatine of Lancaster, signed Alexandrophilus."

Very rare. Sells for £3.

There are other copies bearing the same date, and only differing in the imprint on the Title, which is "Printed by E. G. for R. Best, and are to be sould at his shop neare Graies Inn gate in Houlburne."

TALES and SKETCHES of LANCASHIRE LIFE. By BENJAMIN BRIERLEY (vignette of Daisy Nook). Manchester: John Heywood, 143 Deansgate; London: Simpkin, Marshall, and Co.

Title as above, 1 p. Contents and Tales, 256 pp.

VOL. II.

Title (vignette of Daisy Nook), Contents, Tales, Glossary, and Opinions of the Press, 258 pp.

The two volumes sell for 3s. 6d.

MARLOCKS of MERRITON. By BENJAMIN BRIERLEY. London: Simpkin, Marshall and Co.; Manchester: John Heywood, 141 and 143 Deansgate.

Title as above, Contents, and Marlocks of Merriton, 262 pp.

IRKDALE; or the old house in the Hollow. A Lancashire Story. By BENJAMIN BRIERLEY. Manchester: John Heywood, 141 and 143 Deansgate. London: Simpkin, Marshall, and Co. 1868. 12*mo.*

Title as above, and Irkdale, 275 pp.

This has gone through several editions. 1865, 2 vols. *post octavo,* 21s. A 12*mo* Edition by Tinsley was published at 2s.

AB-O'-TH-YATE on Times and Things. Edited by BENJAMIN BRIERLEY. London : Simpkin, Marshall, and Co.; Manchester: John Heywood, 141 and 143 Deansgate. [1868.]

Title as above, Contents, and By the Way, xii. pp. Ab-o'-th-Yate, 132 pp.

Published at 1s.

ROCHER VALE. A Poem by JAMES BUTTERWORTH. MDCCCIV. *Duodecimo.*

Half-title, Title as above, and Poem, 15 pp.

Scarce. A copy is in the Manchester Free Library.

The RUSTIC MUSE, a Collection of Poems. By J. BUTTERWORTH. Oldham: printed and sold by J. Clarke, Market Place. Sold also by the Author. 1818. *Duodecimo.*

Half-title, Title as above, Dedication, Preface, Title-page to Rocher Vale, and Rustic Muse, 70 pp.

Frontispiece, View of Rocher Vale as it appeared when the Poem was written, taken from Lilly's Nook.

The Poems mostly refer to Lancashire scenes. A copy is in the Manchester Free Library.

The MAYOR of WIGAN, a Tale. To which is added The Invasion, a Fable. By HILLARY BUTLER, Esq.

Α'ΣΚΕ'ΠΤ'ΟΣ.

London: printed for Messrs. Owen, Temple Bar; Wilcox, in the Strand; Davis, in Piccadilly; and John Child, at the Lamb, in Paternoster Row. MDCCLX. *Octavo.*

Half-title, and Title as above, iv. pp. The Mayor of Wigan, etc., 40 pp.

Very scarce. There is a copy in the British Museum.

Published at 1s.

MISCELLANEOUS POEMS by JOHN BYROM, M.A., F.R.S., sometime Fellow of Trinity College, Cambridge, and Inventor of the Universal English Short-hand. In two volumes. Manchester: printed by J. Harrop. MDCCLXXIII. *Octavo.*

VOL. I.

Half-title, and Title as above, ii. pp. Preface, and Contents, vi. pp. Poems, etc., 352 pp.

Frontispiece, Portrait of the Author, engraved by Topham, from an original Sketch by D. Rasbotham, Esq.

VOL. II.

Half-title, Errata, and Title, iii. pp. Contents, vi. pp. Poems, etc., 353 pp.

Many of these poems refer to Manchester.

Published at 10s.

MISCELLANEOUS POEMS. By JOHN BYROM, M.A., F.R.S., sometime Fellow of Trinity College, Cambridge, and Inventor of the Universal English Short-hand. To which are added his Life, and Notes, by the Editor. In two volumes.

VOL. I.

Leeds: printed by and for James Nichols; and sold in London by Cradock and Co., etc. etc.[1] 1814. *Octavo.*

Title as above, Preface, Advertisement, and The Life, xxiv. pp. Contents, and Errata, 2 pp. Poems, 246 pp.

Frontispiece, Portrait as in the Edition of 1773.

VOL. II.

Title, and Contents, iv. pp. Poems, 224 pp.

Published at 12s. Sells for 7s. 6d.

SKETCHES from LIFE—

I. Alice Jevons.

II. The Heiress of Hallstead.

By WILLIAM BYROM. London: published for the Author by Arthur Hall, Virtue, and Co., 25 Paternoster Row. 1852. *Post octavo.*

Title as above, and Preface, iii. pp. Sketches, 156 pp.

[1] A long list here follows.

ODES and MISCELLANIES by ROBERT FARREN CHETHAM. [Quotation 5 lines.] Printed by J. Clarke; sold by Champante and Whitrow, London. 1796.

Title as above, Dedication "to Charles Lawson, A.M., Head Master of the Free Grammar School, Manchester," Letter to C. Lawson, and List of Subscribers, xii. pp. Odes, 184 pp. Errata, 1 p.

Sells for 5s. 6d.

The Subscribers' list contains the names and addresses of many Lancashire people, but the Odes cannot, strictly speaking, be said to refer to the County.

The copy in the Rochdale Free Public Library contains an MS. letter from the author to Lord Folkestone asking his acceptance of "these trifles of a juvenile mind."

Robert Farren was the son of Jonathan Chetham, flour merchant of Stockport. He was educated at the Manchester Free Grammar School, and graduated B.A. at Brazenose College, Oxford, in 1800. He died 13th January 1801, aged 23 years. A small collection of his poems was published in 1795 under the Title of "Poems by Μαθητης."

The SCHOOL CANDIDATES, a Prosaic Burlesque: occasioned by the late Election of a Schoolmaster at the Village of Bondinnoir. [Here follows a quotation from the Dunciad.] Utopia. Printed in the year 1788. [By HENRY CLARKE of Salford.] 18*mo.*

Title as above, etc., ii. pp. School Candidates, 103 pp. A Plate called "An Horoscopical Figure of the Heavens for the Lat. of Bondinnoir, 53° 25′ N. Long. W. of the Royal Observatory of Utopia, 2° 29′, on Friday, Jan. 18th, 1788, at 4 H. P.M. A.T." Two Churches of Manchester; also the Cock Inn, and a Schoolhouse in the foreground.

A copy of this very rare work is in the Library of Mr. J. E. Bailey of Stratford (the author of the Life of Fuller), who is about to republish it. A copy is in the Manchester Free Library, dated 1792.

The Village of Bondinnoir is the Village of Stretford.

Henry Clark wrote "Practical Perspective," 1776. "The Rationale of Circulating Numbers," 1777, and several other pamphlets, copies of which are in the Chetham Library.

A VIEW of the LANCASHIRE DIALECT by way of Dialogue between TUMMUS O WILLIAMS O MARGITS O ROAPHS and MEARY O DICKS O TUMMUS O PEGGYS. To which is added a Glossary of all the Lancashire words and Phrases therein used. By T. BOBBIN, opp'n speyker o' the dialect.

" Heaw arse wood wur I, eh this wark !
Glooar at monny a buk."

Manchester : sold by R. Whitworth, Bookseller; and sold by Mr. Meadows, at the Angel, in Cornhill, London ; Mr. Higginson, Warrington ; Mr. Scolfield, Rochdale ; Mr. Milner, Halifax ; —— Wakefield ; —— Leeds ; Mr. Wilkinson, Printer, Rippenden ; and Mr. William Taylor, Oldham.

This is the Title-page of the First Edition, which is believed to have been published in 1746, and contained 32 pp. 12mo. It was noticed in the "Gentleman's Magazine" (vol. xvi. pp. 527). A copy of it is in the Portico Library, Manchester.

The success of this work induced several printers to issue spurious Editions, and it is now impossible to tell which are the ones authorised by the author. The following Editions have appeared :[1]—

A VIEW of the LANCASHIRE DIALECT by way of Dialogue, etc. etc. Second Edition. Leeds [n. d]. *Duodecimo.*

The Third Edition we have not seen.

* A VIEW of the LANCASHIRE DIALECT, etc., to which is prefixed a Dialogue between the Author and his pamphlet. By TIM BOBBIN, Fellow of the Sisyphian Society of Dutch Loom weavers. The Fourth Edition, corrected and improved, with an addition of above five hundred Lancashire words not in the first impression. 18*mo.*

Title, etc., 32 pp., exclusive of Glossary.

This is a pirated edition, and was printed for J. Robinson, London, and W. Stuart, Wigan. [1750.] Price 6d.

A copy is in the library of the late Dr. Buckley of Rochdale.

The genuine Fourth Edition was published in London, in *duodecimo*, price 6d. [1750.] *See* "The Quack Doctor, a Poem." *Post.*

Scarce. Sells for 7s. 6d.

The Fifth Edition we have not seen.

[1] The Editions marked * are not included in Mr. J. P. Briscoe's Pamphlet, "The Literature of Tim Bobbin. Manchester, 1872."

A VIEW of the LANCASHIRE DIALECT, etc., showing in that speech the comical adventures and misfortunes of a Lancashire clown. To which is prefixed (by way of Preface) a Dialogue between the Author and his Pamphlet, with a few observations for the better pronunciation of the Dialect; with a Glossary, etc. By TIM BOBBIN, Fellow of the Sisyphian Society of Dutch Loom weavers, and an old adept of the dialect [here follows motto as on First Edition]. The Sixth Edition, in which will be several alterations and new adventures, and above eight hundred Lancashire words that never were in any of the five first impressions. Manchester: printed and sold by Joseph Harrop; and by all the Booksellers throughout England and Wales. 1757. *Duodecimo.*

Title as above, and Observations to the Reader, xiii. pp. Dialogue, 51 pp. Glossary, 55 pp. Errata, 1 p.

Contains a rude etching of "Tummus and Meary," "Tim. Bob. inv. et sculp." Scarce. A copy is in the Manchester Free Library. It contains an advertisement stating that the Editions of "Stuart of Preston, Robinson of the Golden Lion, London, Finch of Wigan, and Schofield of Middlewich (the two lately published) are all spurious."

TIM BOBBIN'S TOY SHOP OPEN'D; or his Whimsical Amusements, containing his VIEW of the LANCASHIRE DIALECT, with a large Glossary, etc. The Poem of the Black Bird; or, The Whistling Angel. The Goose; a Poem. By an unknown hand. Corrected by T. B. Etc. etc. Embellished with Copper-plates [three] designed by the author, and engraved by Mr. Barlow of Bolton. Manchester: printed and sold by Joseph Harrop, and by the Booksellers, etc. 1763. *Duodecimo.*

Title, Observations, etc., xiii. pp. Dialogue, etc., 172 pp.

Sells for 15s. A copy is in the Manchester Free Library.

The MISCELLANEOUS WORKS of Tim Bobbin, containing his View of the Lancashire Dialect, etc. Also his Poem of the Flying Dragon, and the Man of Heaton, etc. London: printed and sold in Paternoster Row, and by the Booksellers in Lancashire. 1770. *Duodecimo.*

Title, etc., 39 pp. Glossary, 34 pp.

Sells for 10s. 6d. A copy of this is in the Rochdale Free Public Library.

* Another Edition of the VIEW of the LANCASHIRE DIALECT is mentioned by J. C. Hotten in his Handbook of Topography, etc. Printed in 1773 with Portraits.

A VIEW of the LANCASHIRE DIALECT, with Glossary. By Tummus a Williams, etc. London: printed for the Booksellers. MDCCLXXV. *Octavo.*

Title, etc., 38 pp. Glossary (unpaged), 34 pp.

A copy is in the library of the late Dr. Buckley of Rochdale.

The MISCELLANEOUS WORKS of Tim Bobbin, Esq., consisting of the Lancashire Dialect, with large additions and improvements; also his Poem of the Flying Dragon, and the Man of Heaton, etc. Embellished with eleven Copperplates. Printed for the author and Mr. Haslingden in Manchester, 1775. *Octavo.*

Title, etc., 203 pp. Flying Dragon, 32 pp.

Sells for 10s. It was published at 2s.

Another Edition was published in Manchester in the same year, in two parts. Portraits and Plates. *Duodecimo.*

This is also scarce.

* A VIEW of the LANCASHIRE DIALECT, with Glossary, etc., was published in 1789. Printed for the Booksellers. *Small octavo.* Title, etc., and Dialect, 166 pp. Sells for 7s. 6d.

The MISCELLANEOUS WORKS, etc. Embellished with Ten Copperplates. Manchester: printed for J. Haslingden. 1793. (In two parts.) *Octavo.*

This is the 1775 Edition, with new Title-page.
Sells for 10s. 6d.

* The MISCELLANEOUS WORKS, etc. Manchester, n.d. [17—]. No Plates.

A VIEW of the DIALECT, etc. Printed for the Booksellers. 1797. *Duodecimo.*

Title, etc., 58 pp. Glossary, 14 pp.
A copy of this is in the Rochdale Free Public Library.

A VIEW of the LANCASHIRE DIALECT, etc. London. 1798. *Duodecimo.*

*A View of the Lancashire Dialect, etc. Liverpool: printed and sold by T. Schofield, No. 168 Dale Street. 1802. *Duodecimo.*
Title, Dialogue, and Glossary, 48 pp.

The MISCELLANEOUS WORKS, etc., with Ten Copper Plates. London: printed for J. Haslingden. 1803. *Post octavo.* Sells for 7s. 6d.

A reprint of the 1775 Edition, with Life of the Author by Townley added.

Sells for 7s. 6d. A copy of this Edition is in the Library of Dr. Kendrick, Warrington.

* A VIEW of the LANCASHIRE DIALECT, etc. To which is added the Flying Dragon, etc. Warrington: printed and sold by J. Haddock, Horse Market. 1803.

Title, etc., 58 pp. Glossary, 12 pp.
A copy of this Edition is in the Library of W. H. Rylands, Esq., of Thelwall, near Warrington.

The MISCELLANEOUS WORKS, etc. To which is added a Life of the Author by Richard Townley, Esq. Embellished with Ten Copper-plates. London. 1806. *Duodecimo.*

In three parts. Sells for 6s. 6d. A copy is in the Manchester Free Library.

The MISCELLANEOUS WORKS, etc. Salford. 1811. *Octavo.*

Title, etc., and Works, 240 pp. Again printed in Salford by Cowdroy and Slack. 1812.
These two editions are scarce.

The MISCELLANEOUS WORKS, etc. With a Life by Richard Townley. Embellished with 10 Copperplates. London: printed for T. & J. Allman. 1818. *Duodecimo.*

Title, etc., xxiii. pp. Works, etc., 212 pp. Sells for 10s. 6d.

The WORKS of TIM BOBBIN, Esq., in Prose and Verse. With a Memoir of the Author. By JOHN CORRY. Rochdale : printed for and sold by J. Westall. 1819. *Octavo.*

Title as above, i. p. Contents, iii. pp. Memoir, 2d Title, Observations, and Address, xxix. pp. Works, 494 pp. Eleven Plates.

This is the first Edition which contained the whole of his Works, and is considered the best. Sells for £1. Large paper copies sometimes fetch a much higher price in consequence of a belief that only two such copies were printed. The number of large paper copies was very small, but certainly more than two were printed.

* A VIEW of the LANCASHIRE DIALECT, etc., with Glossary. Rochdale : printed by J. Littlewood for J. Westell [*sic.*] *Octavo.* Price 2s.

This appears to be a reprint of part of the above Edition. After the Title comes the 2d Title and the Observations, which is paged xxi. The pagination then runs on to p. 96 of the collected Works.

The MISCELLANEOUS WORKS, etc. Manchester : printed by J. Slack for T. Sowler, St. Ann's Square. 1820. *Demy octavo.*

Title, etc., and Works, 226 pp. Nineteen Illustrations, executed by J. Slack.

* The LANCASHIRE DIALECT, etc. Preston : printed and sold by L. Clarke, 143 Church Street. 1822. *Foolscap octavo.*

Title, etc., and Dialect, 36 pp. A rude Woodcut of "Tummus and Meary."

The FIRST (2nd) PART of TUMMUS and MEARY, being a VIEW, etc. Manchester : [*circa* 1825.] *Duodecimo.*

A copy is in the British Museum.

TIM BOBBIN'S LANCASHIRE DIALECT and POEMS. Rendered intelligible to general readers by a literal interpretation, and the obsolete words explained by quotations from the most early of the English Writers. London : Hurst, Chance, and Co. 1828. *Foolscap octavo.*

Title, etc., viii. pp. Dialect, etc 184. Five Plates by Cruikshank.
Sells for 12s. 6d.
Reprinted in 1833 by Orlando Hodgson, London.
Sells for 10s. 6d.

The LANCASHIRE DIALECT, etc. To which is added Lancashire Hob and the Quack Doctor, etc. etc. Manchester: William Willis, Old Church Yard. 1839. *Duodecimo.*

Title, etc, 36 pp. *Frontispiece.*

The LANCASHIRE DIALECT, etc., with Glossary. Leeds. 1847. *Duodecimo.*

Title, etc., and Dialect. 47 pp.

DIALECT of SOUTH LANCASHIRE, or TIM BOBBIN'S TUMMUS and MEARY, revised and corrected, with his Rhymes, and an enlarged and amended Glossary. By SAMUEL BAMFORD. Manchester. 1850. *Duodecimo.*

Title, etc., xxiv. pp. Dialect, etc., 241 pp.

Published at 3s. 6d.

The DIALECT of SOUTH LANCASHIRE, etc., 2d Edition. 1854. By SAMUEL BAMFORD. London: J. R. Smith, Soho Square. Title, etc., xxii. pp. Dialect, etc., 266 pp. *Duodecimo.*

Published at 3s. 6d.

The LANCASHIRE DIALECT, etc., with explanatory Notes, etc., by ELIJAH RIDINGS. Manchester: J. Heywood. [1857.] *Octavo.*

Reprinted in 1859. The Engravings are from the original Plates of the 1773 Edition.

The WORKS of TIM BOBBIN, etc., with Memoir by JOHN CORRY. To which is added a rendering into simple English of the Dialogue, etc., with the Idioms and Similes retained, and explanatory Notes, etc. By ELIJAH RIDINGS. Manchester: J. Heywood. 1862. *Royal octavo.* (Illustrated.)

Title, etc., xxxix. pp. Works, etc., p. 40 to p. 534.

Published at 7s. 6d. Large paper, 21s.

This is substantially a Reprint of the 1819 Edition, with the addition of "The Dialogue" rendered into modern English. The same Plates are used.

The LANCASHIRE DIALECT, the Battle of the Flying Dragon, etc. Reprinted from the original Edition. Manchester. [1862.] 16*mo.*

The WORKS of TIM BOBBIN. Manchester: Abel Heywood. [1865.] Price 6d.

The following are without date :—

MISCELLANEOUS WORKS. London. 16*mo.*

Title, etc., and Works, 166 pp.

The POETICAL WORKS of TIM BOBBIN. Leeds and Manchester. *Octavo.*

Title, etc., and Works, 30 pp. Price 1d.

* Illustrated Edition. The LANCASHIRE DIALECT, etc. etc. London: printed and published for the Booksellers. *Post octavo.*

Title, etc., and Works, 36 pp. Glossary, 35 pp. Price 1s.

The Plates (5) are printed on yellow paper.

TUMMUS and MEARY Modernized, etc. Adapted for Public Reading. Manchester. *Octavo.* Price 3d.

LIFE and WORKS. Leeds. *Octavo.*
Title, etc., and Works, 30 pp. Price 1d.

* The LANCASHIRE DIALECT, etc. etc. A New Edition, to which is added a Glossary, etc. London: printed by and for William Cole, No. 10 Newgate Street.

A *Frontispiece* in five compartments.

The LANCASHIRE DIALECT, etc. London: published for the Booksellers by Walker, Otley; Richardson, Derby; Johnson and Heyood,[1] Manchester. Price 6d. *Duodecimo.*

Title, etc., 54 pp. Frontispiece. Woodcut.

[1] On the cover this is "Heywood."

* The MISCELLANEOUS WORKS of TIM BOBBIN, Esq., containing his view of the Lancashire Dialect, with large additions and Improvements, also his Poems, etc. * * Together with other whimsical Amusements in Prose and Verse, some of which were never before published. London: printed for A. Millar, W. Law, and R. Carter, and for Wilson, Spence, and Mawman, York. *Duodecimo.*

Title, Observation, To the Reader, and Works, 666 pp.

Frontispiece, Portrait of Author.
A copy of this is in the Library of the late Dr Buckley, Rochdale.

* The LANCASHIRE DIALECT, etc. To which is added a Glossary, etc. A New Edition, carefully revised and corrected. Embellished with a humorous Frontispiece. Manchester: printed by Hopper and Son, Market Place, and sold by Graham, Thomas, Reddish, Clarke, and Banks, Manchester; Gedge and New, London. *Octavo.*

Title, etc., 129 pp.

Frontispiece, Hob and the Quack Doctor.

* The MISCELLANEOUS WORK, etc. Embellished with Copperplates. Manchester: printed for Hopper and Son. 18*mo.*
Engraved Title, 2 pp. Title, Observation, etc., xii. pp. Works, 204 pp.

Published at 1s. 6d.
A copy is in the Library of the late Dr. Buckley of Rochdale.

* TIM BOBBIN'S TALES, or THOMAS and MARY, rendered into simple English, with the idioms and similes retained. From the original vernacular of John Collier, *alias* Tim Bobbin, Esq. By ELIJAH RIDINGS, author of the "Village Muse," etc. Manchester: James Ainsworth, 93 Piccadilly. *Post octavo.*

Title, etc. 56 pp.

TRUTH in a MASK, or SHUDE-HILL FIGHT, being a short MANCHESTER CHRONICLE of the present Times. Amsterdam: printed in the year 1757. Price 4d. *Duodecimo.*

Title as above, and To the Reader, iv. pp. Truth in a Mask, etc. p. 5 to p. 31.

Written by "Tim Bobbin," and included in his collected Works. Reprinted, Manchester. 1815.

A copy of the original edition is in the Library of Richard Wood, Esq., Manchester.

The FORTUNE TELLER, or the COURT ITCH at LITTLEBOROUGH. By TIM BOBBIN. Published 1771.

Very scarce. Not in his collected works.

The whole of John Collier's MSS., together with his Family Bible, which contains a pedigree of the family, was presented by Canon Raines to the Chetham Library.

A SEQUEL to the LANCASHIRE DIALECT, or part second of the adventures, misfortunes, and losses of a Lancashire Clown. By PAUL BOBBIN, Cousin-German of the famous Tim Bobbin of Merry Memory. Manchester: printed and published by M. Wilson, Barlow's Court, Market Street; sold by John Thomson, 24 Market Street, Messrs. Clarkes, Market Place, and most Booksellers in Town and Country. 1819. *Duodecimo.*

Title as above, and Dialect, 46 pp.

Frontispiece, Portrait of Paul Bobbin, Esq.

JAMES BUTTERWORTH, the author of History of Oldham, etc., was the writer of the above. A copy is in the Manchester Free Library.

Under the same nom-de-plume he published a selection of poems called "A Dish of Hodge Podge."

BEWSEY. A POEM. By JOHN FITCHETT.

> " Laudo ruris amoeni
> Rivos et musco circumlita saxa nemusque."
> " Hor. Ep." x. lib. i.

Warrington: printed by W. Eyres for J. Johnson, No. 73 St. Paul's Church Yard, London. MDCCXCVI. *Folio.*

Title as above, Dedication, and Subscribers' Names, xi. pp. Poems, 32 pp.

A copy is in the Warrington Public Library.

John Fitchett was born in Liverpool 21st September 1776. He practised for many years as a solicitor at Warrington, where he died 20th

October 1838. He published "King Alfred, an epic Poem," and a volume of "Minor Poems."

MARY BARTON. A TALE of MANCHESTER LIFE. By Mrs. GASKELL, Author of "Ruth," "Wives and Daughters," "Sylvia's Lovers," etc. etc. Tenth Edition. London: Chapman and Hall, 193 Piccadilly. 1866. *Duodecimo.*

Half-title, and Title as above, iv. pp. Mary Barton, 323 pp.

Published at 2s.

Other Editions, 2 Volumes, *octavo*, 18s., in 1848. One Volume, 12*mo*, 1861, 2s.

The VICISSITUDES of COMMERCE. A TALE of the COTTON TRADE. [4 lines of poetry.] In two volumes.

Vol. I.

London: Saunders and Otley, Conduit Street. 1852. *Post octavo.*

Title as above, i. p. The Vicissitudes, 288 pp.

Vol. II.

Title, i. p. The Vicissitudes, 340 pp.

Published at 21s.

Afterwards issued under a new Title, as under—

LANCASHIRE LIFE; or, the VICISSITUDES of COMMERCE. A Tale. By THOMAS GRENHALGH. [4 lines of poetry.] New Edition, revised. Liverpool: Edward Howell, Church Street. 1854. *Duodecimo.*

Title and Preface, iii. pp. Lancashire Life, 238 pp.

Frontispiece, Photograph of the Author.

Published at 1s. 6d.

CONISTON HALL; or, the JACOBITES. An historical tale. By the Rev. WILLIAM GRESLEY, M.A., Prebendary of Lichfield, Author of the "Forest of Arden," the "Siege of Lichfield," etc. London: Joseph Masters, Aldersgate Street, and 78 New Bond Street. MDCCCXLIX. 18*mo*.

Title as above, Preface, and Contents, viii. pp. Coniston Hall, 312 pp.

Woodcut View of Coniston Hall.

An Edition was published by Joseph Masters in 1846 at 4s. 6d.

LIVERPOOL, a POEM. By JAMES GROCOTT jun. [Quotation 8 lines.] Liverpool: printed by S. H. Sankey, Lime Street. 1830. *Octavo.*

Title as above, Dedication, and Poem, 18 pp.

Scarce. A copy is in the Library of J. F. Marsh, Esq., Chepstow.

James Grocott jun. was a native of Liverpool. About the year 1820 he became an inmate of the Liverpool Gaol, to which many of his poems relate. He was under the impression that his incarceration was not due to any fault of his own.

He published "The Juvenile, and other Poems," "Almedo," "Reflection," "The Lay of the first Minstrel," etc.

WENDERHOLME, a Story of LANCASHIRE and Yorkshire. By PHILIP GILBERT HAMERTON, Author of a "Painter's Camp," etc. In three volumes.

VOL. I.

William Blackwood and Sons, Edinburgh and London. MDCCCLXIX. The right of Translation is reserved. *Octavo.*

Half-title, and Title as above, iii. pp. Dedication, Preface, and Wenderholme, 317 pp.

VOL. II.

Half-title and Title, iii. pp. Wenderholme, 380 pp.

VOL. III.

Half-title and Title, iii. pp. Wenderholme, 370 pp.

Published at 31s. 6d.

TRADITIONS, SUPERSTITIONS, and FOLK-LORE (chiefly LANCASHIRE and NORTH of ENGLAND); their affinity to others in widely-distributed localities; their eastern origin and mythical significance. By CHARLES HARDWICK, Author of "History of Preston and its environs," "Manual for Patrons and Members of Friendly Societies," etc.

"Thou hast hid these things from the wise and prudent, and hast revealed them unto babes."—MATTHEW xi. 25.

"Every fiction that has ever laid strong hold of human belief is the mistaken image of some great *truth* to which reason will direct its search, while half-reason is content with laughing at the superstition and unreason with disbelieving it."—Rev. J. MARTINEAU.

Manchester: A. Ireland and Co., Pall Mall; London: Simpkin, Marshall, and Co., Stationers' Hall Court. 1872. *Octavo.*

Half-title, Title as above, Dedication, Preface, and Contents, xix. pp. Traditions, and Index, 306 pp.

Frontispiece of "The Spectre Huntsman."

Published at 7s. 6d.

LANCASHIRE FOLK-LORE, illustrative of the superstitions, beliefs, and practices, local customs, and usages of the people of the County Palatine. Compiled by JOHN HARLAND, F.S.A., and T. T. WILKINSON, F.R.A.S. London: Frederick Warne and Co., Bedford Street, Covent Garden; New York: Scribner and Co. 1867. 12*mo.*

Title as above, Preface, and Contents, xii. pp. Folk-lore and Index, 308 pp.

Published at 6s.

A volume full of interest to the lover of old customs and folk-lore.

BALLADS and SONGS of LANCASHIRE, chiefly older than the 19th Century. Collected, compiled, and edited with notes, by JOHN HARLAND, F.S.A. [Small woodcut.] London: Whittaker and Co., Ave Maria Lane. 1865. *Foolscap octavo.*

Half-title, Title as above, Contents, and Preface, xvi. pp. Ballads and Songs, 281 pp.

Published at 5s. Sells for 3s. 6d.

A limited impression on large paper (*Crown quarto*) published at 12s.

LANCASHIRE LYRICS, MODERN SONGS, and BALLADS of

the County Palatine. Edited by JOHN HARLAND, F.S.A., Editor of "Ballads and Songs of Lancashire chiefly older than the Nineteenth Century." London: Whitaker and Co., Ave Maria Lane. 1866. *Foolscap octavo.*

Half-title, Title as above, Preface, and Contents, xiv. pp. Songs, etc., 320 pp.

Published at 5s. Large paper, 21s.

BALLADS and SONGS of LANCASHIRE ANCIENT and MODERN. Collected, compiled, and edited with notes by JOHN HARLAND, F.S.A. Second Edition, corrected, revised, and enlarged. By T. T. WILKINSON, F.R.A.S. London: George Routledge and Sons, and L. C. Gent. 1875.

Title as above, Dedication (List of Subscribers to large paper copies), Introduction, and Contents, xxv. pp. Ballads, etc., 554 pp.

Frontispiece, Portrait of Charles Swain.

Published at 7s. 6d. Large paper, £1 : 1s.

LANCASHIRE LEGENDS, Traditions, Pageants, Sports, etc., with an Appendix containing a rare Tract on the Lancashire Witches, etc. etc. By JOHN HARLAND, F.S.A., and T. T. WILKINSON, F.R.A.S., etc. London: George Routledge and Sons; Manchester: L. C. Gent. 1873.

Title as above, with a view of "The Foldys Cross, Burnley," Dedication, List of Subscribers, Preface, and Contents, xiv. pp. Memoir of J. Harland, Legends, Appendix, and Index, 283 pp.

Published at 6s. Large paper copies, in *Foolscap quarto*, at 15s.
A valuable collection of Lancashire Legends, etc. etc.

PALATINE ANTHOLOGY, a Collection of Ancient Poems and Ballads relating to Lancashire and Cheshire. Edited by JAMES ORCHARD HALLIWELL, Esq., F.R.S., Honorary Member of the Royal Irish Academy, and of the Royal Society of Literature, Fellow of the Society of Antiquaries, etc. London: for private circulation only. MDCCCL. *Quarto.*

Half-title, Title as above, List of Mr. Halliwell's privately printed works, Certificate that only 110 copies were printed [10 of these on thick paper]. Distribution of Copies, and Preface, xiii. pp. Palatine Anthology, 104 pp.

Sells for £1 : 10s. Thick paper copies have been sold for £2 : 2s.

POEMS by MRS. HEMANS. *See* page 210.

POEMS and LETTERS on Several Subjects [by JAMES HEYWOOD], viz.—

I. Poems on Several Occasions.
II. Familiar Letters to several Gentlemen and Ladies.
III. Letters to the Authors of the Spectator, Free thinker Censor, Journal, etc.
IV. Their Answers and Remarks.

[Two Latin Quotations.] London: for W. Meadows at the Angel in Cornhill, F. Stagg in Westminster Hall, and T. Warrel, against St. Dunstan's Church. 1724. *Duodecimo.*

Title as above, and Dedication, iv. pp. Index, xii. pp. Poems, etc., 213 pp. Pages 211, 212, and 213, are printed 215, 216, 217.

Scarce. Sells for 7s. 6d.

This book contains the following articles referring to Lancashire:—A character of the Rev. Mr. Barrow, Head Master of the Manchester School; Lancashire Styles commended; Verses on the death of Mr. Molineux, Mathematician in Manchester. Character of Dr. Wroe of Manchester; and an Epilogue spoken at the last Preston Guild.

A Second Edition of this was printed in 1726.

Title and Dedication, iv. pp. Index, xii. pp. Poems, etc., 249 pp.

The additional matter is principally Letters, and a "Compendious Character of the celebrated Beauties of Manchester, written in the year 1709."

A copy is in the Author's library.

James Heywood was educated at the Manchester School, and afterwards went to London, where he was established as a Linen Draper on Fish Street Hill. He had a habit of twisting buttons off people's coats, which was ridiculed in the "Guardian" (Vol. II.)

OBSERVATIONS and INSTRUCTIONS, Divine and Moral, in verse. By ROBERT HEYWOOD, of Heywood, Lancashire. Edited by JAMES CROSSLEY, Esq., F.S.A. Printed for the Chetham Society. MDCCCLXIX. *Foolscap quarto.*

Chetham Society's Title (Vol. lxxvi.) and List of Council, iii. pp. Title as above, and Introduction, xx. pp. Contents and Half-title, iii. pp. Observations, etc., and Index, 107 pp.

The most pleasant SONG of LADY BESSY, the eldest daughter of King Edward the Fourth, and how she married King Henry the Seventh of the House of Lancaster. With notes by THOMAS HEYWOOD, F.A.S.

"—— Sermones ego mallem
Repentes per humum."

London: printed by Richard Taylor, Red Lion Court, Fleet Street. MDCCCXXIX. *Octavo.*

Title as above, Dedication, and Preface, xvi. pp. The Song, and Notes, 82 pp.

Refers especially to the Stanley Family.

Scarce. A copy is in the Library of Richard Wood, Esq., Manchester.

The POETRY of WITCHCRAFT, illustrated by copies of the Plays on the LANCASHIRE WITCHES by HEYWOOD and SHADWELL. Reprinted under the direction of JAMES O. HALLIWELL, Esq., F.R.S., etc. Brixton Hill: printed for private circulation only. MDCCCLIII. *Large post quarto.*

Title-page as above, Reprint of Plays, etc., 239 pp.

Very scarce.

The Dramatic Works of Thomas Heywood (1600-1655) were published in 1874, with Illustrative Notes and Memoir of the Author, in 6 volumes, price £3 : 3s.

The LATE LANCASHIRE WITCHES, a well received Comedy, lately acted at the Globe, on the Banke side, by the King's Majestie's Actors. Written by THOM. HEYWOOD and RICHARD Broome.

"Aut prodesse solent aut delectare."

London : printed by Thomas Harper for Benjamen Fisher, and are to be sold at his shop at the signe of the Talbot, without Aldersgate. 1634. *Post octavo.*

Very scarce. A Transcript is in the Manchester Free Library. It was reprinted in Helliwell's Poetry of Witchcraft, *quarto.* 1853.

The EARLS of DERBY and the VERSE WRITERS and POETS of the SIXTEENTH and SEVENTEENTH CENTURY. By THOMAS HEYWOOD. Only 64 copies. Privately printed. Manchester. 1825. *Quarto.*

Title and Preface, 3 pp. The Verse Writers, etc., 44 pp.

A copy is in the Chetham Library. See Stanley Papers, Part I. (Chetham Society, vol. xxix.)

ITER LANCASTRIENSE. A POEM, written A.D. 1636. By the Rev. RICHARD JAMES, B.D., Fellow of Corpus Christi College, Oxford. Now first printed from the original Manuscript in the Bodleian Library, Oxford. Edited, with Notes and an Introductory Memoir, by the Rev. THOMAS CORSER, M.A., Vicar of Norton, Northamptonshire.

"Duplico circumdatus æstu
Carminis et Rerum."—MANILIUS.

Printed for the Chetham Society. MDCCCXLV. *Foolscap quarto.*

Chetham Society's Title (Vol. vii.), and List of Council, 3 pp. Title as above, and Introduction, cxii. pp. Iter Lancastriense, and Notes, 84 pp. Errata, 1 p. The First, Second, and Third Reports of the Chetham Society, 13 pp.

ILLUSTRATIONS.

Illuminated folding plate—"Orate pro bono statu Richardi Assheton, etc."
Illuminated plate—"Sir Richard Assheton and Dame Anne, his Wife, anno domini MCCCCXXIIIJ," and Woodcuts on p. 30.
Folding pedigree of Heywood of Heywood.

LIVERPOOL in 1825. A SATIRE. By JEREMY JUMPER, of the Firm of A B C and Co. [Coat of Arms of Liverpool. Printed for the Author by W. Bethell 10 Marshall Street. 1825. *Foolscap octavo.*

Title and Satire, 23 pp. Scarce.

The copy in the Author's Library has the blanks filled in by a former possessor.

REPLY to "Liverpool in Eighteen Hundred and Twenty-five. A Satire."

> "I'll whip the rebel rascal till he's blind—
> Be scarce then, scoundrel, now you know my mind."

Liverpool: printed and sold by Willmer and Co., 25 Lord Street. Sold also by the other Booksellers. 1825. *Duodecimo.*

Title, etc., 20 pp. Scarce.

A copy is in the Library of J. F. Marsh, Esq. of Chepstow.

FAR NORTH: a Novel. By THEO. KENNEDY, with an Illustration by the Writer. Second Edition. London: Whittaker and Co; Simpkin, Marshall, and Co. Ulverston: D. Atkinson, King Street. 1871. *Foolscap octavo.*

Title and Far North, 408 pp.

ORIGINAL POEMS on Miscellaneous Subjects. By CHARLES KENWORTHY. [Three lines from Byron.] Manchester: printed by Cave and Sever, and sold (only) by the Author, 2 Railway Street, Livesey Street. [1847.] *Octavo.*

Title as above, Dedication, and Contents, viii. pp. Poems, 196 pp.

Frontispiece, View of Strangeways Hall, Manchester.

Contains several local poems, amongst others, "A View of Manchester in 1818." "A View of Manchester in 1838." "Collyhurst Hall." "The Manchester Athenæum." "To Junius Smith, Esq., Strangeways Hall."

A 2d Edition was afterwards published, to which is appended a List of Poems, 304 pp.

Subscribers. Title, Contents, and List of Subscribers, xv. pp.

Charles Kenworthy was born at the Red Lion Inn, Church Street, Manchester, 12th September 1773. He was a "pattern designer," and died 31st July 1850.

A DOMESTIC WINTER PIECE, or a POEM EXHIBITING a full VIEW of the AUTHOR'S DWELLING-PLACE in the Winter Season. In two Parts. Interspersed with a great variety of entertaining Reflections. By SAMUEL LAW of Barewise, near Todmorden, Lancashire, Weaver. Leeds: printed by James Bowling. MDCCLXXII. *Post octavo.*

Half-title, Title as above, and Preface, viii. pp. Poems, etc., p. 9 to p. 63. Errata, 1 p.

Rather scarce. Copies sell for 4s. 6d.

A TREATISE of ECLIPSES of the Sun and Moon. For thirty-five years, commencing anno 1715, ending 1749. Containing the Beginning, Middle, and Ending, the Digits Eclipses, etc. * * * By CHARLES LEADBETTER, Teacher of Mathematicks. The 2d Edition, with additions. London, for John Wilcox, at the Green Dragon in Little Britain. MDCCXXXI. *Post duodecimo.*

Title as above, Address, Ode "to Mr. Charles Leadbetter, his Treatise of Eclipses," by George Nickolls, and "Carmen Acrosticon in laudem Authoris," by W. Parr, vii. pp. Errata and Advertisements, 11 pp. Treatise, 176 pp.

Published at 2s. 6d. Sells for 5s. A copy of this is in the Manchester Free Library.

Charles Leadbetter was a native of Cronton in Lancashire, which place is alluded to in the Ode above mentioned. He also wrote "URANOSCOPIA, or the Contemplation of the Heavens, being a Demonstration of the Equation of Time, etc. London, 1735." *Octavo.* Published at 7s. Contains a Portrait of the Author, who was at this time taught "Astronomy, Navigation, Surveying, Gauging, and Dialling at his house at the Hand and Pen, in Cock Lane, Shoreditch, London." He also published in 1737 a Treatise on "Mechanick Dialling, or the New Art of Shadows free from Obscurities, etc." Copies of both these are in the Author's Library.

JOHN MANESTY, the LIVERPOOL MERCHANT, with Illustrations by George Cruikshank. By Dr. W. MAGUIRE. In two volumes. London, 1844. *Post octavo.*

Published at 21s. Is somewhat scarce.

POETICAL TRIFLES, by J. H. MILLS, of the Theatre-Royal, Manchester. . . Manchester: Printed for W. Graham, Bookseller, No. 35 Market-Street-Lane, and sold by him and all the Booksellers in Manchester, by Mr. Broster, Chester, and C. Law, Ave-Maria-Lane, London. 1806. [Printed by J. Aston, Printer, Deansgate, Manchester.] *Duodecimo.*

Title as above, and Trifles, 120 pp.

Contains some local poems.

FRUITS of RETIREMENT, or MISCELLANEOUS POEMS, Moral and Divine. Being some Contemplations, Letters, etc. Written on various Subjects and Occasions. By MARY MOLLINEUX, late of Liverpool, Deceased. To which is prefixed some account of the Author. [Exod. 15-21.] London: printed and sold by T. Sowle, in White-Hart Court in Gracious Street. 1702. *Octavo.*

Title as above, Poems, etc., 216 pp.

Reprinted, 2d Edition, 1702. 3d Edition, 1720. 4th Edition, 1739. 5th Edition, 1761. 6th Edition, 1772.

The last Edition sells for 3s. 6d.

A copy of the 6th Edition is in the Liverpool Free Library, and of the 4th Edition in the Midgley Reference Library, Friends' Meeting House, Manchester.

Mary Mollineux, *neé* Southworth, was the wife of Henry Mollineux of Liverpool. She died 3d January 1695. Her husband was the Author of several Friends' Tracts. See *Post.*

The WAREHOUSE BOY of MANCHESTER. A medical tale in four parts, with Introductory Remarks and Notes, to which is added other Tales in Prose and Verse. By THOMAS NICHOLSON, Author of "A Peal for the People," "The Sabbath Peal," etc. etc. Manchester: printed and published for the Author by Cathrall and Co., Booksellers, Ducie Street, Exchange. Sold by all Booksellers. Entered at Stationers' Hall. *Duodecimo.*

Title as above, and Introduction, xii. pp. Poems, etc., 143 pp.

ROCHDALE, a Fragment, with Notes intended as an Introduction to the History of Rochdale. By WILLIAM NUTTALL.

"Genius rose, with Commerce in his train,
To aid the Labours of the careful Swain;
He form'd the Loom, and bade the Shuttle fly,
He wove the web and mix'd the glowing Dye."

Lancashire, Printer, Rochdale. 1810. *Duodecimo.*

A *Frontispiece*, Title as above, and Address to Lord Byron, vi. pp. Rochdale, 102 pp.

Published at 2s. 6d. Scarce.

Contains some matters of local interest. A copy is in the Rochdale Free Public Library.

The following MSS. of this Author are in the possession of Charles Clay, M.D., Manchester—viz. "The Bard of the British Apennines, or my Grandfather's Legends of Olden Times in Rochdale, with Historical and Biographical Notices" (dedicated to John Roby, Esq.), and "The History of the Town and Neighbourhood of Rochdale, in the County Palatine of Lancaster." Some of the matter contained in these MSS. is embodied in the book above named, and two or three of the Legends are those which have been preserved in "Roby's Traditions of Lancashire."

William Nuttall was a schoolmaster in Rochdale, where he lived until about 1828, when he went to Oldham, where he appears to have got into pecuniary difficulties, and died under painful circumstances. He was three times married. His first wife was Mary, the daughter of William Dutton of Morton Wood, Shropshire, by whom he had issue two daughters, one of whom married Samuel Whittles of Moorbank, Rochdale, who is now living in America, and has in his possession a portrait (oil painting), of William Nuttall. He was the author of "Le Voyageur, or the Genuine History of Charles Manley. Rochdale: Printed and sold by T. Wood, etc. 1806." A copy of this is in the Rochdale Equitable Pioneer's Society's Library.

The PRESTONIAD, a POEM. By ROWLAND OLIVER, Esq.

"Justum et tenacem propositi Virum,
Non vultus instantis Tyranni
Mente quatit solida."

Liverpool: printed by James Smith, and sold by the Booksellers in General. Price 1s. 6d. *Octavo.*

Title as above, and Poem, 42 pp. Scarce.

O FUL, TRU, UN PERTIKLER OKEAWNT o' bwoth wat aw seed, un wat aw yerd we gooin too TH' GREYT EGGSHIBISHUN e LUNDUN, un o greyt deyle o' Hinfurmashum besoide, wele Kalkilatud fur to giv thouse foke o gradely hinseit hinto things, us hassent ad nother toime nur Brass fur to goo un see fur thersels. Kontaining loikewoise O Dikshunayre manefakturt fore o purpus fur thoose as ar noan fur larn't be O FELLEY FRO RACHDI. Thurd Edishun, we o rook ov us pratty pikters us evur ony mon clapt his een on, dun oppo pappur be Mestur Shields, un Mestur Langton did um oppo th' wood.

"Englun expekts evuri mon fur to doo is duti."

Rachde: printed bei Wrigley un Sun; sowd be Hamilton, Adams, un Ko., un Routledge un Ko., Lundun; Abel Heywood un Kelley, un Slater, Manchesstur; G. Philip un Sun, Liverpule, un o Bukesellurs. *Duodecimo.*

Frontispiece, Title as above, Deddykashun, and Preface to First, Second, and Third Edition, 10 pp. Felley fro Rache's, etc., and Dikshunayre, 87 pp.

Price 1s. The First Edition was published in 1851; the Second in 1852, and the Third, with illustrations, by T. J. Shields in 1856.

Mr. OLIVER ORMEROD of Rochdale is the author.

Original POEMS on a Variety of Subjects. By JAMES ORRELL. Bolton: printed and sold by J. Gardner, for the Author. Also sold by G. R. Kaye, Bolton; Mrs. Falkner, Manchester, etc. 1793. *Small quarto.*

Title as above, and Poems, 216 pp.

Contains two or three Poems of local interest.

The OLD CHURCH CLOCK. By RICHARD PARKINSON, D.D., F.S.A., Principal of St. Bees College, and Canon of Manchester. (Woodcut of Church Clock.) Fourth Edition. London: Francis J. John Rivington, St. Paul's Church Yard, and Waterloo Place. 1852. *Duodecimo.*

Half-title, Title as above, and Dedication, v. pp. Introduction, and The Old Church Clock, 262 pp.

Published at 4s. 6d. First Edition was issued in 1843.

ILLUSTRATIONS.

Victoria Bridge, Manchester, *Frontispiece.*
Seathwaite Chapel, *to face* p. 137.

This beautiful story contains a life of Robert Walker of Seathwaite. It has gone through many editions.

HOURS with the MUSES. By JOHN CRITCHLEY PRINCE.

> "Knowledge and truth, and even virtue, were his theme,
> And lofty hopes of Liberty divine."—SHELLEY.

Manchester: J. B. Rogerson. MDCCCLXI.

Title-page as above, Contents, and SKETCH of the AUTHOR'S LIFE, xvi. pp. Dedication, Preface, etc., and Poems, 171 pp. List of Subscribers, p. 173 to p. 183.

The Sixth Edition of this was published in 1866. J. C. Prince is the author of "Autumn Leaves," "Poetic Rosary," and "Miscellaneous Poems."

J. C. Prince was born at Wigan 21st June 1808.

The BARBER'S SHOP. By RICHARD WRIGHT PROCTOR. With illustrations by Wm. Morton.

> "Trifles light as (h)air."—SHAKSPEARE.

Manchester: Thomas Dinham and Co., etc. 1856. *Octavo.*

Title as above, and Preface, viii. pp. The Barber's Shop, 128 pp.

Published at 3s. 6d.

THEN and NOW; or, Ye Chronicles of Ashlynne, a Romance founded on the STORY of the BLACK KNIGHT. By WILLIAM QUARMBY, Author of "The Sea Shell," and other Poems and Songs.

> "Stories of Knights and Ladies fair,
> And chronicles of Eld."—LONGFELLOW.

London: Simpkin, Marshall, and Co., Stationers' Hall Court; Manchester: A. Heywood and Son, 56 and 58 Oldham Street; Ashton: W. Quarmby, 208 Stamford Street. *Post octavo.*

Title as above, Dedication, Contents, and Preface, viii. pp. List of Subscribers, 2 pp. The Chronicles p. 9 to p. 172. Notes, p. 173 to p. 176.

PHASES of DISTRESS; LANCASHIRE RHYMES. By JOSEPH RAMSBOTTOM. Edited by a "Lancashire Lad." Manchester: John Heywood, 143 Deansgate; London: Simpkin, Marshall, and Co. 1864. *Foolscap octavo.*

Title, Preface, and Index, vi. pp. Poems, 105 pp.

Published at 2s.

The Village Muse, containing the complete POETICAL WORKS of ELIJAH RIDINGS. Third Edition.

"The unconquerable mind, and freedom's holy flame."—GRAY.
"One touch of nature makes the whole world kin."—SHAKSPEARE.

Macclesfield: printed by Thomas Stubbs, Stanley Street. Sold by all Booksellers, and by the Author, Four Lane Ends, Whitefield. MDCCCLIV. *Octavo.*

Title as above, Dedication, Preface, Prefaces to the Editions of 1844 and 1850, Contents, Biographical Sketch and Poems, 423 pp.

Sells for 3s. 6d. Contains many "Lancashire Poems."

Elijah Ridings was born in "The Hollows," in Failsworth, near Manchester, 27th November 1802. His parents were silk-weavers.

An ingenious Poem, The DRUNKARD'S PROSPECTIVE, or Burning Glasse. Composed by JOSEPH RIGBIE, Gentleman, Clerke of the Peace of the County Palatine of Lancaster. London: printed for the Author, and are to be sold at the Brazen Serpent, St. Paul's Churchyard. 1656. *Small octavo.*

Title and Introductory Verses, xii. pp. Poem, 29 pp. Commendatory Verses, 11 pp.

This very scarce volume (a copy of which is in the Bodleian Library), contains four metrical Dedications—*1st*, "To the religious and honourable Lady Margaret Houghton, relict of Sir Gilbert Houghton, Knight and Baronet." *2d*, "To his loving, virtuous, and right Worthy Mistress, Ann, daughter of Sir Gualther Blount, Knight and Baronet, wife of James Anderton of Birchley, Esq." *3d*, "To the Right Worshipfull, united in Candor and Knowledge, Richard Shuttleworth of Gauthrop, and John Starkie of Huntroid, Esquires." *4th*, "To the Right Worshipful, truly Noble, and his Worthy honored Friend and Neighbour, Roger Bradshaigh of Haigh, Esquire." At the end of the Poem are Commendatory Verses signed by Ch. Hotham, John Tilsley, James Livesay, Humphrey Maulebone, Ja. Rigbie, and Ch. Carr.

Copies of this work have sold for upwards of £5.

Joseph Rigbie of Aspull was the son of Alexander Rigbie of Wigan. He married Alice, the daughter of Gabriel Houghton of Knowsley. A volume of MS. Poems by this Author (unpublished) is in the Library of Rev. Thomas Corser, M.A., F.S.A. of Stand.

TRADITIONS of LANCASHIRE, by J. Roby, F.R.S.L.

"I know I have herein made myself subject unto a world of judges, and am likest to receive most controulment of such as are least able to sentence me. Well I wote that the works of no writer have appeared to a world in a more curious age than this; and that, therefore, the more circumspection and wariness is required in the publishing of anything that must endure so many sharp sights and censures. The consideration whereof, as it hath made me the more heedy not to displease any, so hath it given me the less hope of pleasing all."—Verstegan, *Rest. dec. Ant.*

In two volumes.

Vol. I.

London: Longman, Rees, Orme, Brown, and Green, Paternoster Row. MDCCCXXIX. *Octavo.*

Engraved Title, 1 p. Title as above, Dedication, Preface, and Contents, xi. pp. Traditions, 329 pp.

LIST OF PLATES.

Mab's Cross, Wigan.	Whalley Abbey.
Burscough Abbey.	Hornby Castle.
Radcliffe Tower.	Collegiate Church, Manchester.

These are all drawn by G. Pickering, and engraved by Edward Finden. The volumes also contain many woodcuts.

VOL. II.

Engraved Half-title, Title, and Contents, vi. pp. Traditions, 331 pp. Advertisement of Second Series, 1 p.

LIST OF PLATES.

Tyrone's Bed, near Rochdale.	Lathom House.
Hoghton Tower.	South Port.
Eagle's Crag, Vale of Todmorden.	Ince Hall, near Wigan.

All drawn by G. Pickering, and engraved by Edward Finden. This volume is also illustrated with woodcuts.

Published at £2 : 2s.; large paper, £4 : 4s. Sells for £2 : 10s.

A 2d Edition of this Series was published in 1830 by Longman, Rees, Brown, and Green, London.

SECOND SERIES (published 1831).

VOL. I.

Title (with date of 1831), Dedication, Preface, Contents, and Introduction, xxvii. pp. Traditions, 330 pp. *Octavo.*

LIST OF PLATES.

Clitheroe Castle.	The Pile of Fouldrey.
"The Thrutch," near Rochdale.	Bewsey, near Warrington.
	Windleshaw Abbey.

VOL. II.

Title (dated 1831) and Contents, 11 pp. Traditions, 340 pp.

LIST OF PLATES.

Clegg Hall, near Rochdale.

Peg O'Nelly's Well, near Clitheroe.	The Lost Farm, near Southport.
Ulverstone Sands.	Rivington Pike.

The plates in both volumes are drawn by G. Pickering, and engraved by Edward Finden. The work is also illustrated with numerous woodcuts.

Published at £2 : 2s.; large paper, £3 : 3s. The 4 vols were also published, with Proof Plates on India Paper, at £6 : 6s. A few copies, with Proofs and Etchings, £10 : 10s. The two series, in a perfect state, are now scarce, and sell for £3 : 10s.; large paper copies, £6. Large paper, with India Proofs and double set of Plates, £13 : 13s.

POPULAR TRADITIONS of LANCASHIRE. By J. ROBY, M.R.S.L. In 3 volumes. Second Edition. London: Colburn. 1840. *Post octavo.*

Published at £1 : 11 : 6. It contains both the original series, but has no plates.

POPULAR TRADITIONS of LANCASHIRE. By J. ROBY, Esq., M.R.S.L. In 3 volumes.

VOL. I.

Third Edition. London: Henry G. Bohn, York Street, Covent Garden. 1843. *Post octavo.*

Title, Preface, Contents, and List of Illustrations, vi. pp. Introduction and Traditions, 318 pp.

ILLUSTRATIONS (Woodcuts).

Portrait of the Author (Steel Engraving), *Frontispiece.*
View of the Street, with steps leading to the Old Church, Rochdale P. 27
Seizure of Robert Dean of Whalley ("Clitheroe Castle") . . 47
Combat ("Mab's Cross") 103
Tournament ("Eagle and Child") 172
Black Knight of Ashton 201
Flight of Henry VI. from Waddington Hall . . . 212

VOL. II.

Title, Contents, and List of Illustrations, iv. pp. Traditions, 348 pp.

ILLUSTRATIONS.

Examination of George Marsh before Sir Roger Barton P. 36
The Seer 100
Earl of Tyrone 133
Imp churning ("Lancashire Witches") 218

Vol. III.

Title, Contents, and List of Illustrations, iv. pp. Traditions, 330 pp.

Illustrations.

Dule upo' Dun . . . . . P. 1
Pursuit of the Robbers ("George Fox") . . 69
Combat ("Raven Castle") 89
Death of Oneida ("Mermaid of Martin Meer") . 145
Suicide of the Maniac ("The Ring and the Cliff") . 180
The Discovery 209
Master Anthony Hardcastle brought before Justice Anderton ("Maid's Stratagem") . . . 258
Opening of the Chest ("Skull House") . . 283

Sells for £1 : 10s.

TRADITIONS of LANCASHIRE, by John Roby, M.R.S.L., illustrated by Engravings on Steel and Wood. In two volumes. Fourth Edition. London: George Routledge and Sons, Broadway, Ludgate. 1867. *Octavo.*

Vol. I.

Half-title, Title as above, Dedication, Contents, Publisher's Preface, Memoir of the Author, Preface to the 1st Series, and Introduction to the 2d Series, xxviii. pp. Tradition, 465 pp.

Vol. II.

Half-title, Title, and Contents, vi. pp. Tradition, 441 pp.

This edition contains all the plates of the first and second Series, with the woodcuts in all the former editions. The only additional plate is a Portrait of John Roby, which forms the Frontispiece to the first volume.

Sells for £2. Large paper copies £2 : 10s.

The fifth Edition is a reprint of the above, published in 1872. It contains all the Plates and Woodcuts in the fourth Edition. It was published at 15s. and 12s., and was sold off at once.

Now sells for 12s.

The LEGENDARY and POETICAL REMAINS of JOHN ROBY.

Author of "Traditions of Lancashire." With a sketch of his literary life and character. By his WIDOW. London: Longman, Brown, Green, and Longmans. 1854. *Post octavo.*

Half-title, Title as above, Preface, and Contents. viii. pp. Sketch of the Literary Life, etc., and Appendix, 376 pp. Portrait, engraved from a Daguerreotype, by Beard. Published at 10s. 6d. Reduced [Bohn], 5s.

John Roby, son of Nehemiah Roby, Master of the Grammar School of Haigh, was born at Wigan on the 5th January 1793. For many years he was a Banker in Rochdale, where he also resided. He was one of the unfortunate passengers who were drowned in the wreck of the "Orion," near Portpatrick, on 18th June 1850.

His first literary production was "Sir Bertram, a Poem, in Six Cantos." 1815.

MUSINGS in MANY MOODS. By JOHN BOLTON ROGERSON. London: Partridge and Co., 34 Paternoster Row; Manchester: George Simms, St. Ann's Square; Liverpool; Edward Howell, 6 Church Street. 1859. *Octavo.*

Title, Preface, and Contents, viii. pp. Poems, 394 pp.

Amongst other Local Poems this contains one entitled, "Chetham College and Manchester Cathedral."

A VOICE from the TOWN, and other POEMS. By JOHN BOLTON ROGERSON, Author of "Rhyme, Romance, and Revery," etc.

[Wordsworth, 4 lines.]

London: Thomas Miller, Newgate Street; Manchester: Bradshaw and Blacklock, Brown Street. MDCCCXLII. *Foolscap octavo.*

Title as above, Dedication, Preface, and Contents, viii. pp. Poems, etc., 200 pp.

John Bolton Rogerson was born in Manchester, 20th January 1809, and died in the Isle of Man, 15th October 1859. He published "Rhyme, Romance, and Revery," 1840; "The Wandering Angel," 1844; "Rogerson's Poetical Works," 1849. His works are only partially local.

MOUNT PLEASANT, a DESCRIPTIVE POEM. [By W. Roscoe.] To which is added an Ode. Warrington: Printed by W. Eyres for J. Johnson, No. 72 St. Paul's Church Yard, London; and S. Crane, Liverpool. MDCCLXXVII. *Quarto.*

Title as above, Half-title, Advertisement, and the Poem, etc., 49 pp. 2d Edition. 1798.

Scarce.

POEMS and other WRITINGS by the late EDWARD RUSHTON, to which is added a SKETCH of the LIFE of the AUTHOR. By the Rev. William Shepherd. London: printed for Effingham Wilson, Royal Exchange. 1824. *Post octavo.*

Title as above, Contents, and Life, xxviii. pp. Poems, etc., 212 pp. An Epistle to Edward Rushton (by W. Shepherd), and an Apostrophe to the Memory of Thomas Noble of Liverpool, 10 pp.

Scarce. A copy is in the Author's library.

The Poems were first published in 1806. Several of them are of local interest. An Epistle to Edward Rushton by his Biographer (the Founder of Shepherd's Library in Preston) is included in the 1824 Edition. Edward Rushton was born in Liverpool 13th November 1756. For some years he was engaged in the African Trade, but having lost his eyesight he returned to Liverpool, where, having lived for some time in poverty, he was established as a Bookseller. In 1805, after an interval of thirty years, he recovered his sight. He died in November 1814.

WOOLTON GREEN, a DOMESTIC POEM, with other Miscellaneous Poems. By John Shaw, of Thistle Nest, Walton, near Liverpool, late of Theatres Royal, York, Hull, Newcastle-upon-Tyne, etc. Dedicated (without permission), to the Right Hon. George Canning. Liverpool: Printed by Perry and Metcalfe, Lord Street, and sold by the Booksellers, and Robinsons and Son, London. 1825. *Duodecimo.*

Half-title, Title as above, Dedication, and Contents, xiii. pp. Poems, 192 pp.

Frontispiece, Portrait of Right Hon. George Canning.
Facing *Frontispiece*, "My Mare Gip."

Sells for 3s. 6d.
A copy is in the Liverpool Free Public Library.

A Picturesque DESCRIPTION of TURTON FAIR, and its pernicious consequences. A Poem. By WILLIAM SHELDRAKE.

> "Quo, quo scelesti ruitis?"—HOR.
> "Unhappy men! the path in which you go
> Will doubtless terminate in endless woe."

London: printed for the Author, and sold by B. Jackson, Bolton. 1789. *Octavo.*

Title as above, Dedication, and Poem, 26 pp.

A copy is in the Library of Mr. W. E. A. Axon, Manchester.
Sells for 5s.

MISCELLANEOUS POEMS, chiefly Amatory, Serious, and Devout, with several Translations from Ancient and Modern Authors. By Sir EDWARD SHERBURNE of Stonyhurst, Knt. Reprinted from the Edition of 1651. With a BIOGRAPHICAL ACCOUNT of the AUTHOR, and observations on his works. By S. FLEMING, A.M.

> "Obscurata diu populo bonus eruet atque
> Proferet in Lucem speciosa."—HOR.

London: printed by Bensley and Son, Bolt Court, Fleet Street, for R. Priestley, 143 High Holborn. 1819. *Duodecimo.*

Title as above, Title of 1651 Edition, Advertisement, and Biographical Sketch, xix. pp. Poems, 207 pp.

Published at 10s. 6d. Scarce. Only 250 copies printed. A copy is in the Author's Library.
The original is excessively scarce; it contains no Memoir.

SCARSDALE; or, LIFE on the LANCASHIRE and YORKSHIRE BORDER. In three volumes.

VOL. I.

London: Smith, Elder and Co., 65 Cornhill. MDCCCLX.

Title as above, and Contents, iii. pp. Scarsdale, 312 pp.

VOL. II.

Title and Contents, iii. pp. Scarsdale, 320 pp.

VOL. III.

Title and Contents, iii. pp. Scarsdale, 331 pp.

Written by Sir JAMES KAY-SHUTTLEWORTH.
Published at 31s. 6d.

SIR WILLIAM STANLEY'S GARLAND, containing his twenty-one years' travels through most parts of the World, and his safe return to LATHAM HALL. Leeds: reprinted for Robinson, Son, and Holdsworth by Inchbold and Gawtress. MDCCCXIV. *Octavo.*

Half-title, Title as above, and Travels, 15 pp.

Only 75 copies were printed in *octavo.* Sells for 7s. 6d. Scarce.
Large paper, *quarto*, only a few printed, sells for £1 : 1s.
A copy of this is in the library of the Right Hon. the Earl of Derby.
Sir William Stanley was the author of "A briefe discourse of Doctor Allen's seditious, Drifts, etc." 1588.

JOHN DRAYTON; being a HISTORY of the early LIFE and DEVELOPMENT of a LIVERPOOL ENGINEER.

"Every man for himself, and God for us all."

In two volumes. London: Richard Bentley, New Burlington Street. 1851. *Post octavo.*

VOL. I.

Title as above, etc., 283 pp.

VOL. II.

Title, etc., 271 pp.

The author of this is Mr. James Stonehouse.

Traditions of the Foreland of the Fylde, Elizabethan Era.

PENNY STONE; or, a Tradition of the Spanish Armada. By the Author of the History of Blackpool, etc. [Arms of Massy, Fleetwood, and Singleton.] Fleetwood: printed for the Author by W. Porter. 1845. *Post octavo.*

Title as above, Address, iv. pp., 78 pp.

This was written by the Rev. WILLIAM THORNBER, B.A. It is somewhat scarce; sells for 4s. 6d.

TALES and LEGENDS of the ENGLISH LAKES and MOUNTAINS, collected from the best and most authentic sources. By LORENZO TUVAR.

> "Holier seems the ground
> To him who catches on the gale
> The spirit of a mournful tale
> Embodied in the sound."

London: Longmans and Co. [1852.] *Duodecimo.*

Title as above, and Preface, ii. pp. Tales, etc., 312 pp.

Frontispiece, Chalk View of Castle Rock in the Vale of St. John; and two other Plates.

Published at 5s. 6d.

A DESCRIPTIVE POEM of the TOWN and TRADE of LIVERPOOL. By JOHN WALKER, Shoemaker. Liverpool: printed and sold by H. Hodgson for the Author, and sold by him at the corner of Sir Thomas's Buildings, Whitechapel. MDCCLXXXIX. *Quarto.*

Title as above, Preface, etc., vii. pp. Poem, 63 pp.

A copy is in the library of Dr. Kendrick of Warrington.

The Second Edition was published in 1801, and a copy of it is in the Manchester Free Library.

PLEBIAN POLITICS, or the principles and practices of certain mole-eyed Maniacs, vulgarly called Warrites, exposed by way of Dialogue betwixt two Lancashire clowns, together with several fugitive pieces. By TIM BOBBIN THE SECOND.

> "Theaw Kon ekspekt no mooar eant ov a pig thin a grunt.—TUM GRUNT.

[Woodcut.] Manchester: printed by W. Cowdroy, "Gazette" Office, Hunter's Lane. Price 1s. *Octavo.*

Title as above, and Preface, iv. pp. Plebian Politics, p. 5 to p. 56. Glossary, 4 pp.

Frontispiece, Portrait of "Tim Bobbin the Second, born 27th July 1728." Scarce.

The author was Robert Walker, who was born at Carrington Barn, in Audenshaw. He died 6th May 1803, and was interred in St. Michael's Church-yard, Ashton-under-Lyne.

POEMS on several occasions. By BRYAN WALLER. [Quotation from Virgil.] London: printed by E. Hodson. Sold by Sewell, Cornhill; also by Deighton, Cambridge, and Walmsley, Lancaster. 1796. *Octavo.*

Title as above, Preface, etc., viii. pp. Poems, 202 pp. The pagination is irregular.

Contains several Poems of local interest. A copy is in the Library of J. F. Marsh, Esq., of Chepstow.

The SPIRIT OF THE DOCTOR, comprising many interesting Poems, selected from the original Manuscript of the late Mr. JAMES WATSON, formerly Librarian of the Portico Library, Manchester, and commonly called Doctor Watson.

> " Sic vita erat; facile omnes perferre ac pate."—TER.
> [And three following lines.]

To which is prefaced a Lithographic Portrait of the Doctor; Memoir of his Life, and various anecdotes relative to him; after and to which are subjoined the " Humors of Trim."

> " Everything in this world is big with jest, and has wit in it,
> And instruction too, if we can but find it out."—STERNE.

Manchester: printed for the Editor by George Cave. 1820. *Octavo.*

Title as above, Address of Corporal Trim, Preface, Life of James Watson, Spirit of Doctor, and Anecdotes, xxxvi. pp.

The Spirit of the Doctor, Epigrams, etc., 51 pp. Humors of Trim, etc. 64 pp.

Scarce. Sells for 5s. A copy is in the Manchester Free Library.

The Editor of this was David William Paynter, the son of Richard Paynter, Attorney of Manchester, who was also the Author of the " Humors of Trim," etc. etc. He died 14th March 1823. James Watson was born in Manchester in 1775, and died (was found drowned in Mersey) in 1820.

SKETCHES of LANCASHIRE LIFE and LOCALITIES. By EDWIN WAUGH.

> " One touch of nature makes the whole world kin."—SHAKSPEARE.

London: Whittaker and Co., Ave Maria Lane; Manchester: James Galt and Co. 1856. *Post octavo.*

Half-title, Title as above, Preface, and Contents, viii. pp. Sketches, 260 pp.

Published at 5s. 2d Edition, 12*mo.* 1867.

This contains "Rambles from Bury to Rochdale." "Tim Bobbin's Cottage." "Highways and Byeways from Rochdale to Top of Blackstone Edge." "The Town of Heywood and its neighbourhood." "The Grave of Gristlehurst Boggart." "Boggart Ho' Clough and Rostherne Mere."

POEMS and LANCASHIRE SONGS. By EDWIN WAUGH. London: Whittaker and Co., Ave Maria Lane; Manchester: Edwin Slater, 129 Market Street. MDCCCLIX. *Foolscap octavo.*

Title as above, Dedication, and Contents, vii. pp. Second Title, Poems, etc., 150 pp. Published at 5s.

The 2d Edition was published in 1870 at 7s. 6d., and contains many additional Poems.

HOME LIFE of the LANCASHIRE FACTORY FOLK during the COTTON FAMINE. By EDWIN WAUGH, author of "Lancashire Sketches," etc. etc.

> "Hopdance cries in poor Tom's belly for two white herrings.
> Croak not, black angel: I have no food for thee."—KING LEAR.

London: Simpkin, Marshall, and Co.; Manchester: John Heywood, 143 Deansgate. 1867. *Duodecimo.*

Half-title, Title as above, Preface, and Contents, viii. pp. Home Life, etc., 277 pp.

First published in 1863 at 3s. 6d.

TUFTS of HEATHER from a LANCASHIRE MOOR.

CONTENTS.

Th' owd Blanket.	Sneck-bant.
Dulesgate.	Yeth Bobs an' scaplins.

By EDWIN WAUGH. Manchester: John Heywood, 141 and 143 Deansgate; London: Simpkin, Marshall, and Co. [1868. In two volumes.] 18*mo.*

VOL. I.

Title as above, and Tales, 304 pp. (each Tale separate Title-page and paging).

VOL. II.

Title and Tales, 381 pp.

Published at 3s. 6d. per volume.

This volume contains "Besom Ben," "Ben an' the Bantam," etc. Most of the Tales in these two volumes were originally published as pamphlets.

JANNOCK; or, the Bold Trencherman. By EDWIN WAUGH, Author of "Sketches of Lancaster Life and Localities," "The Barrel Organ," etc. Manchester: Abel Heywood and Son, 56 and 58 Oldham Street; London: Simpkin, Marshall, and Co., Stationers' Hall Court. Price 1s. *Foolscap octavo.*

Title as above, Half-title, and Jannock, 108 pp.

Published at 1s.

The scene of this Tale is the Head of the Dutton Estuary near Furness.

BESOM BEN. By EDWIN WAUGH. Manchester: John Heywood, 143 Deansgate; London: Simpkin, Marshall, and Co. *Duodecimo.*

Title as above, and Besom Ben, 111 pp.

Published at 1s.

The scene of the tale is laid in Rochdale.

SNOWED UP. By EDWIN WAUGH. Manchester: John Heywood, 141 and 143 Deansgate; London: Simpkin, Marshall, and Co. *Duodecimo.*

Title as above, and Snowed up, 115 pp.

Frontispiece, View of Packer St., Rochdale.

Published at 1s.

OLD CRONIES; or, Wassail in a Country Inn. By EDWIN WAUGH. Manchester:[1] Abel Heywood and Son, 56 and 58 Oldham Street. *Duodecimo.*

[1] Like many of this firm's publications, it has no date, but was published in 1875.

Title as above, and Tale, 100 pp.

Published at 1s.

The scene of this narrative is the Old Boar's Head in Middleton.

MANCHESTER POETRY, with an Introductory Essay. Edited by JAMES WHEELER. *Duodecimo.*

"He that recalls the attention of mankind to any part of learning which time has left behind it, may be truly said to advance the literature of his age."—JOHNSON.

Title as above, Dedication, Introductory Essay, and Contents, xxi. pp. Half-title and Poems, 200 pp.

This volume consists of selections from the works of the Manchester Poets, Byrom, Swain, Bamford, Mort, Gardiner, etc.

Sells for 3s.

The LAYS and LEGENDS of the ENGLISH LAKE COUNTRY. Edited by JOHN PAYN WHITE. London: Bemrose and Son, 10 Paternoster Buildings, etc. 1874. *Crown octavo.*

Published at 6s.

MISCELLANIES, being a selection from the POEMS and CORRESPONDENCE of the REV. THOMAS WILSON, B.D., Rector of Claughton, Incumbent of Clitheroe and Downham, and Master of the Grammar School of Clitheroe; with Memoirs of his Life. By the Rev. F. R. RAINES, M.A., F.S.A., Hon. Canon of Manchester, and Incumbent of Milnrow. Printed for the Chetham Society. MDCCCLVII. *Foolscap quarto.*

Chetham Society's Title (Vol. xlv.) and List of Council, iii. pp. Title as above, Memoirs, and Contents, lxxxvi. pp. Addenda et Corrigenda and Half-title, iii. pp. Miscellanies, 230 pp.

ILLUSTRATIONS.

Frontispiece, Portrait of the Rev. Thomas Wilson.

Monument to the Memory of the Rev. Thomas Wilson, *to face* p. lxxv.

The SONGS of the WILSONS, with a Memoir of the Family, and several additional songs never before published. Edited by JOHN HARLAND, F.S.A. London: Simpkin, Marshall, and Co.; Manchester:

John Heywood, Deansgate. 1865. [This Edition is copyright.] *Foolscap octavo.*

Title as above, Songs, Memoir, and Index, 78 pp.

Published at 1s. A few large paper copies were printed. A Second Edition was published in 1866.

Some of these Songs first appeared in the "Manchester Guardian" in 1839. Many of the songs are in the dialect spoken around Manchester.

In 1847 was published in Manchester, "Songs of the Wilsons. By permission of Mr. William Wilson," 12*mo*, 42 pp.

A PROSPECT of Manchester and its Neighbourhood from Chamber, upon the rising grounds adjacent to the Great Northern Road. A Poem.

"Fuge quo descendere gestis,
Non erit emisso reditus libi; Quid miser egi?"
Quid volui?"—HORACE.

"Breathes there the man with soul so dead."—SCOTT.
[and seven following lines.]

Manchester: Printed by R. and W. Dean, Market Street. 1813. *Octavo.*

Title as above, Dedication, Preface, and Poem, 35 pp.

Published at 2s. A copy is in the Manchester Free Library. The author of this was KINDER WOOD, a Manchester Surgeon, who in 1813 lived in Oldham, near which town is *Chamber.*

DARNETON, or RICH and POOR. A Tale of the Times. By JOHN ELIOTT WOOD.

"Qui laboret orat."

Manchester: Love and Barton, Market Street. MDCCCXLV. *Octavo.*

Half-title, Title as above, Dedication to "John Elliott, Esquire," and Darneton, 61 pp.

The Scene of this Tale is Rochdale, and its author a native of that town.

The RIVER DUDDON, a Series of SONNETS; Vaudracour and Julia, and other Poems. To which is annexed a TOPOGRAPHICAL DESCRIPTION of the COUNTRY of the LAKES in the North of

England. By WILLIAM WORDSWORTH. London: Printed for Longman, Hurst, Rees, Orme, and Brown, Paternoster Row. 1820. *Octavo.*

Title as above, Dedication, Advertisement, and Contents, viii. pp. Poems, p. 1 to p. 212. Topographical Description, p. 213 to p. 321.

Sells for 5s. The Topographical Description was originally published as an Introduction to the Rev. Joseph Wilkinson's Views of the Lakes (*See* p. 35). The above formed the fourth and last volume of the Poetical Works. The Sonnets and the Description have both been frequently reprinted.

THORNE'S (J.) RAMBLES by RIVERS. London. 1844. Contains a notice of the River Duddon.

An HEROIC EPISTLE from the QUADRUPLE OBELISK in the Market Place to the New Exchange. To which are annexed Notes, Historical, Critical, and Bombastical. [Quotation from Shakspeare.] Manchester: Printed and sold by Joseph Aston. 1809. *Octavo.*

Title as above, and Poem, 24 pp. On the 5th page is View of the Exchange..

A copy is in the Manchester Free Library.

A pleasant Comedie of FAIR EM the MILLER'S DAUGHTER of MANCHESTER, with the love of William the Conqueror, as it was sundry times publiquely acted in the Honourable City of London by the Right Honourable the Lord Strange his Servants. London: Printed for John Wright, and are to be sold at his shop at the sign of the Bible in Guiltspur Street, without Newgate. 1631. *Small quarto.*

Title as above, and Comedy, 46 pp. Very scarce.

This comedy was reprinted in Chetwood's "Select Collection of Old Plays," Dublin, 1750, and he states that he had seen three editions, the first without date, and no division into acts. The second dated 1619, with the acts divided, and with some immaterial alterations. Of the 1631 edition there is a copy in the British Museum, and it has been lettered by some old bookbinder as being written by Shakspeare. In Germany, Professor Delius, as a part of his *Pseudo-Shakspere'sche Dramen* (Ebberfeld, 1874), has again reprinted it with Notes on the text of Chetwood, etc. It is printed in *post octavo*, Two Titles, and Vorrede. xiv. pp. Half-title, and Dramatis Personæ, 2 pp. The Comedy, 53 pp.

The TRIAL of the MANCHESTER BARDS and the Bowdon Commemoration. By a Manchester Man.

"Mutavit mentem populus levis et calet uno."—HORACE.
[and two following lines.]

Manchester: Dunnill and Palmer, 3 Bond Street; London: Whittaker and Co.

Half-title, Title as above, and Trial of the Bards, etc., 112 pp. *Post octavo.*

Sells for 3s. 6d.

MEN and MEASURES, or the political Panorama. A Satire.

[Seven lines of Churchill's.]

London: Joseph Thomas, 1 Finch Lane, Cornhill, March 1839. *Royal octavo.*

Half-title, Title as above, 3 pp. Men and Measures, 43 pp.

Published at 2s. 6d. Contains several references to Manchester and Salford.

The FEAST of FOLLY, or the Four Nights' Entertainment. A Poem.

"For sense they little owe to frugal Heaven,
To please the mob they hide the little given."

London: J. M'Cormick; Manchester: Thomas Dewhurst, Market Street. 1837. *Octavo.*

Title as above, and The Feast of Folly, etc., 56 pp.

This is a political poem referring to the late Joseph Brotherton, M.P. for Salford. It is said to have been written by THOMAS DEWHURST, of the firm of Swain and Dewhurst, Manchester. A "Replication" to it appeared in the "Manchester and Salford Advertiser."

LEGENDS of LANCASHIRE.

"Round the fire such Legends go."—Sir W. SCOTT.

London: Whittaker and Co., etc. MDCCCXLI. *Duodecimo.*

Title as above, and Preface, xiv. pp. Legends, 372 pp. On p. 372, "R. Cocker, printer, Market Place, Wigan."

Published at 4s. 6d.

The SIEGE of MANCHESTER, that was to be. A very pretty poem of the last century. Translated by Squire Tristram Ragbotham, a very loyal subject of his present Majesty.

"O my country."

London: printed and published by W. Benbow, 269 Strand, and sold by all other Booksellers. 1820. *Octavo.*

Title as above, Address to the Reader, and Argument, iv. pp. The Siege, 48 pp.

Scarce. A copy is in the Manchester Free Library.

An EPISTLE from the Rector of St. Anne, Westminster, to the Vicar of Rochdale.

"Infœlix quæ tenta animum dementa cepit?
Non Vires alias conversaque numina sentis,
Cede Deo." VIRGIL.

Dedicated, without permission, to the Lord Bishop of London.

"We have conceived,
We have been in anguish,
We have, as it were, brought forth wind."
LOWTH'S "Translation of Isaiah."

London: printed for the Author, and published by J. Bew, Paternoster Row. MDCCLXXIX. Price 1s. *Quarto.*

Title as above, and Dedication, xx. pp. Epistle, 45 pp. Very rare.

Dr. Hind, Vicar of Rochdale, obtained the sobriquet of "The High Priest of St. Anne's."

The RUSHBEARING of ——. A Poem.

"—— Quis talia fando
Temperet a lachrymis." VIRGIL.

Manchester: printed by C. Wheeler for S. Falkner, Old Millgate. *Duodecimo.*

Title as above, and the Poem, 19 pp.

Scarce. A copy in the Library of Richard Wood, Esq., Manchester.

The QUACK DOCTOR. A Poem, in three Parts; to which is added a Humourous Dialogue betwixt the Quack Doctor and his Wife. Preston: printed by [or for] W. Sergent. [1750.] *Small quarto.*

This includes the "Lancashire Hob and the Quack Doctor," written in the Lancashire Dialect. [By TIM BOBBIN.]

Scarce. In J. C. Hotten's Handbook of Topography, priced 7s. 6d. *See* J. Collier, p. 249.

POEMS on various Subjects. [4 lines of Cowper's.] Liverpool: printed by J. M'Creery, and published for the Author at the Subscription Library, Lancaster; also for Mr. Walmsley and Mr. Holt; for Mr. Jones, Mr. Gore, and Messrs. Wright and Ormandy, Liverpool; and for Mr. Johnson, St. Paul's Churchyard, London. Price 7s. in Boards; Hot-pressed 7s. 6d. 1798. *Octavo.*

Title as above, 1 p. Address, List of Subscribers, Contents, and Errata, xiii. pp. Poems, 258 pp. Sells for 5s. 6d.

The List of Subscribers is arranged under the various Towns, and is a valuable record, containing the names of nearly 200 Lancashire people. Amongst other local Poems is "Lancaster Castle by Moonlight."

A copy of this is in the Liverpool Free Public Library.

The FESTIVAL of WIN, celebrated beneath his BROAD OAK, and likewise at his GOOD WICK. Anno Domini MVIIIXI. A Poem in ix. Cantos. Printed by J. Dawson, Stockport. Entered at Stationers' Hall. (NOTE.—Only 25 copies printed.) *Small quarto.*

Title as above, Preface, and Dedication, vi. pp. Festival 50 pp. Explanation, 2 pp.

Only 25 copies printed, one of which is in the Library of Dr. Kendrick, Warrington. The Author was the Rev. William Marriott, author of "The Antiquities of Lyme." The following Pamphlets, referring to the Winwick Broad Oak Festival, were published in 1811, without Title-pages, but with the following Dedications—"This account of the public dinner given to the Gallant Captain Phipps Hornby, of Her Majesty's ship "Le Volage," under the Winwick Broad Oak, by the inhabitants of Winwick-with-Hulme, on Monday, August 26, 1811, is reprinted at their express wish, and most respectfully inscribed to the Rev. Geoffrey Hornby, etc. * * By G. Chippendall." *Small quarto,* 10 pp. "This account of a public dinner given to the Gallant Captain Phipps Hornby, etc. * * by the inhabitants of Warrington, and the gentlemen of its neighbourhood, on Friday, August 30, 1811, is most respectfully inscribed to the Rev.

Geoffrey Hornby, etc. By T. K. Glazebrook, etc. *Small quarto.* 14 pp.

The Rev. Giles Chipperdall was Curate of Winwick, having previously been a Chaplain in the Navy, and lost an arm in the service.

LOYALTY, a LEGEND of SPEKE HALL, Lancashire. A Play, as Licensed by the Lord Chamberlain, and originally performed.

"Aymes Loyaulte."

London: Messrs. Whittaker and Co.; and J. Vincent, Oxford. 1845. *Octavo.*

Title as above, Dedication, and Dramatis Personæ, vi. pp. Loyalty, 59 pp.

A POEM, moral, philosophical, and religious; in which is considered the NATURE of MAN; his origin, his present existence, and his expectations; to which is added an Appendix, containing Bishop Newton's Thoughts on the Final Restitution of Mankind. London: printed for the Author, and sold by Richardson and Co., under the Exchange; and by J. Clarke, Bookseller, Manchester. 1788. *Octavo.*

Title, etc., viii. pp. Poem, etc., 132 pp. Errata, 1 p.

A copy is in the Library of J. F. Marsh, Esq., Chepstow.

This is a poem of local interest. Henry Clarke, Schoolmaster, author of "The School Candidates" [*See* p. 247], is mentioned under the sobriquet of "Thimblewillan;" but, notwithstanding this, the late Mr. Ford attributed to him the authorship.

PART IV.

WORKS PARTLY RELATING TO LANCASHIRE.[1]

ARCHÆOLOGIA; or, Miscellaneous Tracts relating to Antiquity. Published by the Society of Antiquaries of London. *Quarto.*

The First Volume was published in 1770.[2] The following articles refer to Lancashire:—

VOL. I.

An account of the Course of the Roman Roads from MANCHESTER. By THOMAS PERCIVAL. P. 62 to p. 64.

The true situation of COCCIUM. By the Rev. JOHN WATSON, M.A., F.A.S. P. 65 to p. 72.

DUCHY of LANCASTER; a manuscript thereof written in 1590. By Serjeant FLEETWOOD. P. v.

VOL. II.

DUCHY of LANCASTER; its origin. P. 285.

VOL. V.

An account of antiquities discovered in LANCASTER in 1776. By THOMAS WEST, F.A.S. P. 98 to p. 100.

Observations on the Celts, occasioned by the discovery of one in the Ruins of GLEASTON CASTLE. With four plates. By MICHAEL LORT, D.D., F.A.S. P. 106 to p. 118.

---

[1] It is not intended here to include all books which in part refer to the county; but rather to bring under notice certain works which contain much valuable information to the student of Lancashire History.

[2] There were three Editions of Vol. I., the paging of which is slightly different. The numbers above refer to the First Edition.

VOL. VII.

Some account of BARROW HILL near YEALAND, and of Antiquities discovered there. By JOHN COAKLEY LETTSOM, LL. and M.D., F.A.S. P. 414.

An account of nearly nine hundred silver Roman denarii of the Higher Empire, discovered in 1717 between the Villages of CHATBURN and WORSTON. By the Hon. DAINES BARRINGTON, F.A.S. P. 414.

VOL. VIII.

The Church privileged with Sanctuary at Lancaster. P. 41.

VOL. IX.

An account of antiquities in the parish of WARTON. With a Plate. By WILLIAM HUTCHINSON, F.A.S. P. 211 to p. 218.

VOL. XIII.

Observations on Mr. Towneley's Antique Bronze Helmet discovered at RIBCHESTER. With a vignette. By the Rev. STEPHEN WESTON, B.D., F.A.S. P. 223 to p. 226.

A description of a Roman Altar (to Cocideus) discovered at LANCASTER. With a Figure. By the Rev. FRANCIS LEE, A.M. P. 401 to p. 402.

LANCASTER the Longovicum of the Notitia. P. 402.

VOL. XIV.

An explanation of a Carving over a Chimney-piece at SPEKE HALL. With a Plate. By HENRY JOHN HINCHLIFFE, F.A.S. P. 20 to p. 23.

VOL. XVIII.

Account of some Saxon Antiquities found near LANCASTER. With Figures. P. 199 to p. 202.

VOL. XIX.

Great Resemblance of the Dialect of Lancashire to that of Cheshire. P. 17.

Vol. XX.

Badges of the House of Lancaster. P. 105.

LANCASHIRE HERALDS described. P. 164.

LANCASTER SWORD first introduced at the Coronation of Henry IV., being that which he wore on his landing. P. 207.

Vol. XXI.

Descent of the EARLDOM of LANCASTER. P. 201.

Observations on the Arms and Seal of the Town of LIVERPOOL. With a Figure. P. 543 to p. 546.

Vol. XXIV.

Exhibition of the brass bar of a Purse or Pouch found at OVER DARWEN, near Blackburn. P. 353.

The Hoar Stones at LANCASTER. P. 53.

Vol. XXV.

An account of the discovery of an ancient Instrument of brass at ROCHDALE. P. 595 to p. 597.

Vol. XXVI.

Exhibition of assemblage of Impressions from Seals, taken by favour of Lord Holland from the originals in the archives of the Duchy Court of Lancaster.

Vol. XXVIII.

Observations on some ancient pieces of ordnance and other relics discovered in the Island of WALNEY. With two Plates. P. 373 to p. 392.

Vol. XXIX.

Notes on the Runic Cross at LANCASTER. With two Plates. P. 76 to p. 79.

VOL. XXX.

An account of a curious English Poetical Manuscript of the 15th Century preserved in the Chetham Library at MANCHESTER. P. 527 to p. 530.

An account of the discovery of a Roman Urn near BURNLEY. P. 553 to p. 554.

HISTORY of the COTTON MANUFACTURE in Great Britain, with a notice of its early History in the East and in all the Quarters of the Globe.

A description of the Great Mechanical Inventions which has caused its unexampled extension in Britain, and a view of the present state of the Manufacture and the condition of the classes engaged in its several departments. By EDWARD BAINES Jun., Esq. Embellished and illustrated with Portraits of Inventors, Drawings of Machinery, etc. London: H. Fisher, R. Fisher, and P. Jackson. *Octavo.*

Title as above, Dedication, Preface, Order of the Engravings, and Contents, 18 pp. The History and Appendix, 544 pp.

ILLUSTRATIONS (Engravings).

Portrait of Sir Richard Arkwright.
Hall-i'-th'-Wood, Bolton.
Portrait of Samuel Crompton.
Portrait of Sir Robert Peel.
The Exchange, Manchester.
Cotton Factories, Union Street, Manchester.
Cotton Factories of Messrs. Swainson, Birley, and Co., near Preston, and eleven Views of Machinery, also eleven Woodcuts.

Published at 15s. Sells for 4s. 6d.

Mr. Edward Baines is the son and biographer of the late Edward Baines, M.P. for Leeds, and the Author of the "History of Lancashire."

The SOCIAL, EDUCATIONAL, and RELIGIOUS STATE of the MANUFACTURING DISTRICTS, with statistical Returns of the means of education and religious instruction in the manufacturing districts of Yorkshire, Lancashire, and Cheshire, in two Letters to the Right Hon.

Sir Robt. Peel, Bart. With an Appendix containing a Letter to the Right Hon. Lord Wharncliffe on Sir Jas. Graham's Factory Education Bill, also the objections to the amended Bill. By EDWARD BAINES Junr., Author of the "History of the Cotton Manufacture." London: Simpkin, Marshall, and Co., and T. Ward and Co.; Leeds: Baines and Newsome. MDCCCXLIII. *Octavo.*

Title and Dedication, iv. pp. Letters, etc., 76 pp.

Sells for 2s. 6d.

A COLLECTION of the SUFFERINGS of the PEOPLE called QUAKERS for the Testimony of a Good Conscience, from the Time of their being first distinguished by that name in the year 1650 to the Time of the Act commonly called the Act of Toleration granted to Protestant Dissenters in the first year of the reign of King William the Third, and Queen Mary in the year 1689. Taken from the original records and other authentic accounts by JOSEPH BESSE.

VOL. I.

[John xv. 20; Psalms xxxiv. 19, and xii. 5.]

London: Printed and sold by Luke Hinde, at the Bible in George-Yard, Lombard-Street. MDCCLIII. *Folio.*

Sells for £1 : 10s.

This work is complete in two volumes, but the whole of the Lancashire portion is comprised in the pages 300 to 330 of the first volume.

The above is the best Edition. The earlier work, called "An Abstract of the Sufferings of the People, etc., was published in 1733-38 in three volumes 8vo.

A COMPLEAT HISTORY of MAGICK, SORCERY, and WITCHCRAFT. Containing

I. The Tryalls of Several Witches at Salem, in New England.

II. A Narrative of many surprysing and Amazing Sorceries and Witchcrafts practised in Scotland, etc. * *

III. The SURREY DEMONIACK, with all the Testimonies and Informations taken upon Oath relating thereunto.

VOL. II.

London: printed for E. Curll at the Dial and Bible, J. Pembroke at the Buck and Sun, both against St. Dunstan's Church in Fleet Street, and Mr. Taylor at the Ship in Pater-Noster Row. 1716. *Duodecimo.*

Title as above, and Contents, iv. pp. A Compleat History, 235 pp. The portion relating to the Surrey Demoniacks, p. 166 to p. 235.

The work (complete in two volumes) was written by RICHARD BOULTON. It is very scarce. A copy is in the Author's Library.

The POSSIBILITY and REALITY of MAGICK, SORCERY, and WITCHCRAFT demonstrated, or a Vindication of a Compleat History of Magick, Sorcery, and Witchcraft, in answer to Dr. Hutchinson's Historical Essay, now Bishop of Down and Connor, in the Kingdom of Ireland.

IN TWO PARTS.

PART I. Containing an Examination and an Answer of the Positions laid down in that Book.

PART II. An Essay of the Nature of Material and immaterial Substances. How immaterial Substances may affect one another, and alter Matter, or work upon Human Bodies; proved by Reason, Philosophy, and Moral Proof, and the Testimony of Scripture.

By RICHARD BOULTON, sometime of Brazenose College, in Oxford. [Deut. xviii. 10, 11.] London: printed for F. Roberts, near the Oxford Arms, in Warwick Lane. MDCCXXII. Price 2s. *Duodecimo.*

Title as above, Preface, and Contents, xx. pp. Introduction, and A Vindication, 184 pp.

Scarce. A copy is in the Author's Library. The book contains an epitome of the Surrey (or Surey) Demoniac case. *See* PART V., *post.*

The POLITICAL STATE of GREAT BRITAIN, with the most material Occurrences in Europe, for the month of November 1715, containing in particular—

I. An account of the Associations made in England, etc.
II. Declaration of the Lords, etc. * *
III. Proceedings of the Parliament, etc.
IV. Account of the PROGRESS, COUNSELS, and TOTAL DEFEAT

of the REBELS in LANCASHIRE, with a most accurate PLAN of the Town, of Barricades, Batteries, and Attacks at PRESTON, on a large Copperplate.

V. Affairs in Scotland, etc.

VI. Success of the Earl of Sutherland, etc.

By Mr. A. BOYER.

London: printed for John Baker and S. Warren, at the Black Boy, in Paternoster Row. 1715. (Price 1s. 6d.) Where may be had complete Sets bound up in Volumes or single Books, and at the Author's House in Queen's Court, King Street, Covent Garden. *Octavo.*

Title as above. The Political State for November 1715, p. 435 to p. 536.

This forms the tenth volume of the series. The British Museum possesses a complete set of this monthly periodical. Sets have sold for upwards of £40. A copy of the above volume is in the Library of Richard Wood, Esq., Manchester.

BRADSHAW'S MANCHESTER JOURNAL.

VOL. I.

Embellished with a Map and Engravings on Steel and Wood. Manchester: Bradshaw and Blacklock, 27 Brown Street; London: Groombridge, Paternoster Row. MDCCCXLI. *Octavo.*

Title as above, Preface, and Contents, viii. pp. Journal, 424 pp.

PLATES (referring to Lancashire, the others are here omitted).

Victoria Bridge, Manchester.
The Royal Institution, Manchester.
Henshaw's Blind Asylum, and the Deaf and Dumb School, Manchester.
Sir Robert Peel, Bart.
The Public Room of the Town-Hall, Manchester.
Map of the County.
The Crescent and the Adelphi Bleachworks, Salford.
Borwick Hall, near Lancaster.
Dr. Raffles' Chapel, Liverpool.
Fleetwood.
Part of the Market Place, Manchester, in 1821.

VOL. II.

Title, Preface, and Contents, v. pp. Introduction, vii. pp. Journal, 408 pp. No Lancashire Plates.

VOL. III.

Title and Preface, v. pp. Journal, 410 pp.

PLATES (Lancashire).

Darwen Paper-Mills. | Portrait of John Dalton.
Peel Hall, Worsley.

VOL. IV.

Title, Address, Contents, and List of Illustrations, vi. pp. Journal, 376 pp.

PLATES (Lancashire).

Windermere Lake.
Lime Street Station, Liverpool.
Redcliffe Church, and Bason, Liverpool.
The Industrial Schools at Swainton, near Manchester.

These four volumes are all that were published. Copies are in the Manchester Free Library.

BARNABEE'S JOURNALL, under the names of Mirtilus and Faustulus shadowed; for the Traveller's solace, lately published to most apt numbers reduced, and to the old Tune of Barnabe, commonly chanted. By CORYMÆUS.

> "Th' oyle of malt, and juyce of spritely nectar,
> Have made my Muse more valiant than Hector."

224 leaves, with an Engraved Frontispiece by W. Marshall. *Duodecimo.*

This Edition was published about 1650. It is extremely rare. Imperfect copies have sold for £7.

As only a small portion of this work refers to Lancashire, it will not be necessary to detail all the Editions. They were issued as follows:— Second, 1716; third, 1723; fourth, 1774; fifth, 1805, sells for 10s.; sixth, same date, etc. as the fifth.

The seventh, "Barnabae Itinerarium, or Barnabee's Journal. To which are prefixed an Account of the Author, now first discovered, a Bibliographical History of the Former Editions of the Work, and Illustrative Notes." London: printed for J. Harding, St. James's Street, by R. and A. Taylor, Shoe Lane. 1818. Sells for 12s. *Small octavo.*

An Irish Edition published in Dublin in 1762, which is a reprint of the second Edition.

The best Edition is as follows:—

Barnabae Itinerarum, or Barnabee's Journal. By RICHARD BRATHWAIT, A.M. With a Life of the Author, a Bibliographical Introduction to the Itinerary, and a Catalogue of his Works. Edited from the First Edition by JOSEPH HASTLEWOOD.

"E'en in our ashes live their wonted fires."

London. 1820. In 2 volumes. *Duodecimo.*

VOL. I.

Half-title, Title as above, Table of Contents, Illustrations, and Distribution of the whole Impression, Life of the Author, xlv. pp. Introduction, Notes, Collations, and Indexes to both volumes, 459 pp.

LIST OF PLATES.

1. Portrait of R. Brathwait, and Arms, *Frontispiece.*
2. Monument in Catterick Church, p. xl.
3. Medallion and Portrait of R. Braithwait, p. xlv.
4. Woodcut of Queen's College, Horn, also two additional pages of letterpress of Description, paged 88*89.

VOL. II.

Half-title, Title, and Barnabee's Journal (which is almost a facsimile of the 1st Edition), 448 pp. Illustrated with a copy Frontispiece of original Edition by Marshall.

Only 125 copies of this Edition were printed. Sells for £3 : 3s.

An Edition was published in London in 1822, which contains four lithographic prints, and sells for 3s. 6d.

A concise DESCRIPTION of the ENDOWED GRAMMAR SCHOOLS, in ENGLAND and Wales. Ornamented with Engravings. By NICHOLAS CARLISLE, F.R.S. In two volumes.

Vol. I.

London : printed for Baldwin, Cradock, and Joy, Paternoster Row, by W. Bulmer and Co., Cleveland Row. 1818. *Octavo.*

Title, Dedication, and Preface, xliv. pp. List of Subscribers, vi. pp. Description, 858 pp.

The Lancashire portion is comprised between p. 636 and p. 733. Nothing in the Second Volume relates to Lancashire.

The two volumes were published at £2 : 16s. Sell for 15s.

The GREAT CIVIL WAR of the TIMES of CHARLES I. and CROMWELL. By the Rev. Richard Cattermole, B.D., with thirty highly finished Engravings from Drawings by George Cattermole, Esq. London: Henry G. Bohn, York Street, Covent Garden. 1857. *Royal octavo.*

Engraved Title, Title as above, Advertisement, and List of Plates, vi. pp. The Civil War, 279 pp.

Amongst the Plates is "A Sortie from Lathom House."

Sells for 15s.

The WORTHIES of YORKSHIRE and LANCASHIRE, being lives of the most distinguished persons that have been born in or connected with those counties. By Hartley Coleridge. With portraits. London : Frederick Warne and Co., Bedford Street, Covent Garden ; Hull : W. Adams, Market Place. *Octavo.*

Title as above, Contents, iii. pp. Introductory Essay, viii. pp. Worthies, 480 pp.

Sells for 4s. 6d.

Another Edition,

The WORTHIES of YORKSHIRE and LANCASHIRE, being Lives of the most distinguished persons that have been born in or connected with these Provinces. By Hartley Coleridge. London : Whittaker and Co. ; Simpkin, Marshall, and Co. ; John Cross, Leeds ; Bancks and Co., Manchester ; Grapel, Liverpool. 1836. *Octavo.*

Title as above, Dedication, Advertisement, and Introductory Essay, viii.

pp. The Lives, with Half-title, and The Life of Andrew Marvell, 720 pp. Historical and Chronological Index of the Lives of Andrew Marvell, Richard Bentley, Thomas Lord Fairfax, James, seventh Earl of Derby, Lady Anne Clifford, Roger Ascham, John Fisher, Rev. William Mason, Sir Richard Arkwright, William Roscoe, Captain Cook, William Congreve, and Dr. John Fothergill, p. 721 to p. 732.

LIST OF PLATES.

1. Andrew Marvell . . . . . *To face Title-page*
2. Anne Clifford, Countess of Dorset, Pembroke, etc. . . P. 241
3. William Roscoe 481

The termination of the Volume has "End of Vol. I." This is, however, all that was published.

It was first issued by F. E. Bingley, 87 Briggate, Leeds, in 1832, and the remainder, with a new Title-page, was sold by Mr. John Cross.

Published at 16s.

The best Edition was published as follows:—

LIVES of NORTHERN WORTHIES. By HARTLEY COLERIDGE. Edited by his Brother (the Rev. Derwent Coleridge). A New Edition, with the Corrections of the Author, and the marginal observations of S. T. Coleridge. In three volumes. London: Edward Moxon, Dover Street. 1852. *Foolscap octavo.*

VOL. I.

Half-title, Title as above, Preface by the Editor, Advertisement by the Author, and Introductory Essay, xxvii. pp. Contents of Vol. I.—Half-title, "Andrew Marvell." Lives, and Historical and Chronological Index, 397 pp.

VOL. II.

Half-title, Title, Contents, and Half-title, "Lady Anne Clifford," 8 pp. Lives and Index, 389 pp.

VOL. III.

Half-title, Title, Contents of Vol. III., 8 pp. Lives and Index, 389 pp.

Published at 15s.

WORKS PARTLY RELATING TO LANCASHIRE.

A TOUR thro' the WHOLE ISLAND of GREAT BRITAIN. Divided into Circuits or Journeys, giving a particular and entertaining account of whatever is curious and worth observation, viz.—

I. A Description of the Principal Cities and Towns, their Situation, Government, and Commerce.

II. The Customs, Manners, Exercises, Diversions, and Employments of the People.

III. The Produce and Improvement of the Lands, the Trade, and Manufacture.

IV. The Sea Ports and Fortifications, the course of the Rivers, and the Inland Navigation.

V. The Public Edifices, Seats, and Palaces of the Nobility and Gentry.

VI. The Isles of Wight, Portland, Jersey, Guernsey, and other English and Scottish Isles of most note.

Interspersed with useful observations. Particularly fitted for the Perusal of such as desire to Travel over the Island. By a GENTLEMAN [DANIEL DE FOE]. The Fifth Edition. With very great additions, Improvements, and Corrections, which bring it down to the year 1753. In four volumes.

VOL. III.

London: printed for S. Birt, T. Osborne, D. Browne, T. and T. Longman, C. Hitch, L. Hawes, J. Hodges, A. Millar, J. Robinson, and J. and J. Rivington. MDCCLIII. *Duodecimo.*

Title as above and Contents, iii. pp. A Tour, 312 pp. Index (not paged), 18 pp.

From p. 235 to p. 277 contains a Description of the Counties of Lancashire, Westmoreland, and Cumberland. The Lancashire portion is contained on p. 133 to p. 136.

Sells for 6s. 6d.

First printed in 1724. The other Editions appeared in 1732, 1742, 1753, 1769, 1778.

Lowndes says that the "First Edition is the only really valuable one. Defoe is lost in all the others." The Three Volumes of the First Edition sell for £1 : 1s.

This book has often been mistaken for "A JOURNEY THROUGH

ENGLAND; in Familiar Letters from a Gentleman here to his friend abroad." 1722. 2 Vols. *Octavo.*

The author of this was JOHN MACKAY.

LETTERS written from LIVERPOOL, Chester, etc. By SAMUEL DERRICK, Esq., Master of the Ceremonies at Bath. London: printed for L. Davis and C. Reymers. 1767. *Duodecimo.*

In two volumes.—Vol. I., 132 pp. Vol. II., 152 pp.

The portion referring to Liverpool is in the 3d, 4th, and 5th Letters, and gives an interesting description of the town in 1760. Dr. Johnson says of these Letters that "if they had been written by one of more established name they would have been thought very pretty."

Very scarce.

A VINDICATION of the HISTORY of CLEMENCY, with reflections upon the late Proceedings against the Author. In a letter from himself at Paris to a friend in London. To which is added an Edition of the said history, with additions. Addressed to all that ever design to be in arms against the Established Government for their information and benefit.

"Manus hæc Inimica Tyrannis
Semper erit, semperque fuit."
[Jerem. 36-38.]

London: printed in the year 1720. *Post 12mo.*

Title as above, i. p. Letter, xxix. pp. Errata, i. p. The Introduction to History, 24 pp. (unpaged). Second Title, i. p. Preface, 10 p. The History of the Clemency, 167 pp.

Frontispiece, Portrait of Matthias Earbury, "natus 11th July 1690."

A Folding Plate of the Battle of Preston faces the Introduction.

This curious work contains an account of the Battle of Preston. Its author, Matthias Earbury, was a supporter of the Pretender.

It was privately printed, and now sells for 10s. 6d. A copy is in the Author's Library.

The First Edition was printed in London 1717, and only contained the "History of the Clemency."

The HISTORY of the WORTHIES of ENGLAND. Endeavoured

by THOMAS FULLER, D.D. London: Printed by J. G., W. L., and W. G. MDCLXII. *Folio.*

Title as above, etc., iv. pp. Owing to the work having been executed by several printers, the paging is very irregular. The total number of pages is 1018, exclusive of Title, etc. *Frontispiece*, Portrait of T. Fuller. The Lancashire portion is comprised in 18 pp. Other Editions printed in 1684, 1811, and 1840.

SUMMER RAMBLES in Cheshire, Derbyshire, LANCASHIRE, and Yorkshire. Being a sequel to "Manchester Walks and Wild Flowers." By LEO H. GRINDON, Lecturer on Botany at the Royal School of Medicine, Manchester.

SECOND EDITION.

"O how happy here's our leisure!
O how innocent our pleasure!"
[Four more lines.]

Manchester: Palmer and Howe, 1 and 3 Bond Street; London: Simpkin, Marshall, and Co. 1868. *Post octavo.*

Half-title, List of Works by same Author, Title as above, Preface, and Contents, xi. pp. Rambles and Index, 251 pp.

Frontispiece, Palace Hotel, Southport.
Published at 2s. 6d. The first Edition published in 1866 at 4s. 6d.

The BRITISH COTTON MANUFACTORIES, and a reply to an article on the Spinning Machinery contained in a recent number of the "Edinburgh Review." By RICHARD GUEST.

"Error hops with airy and fastidious levity over proofs and arguments, and perches upon assertion which it calls conclusion."—CURRAN.

Manchester: Printed by Henry Smith, St. Ann's Square; sold by E. Thompson and Sons, Market Street, and W. and W. Clarke, Market Place; and Longman, Rees, and Co., London. [1823.] *Post octavo.*

Title as above, and Cotton Manufactures, 230 pp.

Contains much information on the claims of Arkwright.

Sells for 5s.

WORKS PARTLY RELATING TO LANCASHIRE.

A COMPENDIOUS HISTORY of the COTTON MANUFACTURE, with a disproval of the claim of Sir Richard Arkwright to the invention of its ingenious machinery. By RICHARD GUEST. Manchester: Printed by Joseph Pratt, Chapel-Walks, and sold by G. Thompson, Market Street, and W. and W. Clarke, Market Place; London: Hurst and Co., and G. and W. B. Whittaker. 1823. *Quarto.*

Title as above, 1 p., Contents and History, 70 pp. Explanation of Plates, 3 pp. Eleven plates.

Published at 9s.

A HOME TOUR through the MANUFACTURING DISTRICTS of England in the Summer of 1835. By Sir GEORGE HEAD, Author of "Forest Scenes and Incidents in the Wilds of North America. London: John Murray, Albemarle Street. *Octavo.*

Half-title, Title, Advertisement, and Contents, xi. pp. Excursions, 434 pp.

Published at 9s. 6d. Sells for 2s. 6d.

The HISTORY of the REBELLION 1745 and 1746, containing a full account of the rise, progress, and extinction. The character of the Highlanders and the Chieftains. All the Declarations of the Pretender, and the Journal of his marches through England, as published by himself, with observations. Likewise a particular description of all the Battles, Skirmishes, and Sieges, with many incidents hitherto not made public. By an impartial hand, who was Eye witness to most of the Facts. The second Edition, revised and corrected. London: reprinted from the Edinburgh Edition. Edited and sold by R. Griffiths, Bookseller and publisher in Ludgate Street. MDCCXLVIII. *Octavo.*

Title as above, Dedication, and Preface, viii. pp. The History, 126 pp.

The author of this was ANDREW HENDERSON, M.A.

The first Edition was published in 1745. The fifth was published in London in 1753, revised and corrected, with additions. 12*mo.* Sells for 5s. 6d. Contains some interesting details of the Rebellion in Lancashire.

The HISTORY of the REBELLION in the Year 1745. By JOHN HOME, Esq. London: Printed by A. Strahan, New Street Square, for T. Cadell Jun., and W. Davis, in the Strand. 1802. *Quarto.*

Title as above, Dedication, Preface, and Contents, xx. pp. The History and Appendix, 394 pp. Addendum and Directions to the Binder, 2 pp.

PLATES.

Map of Scotland.
The Bust of Charles Edward Stuart.
The Plan of the Battle of Preston (Scotland).
Plan of the Battle of Falkirk.
Plan of the Battle of Culloden.

Sells for 10s. 6d.

The information referring to Lancashire in this work is very slight.

An HISTORICAL ESSAY concerning WITCHCRAFT, with observations upon Matters of Fact, tending to clear the Texts of the Sacred Scriptures and confute the vulgar Errors about that Point. And also Two Sermons, one in Proof of the Christian Religion; the other concerning the Good and Evil Angels. By FRANCIS HUTCHINSON, D.D., Chaplain in Ordinary to His Majesty, and Minister of St. James's Parish in St. Edmunds'-Bury. (Quotation, Psalm xxxi. 6, and 1 Tim. iv. 7.) London: Printed for R. Knaplock at the Bishop's Head, and D. Midwinter at the Three Crowns in St. Paul's Churchyard. MDCCXVIII. *Octavo.*

Half-title, Title as above, Dedication, and Contents, xx. pp. Historical Essay, 230 pp. Two Sermons, p. 231 to p. 270. Books written by the Author, and books printed by R. Knaplock and D. Midwinter, 2 pp.

A second Edition of this work was published in 1720; both are scarce and sell for 7s. 6d.

This interesting work contains notices of the "Witches of Pendle Forest," "The Surey Demoniac," etc. It was written in reply to "A Compleat History of Magic, Sorcery, and Witchcraft." London: E. Curl, 1715-16, 2 volumes. By RICHARD BOULTON. (*See* p. 294.)

MEMOIRS of the REBELLION in 1745 and 1746. By the CHEVALIER DE JOHNSTONE, Aide-de-Camp to Lord George Murray, General of the Rebel Army, Assistant Aide-de-Camp to Prince Charles Edward, Captain in the Duke of Perth's Regiment, and afterwards an Officer in the French Service. Contains a Narrative of the Progress of the Rebellion from its commencement to the Battle of Culloden; the characters of the principal persons engaged in it, and anecdotes respecting them; and various important particulars relating to that contest hitherto either unknown or imperfectly understood; with an account of the sufferings and privations experienced by the Author after the Battle of Culloden before he effected his escape to the Continent, etc. etc. Translated from a French MS., originally deposited in the Scots College at Paris, and now in the hands of the publishers. Third Edition. London: printed for Longman, Hurst, Rees, Orme, and Brown, Paternoster Row. 1822. *Octavo.*

Title as above, Advertisement to the Second Edition, and Introduction, lxxii. pp. Memoirs, 456 pp. *Frontispiece*, Portrait of Charles Edward Stuart. Portrait of James Stuart, son of James II. (facing p. 72). Folding Plan of Skirmish at Clifton Hall (facing p. 1.)

Sells for 10s. 6d. The first Edition appeared in 1820, and the second in 1821. This, though perhaps not very reliable, is one of the most interesting works on the Rebellion, and contains particulars of the passage through Lancashire not to be found elsewhere. Several of the most striking incidents in Mr. W. H. Ainsworth's "The Manchester Rebels," are taken from this volume.

A TRUE HISTORY of the several DESIGNS and CONSPIRACIES against his MAJESTIES Sacred Person and Government as they were continually carry'd on from 1688 until 1697. Containing matters extracted from Original Papers, Depositions of the Witnesses, and Authentick Records, as appears by the References to the Appendix, wherein they are Digested. Publish'd with no other Design then to acquaint the English Nation that notwithstanding the Present Posture of Affairs our Enemies are still so Many, Restless, and Designing, that all imaginable Care ought to be taken for the Defence and Safety of His Majesty and his Three Kingdoms. By R. K. [Quotation from Ovid.] London: printed for the Author, and sold by Abel Roper at the Black Boy against St. Dunstan's Church, in Fleet Street. 1698. *Foolscap octavo.*

Title as above, and Preface, 13 pp. An Account of several Conspiracies, etc., and Appendix, 312 pp. List of Books printed by A. Roper added.

This is quite a Lancashire Book, and contains much valuable information about the *Lancashire Plot.* Sells for 5s. 6d.

WORKS PARTLY RELATING TO LANCASHIRE.

SIR PETER LEGH, a LEGEND of LYME, and other Ballads. Manchester: Edward Slater, 16 St. Ann's Square, and 129 Market Street. 1861. *Post octavo.*

Half-title, Title as above, Dedication, and Introduction, viii. pp. Legends, etc., 88 pp.

Published at 3s.

The Author is John Leigh, Esq., of Manchester. A fourth part of the book refers to Lancashire—viz. "The Hermit of Kersall Cell," and "Incidents in the Life of a Manchester Worthy."

An OLD MAN'S WANDERINGS, or an account of a TOUR through the MANUFACTURING DISTRICTS. Edited by CHARLES LYNE, M.A., Incumbent of Tywardreath and Prebendary of Exeter. London: Simpkin, Marshall, and Co., and Hamilton, Adams, and Co.; Manchester: Simms and Denham. 1846. *Duodecimo.*

Half-title, i. p. Engraved Title, Title as above, Dedication and Introduction, viii. pp. An Old Man's Wanderings, 188 pp. Engraved Frontispiece.

Published at 4s.

The CONDITION of CATHOLICS under JAMES I. FATHER GERARD'S NARRATIVE of the GUNPOWDER PLOT. Edited, with his life, by JOHN MORRIS, Priest of the Society of Jesus. Second Edition. London: Longmans, Green, and Co. 1872. *Octavo.*

Title as above. The Condition of the Catholics and Index, 344 pp. Life of Father Gerrard and Notes, cclxiv. pp.

The first Edition was published in 1871.

Much of this interesting volume refers to Lancashire.

HANDBOOK for SHROPSHIRE, CHESHIRE, and LANCASHIRE. With a Map. London: John Murray, Albemarle Street. 1870. The right of Translation reserved. *Post octavo.*

Title, Preface, Contents, and Introduction, xc. pp. Handbook and Index, 328 pp.

Published at 10s.

WORKS PARTLY RELATING TO LANCASHIRE.

MURRAY'S HANDBOOK to CATHEDRALS. (*See* p. 132).

VIEWS of the SEATS of NOBLEMEN and GENTLEMEN in ENGLAND, WALES, and SCOTLAND. From drawings by J. P. NEALE. London: Published by Sherwood, Neeley, and Jones, Paternoster Row, and Thomas Moule, Duke Street, Grosvenor Square. [1823.]

VOL. VI. contains Views of Ince, Lathom House (2 views), Rufford Hall, Seaforth House, and Woolton Hall.

The entire work is in 11 vols. 1818-1829, which were published at £26 : 8s., reduced to £10 : 10s. Large paper, £52 : 16s., reduced to £21.

MISCELLANEA PALATINA, consisting of GENEALOGICAL ESSAYS illustrative of CHESHIRE and LANCASHIRE FAMILIES, and of Memoir of the Cheshire Domesday Roll. Compiled from the original authorities by GEORGE ORMEROD, D.C.L., F.R.S., F.S.A., of Tyldesley and Sedbury Park, Author of the History of Cheshire. Not published. MDCCCLI. *Octavo.*

Title as above, i. p. Introduction, iv. pp. Title to Memoirs Noreis Family, and Contents, 55 pp. Miscellanea (Part II.) and Contents, p. 56 to p. 116. Memoir of Cheshire Domesday Roll and Index, 28 pp. Addenda and Index, 8 pp.

PLATES.

View of Sedbury	*Frontispiece*
Brasses of Henry and Clemence Norres	P. 33
Pennon, Boswell of Balmuto	35
Bench end with armorial carvings at Childwell Church	47

PEDIGREES.

The Blackrod and Sutton lines of Le Norres	8
The Speke line of Le Norres	14
The same line to the issue of Sir William Norres, living 1567	26
The same line to the termination in heirs-general	36
The Lathom Family	69
The Arderne Family	91

A copy of this rare work is in the Chetham Library (presented by the Author). Copies have been sold for as much as £7, although it is not generally priced so high.

WORKS PARTLY RELATING TO LANCASHIRE.

The NONCONFORMISTS' MEMORIAL; being an ACCOUNT of the MINISTERS who were EJECTED or SILENCED after the RESTORATION, particularly by the Act of Uniformity which took place on Bartholomew-day, Aug. 24, 1662. Containing a concise View of their Lives and Characters, their Principles, Sufferings, and Printed Works. Originally written by the Reverend and Learned EDMUND CALAMY, D.D. Now abridged and corrected, and the Author's Additions inserted, with many farther Particulars and new Anecdotes. By SAMUEL PALMER. To which is prefixed an Introduction containing a brief History of the Times in which they lived, and the grounds of their nonconformity. Embellished with the Heads of many of those venerable Divines.

VOL. II.

[Quotation 2 Chron. xi. 14-16.]

London: printed for W. Harris, No. 70 St. Paul's Church-yard. MDCCLXXV.

Title as above, and Nonconformists' Memorial, 648 pp. Index, 24 pp. The Lancashire portion, p. 79 to p. 111. (Nothing in Vol. I.) Complete in two volumes.

Sells for 10s. 6d.

Second Edition, in three volumes, 1802. The same particulars will also be found in the third volume of "Calamy's "Abridgment of Baxter's History of his Life and Times, or an Account of the Ministers," etc. Four volumes. *Octavo.* 1713-21.

The HISTORY of the LATE REBELLION, with original Papers and Characters of the Principal Noblemen and Gentlemen concern'd in it. By the Reverend Mr. ROBERT PATTEN. London: printed for J. Baker and T. Warner, at the Black-Boy, in Pater-noster-row. 1717. *Octavo.*

Title as above, Dedication, and Preface, viii. pp. History of the Rebellion, p. 1 to p. 144. The History of the Rebellion in Scotland, p. 145 to p. 271. Contains a Map of the Town of Preston, and a full account of the Battle of Preston, etc., with a long list of Prisoners.

Scarce. Sells for 15s. A copy is in the Author's Library.

Robert Patten was the Chaplain to Mr. Foster.

The Second Edition, 1718, is also scarce. The Third and Fourth Editions, 1745, are not quite so difficult to get.

WORKS PARTLY RELATING TO LANCASHIRE.

A TOUR from DOWNING to ALSTON MOOR. By THOMAS PENNANT, Esq. London : printed at the Oriental Press, by Wilson and Co., for Edward Harding, No. 98 Pall Mall, and sold by West and Hughes, No. 40 Paternoster Row. 1801. *Quarto.*

Title as above, Advertisement, Itinerary, and List of Plates, viii. pp. Tour and Index, 195 pp.

LIST OF PLATES.

Painted Glass at Warrington	P. 11	Tomb of Sir——de Musgrave, etc.	P. 124
Orford Hall	12	Wharton Hall	129
Tomb of Sir Thomas Boteler	20	Philip, Duke of Wharton	130
Edward, Earl of Derby	26	Lamerside Hill	131
Charlotte, Countess of Derby	37	Pendragon Castle	131
Sefton Church	48	Brough Church	137
Lydiate Church	31	Appleby Castle	139
Houghton Tower	64	Tomb of the Countess of Cumberland	144
Sir Edward Osbaldiston	66	Three-brother Tree	152
Clitheroe Castle	76	Anne Clifford's Column	154
Ancient Altar at Ribchester	93	Naworth Castle	173
Kirby Lonsdale Bridge	117	Llanercost Priory	177
Dr. Shaw	120	Ben Castle	180
Overton Church	122		

Published at 12s. Sells for 7s. 6d.

The HISTORY of the LATE REBELLION, rais'd against his Majesty King George, by the Friends of the Popish Pretender. Containing an Account as well of the Settlement of the Succession to the Crown of Great Britain in the illustrious Family of Hanover, and the Tory scheme to defeat it during the last four years of the late Queen Anne, as of her Majesty's happy accession, the Rebellious Conspiracy, etc. * * * By a Lover of the Prosperity and Peace of Great Britain. [Quotation 3 lines.] Drumfries :[1] printed by Robert Rae, and sold by him and by John Martin, in the Parliament Closs, Edinburgh ; John Wilson, in Glasgow ; Bailie Duncan, in Kilmarnock ; and other Booksellers. MDCCXVIII. *Small quarto.*

[1] The first book printed in Dumfries, which is spelt as above, Drumfries.

Title as above, Dedication, Address, and List of Subscribers, xii. pp. The History, 388 pp. Index, 8 pp.

This (the 1st Edition) is somewhat scarce. Sells for 10s. 6d. It has been reprinted several times.

This work was written by Peter Rae. Chapter vii. contains a detailed account of the Siege of Preston in 1715, and Chapter x. contains the Trials and Sentences and Executions of the Lancashire Rebels.

WILLS and INVENTORIES from the REGISTRY of the ARCHDEACONRY of RICHMOND, extending over portions of the Counties of York, Westmoreland, Cumberland, and Lancaster. By JAMES RAINE Jun., B.A., Fellow of the University of Durham. Published for the Society by George Andrews, Durham; Whittaker and Co., 13 Ave Maria Lane, T. and W. Boone, 29 New Bond Street, London; Blackwood and Sons, Edinburgh. *Octavo.*

Title as above (with Woodcut of the Seal of Durham University), preceded by a Half-title, on which is printed "The Publications of the Surtees Society." Established in the year MDCCCXXXIV. Vol. xxvi. for the year MDCCCLIII. [Seal of the Society.] Two Titles and Preface, xxv. pp. Wills, etc., and Index, 294 pp. Report of the Society for 1853, 13 pp.

Sells for 15s.

A Complete HISTORY of the REBELLION, from its rise in 1745 to its total suppression at the glorious Battle of Culloden in April 1746. By Mr. JAMES RAY of Whitehaven, Volunteer under His Royal Highness the Duke of Cumberland.

"Non solum nobis nati partim pro Patria."

Wherein are contained The Intrigues of the Pretender's Adherents before the breaking out of the Rebellion. * * * Also an Account of the Family and Extraction of the Rebel Chiefs, especially the Camerons, with the Life of the celebrated Miss Jenny. Likewise the Natural History and Antiquities of the several Towns thro' which the Author passed with His Majesty's Army; together with the Manners and Customs of the different People, particularly the Highlanders. The Tryals and Executions of the

Rebel Lords, etc. Manchester: printed for the Author by R. Whitworth, Bookseller. [1760.] *Duodecimo.*

Title as above, Dedication, and Preface, x. pp. Complete History, 408 pp.

Sells for 5s.

OTHER EDITIONS.

York, 1749. Title, Dedication, and Preface, x. pp. History, 420 pp. *Frontispiece*, Portrait of Duke of Cumberland. Plan of Battle of Prestonpans (p. 54).

Another Edition. Bristol, 1750. There were also several London Editions.

A POEM on the LATE REBELLION, giving an account of the rise and progress thereof from the Young Pretender's first landing in the Isle of Skie to his defeat at the Battle of Culloden. By PHILONADOS ROSSENDALIENSIS. Manchester: printed by R. Whitworth for the Author. Price 3d. *Post octavo.*

Title as above, To the Reader, v. pp. The Poem, p. 6 to p. 24.

Manchester, Wigan, Rossendale, and other Lancashire towns, are mentioned.

Very scarce. Copies have sold for 10s. 6d. A copy is in the Collection of Richard Wood, Esq., Manchester.

The ITINERANT, or Memoirs of an Actor. In three volumes. By S. W. RYLEY.

"The World's a stage," etc.
[and three following lines.]
SHAKSPEARE.

London: printed for Taylor and Hessey, 93 Fleet Street. 1808. *Foolscap octavo.*

VOL. I.

Title as above, Dedication, Preface, Contents, and Itinerant, 326 pp.

VOL. II.

Title, etc., and Itinerant, 332 pp.

VOL. III.

Title, etc., and Itinerant, 398 pp.

VOL. IV.

Title, etc., and Itinerant, 162 pp.

VOL. V.

Title and Contents, iv. pp. Itinerant, 371 pp.

VOL. VI.

Title and Contents, iv. pp. Itinerant, 446 pp.

Scarce. Sells for £1 : 10s.

S. W. Ryley was for many years manager of the Theatre Royal, Manchester, and the above volume contains some curious details referring to many parts of Lancashire.

The HISTORY of the RISE, INCREASE, and PROGRESS of the CHRISTIAN PEOPLE called Quakers, intermixed with several Remarkable Occurrences. Written originally in Low Dutch by WILLIAM SEWEL, and by himself translated into English. Now revised and publish'd with some amendments [and edited by Joseph Besse]. London: printed and sold by the Assigns of J. Sowle at the Bible in George Yard, Lombard Street. 1722. *Folio.*

This is the 1st Edition; three others followed, the last in 1834, 2 vols. octavo, which sells for 10s. 6d.

A TREATISE upon COAL-MINES; or an attempt to explain their general marks of Indication, acknowledg'd and probable, together with particular instances of their public utility; objections to the mode of their discovery, and to their manufacture, obviated, etc. London: printed for the Author; and sold by F. Newbery, in St. Paul's Churchyard. MDCCLXIX. [This is by Dr. WILLIAM SHARP, Vicar of Long Burton.) *Octavo.*

Title as above, and Introduction, vi. pp. Treatise, 106 pp.

Much of this refers to the Lancashire Coal-Fields. A copy of the work is in the Bodleian Library.

The NOBLE and GENTLE MEN of ENGLAND, or Notes

touching the Arms and Descents of the Ancient, Knightly, and Gentle Houses of England, arranged in their respective Counties. Attempted by EVELYN PHILIP SHIRLEY, Esq., M.A., F.S.A., one of the Knights of the Shire for the County of Warwick. [Woodcut of Arms.] Westminster: J. Bowyer; Nicholas and Sons. Second Edition corrected 1860. *Foolscap quarto.*

Half-title, Title as above, and Preface, viii. pp. Notes and Index, 321 pp. The Lancashire Portion, p. 109 to p. 124.

First Edition was published at 25s.; the above at 20s. A copy is in the Manchester Free Library.

Notes on a TOUR in the MANUFACTURING DISTRICTS of LANCASHIRE, in a series of Letters to His Grace the Archbishop of Dublin. By W. COOKE TAYLOR, LL.D., etc., of Trinity College, Dublin, author of "The Natural History of Society," "Romantic Biography of the age of Elizabeth," etc. Second Edition; with two additional Letters on the recent disturbance. London: published by Duncan and Malcolm, Paternoster Row. 1842. *Duodecimo.*

Half-title, Title as above, Preface, and Advertisement to the Second Edition, viii. pp. Notes on a Tour, 331 pp.

Published at 5s.

A compendious ACCOUNT of the Antient and present State of the NORTHERN CIRCUIT. By SAMUEL TYMMS. London: J. B. Nichols and Son, 25 Parliament Street. 1837. *Foolscap octavo.*

Title as above, Dedication, and Northern Circuit, v. pp. The Lancashire portion, p. 1 to p. 43.

Small Map of Lancashire. This volume forms a part of the "Family Topographer."

Published at 5s. Sells for 3s. 6d.

MAGNALIA DEI ANGLICANA; or, ENGLAND'S PARLIAMENTARY CHRONICLE, containing a most exact narration of all the most materiall Proceedings of this renowned and unparalelld Parliament; the armies which have been or are in the severall parts of this land; the manner of the Battails and Seiges of Keinton, Brainford, Stafford, Litchfeild, Cheshire, Lancashire, etc. etc. By JOHN VICARS, etc. London: printed by T. Paine and M. Simmons for J. Rothwell and T. Underhill. Published in Four Parts. The First and Second Parts were reprinted in 1644. *Small quarto.*

The complete work is very scarce.

A TOUR through the NORTHERN COUNTIES of ENGLAND and the Borders of Scotland. By the Rev. RICHARD WARNER. In two Volumes.

VOL. I.

"Σα γαρ ερι κειvα παvτα."

"Creation's Tenant, all the world is thine."

Bath: printed by R. Cruthwell; and sold by G. and J. Robinson, Pater-noster Row, London. 1802. *Octavo.*

Vol. I. contains nothing referring to Lancashire.

Frontispiece, View of Derwent Water.

VOL. II.

Title and Itinerary, iv. pp. Tour (in the form of Letters), 300 pp.

Frontispiece, Ulswater and Gowbray Park.

Sells for 4s. 6d.

The DISPLAYING of supposed WITCHCRAFT; wherein is affirmed that there are many sorts of Deceivers and Imposters, and divers persons under a passive Delusion of Melancholy and Fancy. But that there is a corporeal League made betwixt the Devil and the Witch, or that he sucks on the Witches Body, has carnal Copulation, or that witches are turned into Cats, Dogs, raise Tempests or the like, is utterly denied and disproved. Wherein also is handled The Existence of Angels and Spirits, the truth of Apparitions, the Nature of Astral and Sydereal Spirits, the force of Charms and Filters, with other abstruse matters. By JOHN WEBSTER, Practitioner in Physick.

[Quotation from Galen, lib. 8, de Comp. Med.]

London: printed by J. M., and are sold by the Booksellers in London. 1677. *Folio.*

A page on which is printed "Imprimatur July 27, 1676, Jonas Moore, Soc. Regiæ Vice-Præses." Title as above, Dedication to "Thomas Parker of Braisholme," etc., Preface, and Contents, xv. pp. The Displaying of Witchcraft, 346 pp. Examination of Edmund Robinson of Pendle Forest, etc., before Richard Shuttleworth and John Starkey, Esquires, two of His Majestie's Justices of the Peace within the County of Lancaster the 10th day of February 1633, 3 pp. Errata, i. p.

Scarce. Sells for £1.

This work contains an account of the famous Lancashire Witches. Dr. Webster was born at Thornton Hill, in the parish of Cuxwold, Yorkshire, in 1610, and was buried at the Church of Mary Magdalen, Clitheroe. For Biographical notice of him, see the History of Whalley.

A HISTORY of RICHMONDSHIRE, in the North Riding of the County of York, together with those parts of the Everwickshire of Domesday which form the Wapentakes of Lonsdale, Ewecross, and Amunderness, in the Counties of York, Lancaster, and Westmoreland. By THOMAS DUNHAM WHITAKER, LL.D., F.S.A., Vicar of Whalley, and of Blackburn in Lancashire. In two Volumes. London: printed for Longman, Hurst, Rees, Orme, and Brown, Paternoster Row; Hurst, Robinson, and Co., 90 Cheapside and 8 Pall Mall; and Robinson and Hernaman, Leeds. 1823. *Folio.*

VOL. I.

Title as above, Page with quotation from Camden, Dedication, Advertisement to the Reader, and History of Richmondshire, 442 pp.

LIST OF PLATES.

1. Margaret, Countess of Richmond . . . *Frontispiece*
2. View of Richmond . . . . . . P. 13
3. Interior View of the Keep of Richmond Castle . . 84
4. Keep of Richmond Castle 85
6. Richmond Castle and Town 94
7. South-East View of the Grey Friars' Tower, Richmond . 99
8. St. Agatha's Abbey, Easby 113
9. Interior View of the Hall of St. Agatha Abbey . . 113
10. Ground-plan of Easby Hall 113
11. Aske Hall 115
12. South-East View of Romaldkirk Church . . . 129

13. High Force on Fall of the Tees . . . . P. 142
14. Roman Antiquities found at Rokeby . . . 149
15. South-East View of Eggleston Abbey . . . 151
16. Egglestone Abbey near Barnard Castle . . . 152
17. Junction of the Greta and Tees at Rokeby . . 184
18. Brignell Church 194
19. Wycliffe near Rokeby 197
20. Plan of the Entrenched Lines at Stanwick and Forcet, 1816, made by Thomas Bradley Richmond . . . 207
21. Marrick Abbey 222
22. Monumental Brass in Wensley Church . . . 373
23. Aysgarth Force 393
24. Screen in Aysgarth Church 394
25. Sermer Lake near Askrigg 412
26. Moss Dale Fell 413
27. Hardraw Fall 413
28. Ground-plan of Jervaux Abbey 422

Also 57 Woodcuts printed on the letterpress, none of which refer to Lancashire. 12 separate Pedigrees of Yorkshire families.

VOL. II.

Half-title, Title, iii. pp. History of Richmondshire, 199 pp. Half-title, "An History of Lonsdale, Ewecross, and Amounderness," after p. 200. History of Lonsdale, etc., p. 201 to p. 483. Index to both Volumes, p. 485 to p. 497. Errata, and Directions for placing Plates and Pedigrees to both Volumes, p. 499 to p. 504. Pp. 325 to 335 are repeated with an asterisk, and follow p. 324.

LIST OF PLATES.

1. Brass Plate in Catterick Church . . . . P. 28
2. Court of Hornby Castle 44
3. Brass Plate in Wath Church 184
4. Crook of Lime, looking towards Hornby Castle . . 203
5. Roman Antiquities found near Lancaster . . . 215
6. Gateway of Lancaster Castle 228
7. Ingleborough from Hornby Castle . . . 250
8. Hornby Castle 263
9. Kirby Lonsdale Churchyard 277
10. Heysham and Cumberland Mountains . . . 317

11. Sizergh Hall . . . . P. 333
12. Weathercote Cave half filled with Water . . 342
13. Peel Castle 373
14. Furness Abbey 384
15. Facsimile of a Grant to the Grey Friars, Preston . . 428
16. Umbo of a Shield found at Garstang[1] 457
17. Ashton Hall 475

Besides the above are 54 woodcuts printed on the letterpress (some of which refer to Lancashire), and 58 Initial Letters, and the Arms mentioned in the following

LIST OF PEDIGREES.

1. Lawson, with their Arms . . P. 36
2. Darcy, with their Arms . . . 42
3. Conyers 42
4. Neville, Lord Latimer, with their Arms . 78
5. Danby, with their Arms . . . 98
6. Robinson, Lord Grantham . . 122
7. Wandesford 140
8. Norton, with two Shields of Arms . 182
9. Graham, with their Arms . . 256
10. Harrington, with two Shields of Arms . 250
11. Tunstall 270
12. Bindlosse 311
13. Fleetwood, with their Arms . . 444
14. Brockholes 449
15. Butler 454

This magnificent specimen of typography was published at £25 : 4s., in boards. Sells for from £12 to £20. Large paper copies, with 20 Engravings after J. M. W. Turner, R.A., Proofs on India Paper, published at £50 : 8s., which now sells for £25.

The Author died before this work was published, which accounts for its incompleteness in many important respects.

The VISION, or a View of Terrestrial Objects, with some ACCOUNT of A TOUR from LIVERPOOL to LONDON, with Notes on the New Age of the Millennium; to which is added a Code of Civil and Religious

[1] This Shield was not found at Garstang, but at Kirkham.—See "History of Kirkham," p. 5.

Laws, and also some Memoirs of the Author, with a Portrait, etc. The whole designed to show the one universal reign of Government on Earth. By EPHRAIM WOOD. [Quotation from the Vision, p. 3.] [Johnson, printer, Liverpool.] 1820. *Octavo.*

Title as above, and Memoirs, xxiii. pp. The Vision, p. 1 to p. 19. Select Extracts from "Quakerism unveiled," p. 20 to p. 42. A Tour, p. 43 to p. 106. Select Extracts continued, p. 107 to p. 172. Tour continued, p. 173 to p. 208. Select Extracts, etc., continued, p. 209 to p. 366. Tour continued, and Notes, p. 361 to 401. Notes on the New Age, etc., p. 403 to 436. Supplementary Remarks and Notes, p. 1 to p. 111.

PLATES.

Portrait of "Ephraim," *Frontispiece.*
"Hereunto," *facing* p. i.

Ephraim Wood was a native of Ipswich, afterwards of Liverpool. He was the author of "Quakerism unveiled," and "The Still Voice of Peace."

This curious volume is rarely met with; it contains short notices of Preston, Lancaster, The Lakes, etc. It was published in 18 numbers at 7d. each, and, as a complete work, was sold at 10s. It sells now for about the same price. A copy is in the Author's Library.

A SIX MONTHS' TOUR through the NORTH of ENGLAND, containing an account of the present state of Agriculture, Manufactures, and Population in several Counties of this Kingdom; particularly—

I. The Nature, Value, and Rental of the Soil.
II. The Size of Farms, with Accounts of their Stocks, Products, Population, and various Methods of Culture.
III. The Use, Expense, and Profit of several sorts of Manure.
IV. The Breed of Cattle, and the respective Profits attending them.
V. The State of the Waste Lands which might and ought to be cultivated.
VI. The Condition and Number of the Poor, with their Rates, Earnings, etc.
VII. The price of Labour and Provisions, and the Proportion between them.
VIII. The Register of many curious and useful Experiments on Agricul-

ture, and General Practices in Rural Œconomies, communicated by several of the Nobility, Gentry, etc. etc.

Interspersed with descriptions of the Seats of the Nobility and Gentry, and other remarkable objects. Illustrated with Copperplates of such Implements of Husbandry as deserve to be generally known; and Views of some Picturesque Scenes which occurred in the course of the Journey. [French Quotation.]

VOL. III.

London: for W. Strahan, W. Nicholl, No. 51 in St. Paul's Churchyard; B. Collins, at Salisbury; and J. Balfour, at Edinburgh. MDCCLXX. *Octavo.*

Title as above, Contents, vii. pp. Six Months' Tour, 440 pp.

This work was written by ARTHUR YOUNG, of North Mimms, Hertfordshire. It is in 4 vols. Only this volume refers to Lancashire. It contains the following Plates:—

Views of Waterfalls, p. 146, p. 148, and p. 149.
Two Folding Plates of Plan of Bridgewater Canal (termination), p. 278.
Folding Plate of the Bridgewater Canal, p. 286; and several Plates of Agricultural Implements, etc.

The HISTORY of INLAND NAVIGATION, particularly those of the Duke of Bridgewater in LANCASHIRE and Cheshire, and the intended one promoted by Earl Gower and other Persons of Distinction in Staffordshire, Cheshire, and Derbyshire. Illustrated with Geographical Plans shewing the Counties, Townships, and Villages through which those Navigations are carried, or are intended to be. The whole shewing the Utility and Importance of Inland Navigation. Price 2s. 6d. London: printed for J. Lowndes in Fleet Street. MDCCLXVI. *Octavo.*

Title as above and Dedication, iv. pp. Contents and the History, 88 pp. Folding Map of the Bridgewater Canal, and a Folding Plan of an intended Canal between Liverpool and Hull.

PART II. (or VOL. II.)

Title and Contents, iv. pp. Scheme for an intended Canal from Macclesfield to Mothram, Andrew, etc., 104 pp. Folding Plan of intended

Canal between the interior parts of the Kingdom and the Ports of Bristol, Liverpool, and Hull.

Published at 2s. 6d. each part. The work complete sells for 7s. 6d.

A Second Edition, with additions, published in 1799 at the same price as the above.

The NAMES of the ROMAN CATHOLICS, NONJURORS, and others who refus'd to take the OATHS to his late MAJESTY KING GEORGE. Together with their Titles, Additions, and Places of Abode; the parishes and townships where their lands lay; the names of the then Tenants or occupiers thereof; and the annual valuation of them as estimated by themselves. Transmitted to the late Commissioners. * * * Taken from an original manuscript of a Gentleman who was the Principal Clerk to the Accomptant-General Office belonging to the said Commissioners. * * * London: printed for J. Robinson in Ludgate Street. 1745. *Octavo.*

Title, Dedication, Address, and Contents, viii. pp. The Names, 151 pp. Lancashire, p. 40 to p. 62.

The FIRST REPORT of the ROYAL COMMISSION of HISTORICAL Manuscripts. Presented to both Houses of Parliament by command of Her Majesty. London: printed by George Edward Eyre and William Spottiswoode, Printers to the Queen's most excellent Majesty. For Her Majesty's Stationery Office. 1870.

[C. 55.] Price 1s. 6d.

This only contains a few items referring to the County.

The SECOND REPORT.

[C. 441.] Price 3s. 10d. 1871.

Inter alia contains an account of the MSS. in the Chetham Library, and in the Library at Stonyhurst.

The THIRD REPORT.

[C. 673.] Price 6s. 1872.

The concluding Notice of the MSS. at Stonyhurst, p. 334 to p. 341.

The FOURTH REPORT.—Part I.

[C. 857.] Price 6s. 8d. 1874.

The MSS. of Colonel Towneley, at Towneley Hall, Burnley, p. 406 to 416.

The FOURTH REPORT.—Part II.

Index to the Fourth Report.

The REPORT of the SEPULCHRAL MONUMENTS COMMITTEE.

[C. 558.] Price 7½d. 1872.

Only contains a reference to a Monument (Ralph Assheton) in Middleton Church, and two (Sir Richard and Sir William Molyneux) in Sefton Chapel.

The THIRTIETH ANNUAL REPORT[1] of the DEPUTY-KEEPER of the PUBLIC RECORDS. [25th February 1869.] Presented to both Houses of Parliament by Command of Her Majesty. London : printed by George E. Eyre and William Spottiswoode, Printers to the Queen's most excellent Majesty, for Her Majesty's Stationery Office. 1869. 23,617. Price 3s.

The Lancashire portion is from p. iii. to p. viii., and p. 1 to p. 43.

The THIRTY-FIRST ANNUAL REPORT. 1870. [C. 187.] Published at 2s. 3d. Lancashire parts, p. 1 to p. 41.

The THIRTY-SECOND ANNUAL REPORT. 1871. [C. 374.] Price 2s. 2d.

Vol. I.

Duchy of Lancashire Records, p. 331 to p. 365.

Vol. II.

1871. [C. 374-1.] Price 5s. 6d. This forms Appendix II., and

[1] The Reports issued previous to this contain very little referring to the County Palatine.

consists of CHARITIES; Calendar of Trust-Deeds enrolled on the Close Rolls of Chancery subsequent to 9 Geo. III. c. xxxvi., 1062 pp.

Many Lancashire Charities are referred to.

The THIRTY-THIRD ANNUAL REPORT. 1872. [C. 620.] Price 1s. 10d.

Duchy of Lancaster Records, and Calendar of Rolls of the Chancery of the County Palatine (continued), p. 1 to p. 42.

The THIRTY-FIFTH ANNUAL REPORT. 1874. [C. 1043.] Price 1s. 3d.

Records of the Palatinate of Lancaster, p. iv. to p. x. Duchy of Lancaster Records; Calendar of Ancient Charters or Grants (continued), p. 1 to p. 42; Palatinate of Lancaster; Inventory and Lists of Documents transferred to the Public Record Office, p. 42 to p. 75. List of Documents left at Lancaster and Preston for current business, p. 196 to p. 197.

INDEX to the 28th, 29th, 30th, 31st, 32d, 33d, 34th, and 35th printed Reports.

HISTORIC SOCIETY of LANCASHIRE and CHESHIRE. Proceedings and Papers. Session I. 1848-9. Liverpool: printed under the direction of the Council for the use of the Members. MDCCCXLIX.

Title as above, Advertisement, Contents, and List of Members, xiii. pp. Report of the First Meeting, 16 pp. Proceedings, 160 pp. Index, 6 pp.

This Society issues one volume per year. The following is a list of the principal articles referring to Lancashire:—

VOL. I.

On the Roman Roads in Lancashire, with a particular account of the Tenth Iter of Antoninus. By J. Just.
On the reading of the Lancaster Runic Inscription. By J. Just.
Memoranda relating to Lancaster Castle, etc. By E. Higgin.
On the ruined Chapel at Lydiate, County Lancaster. By W. J. Roberts.

WORKS PARTLY RELATING TO LANCASHIRE.

Account of Certificates given to persons at Wigan to be touched for the King's Evil.
On the Family of Percival of Allerton. By Thomas Heywood, F.S.A.
On the Common Seal of Liverpool. By H. C. Pidgeon.

VOL. II.

Notes on a Roman Road at Warrington. By Dr. Hume.
Some Occurrences during the Rebellion of 1745, principally in Warrington and the neighbourhood. By W. Beamont.
On Charter of Feoffment of Gorton, 1422. By J. Harland.
Deed of Gift of Walter de Scarebreck to the Priory of Cockersand.
On certain Brasses in Cheshire and Lancashire Churches.
A Memoir of the Lancashire House of Le Norreis, or Norres, and of its Speke branch. By George Ormerod, D.C.L.
Notes on Speke Hall. By H. C. Pidgeon.

VOL. III.

Account of the Roman and British Remains found North and East of the River Wyre. By the Rev. W. Thornber.
The Roman Roads of Lancashire. Part II. By John Just.
Notes on the 7th Iter of Richard of Cirencester. By John Robson. Additional Notes by T. Langton Birley.
Evidences of Roman Occupation in the Fylde District. By the Rev. W. Thornber, B.A.
On the Cheshire Watling Street; and other Evidences of Roman Occupation in Lancashire and Cheshire. By John Robson.
Notes on a Visit to Heysham. By John Robson.
On the Seal of Liverpool. By J. G. Nichols, F.S.A.
On the Ancient Domestic Architecture of Lancashire and Cheshire. By Alfred Rimmer.
Description of Lydiate Hall. By W. J. Roberts.

VOL. IV.

British Burial-places near Bolton, Co. Lancaster. By Matthew Dawes, F.G.S.
Traces of the Britons, Saxons, and Danes, in the Foreland of the Fylde. By the Rev. W. Thornber, B.A.
The Danes in Lancashire. By the late John Just.
Historical Notes respecting the Township and Village of Everton. By James Stonehouse.

WORKS PARTLY RELATING TO LANCASHIRE.

The Early History of Warrington and its neighbourhood. By John Robson.

An Account of Warrington Siege, A.D. 1643, etc. By James Kendrick, M.D.

The alleged Royal Visits to Liverpool. By Jos. Mayer, F.S.A.

An Account of the Ancient Hall of Samlesbury, near Preston. By Alfred Rimmer.

Liverpool Churches and Chapels, etc. By Dr. Thom. Part I.

Letters relating to Lancashire and Cheshire before James I., Charles I., and Charles II. By Thomas Dorning Hibbert.

Account of the Free Grant of Warren by Henry VIII. to Thomas Gresley, sixth Baron of Manchester. By John Harland.

A Lancashire Charm in Cypher. By John Harland.

The Old House of Correction, Liverpool. By Richard Brooke, F.S.A.

VOL. V.

An Account of Excavations made at the Mote Hill, Warrington. By Dr. Kenrick.

Historical Notes on the Valley of the Mersey previous to the Norman Conquest. By Thomas Baines, Esq.

Lancashire and Cheshire Men in the Sixteenth Century. By the Rev. A. Hume, LL.D.

Dramatic Places of Amusement in Liverpool a Century ago. By James Stonehouse, Esq.

Liverpool Churches and Chapels. Part II. By the Rev. Dr. Thom.

An Account of Mains Hall near Poulton. By the Rev. W. Thornber, B.A.

Roscoe and the influence of his Writings on the Fine Arts. By Jos. Mayer, Esq., F.S.A.

VOL. VI.

Description of the Antient Fort at Kirby, in Walton. By W. J. Roberts.

Roman Remains in the Fyld District. By the Rev. W. Thornber, B.A.

Account of the Liverpool Election of 1670. By the Rev. A. Hume, D.C.L.

The Royal Warrington Volunteers, 1798. By James Kendrick, M.D.

Gleanings from old Liverpool Newspapers a hundred years ago. By James A. Picton, F.S.A.

Notes, Historical and Ecclesiastical, on the Chapelry of Kirkby in Walton. By the Rev. Thomas Moore, M.A.

Biographical Notice of John Holt (of Walton). By James Stonehouse, Esq. (Notes on the above by James Boardman, Esq.)

Sketch of Mr. John Wyke, with Remarks on the Arts and Manufactures of Liverpool from 1760 to 1780. By J. W. Roberts and H. C. Pidgeon, Esq.

Porcelain and Earthenware Manufacture in Liverpool.

VOL. VII.

A Morning Ramble in Old Warrington. By James Kendrick, M.D.

On the Materials for the History of the two Counties, and the mode of using them. Part II. By John Robson, Esq.

An Account of the Life and Writings of the late J. H. Swale of Liverpool. By Thomas T. Wilkinson, Esq., F.R.A.S.

Remarks on the Flora of Liverpool. By H. S. Fisher.

On the History of the Art of Pottery in Liverpool. By Joseph Mayer, Esq., F.S.A.

On the Lepidopterous Insects of the District around Liverpool. By Charles S. Gregson.

VOL. VIII.

Liverpool Memoranda, touching its Area and Population during the first half of the Present Century. By J. T. Dawson, Esq.

On the Foundation and History of Boteler's Free Grammar School at Warrington. By J. F. Marsh, Esq.

On the Roman Remains recently discovered at Walton-le-Dale, Preston. By Charles Hardwick, Esq.

On the Lepidopterous Insects of the District around Liverpool. By C. S. Gregson.

On the Area and Population of the Manchester District. By J. T. Dawson, Esq.

On the Rise of the Manufacturing Towns of Lancashire and Cheshire. By David Buxton, Esq.

VOL. IX.

On the Language of Lancashire under the Romans. By R. G. Latham, M.A., M.D., F.R.S.

The Castle Hill of Penwortham. By the Rev. W. Thomber, A.B.

On some Fossil Trees recently discovered at Burnley. By J. T. Wilkinson, F.R.A.S.

On the Lepidopterous Insects of the District around Liverpool. By C. S. Gregson.

On the People of the English Lake Country. By A. Craig Gibson, Esq.
On the Population of Lancashire and Cheshire, and its local distribution during the Fifty Years 1801-1851. By J. T. Dawson and T. A. Welton, Esqs.
Historical Sketch of the Liverpool Library. By P. Macintyre, M.D.
Results of an Examination of the Records of the Liverpool Self-registering Tide Gauge for 1854, 1855, and 1856. By Lieut. Murray J. Parks, R.N.

VOL. X.

On the Population of Lancashire and Cheshire, and its local distribution during the Fifty Years 1801-1851. By J. T. Dawson and T. A. Welton, Esqs.
Further remarks on the History of the two Counties and its materials. By John Robson, M.D.
On the Lepidopterous Insects of the Districts around Liverpool. By Mr. C. S. Gregson.
On the Flora of Preston and its Neighbourhood. By Mr. Charles Joseph Ashfield.
Further Memorials of the late J. H. Swale. By T. T. Wilkinson, F.R.A.S.
On the Geology of the Fylde District. By Charles Corey, Esq.
On the Dipterous Insects of the District around Liverpool. By the Rev. H. H. Higgins, M.A.

VOL. XI.

A Historical Sketch of Warrington Academy. By Henry A. Bright, B.A.
On the Population of Lancashire and Cheshire, and its local distribution during the Fifty Years 1801-1851. Part III. By J. T. Dawson and T. A. Welton, Esqs.
On the Diatomaceæ of Liverpool. By Thomas Comber, Esq.
On the popular Customs and Superstitions of Lancashire. By T. T. Wilkinson, F.R.A.S. Part I.
A Sketch of the Origin and Early History of the Liverpool Blue Coat Hospital. By Mr. John R. Hughes.

VOL. XII.

On the Population of Lancashire and Cheshire, and its Local Distribution, during the Fifty Years 1801-1851. By J. T. Dawson and T. A. Welton, Esqs. Part. IV.
On Popular Customs and Superstitions of Lancashire. By T. T. Wilkinson, F.R.A.S.

On the Flora of Preston and its Neighbourhood. Part II. By C. J. Ashfield.

Tumuli at Winwick. By John Robson, M.D.

NEW SERIES, VOL. I.

On the Popular Customs and Superstitions of Lancashire. By T. T. Wilkinson, F.R.A.S.

On the Coleoptera of the District around Liverpool. By C. S. Gregson.

Sketch of the History of the Liverpool Blue Coat Hospital. Part II. By J. R. Hughes.

Books published in Liverpool. By Albert J. Mott.

VOL. II.

Biographical Notices of some Liverpool Mathematicians. By T. T. Wilkinson, F.R.A.S.

Abstract of the principal Mines of the Burnley Coal Fields. By Joseph Whitaker, F.G.S., and T. T. Wilkinson, F.R.S.A.

On the Coleoptera of the District around Liverpool. Part. II. By C. S. Gregson.

VOL. III.

List of the British Roses and Brambles occurring in the Liverpool District. By H. S. Fisher.

An Account of the Life and Writings of the late Henry Buckley. By T. T. Wilkinson, F.R.A.S.

Local Chit-Chat of the "Forty-Five." By Lieutenant-General the Hon. Sir Edward Cust, D.C.L.

VOL. IV.

A Sketch of the History of the Liverpool Blue-Coat Hospital. Part III. By J. R. Hughes, Esq.

VOL. V.

On the Druidical Rock Basins in the Neighbourhood of Burnley. By T. T. Wilkinson, F.R.A.S.

The Pamphlet Literature of Liverpool. By Thomas Dawson, Esq., M.R.C.S.

The Lakeland of Lancashire. No. I. Hawkshead Town, Church, and School. By A. Craig Gibson, F.S.A.

On the Flora of Preston and Neighbourhood. Part IV. By C. J. Ashfield, Esq.
On the Cup-Cuttings and Ring-Cuttings on the Calder Stones near Liverpool. By Professor J. Y. Simpson, M.D.
On the Roman Topography of East Lancashire. By T. T. Wilkinson, F.R.A.S.

VOL. VI.

Changes in the Sea-Coast of Lancashire and Cheshire. By the Rev. A. Hume, D.C.L., LL.D.
Further Observations on the alleged Submarine Forests on the Shores of Liverpool Bay and the River Mersey. In reply to Dr. Hume's Communication, 10th July 1845. By Joseph Boult, Esq., F.R.I.B.A.
On the Miscroscopic Fungi of the District around Liverpool. By R. G. M'Leod, Esq.
The Lakeland of Lancashire. No. 11. Hawkshead Parish. By A. Craig Gibson, Esq., F.S.A.
Notabilia of the Archæology and Natural History of the Mersey District during Three Years, 1863-4-5. Compiled by H. E. Smith.
Ancient British Remains at Over Darwen. By Charles Hardwick, Esq.
Discovery of a Roman Hoard in East Lancashire. By Charles Hardwick, Esq.

VOL. VII.

Historical Sketch of the Forest of Rosendale. By Thomas Newbigging.
Edmund Spenser and the East Lancashire Dialect. By T. T. Wilkinson, F.R.A.S.
Inventory of Whalley Abbey. By Mackenzie E. C. Walcott, B.D., F.R.S.L., F.S.A.
The Lakeland of Lancashire. No. III. The Two Conistons. By A. Craig Gibson, F.S.A.
Archæology of the Mersey District. 1866. By H. Ecroyd Smith.
The Introduced Plants of the Liverpool District. By H. S. Fisher.
Additional Notes on the Ancient Seal of Liverpool. By H. Ecroyd Smith.

VOL. VIII.

On the Ancient Castle at Bury, Lancashire. By Charles Hardwick, Esq.
The Lakeland of Lancashire. No. IV. Yewdale, Tilberthwaite, Little Langdale, Seathwaite. By A. Craig Gibson.
Archæology in the Mersey District, 1867. By H. Ecroyd Smith.

WORKS PARTLY RELATING TO LANCASHIRE.

An ancient British Cemetery at Wavertree. By H. Ecroyd Smith.
The Historical Topography of Aigburth and Garston. By Joseph Boult, F.R.I.B.A.

VOL. IX.

The last popular Risings in the Lancashire Lake Country. By A. Craig Gibson, F.S.A.
Archæology in the Mersey District. 1868. By H. Ecroyd Smith.

VOL. X.

The Burnley Grammar School. By T. T. Wilkinson, F.R.A.S.
The Origin and History of the Warrington Blue Coat School. By John Bowes.
The Early Inhabitants of Lancashire and the neighbouring Counties, and Remains of their Mythology and Local Nomenclature. By Charles Hardwick.
A Littoral Survey of the Port of Liverpool. By Edward Eyes.
Archæology of the Mersey District. 1869. By H. E. Smith.

VOL. XI.

An Essay on Songs and Ballads. Illustrated from Shakespeare and those current in Lancashire. By the late John Harland, F.S.A., and T. T. Wilkinson, F.R.A.S.
Archæology in the Mersey District. 1870. By H. E. Smith.
On Recent Discoveries at the Roman Site at Wilderspool, near Warrington. By James Kendrick, M.D.

VOL. XII.

On the Remains of old Bloomeries formerly existing in Lancashire. By James Kerr, Esq.
The Fee of Makerfield, with an account of some of its Lords, the Barons of Newton. By William Beamont, Esq.
Archæology in the Mersey District. 1871. By H. E. Smith.

VOL. XIII.

More Street, now Moor Street, Liverpool. Its origin, etc. By H. E. Smith.
The Fee of Makerfield. By W. Beamont, Esq.

WORKS PARTLY RELATING TO LANCASHIRE.

Archæology in the Mersey District. 1872. By H. E. Smith.
A History of the Township of Billington, in the Parish of Blackburn. By W. A. Abram.

Vol. XIV.

Extracts from the Register of Ormskirk Church. By James Dixon, Esq.
The Deterioration of the Mersey. By Joseph Boult.
Archæology in the Mersey District. By H. E. Smith.

PROCEEDINGS of the LITERARY and PHILOSOPHICAL SOCIETY of Liverpool. *Octavo.*

The First Volume issued in 1820, and have been published regularly to the present time.

Many articles referring to Lancashire will be found in these volumes.

PROCEEDINGS of the Liverpool ARCHITECTURAL and ARCHÆOLOGICAL Society.

Vol. I.

Sessions 1848-9, and 1849-50. Liverpool: printed for the Society by David Murphy. MDCCCLII.

A few matters of local interest will be found in these Volumes, which have been issued annually to the present time.

A new Series was commenced in 1858.

A DESCRIPTION of the MEMORABLE SIEGES and BATTLES in the NORTH of ENGLAND that happened during the Civil War in 1642, 1643, etc., chiefly contained in the MEMOIRS of GENERAL FAIRFAX, and JAMES, EARL of DERBY. To which is added The LIFE of OLIVER CROMWELL; likewise an impartial HISTORY of the REBELLION.

"No more may Britons against Britons rise."
[And five other lines.]

Bolton: printed by J. Drake. 1785. *Post Octavo.*

Title as above, Address "to the Promoters of this Work," xxiv. pp. Memoir of General Fairfax, p. 25 to p. 67. Siege of Manchester by an Eye-witness, p. 68 to p. 77. Siege of Preston, p. 78 to p.

86. Taking of Bradford, p. 87 to p. 180. Memoirs of James, Earl of Derby, p. 109 to p. 210. Account of Life of Cromwell, p. 211 to p. 244. History of the Rebellion and Appendix, p. 245 to p. 476.

Sells for 7s. 6d.

This was reprinted in Bolton in 1786, with a portrait of Oliver Cromwell and a folding Plate of the Execution of James, Earl of Derby, at Bolton. Sells for 7s. 6d.

Contains many interesting details of the War in Lancashire.

ORIGINAL MEMOIRS of SIR THOMAS FAIRFAX,[1] written by himself during the great civil War, with an Appendix containing the sieges of Bradford, MANCHESTER, and PRESTON. Knaresborough: printed by Hargrove and Son; and sold by them at Knaresborough and Harrogate; Longman, Hurst, and Co., London; Wilson and Son, York, and all other Booksellers. 1810. *Duodecimo.*

Half-Title, Title as above, and Memoirs, 157 pp., Appendix, the Siege of Bradford by Joseph Lister, the Siege of Manchester by an Eye-witness, and the Siege of Preston, p. 158 to p. 221.

Sells for 8s. 6d.

Gives some useful information about the Civil War.

---

[1] The following works contain some slight allusion to the Civil War in Lancashire —viz. "Short Memorials of Thomas, Lord Fairfax, written by himself. London, 1699." Edited by Brian Fairfax. "A Life of the Great Lord Fairfax, Commander-in-Chief of the Army of the Parliament of England. By Clement R. Markham, F.S.A., etc. London, 1870."

PART V.

TRACTS AND PAMPHLETS PRINTED BEFORE 1720.

CIVIL WAR.

* A GREAT VICTORY at Appleby by COL. GENERAL ASHTON, October 9th, 1648, where were taken prisoners at mercy Sir Philip Musgrave, Sir Thomas Tilsey, Sir Robert Strickland, Sir William Huddleston, Sir Thomas Dacre, Sir William Blackstone, 15 Collonels, 9 Lieutenant Collonels, 6 Sergeant Majors, 46 Captains, 17 Lieutenants, 10 Cornets, 3 Ensigns, with a List of their Names, 5 Peece of Ordnance, 1200 Horse, 1000 Arms, and all their Ammunition, Bag and Baggage, October 16th, 1648. This is a true List; a copy whereof was sent from Col. General Ashton, and this day delivered to the Parliament. London: printed for R. Smithurst, near Pye Corner. 1648. *Small quarto.*

* A punctuall relation of the passages in Lancashire this weeke :—

I. Containing the TAKING of HOUGHTON TOWER by the Parliament's Forces, and the perfidious treachery of the Papists, who after they had upon quarter yielded up the Tower, treacherously set fire to a traine of powder, and blew up Captaine Starkey with above a hundred men.

II. How the Earle of Derbie's Forces made an ONSET on the Towne of BOULTON, and was driven off with the losse of an hundred men, and but eight on the Towne side.

* The Tracts marked * are described in "The Lancashire Civil War Tracts," vol. ii. Chetham Society. It has not been thought necessary to attempt to give prices of these Tracts, as all of them are more or less scarce.

III. The TAKING of the TOWNE and CASTLE of LANCASTER, by Sergeant-Major Birch. Printed in the year 1643. *Quarto.*

* An Exact Relation of the bloody and barbarous MASSACRE at BOLTON in the Moors in Lancashire, May 28, by Prince Rupert, being penned by an Eye-Witness admirably preserved by the gracious and mighty hand of God in that day of Trouble. Published according to Order. London: printed by R. W. for Christopher Meredith, August 22, 1644. *Small quarto.*

Title, 2 pp. Relation, 6 pp.

A True Relation of the STRANGE APPARITIONS seen in the Air on Monday, the 25 February, in and about the Town of BOLTON in the MORES, in the County of Lancaster, at mid-day, to the amazement of the Beholders. Being a Letter sent from ELLIS BRADSHAW of the same Town to a Friend in London, with Observations thereupon what probably they may signifie, and what use may be made thereof. London: printed for Tho. Brewster and Gregory Moule, and are to be sold at the three Bibles in the Poultry, under Mildred's Church. 1650. *Small quarto.* 8 pp.

Ellis Bradshaw also wrote "The Quakers' Whitest Divell Unvailed," which was answered by James Taylor of Ardesloe, near Wakefield. (*See* "Smith's Bibliotheca Anti-Quakeriana.")

* The EARLE of DERBY'S SPEECH on the SCAFFOLD immediately before his Execution at BOLTON, in Lancashire, October 15, 1651. Exactly taken in shorthand as it was spoken, and now published for the satisfaction of those that desire to be truly informed. London: printed for Nathaniel Brookes, and are to be sold at his shop at the sign of the Angel in Cornhill. 1651. *Small quarto.*

* Orders concluded by the LORD STRANGE and his adherents at PRESTON, in the County of Lancaster, with some Queries concerning the late differences at Winchester. Printed December 29, 1642. *Quarto.*

* The True relation of the TAKING of the TOWN of PRESTON by Colonell Seaton's forces from Manchester; sent in a letter

from a worthy minister (an eye-witnesse thereof) to an eminent Divine in London. London: printed by J. R. for Luke Fawn, Feb. 14, 1642. *Quarto.*

* A Perfect Relation of the TAKING of the Towne of PRESTON, in Lancashire, by the Parliamentary Forces under the command of Colonell Sir John Seaton, on Thursday the ninth day of February 1642. As it was certified by some Gentlemen of repute in the same county to a Member of the House of Commons, with the names of those that were slain. Together with good news from Cheshire. Ordered by the Commons of Parliament that this Letter be forthwith printed and published. H. Elsynge, Cler. Parl. D. Com. London: printed for Edward Husbands; and are to be sold at his shop in the Middle Temple. Feb. 16, 1642. *Quarto.*

* Original Letter from ALEXANDER RIGBY of PRESTON to the Speaker of the House of Commons, detailing proceedings at the Meeting convened by Lord Derby and the Sheriff of Lancashire on PRESTON MOOR, June 20, 1642, for the purpose of opening the Royal Commission of Array, and also respecting the subsequent seizure of Magazines by the said Earl and Sheriff.[1] *Small quarto.*

PRESTON, Novemb. 7, 1646. The deliberate RESOLUTION of the MINISTERS of the Gospel within the County Palatine of LANCASTER. With their grounds and cautions, according to which they put into execution the Presbyteriall Government upon the present ordinances of Parliament. London: printed for Luke Fawne; and are to be sold by Thomas Smith at his shop in Manchester. 1647. *Small quarto.*

Title, etc., 8 pp.

A copy of this is in the Chetham Library.

* An Impartiall Relation of the late FIGHT at PRESTON, being a Copy of a Letter written (as the tenour of it importeth) by Sir Marmaduke Langdale. Printed in the year 1648. *Small quarto.*

---

[1] The Editor of the Civil War Tracts of Lancashire (Chet. Soc. II.) states that this Tract had probably never before (1844) been printed in its entirety.

VICTORIOUS NEWS from the Earle of Essex, being a true Relation of a famous Battaile fought betwixt His Excellencie and the LORD STRANGE, wherein is declared how the Lord Strange was taken prisoner with 5 other Commanders. 23 Sept. Printed 1642. *Small quarto.*

A DECLARATION of the LORDS and COMMONS assembled in Parliament, in answer to His Majesties Declaration intituled His Majesties Declaration to all His loving subjects, after His late Victory against the Rebels on Sunday the 23 of October 1642. Together with a Catalogue of the names of the divers Colonels, Lieutenant-Colonells, Serjeant-Majors, Captains, and Lieutenants that are Papists and Commanders in the army under the command of the Earl of New-Castle. Ordered by the Lords and Commons assembled in Parliament that this Declaration be forthwith Printed and Published. Hen. Elsyng, Cler. Parl. Dom. Com. London: printed for Edward Husbands and John Franke. 1642. *Quarto.*

Title and Declaration, 12 pp. Petition with the Catalogue as above named, 3 pp.

A copy of this is in the Author's Library.

A DECLARATION and Protestation of the LORDS and COMMONS in Parliament to this Kingdom and the whole World: Wherein (amongst divers of His Majesties late illegall proceedings) is discovered how severall Commissions under the King's authority have been granted to many Papists (herein nominated) for places of command in this warre, with power to raise men and armes, which in sundry places they have performed. Also how Sir John Henderson and Collonel Cockram were sent to Hamburgh and Denmark to raise Forces there and in other forraine parts to bring into this Kingdom. With the names of some who have been proclaimed Rebels in Ireland, now in great favour with His Majesty. For which, and other reasons, they are resolved to enter into a solemne oath and covenant with God, to the utmost of their power, with the hazzard of their lives and fortunes, to defend the truth against the King's popish army and all that shall joyn with them in the prosecution of this wicked designe. Die Sabbathi, Octob. 22, 1642. Ordered by the Lords and Commons in Parliament that this Declaration shall be forthwith printed and published, and read in all Churches and Chappells within the Kingdom of England and Dominion of Wales by the Parsons, Vicars, or Curates of the same. J. Brown, Parliamentorum. London: printed for J. Wright. October 24, 1642. *Quarto.*

Title and Declaration, 7 pp.

Matters of High Consequence; the PETITION of diverse of his Majestie's faithful Subjects in the County of LANCASTER, presented to his Majestie at York by the High Sheriff of Lancaster. With his Majestie's answer and Proclamation. 1642. *Small quarto.*

* A true and full Relation of the TROUBLES in LANCASHIRE between Lord Strange, now Earle of Derby, and the well-affected people of that Countrie, with their valiant Resistance and full Resolution. Also certaine passages between the Earle of Newcastle and Captain Hotham in Yorkshire. Sent to a Rev. Divine in London. London: printed for Edward Blackmoore. December 9th, 1642. *Quarto.* 8 pp.

* Parliamentary Commission for RAISING MONEY FOR THE DEFENCE OF LANCASHIRE, and sending down Colonel Sir John Seaton. From a Broadside in the British Museum, reprinted imperfectly in Rushworth's Collection (Part iii., vol. ii., p. 25). Die September 29, 1642. *Quarto.*

* To the King's Most Excellent Majesty, the Humble Petition of divers RECUSANTS and others in the COUNTY of LANCASTER, that they may be received into his Majestie's Protection, and have their Arms redelivered to them for the defence of his Majestie's Person and their Families. Together with his Majestie's Commission to Sir William Gerard, Baronet, Sir Cecil Trafford, Knight, and other his Majestie's Subjects, RECUSANTS in the same County, charged and commanding them to provide with all possible speed sufficient Armes for the defence of his Majestie's Person or them against all force raised by any colour of any order or ordinance whatsoever without his Majestie's consent. Ordered by the Commons in Parliament that this Petition and Answer bee forthwith prynted and published. H. Elsynge, Cler. Parl. D. Com. London: printed for Edw. Husbands and John Frank, and are to be sold at their Shops in the Middle Temple, and next doore to the King's Head in Fleete Street. 1642. *Quarto.*

* An IMPEACHMENT of High Treason exhibited in Parliament against JAMES, LORD STRANGE, son and heir-apparent of William, Earle of Derby, by the Commons assembled in Parliament, in the names of themselves and all the Commons of England. With an Order of the Lords and Commons in Parliament for the apprehension of the said Lord

to be published in all Churches, Chappels, Markets, and Townes in the County of Lancaster and Chester. 16 Sep. 1642. Ordered by the Lords in Parliament assembled that this Impeachment, with the Order, shall be forthwith printed and published. Joh. Brown, Cler. Parliamenti. Sep. 17. London: printed for John Wright. 1642. *Quarto.*

* Lamentable and Sad Newes from the North, viz., Yorke, LANCASTER, Darby, and Newcastle, sent in a Letter from a Gentleman resident in Yorke, to his friend living in Lumbard Street. Also Strange Newes from Leicester, how Colonell Lumsford, Captain Legg, and Mr. Hastings have appeared in a warlike manner, with a true discovery of their intention, and the manner of the opposition by the Earl of Stainford, Lord Lieutenant of that County. London: printed for G. Tomlinson and T. Watson. 1642. *Quarto.*

* PETITIONS.

"To the Honorable the House of Commons now assembled in Parliament, The Humble Petition of divers Knights, Esquires, Ministers, Gentlemen, and FREEHOLDERS of the County Palatine of LANCASTER. Printed by Felix Kingston, 1641." Presented to the Commons March 12, 1641-2, and preserved in the British Museum's Collection of Broadsides.

* The Humble PETITION of the Knights, Esquires, Ministers, Gentlemen, and FREEHOLDERS in the Countie Palatine of LANCASTER. Presented May 2, 1642. With his Majestie's Letter to the Mayor of Kingston-upon-Hull, 25 April (1) 64 (2). London: printed for Andrew Coe, 1642. *Small quarto.*

* Die Sabbati, 28 Maii 1642.

An ORDER of the Lords and Commons in Parliament to the SHERIFF of the County of LANCASTER, and all other Sheriffs and Lord Lieutenants and Deputy Lieutenants in the Kingdom of England and Dominion of Wales. London: printed for Joseph Hanscott. 1642. *Quarto.*

The PETITION of divers of his Majestie's faithfull SUBJECTS of the TRUE PROTESTANT RELIGION in the County Palatine of

LANCASTER. Presented to his Majestie at York the last of May, by the High Sheriffe of that County, and divers other Gentlemen of Qualitie, and subscribed by 64 Knights and Esquires, 55 Divines, 740 Gentlemen, and of Freeholders and others, 7000. London: printed by Robert Barker, Printer to the King's Most Excellent Majestie, and by the Assignees of John Hill. MDCXLII. *Quarto.*

The above was drawn up by Richard Heyrick, Warder of Manchester. (*Vide* Chet. Soc., Vol. ii. p. 8; and Hollingworth's "Mancunienses," p. 120.)

* HORRIBLE NEWES from LANCASHIRE, Declared in a Letter sent from LANCASTER by one Mr. Benj. Williamson to Mr. Adam Andrewes, Merchant and Inhabit. in the Borrough of Southwarke; wherein is related what Tumuluous uprores the Papists in those parts have lately made to the terror of the Inhabitants of the said County. Also a true Relation how the Protestants rose in armes, and forced them to flye.

Likewise a large Manifestation of the great care of the Sheriffe of Lancaster to disarme the Papists, and to prevent such uprores and tumults. Together with an Order sent from the House of Commons to the High Sheriffe of Lancaster touching the suppressing of the above said tumults. John Browne, Cler. Parl. London: printed for J. Horton. 1642, June 3. *Small quarto.* 8 pp.

* A true Relation of the taking of Roger Manwering, Bishop of St. David's, coming from Ireland in a disguis'd habit in a Ship call'd the Eagle, the 28 of June 1642, by Captaine John Pointz.

Also the relation of the sudden RISING of the LORD STRANGE in LANKASHIRE, and of his intention of taking of the Magazine of LARPOOLE. Likewise concerning the Lord Digby, etc. etc. Henry Elsing, Cler.-Parl.-D. London: printed by Thos. Banks. July 9, 1642. *Small quarto.*

A PIECE of ORDNANCE, invented by a JESUITE, for Cowards that fight by Whisperings, and raise Jealousies, to overthrow both Church and State, which, with the help of a Private Engine, doe more mischiefe at 20 miles distance than stout soldiers at Musket Shot. *Small quarto.*

Secretly printed [1643].

Contains a woodcut of a cannon shaped like a Royalist, his ear the touchhole, into which a Roundhead is blowing.

Refers to Prince Rupert in Lancashire and Cheshire. A copy of it is priced 7s. 6d. in J. C. Hotten's "Handbook of Topography," etc.

* LANCASHIRE'S VALLEY of ACHOR is England's Doore of Hope, set wide open in a brief History of the Wise, Good, and Powerfull Land of Divine Providence, ordering and managing the MILITIA of LANCASHIRE, not onely to the Preservation but Exaltation of a Poor and Praying people in two Hundreds, against and above a considerable Armie of Popish and ill-affected persons in foure Hundreds. Wherein the shift of Piety and Providence, with impiety and humane strength in the weaknesse of means, unto graduail and compleate Victory is laid out; to advance God's praise, and advantage England's Faith. By a well-wisher to the Peace of the Land and Piety of the Church. [Here follow Isaiah, viii. 9, 10; Psalms, xlvi. 7, 11; Jer. xxx. 16, 17.] London: printed for Luke Fawne, and are to be sold at his Shop in Paul's Churchyard, at the signe of the Parrot. 1643. *Small quarto.*

This very scarce Tract is thought by some to have been written by John Angier of Denton.

* A True Relation of the great victory obtained by God's providence by the Parliament's forces in LANCASHIRE, against the forces raised by the King in the Counties of Westmoreland, and Cumberland, where they took Thurland Castle, and in the fight took of the Enemy Col. Huddleston, 2 Captains, an Ensign, 400 prisoners, 7 Colours, killed many, drove many into the Sea, took their Magazine, divers Arms and Horses, and totally routed them.

Sent in a letter by COLONELL RIGBY, a Member of the House of Commons, to the Honorable William Lenthall, Esq., Speaker of the said House. Ordered by the Commons in Parliament that this Relation be forthwith printed and published. H. Elsynge, Parl.-D.-Com. Printed for Edw. Husband, Nov. 20, 1643. *Small quarto.*

A True Relation of two great Victories obtained of the Enemy. The one by Sir William Brereton in Cheshire, the other by SIR JOHN MELDRUM in LANCASHIRE, relating to the death of Col. Marrow, and the list of Prisoners taken in both the Fights, and of about 1800 Horse of Rupert's; as also some remarkable Proceedings of Col. Fox and his

Cubs; with the late Condition of the Lord General's Army in the West. All sent up from good hands to the Parliament and to Citizens of good qualitie. Published according to Order. London: printed for Thomas Underhill, at the Sign of the Bible, in Wood Street. 1644. *Quarto.*

Copie of that LETTER written out of LANCASHIRE which was sent in the name of the Army by two Soldiers to Souldiery of Lancashire, to invite them in to adhere to the [Royalist] Army. [Secretly] printed in the yeare 1647. *Small quarto.*

Contains a list of Officers in the Lancashire Army.

The Engagement or Declaration of the OFFICERS and SOULDIERS of the COUNTY PALATINE of LANCASTER. Together with their Letter to the Reverend Minister of the several Hundreds of that County, desiring them to publish the said Declaration in their Parish Churches, as also the present state and condition of that County, certified in a Letter to a well-affected Citizen in London. Printed May 19, 1648. *Small quarto.*

* The Copy of a Letter from the Duke of Hamilton to the MINISTERS at LANCASTER, with their Answer to the same. Published by authority. London: printed for Edward Husband. Printed by the H. H. of C., August 25, 1648. *Small quarto.*

* The LAST NEWES from the PRINCE of WALES, declaring his further proceedings against the Parliament's Forces, etc. London: printed Annò Dom. 1648. *Small quarto.*

The Tract refers to the North of Lancashire.

* Lt. GENERAL CROMWELL'S Letter to the Honourable WILLIAM LENTHALL, Esq., Speaker of the Honourable House of Commons, of the several great Victories obtained against the Scots and Sir Marmaduke Langdale's Forces in the North; where were slain of the Scot's party about two thousand, above nine thousand taken prisoners, four or five thousand arms taken, the whole Infantry ruined, Duke Hamilton fled into Wales, and Langdale northward, Major-General Vandrusk, Col. Hurry, and Col. Ennis, taken prisoners, who formerly served the Parliament. Ordered by the Commons assembled in Parliament that this

letter be forthwith printed and published. H. Elsynge, Cler. Parl. D. Com. London: printed for Edward Husband, Printer to the Honourable House of Commons, Aug. 23, 1648. *Small quarto.*

* A PARTICULAR of the several VICTORIES, and the Occasions of the Solemn Day of Thanksgiving appointed by both Houses of Parliament to be kept through the Kingdom of England and Dominion of Wales, on Thursday the 7th of September 1648. *Small quarto.*

A particular ACCOUNT of the SEVERAL VICTORIES, with the order for a COLLECTION for MAIMED SOLDIERS. *Small quarto.* 1648.

This refers to a struggle near Lancaster. Henry Ashurst, a Lancashire merchant of Watling Street, was appointed to receive contributions in London for the Lancastrians.

In J. C. Hotten's "Handbook of Topography," etc. A copy of this is priced 18s.

The severall PROCEEDINGS in PARLIAMENT, with accounts of divers Persons being imprisoned by the EARLE of DERBY in the Isle of Man, with orders for seizing the children and servants of the said Earle in Lancashire, and securing them in the garrison of Liverpool. 1650. *Small quarto.*

* Another VICTORY in LANCASHIRE, obtained against the Scots by Major-General Harrison and Collonel Lilburn, with the taking of Lieut.-Gen. David Lesley, Maj.-Gen. Middleton, and other eminent officers and Commanders, with 600 private soldiers, horse, and arms, and a list of the particulars. Also the death of Maj.-Gen. Massey and Duke of Hamilton, and the Scots King going with Hind the great Robber. Together with the manner of my Lord Generall Cromwell's coming, and noble reception by the City of London, and an account of the Scots Prisoners which marched through the City on Saturday last. London: printed by B. A. MDCLI. *Small quarto.*

* Two Letters from Col. Robert Lilburne, the one to the Honourable William Lenthall, Esq., Speaker of the Parliament; the other to his Excellency the Lord Generall, containing the particulars of the totall Rout

and Overthrow of the EARL of DERBY and the Forces under his command in LANCASHIRE on the 25th of August 1651, by the Parliament forces under the said Colonel Robert Lilburne. Imprimatur Her Scobel, Cleric Parliamenti. London : printed for Robert Ibbitson, dwelling in Smithfield, neare Hosier Lane-end. 1651. *Small quarto.*

The HUMBLE ADDRESSE of the Lord Maior, Aldermen, and Common Council of the City of London, on Tuesday last, being the 9th of this instant August, to the Council of State, together with the Lord Whitlock's Speech in answer thereunto. Wherein is discovered the State of the Affairs in Cheshire, LANCASHIRE, Yorkshire, Kent, Sussex, and Surrey, and several other parts of the Nation. London : printed by W. Godbid, over against the Anchor Inne in Litle Brittain. 1659. *Quarto.*

Title, Addresse, etc., 8 pp.

* Good Newes out of Cheshire, being a certaine Relation of the late Passages of that great Malignant, JAMES, EARL of DARBY, how he raised Forces against Parliament, with which, drawing towards the King's Army near Brumicham, in Warwickshire, he was set upon and defeated by the Trained Bands of that County, losing in the fight six hundred of his Cavaliers. London : printed for John Davis. *Small quarto.*

Severall LETTERS of Complaint from the NORTHERN PARTS of the Kingdom, setting forth the Barbarous cruelty and inhumanity of the Scotch Army in destroying whole families and Towns, and carrying away all manner of portable goods, and driving away all cattle into the Kingdom of Scotland. Also their murthering of women in child-bed, and robbing Parents of their deer children more barbarously than the Irish Rebels. To which is added a Declaration of the County of York thereupon * * * London : printed by F. M. *Small quarto.*

Title, etc., 8 pp., contains an Address to the Committee of the County of Lancaster at Manchester.

A copy is in the Chetham Library.

* LANCASTER'S MASSACRE; or, the new way of advancing the Protestant Religion, and expressing loyaltie to the King and Queene,

namely, to cut the throats of Protestant men, women, and children, as lately the Papists and Malignants did at LANCASTER. Related in a letter from a Gentleman of great note in Lancashire to a friend in London, who the Bookseller can name, which letter is here printed verbatim. London: printed for Tho. Underhill at the Bible, in Wood Street, April 1, 1643. *Small quarto.*

With a Woodcut of the Pope riding the seven-headed beast, etc.

LETTERS from the Lord Generall, his Quarters, of a Great Victorie at Malpessie by Sir William Bruerton against 1000 of the Westmoreland Forces; also a parley about the SURRENDERING of LIVERPOOLE, and the particulars thereof, and of 2 shipes of Irish Rebels expected there. 1644. *Small quarto.*

Another great Victory obtained by Lord Lambart against Sir George Booth on Sunday morning last, with the manner of his taking the City of Chester. * * *

As also another desperate Fight at LEVERPOOL; the taking of the Town; the beating and pursuing of the Enemy towards Wales, and the escape of Sir George Booth with 200 Horse to Cherk Castle. London: printed for Edw. Horton. 1659. *Small quarto.*

Title, etc., 8 pp.

A copy is in the Chetham Library.

The KING'S MESSAGE to Winchester. Likewise a true Relation of a famous VICTORY obtained by the Inhabitants of MANCHESTER against the Lord Strange, forcing him to fly to Westchester, where they have besieged him and all his Forces, they having kill'd above a thousand men. Printed for J. H. 1642. *Small quarto.*

A copy is in the Chetham Library.

Jovis, 6th October 1642.

* A Declaration of the Lords and Commons assembled in Parliament in Commendation of the INHABITANTS of the towne of MANCHESTER for their valiant resisting the late Lord Strange, and now Earle of Derbie, and to encourage them in their valour which they have shewed

for their own defence, and to endeavour to suppresse or apprehend the said Earl or any of his Complices, assuring them of allowance and payment for all disbursements or losses in their service.—John Browne, Clerk Parliament. London: printed for Tho. Underhill, at the Bible, in Wood Street.

* A true and faithfull Relation of the BESIEGING of the Towne of MANCHESTER in Lancashire upon Saturday the 24 of September. Together with the manner of the severall Skirmishes and Passages betwixt the Earle of Derby, the besieger, with his 4500 men, and the souldiers in the Town, being only 1000 or thereabout. Also a declaration of the Lords and Commons in Parliament to the Inhabitants of the said Towne. And, lastly, the manner of the raising of the said Siege, having continued until Saturday the 1 of October, as it was credibly represented unto the House of Commons from a godly Minister in the said Towne, and appointed to be printed and published. *Quarto.*[1]

* The LORD STRANGE His demands propounded to the INHABITANTS of the TOWN OF MANCHESTER concerning a pacification and laying down of Armes; with the Valiant Answer and Resolution of the Commanders and Souldiers in denying and withstanding the said Demands. Also the names of the Scots Elders and Ministers chosen by the Commissioners of Scotland to be sent to the Assembly of Divines appointed by the Parliament to be holden at London for the settling of Religion. London: printed for Tho. Cook. October 8, 1642. *Quarto.* 6 pp.

* NEWS from MANCHESTER. Being A True Relation of the BATTELL fought BEFORE MANCHESTER. Wherein Lord Strange lost 120 men, besides 100 taken Prisoners, with the losse of 12 men of the Towne side, whereof six of them were taken Prisoners. Sent in a Letter to a privat Friend. London: printed for Richard Best. 1642. *Quarto.*

* A verie true and credible RELATION of the severall PASSAGES at MANCHESTER on the 15 July last 1642, wherein is specified an Invitation of the LORD STRANGE unto a Banquet, whose life was afterward endangered by SIR THOMAS STANLEY, Baronet, John Holcroft, Esquire, Thomas Birch, Gentleman, as will be attested upon

[1] Copies of many of the Tracts relating to the Siege of Manchester are in the Chetham Library.

Oath ; with the declaration of the better sort of townesmen of Manchester. London : printed by T. Fawcett. July 29, 1642. *Quarto.*

* NEWS FROM MANCHESTER. Being a perfect Relation of the passages which hapned there between LORD STRANGE and the Commissioners for the Militia. Together with the occasion and other circumstances of their skirmishing, and the number and state of those which were slain and wounded. As also how the Magazine for that County is disposed of. Sent in a Letter from M. Jo. Rousgore, an eye-witness, and an Inhabitant of the said Town of Manchester. July 23. Printed for T. N. 1642. *Quarto.*

* MANCHESTER'S RESOLUTION against the LORD STRANGE, with the Parliament's endeavour and care for the prevention of such sad Calamities that may ensue upon the Nation, by their severall Votes resolved upon in the House of Peers and in the House of Commons, for the securing the Kingdome of England and the Dominion of Wales. John Brown, Cler. Parliament. Also a remarkable passage concerning his Majesty's blocking up of Hull, July 12. London : printed for A. Coe, 1642. *Quarto.*

* To the King's Most Excellent Majesty : The Humble Desires of The High Court of Parliament. Declaring the Grounds and chief Motives that induce them to proceed in this Course of Raising a Guard to defend themselves against all such as should oppose them. With the Grounds of their Fears, collected into severall Hedds. Also HORRIBLE NEWS FROM MANCHESTER, declaring a great Skirmish betwixt the LORD STRANGE'S FORCE and the Followers of the Deputy-Lieutenant, July 19 [an error for 15]. Whereunto is annexed the Parliament's Protestation to the King's most Excellent Majesty. Ordered that this be printed and published. John Brown, Cler. Parl. ; Hen. Elsing, Cler. Parl. D. Com. July 23. London : printed for A. Coe. *Quarto.*

* Severall Letters from the Committees in severall Counties to the Honourable William Lenthall, Esquire, Speaker of the House of Commons, read in both Houses of Parliament, June 27, 1642. Wherein (amongst divers other Passages very remarkable) is related how the TOWNSMEN of MANCHESTER PUT THEMSELVES INTO ARMS and stood upon their defence against LORD STRANGE and his Forces, who came to seize on the Magazine. With an intercepted Letter from Sir Edward

Fitton to Sir Thomas Ashton at York, discovering a fowl design of the malignant Party. Whereunto is added several Votes of both Houses. Die Lunæ, 27 Junii 1642. Ordered by the Lords and Commons in Parliament that these votes and four Letters be forthwith printed and published. John Brown, Clerk Parliamentorum. London: printed for Joseph Hunscott and John Wright. 1642. *Quarto.*

* Lieutenant-General Cromwell's Letter concerning the Total Routing of the Scots Army, the taking of Four Thousand Arms and almost all their Ammunition. With another LETTER written from MANCHESTER to SIR RALPH ASHTON, a Member of the Honourable House of Commons, concerning the said Victory. Ordered by the Commons assembled in Parliament that these Letters be forthwith printed and published. H. Elsynge, Cler. Parl. D. Com. London: printed for Edward Husband, Printer to the Honourable House of Commons. August 22, 1648. *Small quarto.*

The beginning of Civil-Warres in England, or a Skirmish between the LORD STRANGE and the Inhabitants of MANCHESTER in Lancashire, July 4. With the number of the men that were slain and wounded on both sides, and a catalogue of the Officers that were in the Skirmish. The occasion whereof was through the Lord Strange's resolution to take away their Magazine by force, having received many forces from Yorke. Likewise a Letter which the Lord Strange sent to the Gentry of Manchester, July 5, with their answer to the said letter, together with the Parliament Declaration and Order concerning the aforesaid Lord. Lond. 1642. *Small quarto.* 8 pp.

This Tract is not the same as the last named, though *Ormerod* considers it only another edition of it. (*See* "Civil War Tracts of Lancashire," Chetham Society, II. p. 25.)

A copy is in the Library of the Right. Hon. the Earl of Derby.

* His Majesties Desires and COMMANDS to all the TRAYNED BANDS and others on this side Trent and Dominion of Wales to be in Readinesse with Horse and Arms to serve his Majesty for defence of the Kingdome, and to be in such readinesse that they may be able to march at 24 houres warning at the furthest. Signed with his Royal Signet at

the Court of Yorke, and published by his Majesties speciall Command. With the Sheriffs of Yorkshire's Propositions to the Gentry and Commonalty of that County, July 1, 1642. Likewise a Letter which came from MANCHESTER read in the House of Commons concerning a great Troop of Horse lately come from York under the command of Lord Strange, and the Parliament Resolution concerning the same. Hen. Elsyng, Cler. Parl. D. Com. July 6. Printed for John Norton. 1642. *Small quarto.*

* A true and exact Relation of the several Passages at the SIEGE of MANCHESTER between Lord Strange his forces and the Towne, wherein is evidently seene the wonderfull mercy of God in their deliverance. Written by one that was an eie-witness and an Actor in most of that Service. Also a Protestation of Master Hotham and divers others Knights and Gentlemen against the 14 Articles of Pacification and Neutrality. London: printed for Edward Blackman, at the Angel in Paul's Church Yard. Oct. 12, 1642. *Small quarto.*

* A continuation of the LATE PROCEEDINGS of His Majesties Army at Shrewsbury, Bridgenorth, MANCHESTER, etc. Written by a good hand from the Army. London: Batt, Oct. 12, 1642. *Small quarto.*

* A DECLARATION and SUMMONS sent by the Earl of Newcastle to the Town of MANCHESTER to lay down their arms; with the resolute Answer of the Commanders-in-Chief and Souldiers in Manchester to spend their blood for the honour of the King, the Protestant Religion, and the Priviledges of Parliament against the Papists and Malignants now under his Lordship's command. Imprimatur John White. London: printed for Peter Cole, and are to be sold at the Glove in Cornhill. July 15, 1643. *Small quarto.*

* Good Service hitherto ill rewarded, or an Historical Relation of eight years Services for King and Parliament done in or about MANCHESTER. By Lieut.-Col. JOHN ROSWORM. London: printed in the year 1649.

Reprinted for the Editor (John Palmer) by John Leigh, Market Street, Manchester, in 1822. *Small quarto.*

* Manchester's Joy for DERBIES OVERTHROW, or an exact

relation of a famous Victory obtained by the MANCHESTER FORCES against the Lord Strange, Earle of Derby, at WARRINGTON, in Lancashire, where the said Earle was beaten into a Steeple, with the losse of many of his men, with a true declaration of what ensued thereupon. Published to prevent misinformation. Printed for Bernard Hayward. 1643. *Small quarto.*

* Exceeding Joyfull NEWS out of LANCASHIRE, Nottinghamshire, and Lincolnshire, or an Extract of certain letters from thence, being a True Relation of the Parliamentary Forces taking the Townes of WARRINGTON and Whitchurch, with the names of the chief Commanders on both sides; the number of men that were slain, and the ordnance, Armes, Ammunition, and prisoners that were taken. The clearing LANCASHIRE of King's Forces, and the manner of besieging of Newark by the Nottingham and Lincolnshire forces, and what hath been done there since the sieges, and the probability of taking the said towne. London: printed for Robert Wood. 1643. *Small quarto.*

* A True Relation of a great and wonderfull VICTORY obtained by CAPTAIN ASHTON and the Parliament Forces against the Earl of Derby at WHALLEY in Lancashire. As it was certified in a letter from a Gentleman there to a Member of the House of Commons. For which great mercie they have appointed a day of Thanksgiving. London: printed for Edw. Husbands, and are to be sold at his shop in the middle Temple. May 8, 1643. *Small quarto.*

* A true representation of the present sad and lamentable condition of the COUNTY of LANCASTER, and particularly of the towne of WIGAN, ASHTON, and the parts adjacent. May 24, 1649. *Small quarto.*

* A Great Victory by the Blessing of God obtained by the Parliament forces against the Scots forces commanded by the Earl of Derby on the 25 of August 1651, near WIGGON, in Lancashire, certifyed by a letter from Col. Lilburne and two letters from Chester, also a Letter from Col. Birche to Mr. Speaker. Imp. Hen. Scobel, Cler. Par. *Small quarto.*

MASTER RIGBY'S SPEECH in Answere to the Lord Finch, of

that he delivered before the House of Commons, in behalfe of himselfe. Printed, 1641. Iune 29. *Small quarto.*

Title, 2 pp. Speech, 4 pp.

Alexander Rigby of Middleton, M.P. for Wigan (the eldest son of Alexander Rigby of Wigan), was born in 1594, and died 19th August 1650. The above Speech is reprinted in Campbell's "Lives of the Chancellors, vol. ii. p. 579, and in the "History of Goosnargh," p. 144, which also contains a pedigree and account of the Rigby family of Middleton.

MASTER RIGBY'S SPEECH in answer to the Lord Finch, of that he delivered before the House of Commons, in behalf of himself. With a Conspiracie discovered: or, The Report of a Committee to the House of Commons in Parliament of the Examination of divers of the Conspirators and others in the late Treason, June the 17th, 1641.

1. Concerning the Tower.
2. Wherein the French are concerned in this Conspiracy.
3. Of provoking the Army against the Parliament by false Reports.

Printed in the yeare 1941 (*sic*). *Small quarto.*

Title, ii. pp. Speech, 6 pp.

Copies of the two last named are in the Bodleian.

XXV. QUERIES propounded to the COMMONS of ENGLAND, etc. (Preceded Title-page)—"To the Right Worshipfull and much honoured Colonells—

Ralph Assheton }
Richard Holland } Esquires.

and the rest of the Colonells, Commanders, Officers, and Souldiers in the Countie Palatine of Lancaster." *Quarto.*

Title, i. p. Queries, 14 pp.

A copy of this is in the Chetham Library.

* A True and Perfect Diurnall of all the CHIEFE PASSAGES in LANCASHIRE from the 3 July to the 9. Sent to five Shopkeepers in London from a friend, July 9, 1642. Printed for T. U. 1642. *Quarto.*

* The BEGINNING of the Civil Warres in England; or, TERRIBLE NEWES from the NORTH. Printed by order of Parliament, July 9, 1642.

PROTESTATION of the LORDS and COMMONS; wherein, amongst divers of His Majestie's late illegal proceedings is discovered his friendlinesse for profest Papists. 1642. *Small quarto.*

Refers to Papists in Lancashire, etc.

LANCASHIRE DURING THE CIVIL WAR.

The following Tracts contain more or less details concerning the County at this time:—

The MODERATE INTELLIGENCER communicating the affairs of the Kingdom. (Contains Letters from Lancashire.) 1648.

THREE LETTERS written by ROGER WILBRAHAM of Namptwich, concerning the surrender of many Scottish Lords to the High Sheriffe of the County of Chester, etc. 1648. *Small quarto.*

Contains a list of the officers, etc., taken prisoners at Warrington Bridge.

The PARLIAMENTARY INTELLIGENCER, July 1660.

Contains a Letter from Bury, in Lancashire, respecting the ceremony of proclaiming Charles II. King.

The PARLIAMENTARY INTELLIGENCER, 1662.

Contains the Petition of the Mayor, Bailiffs, and Burgesses of the Town of Preston to Charles II. on the surrender of the Fee Farm Rent purchased by the town.

DECLARATIONS and REMONSTRANCES of the King's Majestie's Loyall Subjects concerning the Army under Lord Gen. Fairfax, and the discontents and jealousies thereof, etc. etc. Secretly printed 1648.

Alludes to the Army before Preston.

A PERFECT DIURNALL of some Passages in Lancashire and Yorkshire; the Barrbarous Cruelty of Prince Rupert in the towne of Bolton; the Relief of Lancaster; Sir W. Brereton, Commander-in-Chief of the Forces in Cheshire and Lancashire, etc. 1644. *Small quarto.*

A PERFECT DIURNALL of Passages in Parliament, etc. 1649.

Contains a Petition from Blackburn Hundred, etc.

STAR CHAMBER CASES, showing what causes properly belonged to the cognizance of that Court, etc. 1641.

Contains an account of Thomas Worsley, who seized, in the right of his wife, certain lands in Lancashire.

DAGON DEMOLISHED; or, Twenty admirable examples of God's severe Justice and Displeasure against the SUBSCRIBERS of the late ENGAGEMENT against our Lawfull Soveraign King Charles the Second and the whole House of Peeres in these words:—*I do declare and promise that I will be true and faithfull to the Common-wealth of England as it is now established without a King or House of Lords.*

Also against some of the Judges of the late King in the High Court of Injustia.

Published to reclaim such Fanatique persons who have been too forward to promote this wicked, destructive Engagement; and still designe it, which hath wounded the consciences of so many Godly Christians in this Kingdom. By that late worthy Patriot of his Country Mr. JOHN VICARS.

[Quotation, Eccles. x. 20.]

London: printed by T. Mabb for Edward Thomas; and are to be sold at the Adam and Eve, in Little Britain. 1660. *Small quarto.*

Title as above, The Stationer to the Reader, and Dagon Demolished, 16 pp.

Scarce. Sells for 6s. 6d.

Amongst the twenty examples are the following Lancashire men—viz. Mr. Midgeley, a Schoolmaster in *Ouldam*, Mr. James Ashton of *Chadarton*, Mr. Bray, Minister of *St. Michael's*, the Constable of *Shaw*, and *Barron Rigby* [*i.e.* Alexander Rigby of Middleton].

THE SUREY DEMONIAC TRACTS.

The SUREY DEMONIACK, or an account of SATAN'S STRANGE and DREADFUL ACTINGS in and about the BODY of RICHARD DUGDALE of SUREY near WHALLEY in Lancashire, and how he was Dispossest by Gods blessing on the Fastings and Prayers of divers Ministers and People. The Matter of Fact attested by the Oaths of several credible Persons before some of His Majesties Justices of the Peace in the said County. London: printed for Jonathan Robinson, at the Golden Lyon in St. Paul's-Church-Yard. 1697. *Small quarto.*

Title as above and Preface, viii. pp. Some Account, 64 pp.

The compilers of this Tract were Thomas Jolly and John Carrington.

The SUREY IMPOSTER; being an ANSWER to a late Fanatical Pamphlet entituled The SUREY DEMONIACK. By ZACH. TAYLOR, A.M., and one of the King's Preachers for the County Palatine of Lancaster. [Prov. xviii. 17.] London: printed for John Jones at the Dolphin and Crown in St. Paul's Church-yard; and Ephraim Johnson, Bookseller in Manchester. MDCXCVII. *Small quarto.*

Title as above and Address to the Dissenting Minister, vi. pp. An Answer, 75 pp.

A *Frontispiece* Portrait of the Surey Impostor.

A VINDICATION of the SUREY DEMONIACK as no Impostor; or a REPLY to a certain pamphlet Publish'd by Mr. Zach. Taylor, called the Surey Impostor. With a further clearing and confirming of the Truth as to Richard Dugdale's Case and Cure. By T. J. [Thomas Jolly], one of the Ministers who attended upon that affair from first to last; but replies only as to matter of fact, and as he therewithal is more especially concerned. To which is annexed a brief Narrative of the Surey Demoniack, drawn up by the same author, for the satisfaction of such who have not seen the former narrative. [2 Cor. vi. 4 to 11.] London: printed for Nevill Simmons in Sheffield, Yorkshire, and sold by G. Conyers at the Ring in Little Britain, London. 1698. *Small quarto.*

Title as above and Preface, pp. i.-vi. A Vindication, etc., pp. 7 to 80.

The Lancashire Levite rebuk'd, or a VINDICATION of the DIS-

SENTERS from Popery, Superstition, Ignorance, and Knavery, unjustly charged on them by Mr. Zach. Taylor in his book entitled "The Surey Impostor," in a letter to himself. By AN IMPARTIAL HAND. With an abstract of the Surey Demoniack. London: printed by Rich: Janeway Jun., and sold by Richard Baldwin in Warwick Lane. 1698. *Small quarto.*

Title as above and Address, iv. pp. A Letter to Mr. Z. Taylor, 32 pp.

POPERY, SUPERSTITION, IGNORANCE, AND KNAVERY very unjustly by a Letter in general pretended, but as far as was charg'd, very fully proved upon the Dissenters that were concerned in the Surey Imposter. By ZACH. TAYLOR. London: printed for John Jones at the Dolphin and Crown in St. Paul's Church-yard. 1698. *Small quarto.*

Title as above and Letter to Apostate Friend, N. N., 28 pp.

Copies of the five last-named Tracts are in the Chetham Library.

The LANCASHIRE LEVITE REBUK'D; or a farther vindication of the Dissenters from Popery, Superstition, Ignorance and Knavery; unjustly charged on Them by Mr. ZACHARY TAYLOR, in his Two Books about the Surey Demoniack. In a Second Letter to Himself. London: printed by R. J., and sold by A. Baldwin, near the Oxford-Arms in Warwick-Lane. 1698. *Small quarto.*

Title as above and Preface, vi. pp. The Lancashire Levite, etc., 26 pp.

A copy of this is in the Bodleian Library.

POPERY, SUPERSTITION, IGNORANCE, and KNAVERY CONFESS'D and fully Proved on the Surey Dissenters. From the Second Letter of an Apostate Friend to Zach. Taylor. To which is added A refutation of Mr. T. Jollie's vindication of the Devil in Dugdale; or The Surey Demoniack. London: printed for W. Keblewhite at the White-Swan, and J. Jones at the Dolphin and Crown in St. Paul's Church-yard. 1699. *Small quarto.*

Title as above, Preface, Popery, etc., 40 pp., including the first leaf, on which is a woodcut of the Surey Impostor.

The Refutation of Mr. T. Jolly's Vindication of the Devil in Dugdale, or the Surey Demoniack. London: printed [as above].

Title and Refutation, 20 pp. (being sheet F of the preceding Tract).

Copy in the Bodleian Library.

THE DARRELL TRACTS.

A DISCOVERY of the FRAVDVLENT PRACTISES of IOHN DARREL, Bacheler of Artes, in his proceedings concerning the pretended Possession and dispossession of William Somers at Nottingham: of Thomas Darling, the boy of Burton, at Caldwall: and of Katherine Wright at Mansfield, and Whittington: and of his dealings with one Mary Couper at Nottingham, detecting in some sort the deceitfull trade in these latter dayes of casting out Deuils.

"We may not do euill that good may come of it."—ROM. iii.

"Dum per mendacium tenditur vt doceatur fides, id demum agitur, vt nulli habenda fides."—AUG. AD CONSENTIUM, Cap. 4.

London: imprinted by Iohn Wolfe. 1599. *Small quarto.*

Title as above and To the Reader, viii. pp. A Discovery, pp.

The Copy in the Bodleian Library is not quite perfect. A considerable portion of this refers to Lancashire. A copy of this lately sold for £2 : 5s.

The TRIALL of MAIST. DORRELL, or A Collection of Defences against Allegations not yet suffered to receive convenient answere. Tending to cleare him from the Imputations of teaching Somners and others to counterfett possession of Divells. That the mist of pretended counterfetting being dispelled, the glory of Christ, his royall power in casting out Divels (at the prayer and fasting of his people) may evidently appeare. 1599. *Duodecimo.*

JOHN vii. 11.—"Doeth our Law iudge a man before it heare him, and know what he hath done?"

PROVERB xiv. 15.—"The foolish will beleeue euery thing, but the prudent will consider his steppes."

Title as above, i. p. Dedication, i. p. To the Reader, viii. pp. The Triall, 103 pp.

A copy of this is in the Chetham Library.

A SVRVEY of CERTAINE DIALOGICAL DISCOURSES: written by IOHN DEACON and IOHN WALKER, concerning the doctrine of Possession and Dispossession of Diuels. Wherein is manifested the palpable ignorance and Dangerovs errors of the Discoursers; and what according to proportion of God his truth, every Christian is to hold in these poyntes. Published by Iohn Darrell, minister of the gospell. Imprinted 1602. *Small quarto.*

TITUS i. 10, 11.—"There are many disobedient and vaine talkers, and deceiuers of mindes, teaching thinges, which they ought not, for filthy lucre's sake, whose mouthes must be stopped.

Title, and to the Reader, x. pp. A Survey, 78 pp.

The REPLIE of IOHN DARRELL to the Answer of IOHN DEACON and IOHN WALKER, concerning the doctrine of the Possession and Dispossession of Demoniakes. Imprinted 1602. *Small quarto.*

ECCLESIASTES iv. 1.—"I turned, and considered all the oppressions that are wrought vnder the sun; and behold, the teares of the oppressed, and none comforteth them; and loe the strength is of the hand of them that oppresse them, and none comforteth them."

Title and Dedication, x. pp. The Reply, 58 pp.

Copies of the two last named are in the Bodleian Library.

A trve NARRATION of the STRANGE and GREVOVS VEXATION of the DEVEL, of PERSONS in LANCASHIRE, and William Somers of Nottingham.

Wherein the doctrine of possession and dispossession of Demoniacks ovt of the word of God is particularly applyed vnto Somers and the rest of the persons controuerted; together with the vse we are to make of these workes of God. By JOHN DARRELL, Minister of the word of God. Printed 1600. *Quarto.*

"He that is not with me is against me; and he that gathereth not with me, scattereth."—MATT. xii. 30.

Title as above, Dedication, viii. pp. The true Narrative, 165 pp.

Secretly printed, of great rarety, copies having sold for £1 : 15s.
A copy is in the British Museum.

A DETECTION of that sinnefvl, shamfvl, lying, and ridicvlovs discovrs of SAMVEL HARSHNET, entittvled a discoverie of the fravvdvlent practises of John Darrell, wherein is manifestly and apparantly shewed in the eyes of the world, not only the vnlikelihoode but the flate impossibilitie of the pretended counterfayting of William Somers, Thomas Darling, Kath. Wright, and Mary Couper, togeather with the other 7 IN LANCASHIRE, and the supposed teaching of them by the saide John Darrell. Imprinted 1600. *Quarto.*

PSALM vii. 14.—"Behold he shall travaile with uickednes, for he hath conceived mischiefe, but he shall bring fourth a lye."

Title as above, Address, x. pp. Detection, etc, 208 pp. Contents, 3 pp.

Very rare; copies have sold for £2 : 5s. A copy is in the Manchester Free Library.

Samuel Harsnet was Archbishop of York.[1]

DIALOGICALL Discourses of Spirits and Divels, Declaring their proper essence, natures, dispositions, and operations: their possessions and dispossessions: with other the Appendantes, peculiarly appertaining to those speciall points. Very conducent and pertinent to the timely procuring of some Christian conformitie in iudgement: for the peaceable compounding of the late sprong controuuersies concerning all such intricate and difficult doubts. By {JOHN DEACON, JOHN WALKER,} Preachers.

(Deut. xiii. 1, 2, 3; and Matth. xxiv. 23, 24; and quotation from Augustine "De Trinitate," with translation.) Propugnaculum Vitæ patientia. Londini: jmpensis Geor. Bishop. 1601. *Small quarto.*

Title and Preface, xvi. pp. Dialogical Discourses, 356 + xii.

A copy in the Chetham Library.

[1] A declaration of egregious Popish Impostures, to withdraw the harts of his Maiesties Subjects from their allegeance, and from the truth of Christian Religion professed in England, vnder the pretence of casting out of deuils. Practised by Edmunds, alias Weston a Iesuit, and diuers Romish Priestes, his wicked Associates. Whereevnto are annexed the copies of the Confessions and Examinations of the parties themselves, which were pretended to be possessed and dispossessed: taken uppon oath before his Maiesties Commissioners, for causes Ecclesiasticall. At London: newly printed by Ia. Roberts, dwelling in Barbican. 1605.

The above has not been printed; it was written by Bishop Harsnet, and the MS. is in the Bodleian Library. It is contained in 286 pp. *quarto.*

A Svmmarie Answere to al the Material points in any of Master Darel his bookes. More Especiallie to that one booke of his, intitvled, the Doctrine of the possession and dispossession of Demoniaks out of the word of God. By { JOHN DEACON, / JOHN WALKER, } Preachers. (Exod. vii. 11, 12, 13; Aug. Chrysost. Engubinus.) Propugnaculum Vitæ patientia. Londini: Geor. Bishop. 1601.

Title and Preface, xxxii. pp. Discourse, 240 pp. Table, viii. pp.
A copy in the Chetham Library.

An Astrological prediction of the occurrences in England, 1648, 1649, and 1650, concerning these particulars. [The first 5 do not refer to Lancashire].

VI. What may succeed the apparition of THREE SUNS in LANCASHIRE, seen of many[1] the 28 Febr. last, and described by Jer. Shakerly, of Pendle Forest. By WILLIAM LILLY, Student in Astrology. London: printed by T. B. for John Partridge and Humphrey Blunden; and are to be sold in Blackfriers going into Carter Lane, and at the Castle in Cornhill. 1648. *Small quarto.*

The Article on Lancashire is included in the first 28 pages. The whole work consists of 71 pages, and has a Woodcut of the three suns.
Rare. Sells for 7s. 6d.

TRACTS RELATING TO QUAKERS (OR FRIENDS).

The QUAKER-JESUITE; or, Popery in Quakerisme. Being a clear Discovery. 1. That their doctrines, with their Proofs and Arguments, are fetcht out of the Council of Trent, Belarmine, and others. 2. That their practises are fetcht out of the Rules and Practises of Popish Monks. With a serious admonition to Quakers to consider their ways, and return from whence they are fallen. By WILLIAM BROWNSWORD, Minister of the Gospel at Kendal. London: printed by J. M., and are to be sold by Miles Harrison, Bookseller in Kendal. 1660. *Small quarto.*

16 pp.

[1] This is probably the Geoffry Shakerly, who was M.P. for Wigan in 1640, and who was the prototype of Shadwell's "Sir Jeffery Shacklehead" in "The Lancashire Witches."

This Tract was answered by John Story in his "Babilon's Defence broken down." *See* "Smith's Bibliotheca Anti-Quakeriana."

William Brownsward was, in 1658-9, described as "Clerke, formerly of Preston, now Minister of Kendal" ("Preston White Book"), and in 1649 as "Pastor of Douglas," in the Parish of Eccleston. He signed the Paper known as "The Agreement of the People" in 1650 (*see* "History of Kirkham," p. 105).

The Christian's Testimony against Tythes. In an account of the great Spoil and Rapine committed by the Bishop of Chester's Tythe-Farmer at CARTMELL, in LANCASHIRE, upon the People called Quakers in the years 1677 and 1678. Printed in the year 1678. *Small quarto.*

Title, etc., 16 pp.

Thomas Atkinson, a native of Lancashire, was the author of this Tract. In 1684 he published "An Exhortation to all People." He was then in his 80th year.

Divers Queries of great importance propounded by THOMAS ATKINSON of CARTMELL, in Lancashire, to GABRIEL CAMELFORD, Parson of Stafley Chapel. With his answers to them. Also Replies to the Answers therein is lay'd open the subtilty and deceit of the Priest, and his Inventions, Snares, and Baits, etc.

This was replied to by George Fox and Richard Hubberthorn in a Tract entitled "Truth's Defence," etc. 1653.

Gabriel Camelford was Curate of Stavely Chapel, in the Parish of Cartmel, from which he was ejected. He died 1676.

The Cry of Oppression (No. 2). In a few instances of the late Distresses and Levies made upon some of the peaceable People called Quakers, in the Counties of York and LANCASTER, on account of their tender consciences, and for their Religious Meetings, briefly stated. London: printed in the year 1683. *Folio.* 4 pp.

The Cry of the oppressed for Justice; or the case of THOMAS RUDD, who was Imprisoned and Whipped through several streets of the

TOWN of LEVERPOOL, in the County of Lancaster, by order of the then Mayor of said town, for going through the streets thereof, and exhorting the people to fear God. With a Letter written by the said Thomas Rudd to THOMAS SWEETING, Mayor of LIVERPOOL. London : printed and sold by T. Sowle, in White Hart Court, in Gracious Street, and at the Bible, in Leadenhall Street. 1700. *Small quarto.*

16 pp.

Thomas Rudd was a miller of Wharfe, near Settle, in Yorkshire, where he was buried in 1719.

Light sown for the Righteous, and Gladness for the Upright in Heart. This is to go abroad among all people who are honest-hearted, especially amongst the INHABITANTS of FOURNS FELLS, in LANCASHIRE, and among all who have known me after the flesh, that all honest people may see what I was in profession, and what I am now by the Grace of God. London : printed for Thomas Simmons, at the Bull and Mouth, near Aldersgate. 1657. *Small quarto.*

40 pp.

Written by Thomas Rawlinson of Furnessfells, Lancashire. A copy of this is in the Midgly collection, Friends' Meeting House, Manchester.

An answer to Scandalous Paper, wherein were some Queries Given to be answered. And likewise therein is found many Lies and Slanders, etc. * * Dated from Dorchester, in New England, August 17, 1655, subscribed Edward Breck, which was directed to a People at RAINFORTH, in LANCASHIRE, which he calls a Church of Christ. London : printed for Giles Calvert, etc. * * 1656. *Small quarto.*

40 pp.

Living Words through a Dying Man, being a Melodious Song of the Mercies and Judgments of the Lord, sung by a Disciple of Christ on his Dying Bed, when the Pangs of Death upon his outward man. By one who died a prisoner for the Testimony of Jesus, FRANCIS PATCHET. Printed in the year 1678. *Foolscap octavo.*

12 pp.

He was a native of Scotforth, in Lancashire, and died in the Fleet, where he was a prisoner for non-payment of Tythes, in March 1677.

The Revelation of Jesus Christ unto JOHN MOORE, in the Fourth Moneth, in the year 1658. London: Printed for Thomas Simmons, at the Bull and Mouth, near Aldersgate. 1458. *Small quarto.* 8 pp.

John Moore was a native of Carhouse, in the parish of Garstang, Lancashire, and the author of "The True Light," "The Great Trumpet," "A Jesuitical Designe Discovered, in a piece called the 'Quaker's Pedigree,'" and other Friends' Books.

Popery exposed by its own Authors, and Two Romish Champions checked for their hot and rash onsets and attempts against the people called Quakers: being an answer to the large demands and false accusations, assertions, and doctrines contained in several manuscripts of JAMES WATMOUGH, of BLACKROAD, in LANCASHIRE, and his abettor, Matthew Hall, Papists * * As herein is also a defence of some printed Books, formerly written by Francis Nowgill (one of the People called Quakers), deceased. * * Written in true Love to all People whomsoever. By a lover of Truth, HENRY MOLLINEUX. London: Printed by the assigns of J. Sowle, at the Bible, in George-Yard, in Lombard Street. 1718. *Octavo.*

Title, etc., 256 pp.

A copy of this is in the Friends' Meeting House, Manchester (Midgley Reference Library). Henry Mollineux was a native of Liverpool. *See* page 266.

A Serious Remembrancer to Live well, written Primarily to Children and Young People; Secondarily, to Parents, useful (I hope) for all; Lastly, Confessions, Remarks of the Death of JONAH LAWSON, who finished his course upon earth the 22d day of the Month called February 1683, in the 14th year of his age.

[Three Lines of poetry.]

[By THOMAS LAWSON.] London: Printed in the year 1684. *Small octavo.* 32 pp.

Jonah Lawson was the son of Thomas Lawson, who was the son of Sir Thomas Lawson and Ruth his wife. He was born 10th December 1630, and was for some time the curate of the church at Rampside, in the parish of Dalton-in-Furness. He afterwards joined the Society of

Friends. He was a skilled botanist, and was the author of several Friends' Books. "Dagon's Fall," "A Mite into the Treasury," were from his pen.

The Immediate Call to the Ministry of the Gospel witnessed by the Spirit, with a true Declaration of the Persecution and Suffering of RICHARD HUBBERTHORNE, James Parnell, Ann Blaykling. By WILLIAM PICKERING, who is Mayor of Cambridge. [Part written by JAMES PARNELL.] London: Printed for Giles Calvert, at the Black Spread Eagle, at the West end of Paul's. 1654. *Small quarto.* 8 pp.

Something that lately passed in Discourse between the King and R. H. (RICHARD HUBBERTHORNE). Published to prevent the mistakes and Errors in a Copy lately printed contrary to the knowledge or intention of the party concerned, and not only so, but also misprinted and abused in several particulars, therefore it was thought convenient fo [*sic*] the removing of Erors and mistakes, to be reprinted in a more true form and order for the satisfaction of others.—R. H. London: Printed for P. L. for G. C.; and are to be sold at his shop, at the Black Spread Eagle, west end of Paul's. 1660. *Small quarto.*

Title as above, 1 p. Discourse, 6 pp.

Another Edition, with the same date but different type, was published in which the word "copy" on title-page was spelt "coppy;" in other respects it was identical with the above. It was also reprinted by the Manchester Tract Society.

The edition which R. H. says was published without authority had the following Title:—"An account of several Things that passed between his Sacred Majesty and Richard Hubberthorne, Quaker, on the 4th of June 1660, after the delivery of George Fox his letter to the King." London: Printed for M. S., and are to be sold at the Booksellers' Shops. *Small quarto.* 10 pp.

Contains some allusions to Lancashire.

The cause of Stumbling removed from all that will receive the Truth, and from before the Eyes of the wise men of London. In a Treatise shewing the difference between the spirit of a man which is the candle of the Lord and the light which hath enlightened every man that cometh into the World. * * * Given forth from the Lords' servant, RICHARD HUBBERTHORNE.

[Three Texts of Scripture.]

London: Printed for Thomas Simmons, * * 1657. *Small quarto.*

Title, Address, and Cause of Stumbling, 29 pp.

A COLLECTION of the several BOOKS and WRITINGS of that Faithful Servant of God, RICHARD HUBBERTHORN, who finished his Testimony (being a Prisoner in Newgate for the Truth's sake) the 17th of the 6th Month, 1662. [Rev. xiv. 13.] London: printed and are to be sold by William Warwick. *Small quarto.*

Title as above, and Collection, 376 pp.

Richard Hubberthorn was a native of Yelland in Lancashire. A Memoir of him is in "Biographical Notices," by Henry Fuke, vol. ii. p. 123.

The Quaker's Wilde Questions objected against the Ministers of the Gospel, and many Sacred Acts and Offices of Religion. With brief Answers thereunto. Together with—

A Discourse.
1. Of the Holy Spirit of God, His Impressions and Workings on the Souls of Men.
2. Of Divine Revelation, Mediate and Immediate.
3. Of Error, Heresie, and Schism; the Nature, Kindes, Causes, Reasons, and Dangers thereof; with Directions for avoiding the same.

All very seasonable for these times. By R. SHERLOCK, B.D., at BORWICK-HAL in Lancashire. [Matt. xiii. 24, 25. Greek Text.] London: printed by E. Cotes for R. Royston at the Angel in Ivie Lane. 1656. *Small quarto.*

Title as above, Dedication to Sir Robert Bindlosse, Bart., and Table of Contents, xii. pp. (unpaged). The Quaker's Wilde Questions Answered (with facsimile of direction of the Letter containing the Questions), 25 pp. Title-page to 1st Discourse, Dedication to Lady Rebecca Bindlosse, and Errata's (*sic*), vi. pp. Discourse, 68 pp. Title to the 2d Discourse, i. p. Introduction to the 2d Discourse, p. 69-72. Discourse, p. 73-168. The Grounds and General Heads of 3d Discourse, p. 169-172. Discourse, p. 173-244. A Catalogue of books printed for Robert Royston, 4 pp.

A copy of this is in the Chetham Library.

A Reply to a Book set forth by one of the blind Guides of England, who is a Priest at Barwick-Hall in Lancashire, who writes his name R. SHERLOCK, Batchelor of Divinity, but he is proved to be a Diviner and Deceiver of the People. Which Book is in answer to some Queres set forth to him by them whom he calls Quakers. Dreadfull powerfull God! Praises to thee for ever, Amen. Thy Servant, RICHARD HUBBERTHORNE. London: printed for Giles Calvert. *Small quarto.* 32 pp.

A Brief Discovery of a threefold Estate of Antichrist now extant in the World—viz. a Description of (1) The True and False Temple; (2) The False Ministry; and (3) The false churches. Whereunto is added the trial of one GEORGE FOX in LANCASHIRE, with his answer to eight articles exhibited against him, being sent in a letter for Kellet to some Friends in Yorkshire. Also certain Queries upon a petition lately presented to Parliament from divers Gentlemen and others in Worcestershire, etc. London: printed for Giles Calvert, Black-Spread-Eagle, at the West End of Paul's. 1653. *Small quarto.*

Written by Thomas Aldam (of Warnsworth near Doncaster), Benjamen Nicholson, John Harwood, and Thomas Lawson.

A true Testimony from the People of God (who by the world are called Quakers) of the Doctrines of the Prophets, Christ, and the Apostles, which is witnessed unto by them who are now raised up by the same Power and quickened by the same Spirit and Blood of the Everlasting Covenant which brought again our Lord Jesus from the dead. Published for this end—viz. That all sober minded People may see the Unity and Agreement of our doctrine, etc. * * * By M. F. [MARGARET FELL.] London: printed for Robert Wilson, and are to be sold at his Shop at the sign of the Black-Spread-Eagle and Wind-Mill in Martins L'Grand. 1660. *Small quarto.*

Title and To the Reader, iv. pp. True Testimony, 28 pp.

A Declaration and an Information from us, the People of God, called

Quakers, to the present Governors, the King, and both Houses of Parliament, and all whom it may concern. This was delivered into the King's hand the 22 day of the Fourth Moneth by M. F. [Margaret Fell.] London: for Thomas Simmons and Robert Wilson. 1660. *Small quarto.*

Title as above and Declaration, 28 pp.

On the last page is a note, in which the authoress says: " I was moved of the Lord to leave my House and Family, and to come Two Hundred Miles to lay these Things " before the King.

A copy of this scarce Tract is in the Author's Library.

Women's Speaking justified, proved, and allowed of by the Scriptures, all such as speak by the Spirit and Power of the Lord Jesus, and how women were the first that preached the Tidings of the Resurrection of Jesus, and were sent by Christ's own command before he ascended to the Father.—John xx. 17.

[4 Texts of Scripture.]

London: printed in the year 1666. *Small quarto.*

Title as above, and Tract, 16 pp.

This was written by Margaret Fell. Her initials appear on p. 12.
Reprinted, with additions, 1667 (London).
Translated into Dutch, 1668 (Amsterdam).

The Examination and Tryall of MARGARET FELL and GEORGE FOX (at the severall Assizes held at Lancaster); also something in answear to Bishop Lancelot Andrew's Sermon concerning Swearing. [By GEO. FOX.] Printed in the year 1664. *Small quarto.*

Title, etc., 34 pp.

Reprinted in the Harleian Miscellany, Vol. VI. 1810.
See Life of Margaret Fell.

Antichrist's strongest Hold overturned; or, the Foundation of the Religion of the People called Quakers Bared and Razed. In a debate had with some of them in the CASTLE at LANCASTER, and in an additional Account of the Light within. Wherein is shewed, etc.

* * * All of which is published (at the desire of certain friends, some of whose Letters are prefixt) for the common benefit. By J. W. [*i.e.* JOHN WIGGAN, a Baptist of LANCASHIRE.] London: printed for the Author in the year 1665.

Title, etc., 39 pp.

This is an answer to JOHN WIGGAN'S BOOK spread up and down in LANCASHIRE, Cheshire, and Wales, who is a Baptist and a Monarchy man. Wherein may be seen how he exalts himself against Christ, the Light that doth enlighten every man, etc. From the prisoners at Lancaster, whom he then opposed, being then a Prisoner Thomas Curwen [of Lancashire], William Houlden, Henry Wood, William Wilson. Also here is an answer to his Appendix annexed to the Book by MARGARET FELL [Part by GEO. Fox]. London: printed in the year 1665. *Small quarto.*

Title, etc., 160 pp.

As a continuation of this book appeared "Some Scriptures, which overturns John Wiggan's Assertions. By Henry Wood. With a Postscript by G. Fox."

A true Declaration of the Bloody Proceedings of the Men of Maidstone, in Kent, against JOHN STUBBS and WILLIAM CATON. 1655. *Small quarto.* 8 pp.

Written by the two sufferers.

Truths Caracter of Professors and their Teachers, which, by looking through may bring to their remembrance the dayes of old, and how it was then with them, which may evidently shew unto them what hath befallen them since they degenerated from the measure of God which some of them had in them. * * * Here is also something in answer to some remarkable particulars which were extracted out of above thirty addresses, which were presented to Richard Cromwell when he was protector, and were published to the nation in the Diurnals as one by Tho. Godwin by the appointment of the officers and messengers of above a hundred Congregational Churches and others from some of the Churches of the baptized people, but most of them were from the parochial priests and others that joyned with them from most of the counties in the nation, whereby their hypocrisie and deceit, their folly and their flatteries, are made palpably manifest to their shame and confusion of face. By one that is appointed of the Lord to make War in Righteousness under the Banner of the Lamb in the Truth's behalf, both against the Beast and false prophet known unto men by the name of WILLIAM CATON.

[Three texts of Scripture.]

London: printed for Thomas Simmons at the sign of the Bull and Mouth, near Aldersgate. 1660. *Small quarto.*

Title as above, Epistle to the Reader, and Tract, 56 pp.

On pages 49-50 are the addresses of "The priests and others of Lancaster, Liverpool, Preston, and Wiggan, in Lancashire" to W. C.

The Testimony of a Cloud of Witnesses who in their Generation have testified against that horrible Evil of Forcing of Conscience, and Persecution about Matters of Religion. Whose Testimony may be seasonable and sutable for the present state of the wise and learned in England, whether of the magistrates or of the clergy; and may serve as a timely Warning to them all of defiling their hands with that horrible, filthy thing, which is already in part committed in the Land. Composed together, and Translated into English by a living Witness against the aforesaid Evil, WILLIAM CATON. [Gen. ix. 27; Rev. xii. 11.] Printed in the year 1662. *Small quarto.*

Title as above, Epistle to the Reader, xii. pp. The Testimony, 51 pp.

Probably printed in London, but it is dated from "Germany, but Transcribed in Amsterdam the second month 1662."

The Moderate Enquirer resolved in a plain description of several Objections which are summed up together, and treated upon by way of Conference concerning the contemned people commonly called Quakers, who are the Royal Seed of God, and whose Innocency is here cleared in the Answers to the many objections that are frequently produced by their opposers. Which may be profitable for all to read that have anything against them, and useful for all such as desire to know the certainty of those things which are most commonly reported of them. Written in the behalf of the Brethren in Vindication of Truth. By W. C. (William Caton).

[Two texts of Scripture].

Printed in the year 1671. *Small quarto.*

Title as above, i. p. To the Reader, and Tract, 36 pp.

A Journal of the LIFE of that faithful Servant and Minister of the Gospel of Jesus Christ, WILL CATON. Written by his own hand [Edited by GEORGE FOX.] London: printed for Thomas Northcott, in George-yard, Lombard-street. 1689. *Small quarto.*

Second Edition, with some addition, *Foolscap octavo.* London. 1839. Title, etc., 88 pp.

This Tract will be found in Midgley Reference Library, Friends' Meeting House, Mount Street, Manchester.

A Notice of W. Caton is also in Luke's "Biographical Notices," Vol. II., p. 205.

William Caton was born in Lancashire about the year 1636, and was intimately associated with the Fells of Swarthmore. He subsequently went to Holland, where he married Annekin Dirricks, at Amsterdam, in 1662.

He was the author of a large number of Friends' Tracts written in Dutch and English, for particulars of which see "Smith's Cat. of Friends' Books."

God's Protecting Providence evinced in the remarkable Deliverance of ROBERT BARROW from the Inhuman Cannibals of Florida, etc. Faithfully related by JONATHAN DICKENSON. Philadelphia. 1699. *Small quarto.*

Title, etc., 108 pp.

This was reprinted by Jonathan Dickenson in 1700. London: T. Sowle. *Octavo.* And again in 1720, 1759 [n.d.], 1787, and 1790 [the Seventh Edition].

Robert Barron was born in Lancashire, and died on the 4th April 1697, and was buried in the Friends' Burial Ground, Philadelphia.

The Life, and Death, and Sufferings of ROBERT WIDDERS of

KELLET, in Lancashire, who was one of the Lord's Worthies, together with several Testimonies of his Neighbours and Friends concerning him. London: first printed in the year 1688. *Small quarto.*

Title as above, i. p. Life, etc., 35 pp.

A MS. copy of this very rare work is in the possession of Mr. John Yeardley of Rochdale.

Robert Widders died 20th January 1686, aged 67.

"The persecution of them [*sic*] People they call Quakers in several Places in LANCASHIRE." Here follows the Text (there is no Title), which is contained in 15 pp., and is signed Thomas Holme. On the last page is, "London: printed for Giles Calvert, at the Black Spread Eagle, near the West end of Paul's. 1656. *Small quarto.*

Very rarely met with. There is a copy in the Chetham Library.

This Tract was the joint production of William Simpson, Leonard Addison, John Branthwait, Isaac Yeats, Thomas Holme, Leonard Fell, and William Addamson (*see* Smith's Catalogue of Friends' Books). It was first printed without date.

A warning to Souls to beware of Quakers and Quakerism. By occasion of a late Dispute at Arley, in Cheshire, between JOHN CHEYNEY, a Christian Minister, and ROGER HAYDOCK, a Sect-master and Speaker to the Quakers, on Tuesday, Jan. 23, 1676.

[2 Tim. iv. 3.]

London: printed for Dormen Newman, at the King's Arms, in the Poultry. 1677. *Small quarto.*

Title as above, and Warning, 25 pp.

A Copy in the Chetham Library. Rare.

Quakers' Principles Quaking, or pretended Light proved Darkness, and Perfections proved to be greater Imperfections. In answer to a written Paper subscribed with the name of Thomas Holme, and scattered through the Country about LIVER-POOL, in Lancashire. Modestly propounded by RALPH HALL, an affectionate Lover of Truth, admirer of sincere saving Light, ardent desirer of perfection.

[Isa. v. 20; Jude 10.]

London: printed by R. I., and are to be sold by Edm. Paxton, near Doctors' Commons, and Tho. Parkhurst, over against the great conduit in Cheapside. 1656. *Small quarto.*

Title as above, Epistle to the Reader, signed ZACH. CROFTON, viii. pp. The Quakers' Paper, 4 pp. The Quakers' Principles, p. 5-28.

A scarce Tract, a copy of which is in the Chetham Library.

An ANSWER to a Book Titled "QUAKERS' PRINCIPLES QUAKING," subscribed by the name of one Ralph Hale, with an Epistle (so-called) to the Reader, subscribed with the name of one Zachariah Crofton. A principle of darkness, deceit, and confusion, in Ralph Hale and his Fellow labourer in Latham's Work. Zachariah Crofton is discovered by the Quakers' principle, and the Quakers' principle doth stand against the Power of darkness and all the false principles in the World, them to discover and lay open, etc. London: printed for Giles Calvert, and are to be sold at his shop, etc. etc. 1656. *Small quarto.*

The writer of this was William Adamson, of Liverpool.

A SHORT RELATION concerning the LIFE and DEATH of that man of God and faithful Minister of Jesus Christ, WILLIAM SIMPSON, who laid down his Body in the Island of Barbadoes, the eight Day of the twelfth month MDCLXX.

[2 Kings ii. 12 and Rev. xiv. 13.]

Printed in the year 1671. *Small quarto.*

Title as above, "A short account" (signed by William Fortescue). "A few lines more concerning, etc.," and "Going Naked a Signe," by William Simpson. 15 pp.

This is a very rare and curious Quaker Tract. A copy is in the Author's Collection.

William Simpson was a native of Lancashire, and in the above Tract it is stated that he was made "to go through Markets, to priests'-houses, and to great men's houses, and Magistrates'-houses, and to Cambridge, stark naked, as a sign to them shewing how God would strip them of their Power."

He was the author of several Friends' Tracts. Amongst them were "A Declaration unto all, Priest and People;" "From one who was moved of the Lord God to go a sign among the Priests, etc. * and naked from Salvation and Immortality, but as black as spiritual Ægyptians, etc.;" "A Discovery of Priests and Professors."

An Epistle for the strengthening and confirming of Friends in their most Holy Faith. *Small quarto.*

No Title. Epistle, 6 pp. Signed by LEONARD FELL, and dated the 10th of the 11th moneth 1670.

He says that in the North part of the Nation the informers are "either High-way-men, or such as have been arraigned for Fellony, or are come out of Gaols, or idle Fellows that have spent their estates if they had any."[1]

MISCELLANEOUS TRACTS.

EYE-SALVE FOR ENGLAND, or the good Trappan debated in a plain and faithful narrative of the horrid and unheard-of Designs of some Jesuits and Deputy-Lieutenants in Lancashire, treacherously to ensnare the Lives and Estates of many Persons of Quality in that County, as also in the County of York and Chester. By EVAN PRICE, who suffered long and grievous imprisonment there for not complying with them to carry on their wicked and pernicious designs.

[Seven Texts of Scripture.]

London: Printed in the Year 1667. *Small quarto.*

Title as above, and Address to the Reader, 4 pp. The Narrative, 8 pp.; amongst the Lancashire people named are Major Robinson, Captain James Howarth, Mr. Sharples, Sir Richard Houghton, and Nicholas Moseley.

A Copy is in the Chetham Library.

Hieromachia; or, a True, Sincere, and Impartial Account of a certain Dispute that happen'd August 1st, 1717, between K——, a Presbyter, etc. etc. By W. A., Schoolmaster, etc.

To which is added

The LANCASHIRE TUBSTER; or, a Dialogue between Obadiah

[1] For a notice of other Tracts written by R. Hubberthorne, Margaret Fell, William Caton, etc. (which do not refer to Lancashire), *see* "Smith's Catalogue of Friends' Books."

Cantwell, a Jockey, and Tarpides, his inspired Ass; after which he meets with Tom Squab, a Dissenting Brother, and then with his Son Ephraim, a Tub Teacher, and Daughter Jude, who reflect upon each other in opprobrious Matters of Fact. Written by a Lover of Truth. [Three *Quotations*.] London: Printed for the Author, 1719. Price Fourpence.

Title and Preface, and Hieromachia, etc., 24 pp.

Very rare.

A LETTER out of LANCASHIRE to a friend in London, giving some account of the late Tryals there, together with some seasonable and proper remarks upon it. Recommended to the Wisdom of the Lords and Commons assembled in Parliament. [Jer. v. 25; Luke xx. 20.] Printed in the year 1696. *Small quarto.*

Title, etc., 16 pp.

A Copy is in the Library of James Crossley, Esq., F.S.A., Manchester. This was written by THOMAS WAGSTALL (the son of a Warwickshire man), who was born 15 Feb. 1645, and died 17 October 1712. He was Rector of Martin's Thorpe, in Rutland, in 1669, and Chancellor of Lichfield Cathedral in 1684. At the Revolution he was deprived of his preferments, and practised in Physic.

The DEVIL TURN'D CASUIST; or the Cheats of Rome Laid Open, in the Exorcism of a Despairing Devil, at the house of THOMAS PENNINGTON in ORREL, in the Parish of Wigan, and County of Lancaster. By ZACHARV TAYLOR, M.A., Chaplain to the Right Reverend Father in God, Nicholas, Lord Bishop of Chester, and Rector of Wigan.

Spectatum admissi! Risum teneatis.

London: Printed for E. Whitlock, near Stationers' Hall, MDCXCVI. *Small quarto.*

Title as above, and Dedication xiv. pp. The Devil, etc., 16 pp.

A Copy of this very rare work is in the Bodleian Library.

A True Discourse concerning the certaine possession and DISPOSSESSION of SEVEN PERSONS in one familie in Lancashire, which also may serve as part of an answere to a fayned and false discoverie which speaketh very much evill, as well of this as of the rest of those great and mightie workes of God, which bee of the like excellent nature. By GEORGE MORE, Minister and Preacher of the Worde of God, and now (forbearing witnesse vnto this, and for iustifying the rest), a prisoner in the Clinke, where he hath continued almost for the space of two yeares. 1600.

Remember thou magnifie the worke of God which men beholde.—Iob xxxvi. 24.
We speake that we know, and testifie that which we have seene; but ye receive not our testimonie.—Ioh. iii. 11.

Title as above. To the Reader and Discourse, 85 pp. *Duodecimo.*

A copy of this is in the Bodleian Library.

A PLEA for NON-SUBSCRIBERS; or, the Ground and Reasons of many Ministers in Cheshire and LANCASHIRE, and the parts adjoining for the refusal of the late engagement modestly propounded either for receiving of satisfaction which they most desire, or of indemnitie till satisfaction be laid before them, which they cannot but expect. 1650. *Small quarto.*

A Copy of this is in Queen's College Library, Cambridge.

The Miraculous Child; or, WONDERFUL NEWS from MANCHESTER. A most true and certain account how one CHARLES BENNET, a child of but Three Years old (on the 22d of June 1679) could speak Latin, Greek, and Hebrew, though never taught those Languages, and answer all Questions relating to the Bible, etc., in a wonderful manner, and is now brought up to be presented to the King, having all along the journey been visited at Coventry and other places by most of the Ministers and other learned men, to whom he gives such satisfaction, that they depart with wonder and amazement. If any question the certainty of the relation, let them repair to Mr. Nightingale's at the Bear Inn in West Smithfield (where the child now resides), and they may be abundantly satisfied. London: Printed for F. L., 1679. Reprinted by A. Swindells, Manchester [1820.] *Octavo.*

Title and reprint, 8 pp. The original was in one sheet quarto. Of the reprint only "40 copies were printed for sale, and 10 to give away." A copy without Title is in the Manchester Free Library. A complete copy is in the Library of Richard Wood, Esq. of Whalley Range, Manchester.

The Manner of the Solemnity of the King's CORONATION at

MANCHESTER in Lancashire, April 23, 1661. [On the same page the texts commence with] "Worthy Sir," and on the foot of the last page is "Your affectionate Kinsman and Servant, WILLIAM HEAWOOD, Manchester, May 7, 1661." *Quarto.*

8 pp. A copy is in the Chetham Library.

Reprinted in Manchester 1861 and 1863. [*See* p. 130.]

The KING'S MAIESTIES DECLARATION to His Subjects concerning LAWFUL SPORTS to be used. London: printed by Bonham, Norton, and John Bill, Deputie Printers for the King's most Excellent Maiestie. MDCXVIII. Reprinted by G. Smeeton, St. Martin's Church Yard, Charing Cross. 1817. *Foolscap quarto.*

Title as above (printed in colours), and Declaration, 11 pp.

This reprint of a scarce Tract, having special reference to Lancashire, was published at 2s., and sells for 3s. 6d. Other reprints were issued in 1709 and 1860.

Case between Sir DARCY LEVER, Knight, Appellant, and JOHN ANDREWS, Gent., Respondent. *Folio.*

The Appellant's case, with pedigrees, 4 pp. The Respondent's case, 4 pp.

Refers to Lands in Manchester owned in 1612 by John Hunt and Robert Lever. Sells for 7s. 6d.

The Paper called the AGREEMENT of the PEOPLE taken into consideration, and the Lawfulness of Subscription to it examined and resolved in the negative by the MINISTERS of CHRIST in the Province of LANCASTER. Published by them especially for the satisfaction of the Conscience and guiding of the practise of our entirely honored and beloved the People of our several Churches committed to our Charge; and for the general good of this Church and Nation. London: printed for Luke Fawne, and are to be sold at his shop at the signe of the Parrot in Paul's Church-yard. 1649. *Quarto.*

Title, i. p. The paper, etc., 36 pp.

This Tract is scarce, and is of peculiar value, as it contains the names and stations of fifty-four Lancashire ministers.

The BISHOP of CHESTER'S CASE with relation to the Wardenship of Manchester. To which is shewn that no other Degrees but such as are taken in the University can be deemed Legal Qualification for any Ecclesiastical Preferment in England. [Woodcut.] Oxford: printed at the Theatre. MDCCXXI. *Folio.*

Title as above, and Preface, iv. pp. The Bishop's Case, 51 pp.

Considerations on the English Constitution in the Church and State relating to the Lord Bishop of Chester's Case, etc. Wherein—

I. The Prerogative Royal of the Imperial Crown of the Realm of England.

II. The Prerogative Powers and Privileges of the Archbishop of the Archiepiscopal See of Canterbury; and

III. The Legal Rights, Privileges, and Liberties of the Reverend Presbyters of the Church of England are demonstratively asserted and defended against Universities usurping sole Power of granting degrees, etc., as claimed in an Essay for that purpose lately made by that learned Person in a Book entitled the "The Bishop of Chester's Case with relation to the Wardenship of Manchester.

[Pro. xviii. 17.]

London: printed for J. Roberts, near the Oxford Arms, Warwick Lane. MDCCXXI. *Folio.*

Title as above, Dedication, and Consideration, 32 pp.

The Bishop of Chester's Case with relation to the Wardenship of Manchester, in which is shewn that no other degrees but such as are taken in the Universities can be deemed Legal Qualifications for any Ecclesiastical Preferment in England. Cambridge: printed at the University Press by Corn. Crownfield, printer to the University of Cambridge. MDCCXXI. *Folio.*

Title as above, and Preface, iv. pp. The Bishop's Case, 52 pp.

Copies of the above three scarce Tracts are in the Chetham Library.

In one of Ford's (of Manchester) Catalogues, occurs the following:—"A Collection of curious Papers relative to the Bishop of Chester and the Wardens of Manchester. Printed for the Author. n. d. The writers of these curious papers, which were not published, were the celebrated Dr. Byrom and Mr. Kenyon, and the date 1727."

A Collection of Curious Papers. First, a new Method of reasoning, by the B—p of C—r. Secondly and Thirdly, Two Essays, by an admirer of his L—p, in order to improve and illustrate the said Method. The fourth proves the method to be inconclusive, and, consequently, that it could not be the work of that learned Divine. The last shews that he has been engaged in a matter of much greater moment than to trouble himself about any method of Reasoning. [Three Quotations.] Printed for the Author. *Quarto.*

Title, etc., 20 pp.

A copy is in the Chetham Library. It of course refers to the Bishop of Chester.

The HARMONIOUS CONSENT of the MINISTERS of the Province within the County Palatine of LANCASTER, with the Reverand Brethren the Minister of the Province of London in their late Testimonie to Trueth of Jesus Christ and to our solemn League and Covenant. And also against the Errours, Heresies, and Blasphemies of these Times, and the Toleration of them. London: printed by J. Macock for Luke Fawne at the sign of the Parrot, at Paul's Churchyard. MDCXLVIII. *Small quarto.*

Title, etc., 30 pp.

A copy is in the Chetham Library. It was reprinted in the "History of the Manchester Foundations," vol. i. p. 395. Its author was Richard Heyrick.

The Copy of a LETTER from DUKE HAMILTON to the MINISTERS at LANCASTER, with their Answer to the Same. Published by Authority. London: printed for Edward Husband, Printer to the Honourable House of Commons. August 25, 1648. *Small quarto.*

Title as above, ii. pp. Letter, 6 pp.

A copy of this is in the Bodleian Library.

The NON-CONFORMIST'S PLEA for Uniformity, being the Judgment of Fourscore and Four MINISTERS of the County Palatine of LANCASTER, Of a whole Provincial Assembly of Ministers and Elders in and about London, And of several other eminent Preachers, English, Scottish, and New English, concerning Toleration and Uniformity in matters of Religion, Together with a Resolution of this difficult Question, Whether the Penalty of the Law ought to be inflicted on those who pretend and plead Conscience in opposition to what the Law commands ?

"Video meliora probaque, Deteriora sequor."

Mr. Case Farewel-Serm. on Rev. ii. 5.—"Time was when the name of a Toleration have made Christians to have trembled."

London : printed for Henry Browne at the Gun in St. Paul's Church-yard. 1674. *Small quarto.*

Title as above, etc., 22 pp.

A copy of this is in the Rochdale Free Public Library.

A true purtraiture of Sundrie Coynes found at CROSBIE-LITLE. Published in 1611.

The Case at large of DUKE HAMILTON [of Ashton Hall, Lancashire] and the LORD MOHUN—viz. I. A Full and exact Relation of the Duel fought in Hyde Park on Saturday, Nov. 15, 1712, with the Grounds and Management of the Quarrel. II. The Authentick Depositions at large taken at the Coroner's Inquest, and at the Earl of Dartmouth's Office before a Committee of Council. III. The Particular Wounds of the Peers upon searching their Bodies by Dr. Roujat, M. Buissiere, and M. la Fage. The Third Edition. London : printed for E. Curll at the Dial and Bible against St. Dunstan's Church in Fleet Street. 1712. Price 6d. Where may be had Mr. Thornhill's Tryal for the Murther of Sir Cholmley Deering. Price 2d. *Foolscap octavo.*

Title as above, etc., xi. pp. The Depositions, etc., 14 pp.

A copy of this is in the Author's Library.

STRANGE NEWS of a Prodigious Monster born in the Township of ADLINGTON, in the Parish of Standish, in the County of Lancaster, April 17th, 1613, testified by the Rev. Divine W. LEIGH, D.D., and preacher of God's Word at Standish aforesaid. Printed by J. P. for S. M. 1613. *Small quarto.*

Title, etc., 14 pp. On the Title-page is a Woodcut of the Monster.

A copy of this is in the Bodleian Library.

Strange Signs from Heaven, seene and heard in Cambridge, Suffolke, and Norfolke, on and upon the 21 Day of May last past in the afternoon, 1646.

MIRACULOUS WONDERS seene at Barnstable, KIRKHAM, Cornwall, and Little Britain in London. Whereunto is annexed Severall apparitions seene in the aire at the Hague, in Holland, upon the $\frac{21}{31}$ day of May last past, about one of the clocke in the afternoone. This is Licensed and Published according to order. London: printed by T. Forcet, dwelling in Old Fish Street, in Heydon Court. 1646. *Quarto.*

Title and Strange Signs, 8 pp.

This exceedingly rare tract was reprinted (n. d.), but the reprint is also very scarce. The portion referring to Lancashire is quoted in Vicar's "Jehovah Jireh," and in the "History of Kirkham" (*see* page 20). A copy of the original is in the British Museum. A copy of the reprint is in the author's Library. The portion referring to the Miraculous Monster born in Kirkham was published as a distinct Tract in 1646, with a curious Woodcut of the Monster. A copy is in the British Museum.

A SOLEMN EXHORTATION made and published to the Several Churches of Christ within the PROVINCE of LANCASTER, for the excitation of all Persons therein to the practice of their duties requisite to the effectual carrying out of Church Discipline, etc., by the Provincial Synod assembled at Preston, Feb. 7, 1648. London: printed by Luke Fawne, at the sign of the Parrot, in Paul's Church Yard, and are to be sold by Thomas Smith, at Manchester, MDCXLIX. *Small quarto.*

Title, etc., 16 pp.

A copy of this is in the Chetham Library.

The RANTER'S LAST SERMON, with the manner of their Meetings, Ceremonies, and Actions; also their damnable Blasphemous and Diabolical Tenents, delivered on an Exercise near Pissing Conduit. Printed in the year 1654. *Small quarto.*

The author, JOHN MOON, was a reformed "Shaker," of Liverpool. He gives an account of a meeting at Bolton between the Devil and a Mr. Smith, a Ranter. Very rare.

A true Copy of the PETITION of TWELVE THOUSAND and five

hundred and upward of the well affected Gentlemen, MINISTERS, FREEHOLDERS, and others, of the County Palatine of LANCASTER, to the Right Honourable the House of Peers and the Honourable the House of Commons, Together with some true and materiall Observation concerning the said Petition. * * * As also a particular, clear, and satisfactory answer to the said animadversions. * * By JOHN TILSLEY, Minister of the Gospel at Dean Church, in Lancashire, one of the Avouchers of the Petition. Together with an answer of the Right Hon. the House of Peers. London : printed by John Meacock for Luke Fawne, etc. 1646. *Small quarto.*

Title 1 p. Petition, etc., 22 pp.

A copy is in the Chetham Library.

A LETTER from a GENTLEMAN in MANCHESTER to his Friend, concerning a Notorious Blasphemer who died in Despair, etc. Licens'd, Decemb. 28th, 1694. *Small quarto.* 4 pp.

Dated at the end, "Manchester, Decemb. 10, 1694." London: printed for John Whitlock, near Stationers' Hall. 1694.

Relates the death of T. B., of Downham, near Clithero, in Lancashire, who died on the 7th September 1694.

Very scarce. A copy is in the Library of William Harrison, Esq., of St. John's, Isle of Man.

PART VI.

SERMONS AND THEOLOGICAL TREATISES.[1]

The History of Saul and David and the xiiith of Romans, consider'd in a Thanksgiving Sermon preach'd at Manchester, Nov. 14, 1716, at the Request of the Young Men there who were minded to commemorate the Day of their own and these Kingdom's Deliverance from the Rebels by means of the compleat Victory obtain'd over them at Preston, in Lancashire, by his Majesty's Forces, Nov. 14, 1715. By JEREMIAH ALDRED, V.D.N. [Prov. xxviii. 15.] London: printed and sold by Eman. Mattheus at the Bible in Pater-noster-row; and John Whitworth, Bookseller in Manchester. 1716. Price 6d. , *Octavo.*

Title as above, and Sermon, 40 pp.

A copy is in the Manchester Free Library.

Prima the First things in reference to the Middle and Last Things of the Doctrine of Regeneration, the New Birth, the very beginning of a godly life. Delivered by ISAAC AMBROSE, Minister of the Gospel at Preston, in Amounderness, in Lancashire.

[1 Cor. v. 17.]

London: printed by J. F. for J. A.; and are to be sold by Nath. Webb and Wm. Grantham at the Greyhound, in Paul's Ch.-Yard. MDCL. *Small quarto.*

Title, Dedication, and Appendix, viii. pp. Prima, etc., 72 pp.

Reprinted 1654, and afterwards in Ambrose's Collected Works. See *Post.*

[1] It is perhaps not necessary to state that only Sermons, etc., which *refer in some way* to the County are included. Sermons *simply written by natives, and not preached in or referring to* Lancashire, are therefore purposely omitted.

The Doctrine and Directions, but more especially the Practice and Behaviour of a Man in the act of the New Birth. A Treatise. By way of Appendix to the former. By ISAAC AMBROSE, Minister of Christ at Preston, in Amounderness, in Lancashire. London: printed by J. F. for Nathl. Webb and Wm. Grantham at the Greyhound, in Paul's Ch.-Yard. MDCL. *Small quarto.*

Title and Contents, iv. pp. The Doctrine, etc., 70 pp.

Redeeming the Time. A Sermon preached at Preston, in Lancashire, January 4th, 1657, at the Funerall of the Honourable Lady the Lady Margaret Houghton. Revised and somewhat Enlarged; and at the importunity of some Friends now published. By ISAAC AMBROSE, Preacher of the Gospel at Garstange, in the same County. London: printed by T. C. for Nath. Webb and William Grantham, at the Black Bear, in Paul's Church-yard, near the little North-Door of Paul's. 1658. *Quarto.*

Title as above, Advertisement, Addresses to the relations of Lady Houghton, and to the Reader, iv. pp. Sermons, 32 pp.

A copy of this is in the Author's Library.

Looking unto Jesus. A view of the Everlasting Gospel; or, the Soul's eyeing of Jesus, as carrying on the Great Work of Man's Salvation from first to last. By ISAAC AMBROSE, Minister of the Gospel.

"Look unto me, etc."—ISA. xlv. 22.

London: printed by Edward Mottershed for Nath. Webb and Wm. Grantham at the Black Bear, in St. Paul's Ch.-Yard, near the little North-door. 1658. *Small quarto.*

Title, Dedication, and Table of Contents, xii. pp. Looking unto Jesus, 1062 pp.

Several times reprinted.

The Great Ordinances of Jesus Christ, viz.—

I. War with Devils.
II. Ministration of and Communion with Angels.
III. Looking unto Jesus.

By ISAAC AMBROSE, Minister of the Gospel.

THE FIRST VOLUME.

[Woodcut with the words "Royal Oake].

London: printed by J. H. for Nathaniel Webb at the Royal Oake, near the little North door in St. Paul's Church Yard. 1662. *Small octavo.*

Title, Second Title, Dedication, and Contents, xiv. pp. War with Devils, etc., 334 pp. Third Title, "Looking unto Jesus," Dedication, and Contents, xviii. pp. Looking unto Jesus, 252 pp. (misprinted 152).

VOL. II.

Two Titles, iv. pp. Looking unto Jesus continued, p. 255 to p. 1062, followed by a List (6 pp.) of books sold by the Publishers.

VOL. III.

Title, "Prima Media," Second Title, *dated* 1650, Dedication, and Contents, x. pp. The New Birth, etc., 70 pp. Third Title, and Dedications, xxxii. pp. The Believer's Priviledges, 510 pp. Errata, i. p. Fourth Title, "Ultima," Dedication, and Contents, vi. pp. Life's Lease, 222 pp.

A copy of this is in the Chetham Library. The collected works of I. Ambrose were published in folio, London, 1689. In 1701, London (folio), with Portrait. Glasgow, 1796, 4 vols. octavo. Manchester, 1799, 2 vols. octavo, with Portrait and Sketch of his Life by John Wesley.

Helpe to Better Hearts for Better Times, in severale Sermons by the Rev. JOHN ANGIER, Pastor of Denton Chapel, in Lancashire. London. 1647. 12*mo.*

Very scarce. *See* Lancashire "Valley of Achor," page 340.

The County Parsons Admonition to his Parishioners against Popery, with directions how to behave themselves when any one designs to seduce them from the Church of England. By WILLIAM ASSHETON, D.D., Rector of Beckenham, in Kent, and Chaplain to his Grace the Duke of Ormond. London: printed for B. Aylmer at the Three Pigeons, against the Royal Exchange, in Cornhill. 1706. *Royal* 32*mo.*

Title as above, and Address to Inhabitants of Lancashire, viii. pp. Admonition, 71 pp. List of Books printed by B. Aylmer, 6 pp.

Dr. Assheton wrote several other works, but which do not relate to Lancashire. His "Seasonable Apology for the Honours and Revenues of the Clergy, London, 1676," contains his portrait.

See Life of W. Assheton, page 193.

God's Lift up Hand for Lancashire, presented in a Sermon preached before the Honourable Committee of the County of Lancaster upon the 18th December 1645. Being a Solemne Day of Thanksgiving to God for clearing of the County and in subduing the enemies thereof. By NEHEMIAH BARNET, Minister of Lancaster. London: printed by W. Wilson for John Williams; and are to be sold at the Crown, in Paul's Churchyard. 1646. *Duodecimo.*

Title as above, and Sermon, 47 pp.

Scarce.

A Sermon begun to a ship's company at the New Meeting House upon Thursday, Dec. 13, 1711, at Leverpool, on the seaman's character and calling considered and improved. Dedicated to Mr. Brian Blundell, Captain of the Cleveland. By CHRISTOPHER BASNETT.] London. 1712. *Octavo.*

Ford describes this in 1832 as curious and scarce.

Church Officers and their Missions. A Sermon preach'd at a Public Ordination. By C. BASSNETT, Minister of the Gospel in Leverpoole.

[1 Tim. iii. 1.]

London: printed for John Clark, at the Bible and Crown in the Poultry, near Cheapside. 1717. Price 4d. *Octavo.*

Title as above, Dedication to the Rev. Brethren of Bolton and Warrington Districts, and Sermon, 32 pp.

This Sermon was preached at St. Helen's, on the occasion of the ordination of Dr. Henry Winder and Mr. Mather.

A copy is in the Manchester Free Library.

"Zebulon's Blessing Open'd," etc., by C. Bassnett, being a Volume of Sermons, was published in 1717.

The Rev. Christopher Bassnett was the minister of St. Matthew's Church, Liverpool, from 1707 until his death in 1744.

JOHN BRERELEY, *alias* ANDERTON of LOSTOCKE, Protestant's Apology for the Roman Church. London. [1608.]

He also published Liturgie of the Masse.

Printed at Cologne, 1620.

The Author's real name was James Anderton. He was of Lostock, near Bolton.

The Excellency, Necessity, and Usefulness of Patience; as also The Patience of Job, and The End of the Lord; or, The Glorious Success of Gracious Suffering. In Two Treatises, very seasonable for our present Times. By WILLIAM BELL, Mr. of Arts, late Preacher of the Word at Hyton in Lancashire. Whereunto is added a Preface by Mr. Richard Baxter. London: printed for Nevil Simmons, at the Prince's Arms in St. Paul's Church Yard. 1674. *Octavo.*

Title as above, Address to Reader, and Contents, xxxii. pp. Sermon, 72 pp.

[On sheet F. 5. begins a new title and pagination.]—The patience of Job and the end of the Lord; or, The Glorious Success of Gracious Suffering opened and applied. By William Bell, Master of Art, and sometimes Preacher of the Word at Hyton in Lancashire. [Psal. xxxvii. 7. Rom. v. 3, 4, 5.] Dum spiro spero, Imò dùm Expiro. London: printed for Nevil Simmons, at the Prince's Arms in St. Paul's Church-yard. 1674. *Octavo.*

Title and Dedication, iv. pp. Sermons, 92 pp.

Copies of these in the Bodleian Library.

Incomparable company keeping; or a conversation on Earth in Heaven. London. 1656. 12*mo.*

Enoch's Walk; being the substance of sundry Sermons digested into a Treatise. London: printed and sold by George Eversden [*ante* 1660]. *Octavo.*

Both these (by the same Author) are very scarce.

The Rev. William Bell was a Lancashire Queen's Preacher and clergyman at Huyton, from whence he was ejected in 1662. He afterwards lived at Sinderland near Ashton-under-Lyne. In 1672 he returned to Huyton, where he died in 1681, aged 74 years.

BROWNSWORD, WILLIAM. *See* p. 358.

A Warning-Piece for the Unruly. In two Sermons at the Metropolitical Visitation of the Most Rev. Father in God Rich., Lord Archbp. of York, held at Preston in Amounderness in Lancashire, and there preached May 8. The former on that day, the latter the day following. By SETH BUSHELL, D.D. [A Greek Quotation.] London: printed for Will. Cademan at the Pope's Head, in the Lower Walk of the New Exchange in the Strand, and Tho. Passengir at the Three Bibles on London Bridge. 1673. *Small quarto.*

Title as above and Dedication to 1st Sermon, iv. pp. 1st Sermon, 19 pp. 2d Sermon, 22 pp.

A copy of this is in the British Museum.

The Believers Groan for Heaven. In a Sermon at the Funeral of the Honble. Sir Rich. Hoghton of Hoghton, Bt. Preached at Preston in Amounderness in Lancashire, Feb. 14, 1677. By SETH BUSHELL, D.D. [Two Greek Quotations.] London: printed for Tho. Sawbridge at the Three Fleurs-de-Luces in Little Britain, and Philip Burton at Preston in Lancashire. 1678. *Small quarto.*[1]

Title and Preface, ii. pp. Sermon, 29 pp.

A copy of this is in the British Museum.

Reprinted in 1679.

Cosmo-Meros. The Worldly Portion, or the Best Portion of the Wicked and their Misery; or the enjoyment of it opened and applyed. Together with some Directions and Helps in order to a Heavenly and better Portion, enforced with many useful and Divine considerations. By SETH BUSHELL, D.D. [Two Quotations.] London: printed for Will. Thackeray at the Angel in Duck Lane. Anno Dom. 1682. 18*mo.*

Title, Dedication (to Sir Charles Hoghton of Hoghton, Bart.), To the Reader, xv. pp. The Worldly Portion, 367 pp.

[1] This London printed sermon has erroneously been called the earliest example of the Preston Press. *See* p. 388.

A copy of this Sermon is in the possession of the Rev. Canon Raines, M.A., F.S.A.

Dr. Bushell also published "The Great Mystery of the Great Whore unfolded." London. 1696. *Folio.*[1]

Seth Bushell was the only son of Adam Bushell of Cuerdale in Lancashire, and was born in 1621. In 1650 he was the minister of Euxton, and was afterwards vicar of Preston, where he remained until his appointment to the vicarage of Lancaster in 1682. He died in 1684. For a notice of him and his family, *see* Fishwick's "History of Goosnargh."

A Sermon preached before the right honourable Earle of Darbie, and divers others assembled in his honor's Chappell at Newparke in Lankashire, the second of Januarie, anno humane Salut. 1577.

GALA. vi.—"Dum tempus habemus operemur bonum."

"Whyle we have time let us doo good."—GALA. vi.

Imprinted at London by Thomas Easte, the xiiii. day of March 1577. *Small octavo.*

Title and Sermon, 86 pp.

A copy of this (which is probably unique), is in the Library of the Right Honourable the Earl of Derby.

The author of the above was JOHN CALDWELL, B.A., the Rector of Winwick, to which living he was instituted 7th January 1575. In 1570 he was presented to the Rectory of Mobberley. He was born at Burton-upon-Trent, and he died at Clyfton Convill in Staffordshire 30th June 1595, where he was buried the next day.

An answere made by OLIUER CARTER, Bacheler of Diunitie, unto certain Popish Questions and Demaundes. [1 Cor. ii.] Imprinted at London for George Bishop, 1579. 18*mo.*

Title as above, Dedication to Lord Henrie, Earle of Darbie, etc., xxxvii. pp. An Answere, 82 pp.

This exceedingly rare work is in the Library of the Rev. Canon Raines, M.A., F.S.A.

[1] Wood's "Athen. Oxon.," vol. iv. p. 162.

Oliver Carter was a Fellow of the Manchester College, and was buried at Manchester 20th March, 1604-5. Hollingworth says that "his sons did walk in the Godly ways of their Father." One of them was preferred to a Bishopric in Ireland.

Funeral Sermon on Death of Rev. H. Newcome. By the Rev. JOHN CHORLTON. London: printed by T. P., and are to be sold by Zachery Whitworth, Manchester, 1696. *Octavo.*

Frontispiece, Portrait of Mr. Newcome.

This Sermon was preached by Mr. Chorlton in accordance with a clause in the Will of the Rev. Henry Newcome. (*See* Auto. of Henry Newcome, Chetham Soc., xxvii.)

The Everlasting High-Priest Consider'd and Improv'd in a Sermon Preach'd at the Interment of the Late Reverend Mr. John Chorlton, Minister of the Gospel in Manchester, May 19, 1705. By JAMES CONINGHAM, A.M. London: printed by R. Tookay, and are to be sold by B. Bragge at the Blew Hall in Ave Mary Lane, 1705. *Octavo.*

Title as above, and Dedication, vi. pp. Sermon, 36 pp.

A copy of this is in the British Museum.[1]

Two Sermons of Hypocrisie, and the vain hope of Self-deceiving Sinners; together with an inspection into the manners and conversations of the people called Quakers, etc. London: Printed for R. Butler, next door to the Lamb and Three Bowls in Barbican. [By JOHN CHEYNEY.] 1677. *Octavo.*

Very scarce.

A Call to Prayer, in Two Sermons on that subject lately Preached to a Country Auditor, with an account of the Principles and Practice of the Quakers in matter of Prayer subjoined. Wherein is showed that the Quakers Religion is much wanting in Prayer, and they themselves grosly guilty of not calling upon God, and of the Fathering much impiety upon

[1] James Coningham also published a Sermon preached at Salters' Hall to the Societies for Reformation of Manners in the Cities of London and Westminster, on Monday, June 28, 1714. Published at their request. London: printed for John Lawrence, at the Angel on the Poultry, 1714. Price 6d. *Octavo.*

the Spirit of God, alledging him in defence of their Prayer-less course. By the author of The Skirmish upon Quakers. Printed in the year 1677. [JOHN CHEYNEY.] *Small octavo.*

Title-page as above, and Sermons, 164 pp.

John Cheyney was an Episcopal Priest near Warrington. *See* Quaker Tracts, p. 369.

Job's Assurance of the Resurrection: a Sermon preached at Winwick, in the County Palatine of Lancaster, June 25, 1689, at the Funeral of the Reverend Richard Sherlock, D.D., late Rector there. By THO. CRANE, M.A. (Licens'd June 2, 1690.) Z. Isham. London: printed for Philip Burton, Bookseller in Warrington, 1690.[1]

Title as above, and Address, iv. pp. Sermon, 30 pp. Notice of Richard Sherlock, 2 pp.

A copy of this is in the Chetham Library.

The Protestant Religion is a sure Foundation and Principle of a True Christian and a Good Subject, a Great Friend to Humane Society, and a Grand Promoter of all Virtues, both Christian and Moral. The Second Edition. By CHARLES, EARL of DERBY, Lord of Mann and the Isles. *Small quarto.* London: 1671.

Title, Dedication, and "To the Reader," 16 pp. "A Dialogue between Orthodox, a Royalist," etc., 42 pp.

Truth Triumphant, p. 42 to p. 58.

The first Edition is without the author's name or date, but believed to have been published in 1669. (*See* Censura Literaria, vol. viii. p. 235.)

Mr. Park had never seen either edition. (*See* Royal and Bible Authors, vol. iii. p. 128.)

Both of these editions are in the Library of the Right Honourable the Earl of Derby.

The Defence of sound Positions and Scriptures for the Congregational way justified, or an answer to an Epistle written by Mr. Richard Hollingworth unto S. E. and T. T., wherein he (in many particulars)

[1] This has been called the first example of the Warrington Press. It is, however, clear that it was printed in London. Philip Burton was established as a bookseller in *Preston* in 1679. *See* Seth Bushell.

chargeth them with injurious dealing against God and against himself, in that book of theirs called a Defence of sundry positions, etc., containing a vindication from such charges. * * Also a brief answer to his large (if not unreasonable demand) to have Scripturall or rationall Answ. given to his 112 Queres.

By SAM. EATON, Teacher, } of the Church of Duckinfeild,
TIM. TAYLER, Pastor, } in Cheshire.

Published according to order. London. 1646. *Small quarto.*

Title and Address, iv. pp. Defence, 46 pp.

A copy is in the Chetham Library.

SAMUEL EATON published, according to Calamy, two Sermons, entitled "The Mystery of God Incarnate," and "a Vindication of the Mystery of God Incarnate."

Samuel Eaton was the son of Richard Eaton, of Great Budworth, in Cheshire. He was educated at Oxford, and took orders, but afterwards left the Church and became a minister at Dukenfield. He died 9th January 1664. He was the author of a Tract entitled "The Quakers confounded, etc." [*See* Smith's "Bib. Anti-Quakeriana."]

A Sermon preached at Ashby De-la-Zouch, in the Countie of Leicester: At the Funerall of the Truely Noble and Vertuous Lady Elizabeth Stanley, one of the Daughters and Co-heires of the Right Honourable Ferdinand, late Earle of Derby, and late Wife to Henrie, Earle of Huntingdon, the Fifth Earle of that Familie, the 9 of February A.D. 1633, by J. F. London. 1635. *Small quarto.* 44 pp.

A copy of this is in the Library of the Right Hon. the Earl of Derby.

A Sermon, preached at Manchester, upon the 9th September, being the Day of Thanksgiving for our Deliverance from the Late Conspiracy. By E. FORENESS, Presbyter of the Church of England. London: printed by Miles Flesher for William Abbington, near Ludgate. 1683. *Octavo.*

Title as above and Dedication, iv. pp. Sermon, 25 pp.

A copy of this is in the Manchester Free Library.

He also published a Funeral Sermon, preached on the death of Sir Robert Leicester of Tablet, Bart., at Great Budworth, in Cheshire.

Dr. Hibbert, in his "History of the Manchester Collegiate Church," refers to the above-named Thanksgiving Sermon in the following words: "On this occasion neither Dr. Stratford nor Mr. Wroe occupied the pulpit of Manchester; and as temperance was not the order of the day, the violent tories of the town were disposed to receive their lesson on the doctrine of non-resistance from impassioned preachers of a more vulgar stamp, amongst whom they readily found a teacher well adapted to their taste in the person of Mr. Foreness, known to Manchester from his having received his education at the Grammar School of that town."

An Exercitation concerning vsvrped power, wherein the Difference betwixt Civill Authoritie and Vsurpation stated that obedience due to lawfull Magistrates is now owing or payable to ursurped Powers is maintained, etc. * * By one studious of Truth and Peace both in Church and State. [EDWARD GEE.] No Printer's name or date. *Small quarto.*

Title as above, Contents, and Advertisement, iv. pp. Exercitation, 88 pp.

A Vindication of the Oath of Allegiance, in answer to a paper disperst by Mr. Sam. Eaton, pretended to prove the Oath of allegiance voyd and non obliging. Wherein his position against it is examined and confuted. By the Author of the Exercitation concerning ursurped Powers. [EDWARD GEE.]

[Pro. xx. 25.]

Printed in the year 1650. *Small quarto.*

Title as above and Vindication, 48 pp.

Copies of the two last-named are in the Library of James Crossley, Esq., F.S.A., of Manchester.

A Treatise of Prayer and of Divine Providence as related to it. With an Application of the general Doctrine thereof unto the Present time and state of things in the Land, so far as Prayer is concerned in them. Written for the Instruction, Admonition, and Comfort of those that give themselves unto Prayer, and stand in need of it in the said respects. By EDWARD GEE, Minister of the Gospel at Eccleston, in Lancashire.

[Psal. lxxx. 4.]

London: printed by J. M. for Luke Fawn, and are to be sold at his Shop, at the sign of the Parrot, in Paul's Church-yard. 1653. *Duodecimo.*

Treatise, exclusive of Title and Address to the Reader, 499 pp. (*See* Bib. Notices of Church Libraries of Turton, etc., Chet. Soc. xxxviii. 178.) A 2d Edition was published in 1666.

Steps of Ascension to God, or a Ladder to Heaven. [EDWARD GEE.] Of this the 27th Edition was published in London, 1677.

He also wrote The Divine Right and original of the Civill Magistrate from God [as it is drawn by the Apostle Paul in these words, Rom. xiii. 1]. Illustrated and vindicated in a Treatise (chiefly) upon that Text, wherein The procedure of Political Dominion from God by his ordination; The direct line of the said Ordination descendeth from him upon the person of the Magistrate, etc. * * * London: printed for George Eversden, at the Maidenhead, at Paul's Church-yard. 1658. *Duodecimo.*

Title, Preface, Errata, etc., xliii. pp. The Divine Right, etc., 372. Contents, 11 pp.

A copy is in the Chetham Library.

Edward Gee was the Presbyterian Minister at Eccleston, where, in 1640, he married Elizabeth Raymond. In 1654 he was one of the Committee to examine incompetent Ministers and Schoolmasters in Lancashire. In 1656 he was sent prisoner to London. On his release he returned to Eccleston, where he was buried 29th May 1660. He was one of the Divines who signed the "*Agreement of the People.*"

There was an Edward Gee (the son of a shoemaker), who was born in Manchester in 1659; and after taking his M.A. at Cambridge, became Rector of St. Benedict's Church, Paul's Wharf, London, and Chaplain to William III. He was the Author of the "*Jesuits' Memorial,*" and other works.

Three Sermons preached in Lent and Summer Assises last at Lancaster, and on one of the Lords Days, in the Guild of Preston. Wherein the Nature of Subjection to the Civil Magistrate is explained, the Duty proved, and the Clergy justified in pressing the same upon their Fellow Subjects. By THOMAS GIPPS, Rector of Bury, in Lancashire, Chaplain to the Right Honourable the Earl of Darby, and sometime Fellow of Trinity Colledge, in Cambridge.

[4 lines of quotations.]

London: printed by H. H. for Walter Kettilby, at the Bishop's Head, in St. Paul's Church Yard. 1683. *Quarto.*

Title and Preface, viii. pp. Sermons, 80 pp.

A Sermon against corrupting the Word of God, preacht at Christ's Church, in Manchester, upon a publick occasion, on the 11th day of July 1696, by THOS. GIBBS, etc. London: printed for Ephraim Johnston, Bookseller in Manchester. 1697. *Small quarto.*

Title, etc., iv. pp. Sermon, 28 pp.

A copy is in the Library of James Crossley, F.S.A., Esq., of Manchester.

The Rector of Bury's reply to the Minister of Oswestry's answer, in a second letter to a friend. n. d. [1697.]

Remarks on "Remarks," or the Rector of Bury's Sermon Vindicated. His charge against dissenters for corrupting the Word of God justified and confirmed. By THOS. GIPPS, Rector of Bury, Lancashire. Also the absurdities and Notorious Falsities of Mr. Owen detected. London: for Ephraim Johnston, Bookseller, Manchester.[1] *Small quarto.*

Title, etc., 64 pp. Very scarce.

Tentamen Novum Continuatum: or, An Answer to Mr. Owen's Plea and Defence, wherein Bishop Pearson's Chronology about the Time of St. Paul's constituting Timothy Bishop of Ephesus and Titus of Crete is confirmed; all Mr. Owen's Arguments drawn from Antiquity are overthrown. By THOS. GIPPS, Rector of Bury in Lancashire. Manchester: Ephraim Johnston. 1699. *Small quarto.*

Title, etc., 132 pp.

The Second part of Tentamen Novum, etc. 1669. *Small quarto.*

Title, etc., 137 pp. Errata, 1 p.

Thomas Gipps was appointed Rector of Bury in 1674, and died there in 1712.

---

[1] Ephraim Johnston was one of the early Manchester booksellers whose name appears on several works bearing date 1694-1701.

Rest from Rebels, or the Blessing and Duty of Churches; Consider'd in a Sermon, most of which was preach'd at a Provincial Assembly of Ministers, held at Manchester, May the 18th, 1716. By JAMES GRIMSHAW, Minister of the Gospel in Lancaster. London: printed in the year 1716. *Octavo.*

Title and Sermon, 40 pp.

A copy is in the Manchester Free Library.

The Censures of the Church Revived. In the defence of a short Paper published by the First Classis within the Province of Lancashire, in the severall Congregations, * * * but since printed without their privity or consent. * * * London: printed for George Eversden, at the signe of the Maiden-head, in Paul's-church-yard. 1659. *Small quarto.*

Title, Dedication, and Preface, xxi. pp. The Narrative, 34 pp. The Paper published by the First Classis, 12 pp. An Answer, etc., pp. 13-352.

The author of this was the Rev. JOHN HARRISON, the son of "a gentleman of good position, of Wigan," sometime Minister of Walmsley Chapel, and afterwards of Ashton-under-Lyne. He resigned his living in 1662. He died 1669, aged 57.

Deaths Advantage little regarded; or the soules solace against sorrow. Preached in two funeral Sermons at Chilwal in Lancashire, at the buriall of Mistris Katherine Brettergh, the third Iune 1601. The one by WILLIAM HARRISON, one of the Preachers appointed by her Maiestie for the Countie Palatine of Lancaster; the other by WILLIAM LEYGH, Bachelor of Diuinitie, and Pastor of Standish. Whereunto is annexed the Christian Life and godly Death of the said Gentlewoman. The second Edition, corrected and amended. [Phil. i. xxi. Rev. xii. 17.] At London, Imprinted by Felix Kynston, and are to be sold by Arthur Iohnson. 1612. *Duodecimo.*

Title as above and Dedication, ii. pp. Death's Advantage, 84 pp. 2d Title and Dedication, iv. pp. The Soules Solace, 77 pp. 3d Title [as follows:—" A Briefe discourse of the Christian Life and Death of Mistris Brettargh, late wif of Master William Brettargh of Brettinghoult, in the Countie of Lancaster, Gent., who departed the world the last of May 1601. With the manner of a little conflict she had with Satan, and blessed conquest by Christ, before her Death, to the great glory of God and comfort of all beholders."] and Address, x. pp. A Postscript, etc., viii. pp. The Life, 38 pp.

Of this very rare book a copy is preserved in the Library of the Rev. Canon Raines, M.A., F.S.A.

William Brettargh, of Bretargh Holt, died in 1609.

The difference of Hearers; or an Exposition of the Parable of the Sower, delivered in certain Sermons at Hyton, in Lancashire. By WILLIAM HARRISON, Her Majesty's Preacher there. Together with a Postscript to the Papists in Lancashire, containing an apologie for the points of controversie touched in the sermons Luk. viii. 18. *Tak heede how yee heere.* London: printed by T. C. for Arthur Johnson, dwelling at the signe of the White Horse, near the great North Doore of Paul's. 1614. *Duodecimo.*

Title as above, Sermons, and Postscript, 402 pp.

A copy of this scarce volume is in the possession of the Rev. A. B. Grosart of Blackburn.

William Harrison was Rector of Eccleston, near Chester. William Leigh, B.D., was Rector of Standish until the time of his death in 1639. He was Chaplain to the Earl of Derby and to the Earl of Ferdinando, and tutor to Prince Henry. He married Mary, the daughter of John Wrightington, of Wrightington, and left issue. (*See* "History of Kirkham," p. 187.)

Contemplations and devotions on the several passages of our blessed Saviour's death and Passion, with dedication to my Lord Strange. By CHARLES HERLE, Rector of Winwick. London. 1631.

Very scarce.

A Fvller Ansvver to a Treatise written by Docter Ferne, entitvled "The resolving of conscience," etc. Done by another author, and by him revised and enlarged by occasion of some late pamphlets complaining in the name of the City against the Parliament. London: printed for John Bartlet, and are to be sold at the signe of the Gilt-Cup in Paul's Churchyard, near to Austen's Gate. 1642. [By CHARLES HERLE.] *Small quarto.*

Title as above, etc., 20 pp. Reprinted in 1642. 24 pp.

A Payre of Compasses for Church and State. Delivered in a Sermon preached at St. Margaret's in Westminster, before the Honble. House of Commons, at their Monethly Fast, November the last, 1642. By CHARLES HERLE, Rector of Winwicke in Lankashire. Published by Order of that House. London: printed by G. M. for John Bartlet, at the Signe of the Guilt-Cup, neare S. Austins-Gate. 1642. *Small quarto.* 48 pp.

The Independency of Scripture of the Independency of Churches. A Sermon. By MASTER HERLE, a Lancashire Minister. London: T. Brudenell. 1643. *Small quarto.*

David's Song of Three Parts, delivered in a Sermon preached before the Right Honourable the House of Lords at the Abby-church, in Westminster, upon the 15th day of June 1643, being the day appointed for publike Thanksgiving for God's great deliverance of the Parliament, Citie, and Kingdome from the late mischievous conspiracy against all three. Ordered by the said House to be published. By CHARLES HERLE, Pastor of Winwicke in Lancashire, the Preacher thereof. [Isai. xxxiii. 11.] London: printed by T. Brudenell for N. A., and are to be sold at the Angell and Bible in Lumber Street. 1643. *Small quarto.*

Title as above, i. p. Sermon, 29 pp.

An Answer to Dr. Ferne's Reply entitled Conscience Satisfied, especially to as much of it as concerned that answer to his Treatise which went under the name of the "Fuller Answer." By the same Author. London: printed by Tho. Brudenell for N. A., and are to be sold at the Angell and Bible in Lumber Street. [17 May] 1643. [By CHARLES HERLE.] *Small quarto.*

Title, etc., 37 pp.

Ahab's Fall by his prophet's flatteries; being the substance of Three Sermons. * * * The first sermon preached before the Commons House of Parliament; the second before the Lord Mayor of London, and the Aldermen, his Brethren; the third at the Abbey Church in Westminster, where it was much acquarrelled by some, and as much desired to be published by others. Printed by R. A. for J. Wright in the Old Baily [May 30], 1644. [By CHARLES HERLE.] *Small quarto.*

42 pp., exclusive of Epistle Dedicatory.

A copy of this is in the British Museum.

Abraham's offer God's offering; or, a Sermon preached before the Right Honourable the Lord Mayor, together with the Aldermen, his Brethren, at Christ Church, on Easter Tuesday last, being the day of Publique Thanksgiving. By C. HERLE. London: printed for Peter Cole at the signe of the Printing Presse at the Royall Exchange. 1644. *Small quarto.* 23 pp.

A copy of this is in the Bodleian Library.

David's Reserve and Rescue, in a Sermon preached before the Honourable the House of Commons, on the Fifth of November, 1644. By C. HERLE, Pastor of Winwicke, in Lancashire. Published by order of the said House. London: printed for John Wright in the Old Baily, 1645. *Small quarto.*

Epistle Dedicatory unpaged. Sermon, 18 pp.

A copy in the British Museum.

Another Edition.

"David's Reserve and Rescue," in a Sermon before the Honourable the House of Commons, on the 5th Nov., 1644. By CHARLES HERLE, Pastor of Winwicke in Lancashire. Published by order of the said House. London: Printed for John Wright, at the signe of the King's-head in the Old Baily. 1646. *Small quarto.*

24 pp.

Worldly Policy and Moral Prudence. The Vanity and folly of the one. The solidity and usefulness of the other. In a moral discourse. By CHARLES HERLE, minister of God's Word at Winwick in Lancashire. London: printed for Sa. Gellibrand at the Ball in Paul's Church-yard, 1654. *Foolscap 12mo.*

Title, Table, etc., 208 pp. List of Books sold "at the Ball," pp. 209-212. Published at 2s. 6d.

Detur Sapienti. In a Treatise of the Excellency of Christian Wisdome above that of Worldly Policy and Morall Prudence in two former Treatises. By C. HERLE, etc. London: printed for Samuel Gillibrand at the Ball in Paul's Churchyard. 1655. [Feb. 27, 1654.] *Octavo.*

242 pp.

In 1655 the two last works were published in one volume under the following Title:—

Wisdome's Tripos, or rather its Inscription, Detur Sapienti, in three Treatises.

I. of Worldly Policy.
II. of Moral Prudence.
III. of Christian Wisdom.

The Vanity of the First.
The Usefulness of the Second.
The Excellency of the Third.

By CHARLES HERLE, minister of God's Word at Winwick in Lancashire. London: printed for Samuel Gellibrand at the Ball in Paul's Churchyard. 1655. 12*mo.*

460 pp.

In this edition a set of verses is added to each Treatise.

Charles Herle was born at Prideaux-Herle, Cornwall, in 1598, M.A. of Exeter College, Oxford (1618). In 1643 he was elected one of the Assembly of Divines. After the execution of Charles I. he retired to his Rectory at Winwick in Lancashire, and died there in September 1659.

Three Sermons preached at the Collegiate Church, Manchester. The first on Psal. cxxii., ver. 6, July 8, 1640, the publick Fast Day, etc. * * * The second on 2 Thess. ii. 15, November 5, 1638. * * * The third on Genesis xlix., vers. 5, 6, 7, November 5, 1630. * * * By RICHARD HEYRICKE, Warden of the said College. London: printed by T. B. for Luke Fawne, and are to be sold at the sign of the Parot in Paul's Churchyard. 1641. *Duodecimo.*

Copies of these Sermons are in the Chetham Library.

Title as above, and Dedication, xxiii. pp. (not numbered.) Sermons, 173 pp.

The copy in the Chetham Library has the autograph of J. Heyricke, 1674-5. In the dedicatory Epistle is the following passage:—

"The masse hath outfaced our Christian meetings. Jesuites have jeered our ministers. Manchester, the Goschen of their Egypt, is darkened with the blacknesse of it."

Queen Esther's Resolve: a Sermon preached before the Honourable House of Commons at the monethly fast, May 27, 1646. By RICHARD HEYRICKE, Warden of Christ College in Manchester in Lancashire, and one of the Assembly of Divines. London: printed for Luke Fawn, and are to be sold by Thomas Smith at his shop in Manchester, 1640.

[On the Coronation of Charles II.]

A Sermon preached at the Collegiate Church, Manchester, on Tuesday, April 23, 1661. By RICHARD HEYRICKE. London: printed for Ralph Shelmerdine,[1] Manchester.

Richard Heyricke was the son of Sir William Heyricke of Beaumanor Park, Leicestershire. He was one of the Wardens of the Manchester Collegiate Church from 1636-1646, and 1660-1667. He died 6th August 1667, aged 67, and was buried in the chancel of the Collegiate Church. For extracts from R. Heyricke's sermons and biographical notice, *see* Hibbert's *History of the Collegiate Church of Manchester.*

Christ Displayed as the Choicest Gift and Best Master. From John iv. 10, John xiii. 13. Being some of the last Sermons of that faithful and industrious servant of Jesus Christ, Mr. NATHANIEL HEYWOOD, sometime minister of the Gospel at Ormeschurch in Lancashire. London: printed for Tho. Parkhurst at the Bible and Three Crowns in Cheapside, near Merar's Chappel, 1679.

The Dedicatory Epistle is written by Mr. Oliver Heywood.

Nathaniel Heywood was the brother of Oliver Heywood (*see* p. 211). He was born at Little Lever, near Bolton, in 1633. He was Vicar of Ormskirk from 1657 until his ejection in 1662. He died in 1677.

The Office and Use of the Moral Law of God in the Days of the Gospel justified and explained at large by Scriptures, Fathers, and other orthodox Divines. By WILLIAM HINDE, A.M., Fell. Qu. Coll., Oxon, and Preacher at Bunbury, Cheshire. 1623. *Foolscap octavo.*

Title as above, Dedication, and Advertisement, 10 pp. Antinomus Anonymus, or a Scandalous Pamphlet of a namelesse aduersary, etc., 8 pp. The Office and Use, 140 pp.

[1] Ralph Shelmerdine was the son of William Shelmerdine, who was also a Manchester bookseller. He died 1699.

A side note to Antinomus Anonymus states that "this pamphlet was directed and sent unto a religious and gracious Gentleman, Mr. John Foxe, late Steward to the Right Hon. the Earle of Darby, of his L. of Berry and Pilkington, in Lancashire.

Very rare. A copy is in the Library of the Rev. Canon Raines, M.A., F.S.A.

Certain Queres modestly (though plainly) Propounded to such as affect the Congregational Way; as specially to Master Samuel Eaton and Mr. Timothy Taylor; with an Epistle also directed to them concerning their late book intituled A Defence of Sundry Petitions, etc. By RICHARD HOLLINGWORTH, Mancuniensis.

[The following texts are here quoted:—Deut. v. 32; Isa. viii. 20; and Matt. vi. 23.]

London: printed by Ruth Raworth for Luke Fawn, and to be sold at the signe of the Parrot, in Paul's Church-yard. 1646. *Small quarto.*

Title, etc., 31 pp.

Of this scarce pamphlet a copy is in the Chetham Library.

A rejoinder to Master Samuel Eaton and Master Timothy Taylor's Reply; or, an answer to their late book called a Defence of sundry positions and Scriptures, etc. With some occasionall animadversions on the Book called the Congregational Way justified. For the satisfaction of all that seek Truth, in Love especially for his dearly beloved and longed for, the Inhabitants in and near to Manchester, in Lancashire. Made and published by RICH. HOLLINGWORTH, Mancuniens.

"The Lord will show who are His, and who are holy."

London: printed by T. R. and G. M. for Luke Fawn; and are to be sold at the signe of the Parrot in Paul's Church-yard. 1647. *Small quarto.*

Title as above, and Contents, ii. pp. Rejoinder, 108 pp.

Very scarce.

The Holy Ghost on the Bench other Spirits at the Barre and Judgement of the Holy Spirit of God upon the Spirit of the Times. Recorded in Holy Writ, and reported by RICHARD HOLLINGWORTH, Mancuniens. The Second Edition much corrected. London: printed by J. M. for Luke Fawn, etc. * * 1657. 18*mo.*

Title, Address, Epistle, and Contents, xiv. pp. The Holy Ghost, etc., 113 pp.

A copy is in the Chetham Library.

A full and true Account of the Penitance of John Marketman during his imprisonment in Chelmsford Goal for murthering his wife, etc. ;. to which is prefixed a Sermon preached before him by RICHARD HOLLINGWORTH (of Manchester). 1680.

This is from one of J. Ford's Catalogues, 1818. We have not met with a copy of it.

Richard Hollingworth also wrote "The main points of Church Government plainly and modestly handled by way of Question and Answer, usefull to such as either want money to buy, or Leasure to read large Tracts. Printed by J. M. for Luke Fawne; and are to be sold by Thomas Smith at his Shop, Manchester. 1649. 12*mo.*

Title, etc., 58 pp.

Richard Hollingworth, the Author of "An History of the Towne of Manchester," was a Fellow of Christ College, Manchester. He died 11th November 1656.

A Sermon preached in St. Peter's Church, Liverpool, for promoting the Charity School lately erected in that place. By Rev. ROBERT HORROBIN, Curate of Warrington. Printed by S. Terry, in Dale Street, Liverpool. 1718. *Octavo.*

A Discourse concerning the Redeemer's dominion over the Invisible World and the entrance thereunto by Death. Some part whereof was preached on the occasion of the Death of John Hoghton, Esq., eldest Son of Sir Charles Hoghton, of Hoghton Tower, in the County of Lancaster, Bart. By JOHN HOWE, Minister of the Gospel. London : printed for Tho. Parkinson of the Bible and Three Crowns in Cheapside, near Mercer's Hall. 1699. 12*mo.*

Title as above, and Dedication to Sir Charles and Lady Mary Hoghton, xxxi. pp. Sermon, 213 pp.

John Howe, the son of the minister of Loughborough, in Leicestershire, was born in 1630. He was prepared for the University at the Warrington Grammar School, and after becoming a Fellow and Chaplain of Magdalen College he was ordained (after the Presbyterian form) at Winwick. He subsequently was minister of Great Terrington, Devonshire, and Chaplain to Oliver Cromwell.

A short and plain Way to the Faith and Church, composed many years since by that Eminent Divine Mr. RICHARD HUDLESTON of the English Congregation of the order of St. Benedict, and now published for the common good by his Nephew, Mr. JOHN HUDLESTON, of the same Congregation. To which is annexed His late Majesty King Charles II.'s Papers found in his Closet after his Decease. As also a brief account of what occurred on His Death-bed in regard to Religion.

Permissu Superiorum.

London: printed by Henry Hills, Printer to the King's most Excellent Majesty for his Household at Chappel; and are to be sold at his Printing-house on the Ditch-side in Black-Friars. 1688. *Foolscap* 12*mo.*

Title as above, Dedication "To the Queen Dowager" and "To the Reader," xiv. pp. A Short and Plain Way, etc., 91 pp. Catalogue of Books printed by H. Hills, 3 pp.

Richard Hudleston was the son of Andrew Hudleston of Farrington Hall, Lancashire.

A copy of this is in the Author's Library.

A Sermon Preach'd at the Funeral of the Right Honourable Dorothea Helena, Countess Dowager of Derby, at the Parish Church of Ormskirk in Lancashire, on Friday, April 16th, 1703. By RICHARD HUNTER, A.M. London: printed for A. and J. Churchill at the Black Swan in Paternoster-row. 1703. *Small quarto.*

Half-title, Title as above, and Dedication, vi. pp. Sermon, 26 pp.

Melchizedech's Anti-type, or the Eternall Priest-hood, and all sufficient Sacrifice of Christ. With the scrutiny of the Masse. Containing an exact examination and sound confutation of the Romish Sacrifice. By JOHN LEWIS, Mt. of Artes of Sydney Sussex Colledge in Cambridge, and one of His Maiesties Preachers, authorized for the County of Lancaster.

[1 John iv. 1 and 1 Thess. v. 21.]

London: printed by Nicholas Okes for Richard Whitakers, and are to be sold at his shop in Paule's Church-yard, at the signe of the King's head. 1624. *Small quarto.*

Title as above, Dedication to James, Lord Strange, Address to the Reader, etc., viii. pp. Melchisedech's Antitype, 233 pp. Faults escaped, 1 p. Very scarce.

A copy is in the Author's Library.

John Lewis was for a short time Vicar of Preston in Lancashire. He married Anne, the 2d daughter of Richard Moore, of St. Edmundsbury, in Suffolk.

A Sermon, preached at Childwall Church, Lancashire, the 3d June 1601, on the death of Mrs. Katherine Brethargh. By the Rev. WILLIAM LEYGH, B.D., Pastor of Standish. London: Imprinted by Felix Kynston. 1602.

A Soul's solace against sorrow.

London. 1617.

William Leigh, B.D., was Rector of Standish from 1586 to the time of his death in 1639. He was Chaplain to Henry, the Earl of Derby, and Tutor to Prince Henry. From him descended the Leighs of Singleton Grange, in Kirkham. *See* p. 393.

Enchiridion Judicum, or Jehosophat's Charge to the Judges, opened in a Sermon before the Right Honourable the Judges and the Right Honourable the Sheriff of the County Palatine of Lancaster. Together with Catastrophe Magnatum, in a Sermon meditated on the Fall, and preached at the Funeral of the Right Worshipful John Atherton of Atherton, Esq., High Sheriff of the County Palatine of Lancaster. By JOHN LIVESEY, Minister of the Gospel at Atherton. London: printed by R. J. for Tho. Parkhurst, etc. * * 1657. *Small quarto.*

Title as above, 1 p. Dedication and 1st Sermon, 174 pp. [wrongly numbered 574]. 2d Sermon, p. 175 to p. 310.

Copies of both these are in the Chetham Library.

ΨΥΧΗΣΗΜΙΑ, or the greatest Loss; or Matth. xvi., xxvi. In a short discourse occasioned by the doleful loss of an eminently pious and learned Gentleman—viz. Mr. Humphrey Chetham, who died at Turton Tower Feb. 13, was interred at Manchester the 18th 165$\frac{8}{9}$, aged twenty three years seven months. [Three Latin Quotations.] London: printed by J. B. for Tho. Parkhurst, at the Three Crowns in Cheapside, over against the great conduit. 1660. *Duodecimo.*

Title as above, Contents, and Dedication, xviii. pp. (not numbered). The Sermon, 198 pp.

This Sermon was written by the Rev. JOHN LIVESEY, Minister at Atherton. Humphrey Chetham was the son of George Chetham, then High Sheriff of the County of Lancaster.

A copy is in the Chetham Library.

John Livesey resigned his living at Atherton on his appointment to the Vicarage of Great Budworth, Cheshire.

Roman Catholics uncertain whether there be any True Priests or Sacraments in the Church of Rome; evinced by an argument urg'd and maintain'd (upon their own Principles) against Mr. Edward Goodall, of Prescott in Lancashire. By THOMAS MARSDEN, Vicar of Walton in the same County. The Treatise divided into Two parts. The first being Explicative of Terms. The second Argumentative. London: printed for Walter Kettilby, at the Bishop's Head in St. Paul's Church-yard. MDCLXXXVIII. *Small quarto.*

Title as above, Preface, and Contents, viii. pp. Roman Catholics, etc., 136 pp.

A copy of this is in the Bodleian Library.

Thomas Marsden, of Brazenose College, Oxford, was afterwards chaplain to the English Merchants at Lisbon. (*See* "Chetham Popery Tracts," vol. i. p. 211.)

ΨΥΧΟΣΟΦΙΑ, or Natural and Divine Contemplation of the Passions and Faculties of the Soul of Man. In three Books. By NICHOLAS MOSLEY, Esq. [1 Pet. ii. 11. Ign. Epist.] London: printed for Humphrey Mosley, at the Prince's Arms, St. Paul's Church Yard. 1650. 16*mo.*

Title as above, Dedication to "my honoured kingsman Robert Booth," and To the Reader, 21 pp. Contemplations, 109 pp. Dedication "to his loving Brother Edward Mosley," viii. pp. 2d Part, p. 113 to p. 214. Dedication to Humphrey Chetham, iv. pp. 3d Part, p. 215 to p. 270.

A copy of this is in the Library of the Rev. Canon Raines, M.A., F.S.A.

Robert Booth was the son of Humphrey Booth of Salford by his wife Ann, daughter of Oswald Mosley of Ancoats; and Nicholas Mosley was his son and heir. He was born 1611, and was buried at the Collegiate Church, Manchester, in 1672.

John Goodhand Holt, a Plant of Paradise; being a Sermon preached at St. Martin's in the Fields, on the young son, only child, and hopefull heir of Thomas Holt of Gristlehurst, in the County of Lancaster, Esq. By R. MOSSOM. *Small quarto.*

With a Portrait by Logan. Very rare.

A Thanksgiving Sermon preached at Manchester, November 14, 1718, being the anniversary of the Surrender of the Rebels at Preston to the King's Forces. By J. MOTTERSHEAD. Printed (with some Inlargements) at the request of the Auditors. [Psal. cvii. 8, 15, 21, 31.] London: printed and sold by Eman. Matthews, at the Bible in Paternoster Row; and John Whitworth, Bookseller in Manchester. 1719. Price 4d.

Title as above, and Sermon, 28 pp.

A copy of this is in the Author's Library.

The Prospect of Heaven the support of afflicted Christians, consider'd and improv'd in a funeral Sermon at St. Hellen's Chappel (some time ago) upon the death of Edward Potter of Rainhill (a young man), who died beyond sea. By the late Reverend Mr. JAMES NAYLOR; and now, upon the request of the deceased's father, prefac'd and publish'd by Charles Owen.[1] Printed at Leverpoole for Daniel Birchall, Bookseller in Castle Street. 1713.

This is the earliest specimen of the Liverpool Press which we have met with. It contains 32 pp., roughly printed. The first 28 pp. are in Longprimer type, and the 4 last pages are in Brevier. A copy is in the Library of J. A. Picton, Esq., F.S.A., of Liverpool.

The Sinner's Hope as his priviledge and duty, or his worst condition stated, cleared, and improved. Tending as well to the startling and inviting of the Wicked from his Sinfull and Wretched course, etc., etc. Being the substance of severall Sermons preached by HENRY NEWCOME, M.A., and one of the Ministers of the Gospell at Manchester, in

[1] No Preface is prefixed.

the county of Lancaster. London : printed by E. C. for George Eversden, at the Sign of the Maiden-head, in Paul's Church-yard. 1660. 12*mo.*

Title and Address from Richard Herrick, Isaack Ambrose, and John Angier, The Epistle Dedicatory, and the Epistle to the Reader, xxxi. pp. (unpaged). Sermons, 187 pp., followed by errata, 1 p. List of Books printed by Eversden 2 pp. Letter from Edm. Calamy, 1 p.

A copy of this is in the Author's Library.

Vrsurpation defeated and David restored : a Sermon preached at the Collegiate Church, Manchester, on His Majesty's restoration. By the Rev. H. NEWCOME. 1660.

A copy of this is in the Chetham Library.

Henry Newcome also published—

A Discourse on Psalm cv. 8 with 1 Chron. xvi. 15.
A Help to Duty in and right Improvement of Sickness.
A Discourse on Job v. 6, 7, 8.
A Treatise on rash and Sinful Anger, from Prov. xxv. 28.
The Covenant of Grace effectually remembered.[1]

This distinguished Divine was the fourth son of the Rev. Stephen Newcome, Rector of Caldecot, in Huntingdonshire. He was born in 1627, and in 1648 married Elizabeth, the daughter of Mr. Peter Manwaring, of Smallwood, in Cheshire. He was sometime Rector of Gawsworth, from whence he came to Manchester, in 1656, upon the death of Mr. Richard Hollingworth (assistant to the Rev. Richard Heyrick), whom he succeeded. Subsequently his congregation built him a Chapel in Cross Street, where he ministered until his death, 17th September 1695. He was buried in his Chapel. For a full detail of him and his family, *see* Chetham Society, volumes 18, 26, and 27.

Some motives, purely Christian, to Alms Deeds. Recommended in a Sermon Preach'd before the Lord Bishop of Chester and the Clergy of that Archdeaconry, at their Anniversary Meeting for Relief of Widows and Orphans of the Poor Clergymen, at Warrington, on June 5th, 1711. By HENRY NEWCOME, M.A., Rector of Middleton, in Lancashire.

[Latin Quo.]

[1] See Slate's "Select Non-Conformists' Remains."

London: printed for John Wyat, at the Rose, in St. Paul's Churchyard and William Clayton, Bookseller, Manchester. 1711. *Octavo.*

Title and Dedication, iv. pp. Sermon, 20 pp.

A copy of this is in the Library of James Crossley, Esq., Manchester.

A Serious Admonition to all Despisers of the Clergy. In a Sermon preach'd before the Right Reverend Father in God, William, Lord Bishop of Chester, at his Triennial Visitation, held at Manchester, in the County Palatine of Lancashire, July 19, 1712. By HENRY NEWCOME, A.M., and Rector of Middleton, in Lancashire. London: printed for W. Clayton, Bookseller in Manchester, and sold by D. Midwinter, in St. Paul's Church-yard. 1712. *Octavo.*

Title as above, and Dedication, xi. pp. Sermon, 24 pp.

A copy of this is in the Bodleian Library.

A second Edition was published in 1713. It was probably printed in London, and was sold by "R. Scofield, Bookseller, Rochdale."

We have not met with this edition, and quote from J. C. Hotten's Handbook of Topography. There is no reason to believe that a Press existed in Rochdale so early as this.

This Rector of Middleton was the son of the Rev. Henry Newcome, of Manchester. Previous to his appointment to Middleton, he was Rector of Tattenhall in Cheshire. He was the author of a work entitled, "The compleat Mother, or an earnest Persuasive to all Mothers (especially those of rank and Quality) to Nurse their own children, London, 1695," and is believed to have written, "Why no Christian Parent can consent that his children be brought up contrary to the Judgment of his own conscience in matters of faith and religion," and also a treatise "For and against Transubstantiation."

The Scene of Delusions open'd in an Historical Account of the prophetick Impostures in the Jewish, Christian, and Pagan World, wherein the pretensions of the new Prophets are considered and confuted. By CHARLES OWEN, V.D.M. London: printed for John Lawrence at the Angel in the Poultry; and Henry Eires, in Warrington. 1712. *Duodecimo.*

A copy of this is in the Library of J. F. Marsh, Esq., of Hardwick House, Chepstow.

Hymns Sacred to the Lord's Table. Collected and Methodiz'd by CHARLES OWEN.

[Mat. xxxi. 30; Eph. v. 19].

Leverpoole: printed by S. Terry for Daniel Birchall; and sold by Nat. Cliff and D. Jackson at the Bible and Three Crowns in Cheapside; and S. Matthew's at the Bible in Paternoster Row. London. MDCCXII.[1]
Foolscap octavo.

Title and Hymns, 76 pp.

A copy is in the Library of W. Robson, Esq., of Warrington.

Donatus Redivivus; or, a Reprimand to a modern Church Schismatick. London. 1714. [By CHARLES OWEN.]

This was republished under the title of "Rebaptization Condemned." London. 1716.

Plain Dealing; or, Separation without Schism, and Schism without separation. By CHARLES OWEN. London. 1715.

A copy is in the Bodleian Library. Republished many times; the Twelfth Edition in 1727.

Validity of Dissenting Ministry. By CHARLES OWEN. London. 1716. *Octavo.*

A Vindication of Plain Dealing from the Aspersions of Two Country Curates contained in a Pamphlet entitled Plain Dealing[2] proved to be plain lying. By CHARLES OWEN. London. 1716. *Octavo.*

A copy is in the British Museum.

Plain Reasons. I. for Dissenting from the Communion of the Church of England; II. Why Dissenters are not and cannot be guilty of Schism,

[1] This book is inserted here as being the earliest known specimen of the Liverpool press.

[2] Plain Dealing Proved to be Plain Lying, being a collection of Falsehoods and Prevarications published in a Scandalous Libel against the Church of England by Charles Owen, against whom an Indictment was found at the last Assizes at Lancaster. London. 1715. *Octavo.*

etc. By a true Protestant [CHARLES OWEN]. London. 1717. Third Edition.

This went through at least twenty-three Editions.

The Jure Divino Woe exemplify'd in the remarkable punishment of Persecutors, False Teachers, and Rebels. A Thanksgiving sermon preached from Jude ii. at Manchester, November 14, 1717, being the ever Memorable Day of our Happy Deliverance from the late Rebellion. By CHARLES OWEN. With an Appendix.
[Rev. ix. 12.]
London: printed and sold by Emanuel Matthews at the Bible in Pater-noster-row. 1717. Price 6d. *Octavo.*

Title as above, Address, and Sermon, 30 pp. Appendix, p. 31 to p. 38. List of Books printed by E. Matthews, 2 pp.

The Appendix contains a complete reprint of "The Book of Sports," published by King James I. Scarce.

A copy of this is in the Manchester Free Library.

A Funeral Sermon for the Reverend Mr. Tho. Risley, A.M., and some time Fellow of Pembroke College in Oxford. With some short Memoirs of his Life. By CHARLES OWEN. London: printed for Eman. Mathews at the Bible in Paternoster Row; and J. Harrison at the Royal Exchange. 1716. Price bound, 6d. *Octavo.*

Title as above, and Dedication, vi. pp. Sermon, 54 pp.

The Vanity of Human Illustra——, the Similitude of Nothing. A Discourse occasion'd by the Death of Mrs. Mary Lythgoe, a young woman near Warrington. By CHAS. OWEN, D.D. Manchester: printed by R. Whitworth, Bookseller. *Octavo.*

Title and Sermon, 38 pp.

A copy of this is in the British Museum.

The Dissenters' Claim of Right to a Capacity for Civil Office. London: 1717. *Octavo.*

A copy is in the British Museum.

The Danger of the Church and Kingdom from Foreigners considered. London: 1721. *Octavo.* Reprinted 1750.

An Alarm to Protestant Princes and People who are all struck at in the Popish cruelties at Thorn, etc. London: 1725.

Religious Gratitude. Seven Practical Discourses. 12*mo.* 1731.

A Funeral Sermon. London: 1746. *Octavo.*

A Sermon on Marriage. London: 1758.

A Sermon on the Queen's Death (1 Aug. 1714) on the Text 1 Kings xvi. 20.

The Character and Conduct of Ecclesiastics in Church and State, from the First Plantation of this Island to the Accession of the Royal House of Hanover. Taken from a MS. of Dr. Charles Owen. Shrewsbury, 1768. 12*mo.*

The whole of these and a few others are generally attributed to CHARLES OWEN of Warrington, but we are inclined to agree with Mr. W. H. Alnnutt (from whose list in Notes and Queries, v. i. 90, and viii. 355, we have extracted several of the above), that they were written by two men who were perhaps father and son.

Charles Owen of Warrington was the son of John Owen of Abernaut, and brother of James Owen of Oswestry (*see* p. 410.) He was for some years minister of the Presbyterian Chapel in Warrington, where he died 1745-6, and his Funeral Sermon was preached there on the 23d February in the same year by the Rev. James Owen of Rochdale, who is believed to have been his nephew.[1] Charles Owen also wrote "Some account of the Life and writings of the late pious and learned Mr. James Owen, minister of the Gospel in Salop. London: printed for John Lawrence at the Angel in the Poultry. MDCCIX.

[1] James Owen of Rochdale published "National Gratitude, etc., preached at Rochdale Nov. 5 1752." "The End of all Perfection, preached at Rochdale on the death of Mr. James Hardman, merchant, 1746." "Jacobite and Nonjuring Principles freely examined, etc.," being a reply to Dr. Deacon, and "Dr. Deacon tryed before his own Tribunal, 1748."

Remarks on a Sermon preached by Thos. Gipps, Rector of Bury, on the 11th July 1696, wherein the Dissenters are vindicated, etc. * * By J. O. [JAMES OWEN], minister of the Gospel at Oswestry. London: printed for Zachery Whitworth, Bookseller in Manchester. 1697.

A further Vindication of the Dissenters from the Rector of Bury's unjust accusation, wherein his charge of their being corruptors of the Word of God is demonstrated to be false and malicious. By JAMES OWEN, minister of the Gospel at Oswestry. London: printed by S. Bridge for Thomas Parkhurst. 1699. *Small quarto.*

Title and errata, iv. pp. Vindication, 37 pp.

Postscript or further vindication of the Dissenters, etc. etc. By JAMES OWEN, etc. A 2d Title-page to the above, and the paging continued from p. 38 to p. 70.

A copy is in the Library of James Crossley, Esq., F.S.A., of Manchester.

An Answer to the Rector of Bury's Letter to his friend, wherein is show'd that he has effectually though unwillingly acquitted the Dissenters from his malicious charge of their being corrupters of the Word of God. That his attempts against the Titles of the Psalms and Hebrew Bible are Feeble and Inconsistent. By JAMES OWEN.

[Two Latin Quotations.]

London: printed by S. Bridge for Tho. Parkhurst at the Bible and Three Crowns in Cheapside, near Mercers-Chapel. 1699. *Quarto.*

Title as above, 1 p. An Answer, 22 pp.

A copy of this is in the Author's Library. It contains a story told by Colonel Fairfax in a public-house in Rochdale to Mr. Piggot (the Vicar of Rochdale) and Mr. Milne.

James Owen, the son of John Owen of Abernaut, was born at Bryn, near Carmarthen, on 1st November 1654, and died at Salop 8th April 1706.

A Life[1] of him (which contains his Portrait) was published in 1709, a copy of which will be found in the Chetham Library. He was the author of several other Tracts, which do not in any way refer to the County Palatine.

[1] Written by his brother, Charles Owen, of Warrington, *see* p. 409.

A plain representation of the Transubstantiation as it is received in the Church of Rome, with the sandy foundations it is built upon, and the arguments that do clearly evert and overturn it. By a Country Divine [HENRY PENDLEBURY]. London: printed for J. Johnson. 1687. *Small quarto.*

Title as above, etc., 68 pp.

This was printed under the direction of Archbishop Tillotson.

Invisible Realities the real Christian's greatest concernment, In several Sermons on 2 Cor. iv. 18. By HENRY PENDLEBURY, A.M., late Minister of the Gospel at Rochdale in Lancashire, Author of the "Plain Representation of Transubstantiation." London: printed by J. D. for Ann Uinsworth,[1] of Manchester, and sold by Jonathan Robinson at the Golden Lion in St. Paul's Church-yard. 1696. *Duodecimo.*

Title, Dedication signed by John Chorlton (*see* p. 388), Account of the Life of the Author, xvi. pp. Invisible Realities, 127 pp. Second Title, "The Books opened,[2] being several Discourses on Rev. xx. 14. By HENRY PENDLEBURY," etc. etc. Epistle to the Reader, signed R. S. [Robert Seddon, of Bolton], and the Books opened, 116 pp.

A copy of this is in the Library of the Rev. Canon Raines, M.A., F.S.A., Milnrow.

The Barren Fig Tree, or a practical Exposition of the Parable, Luke xiii. 6, 7, 8, 9; very useful for the awakening of those that remain unprofitable under Gospel Priviledges and Vineyard Enjoyments. By HENRY PENDLEBURY, Minister of the Gospel at Rochdale in Lancashire. London: printed by R. Janeway Jun., for Ed. Giles, Bookseller in Norwich, near the Market Place. 1700. *Duodecimo.*

Title, Preface, and Exposition, 183 pp. Errata, 1 p. List of Books Printed for E. Giles, iv. pp.

A copy of this is in the Manchester Free Library.

---

[1] Ann Uinsworth was the widow of John Uinsworth, of Manchester. He was buried at the Collegiate Church there 19th August 1688, and his widow 14th Feb. 1699.

[2] The Books opened, etc., was published in a distinct work by the same publishers and the same date.

Sermons, by HENRY PENDLEBURY, of Rochdale. Second Edition, with Preface and Dedication, by Messrs. Chorlton and Coningham of Manchester. 1711.

In 1768 was published, edited by Archbishop Tillotson, HENRY PENDLEBURY'S "Sacrificum Missaticum, Mysterium Iniquitatis, or a Treatise concerning the sacrifice of the Mass, with a short account of the Author's Life." London: printed for W. Griffin. *Octavo.*

Title, Treatise, and List of Subscribers, 50 pp. Life, etc., 180 pp.

Henry Pendlebury was born at Jokin, in the parish of Bury, 6th May 1626. He was "perfected for the University at the Bury School," and became a graduate of Christ's College, Cambridge. In 1651 he was appointed Minister to Holcombe Chapel, near Bury, from whence he was ejected in 1662. He is subsequently described as "Minister of the Gospel at Rochdale." He died 18th June 1695, in the 70th year of his age, and was interred in the church yard of the parish church of Bury, where there was (previous to the rebuilding of the church) a tombstone to his memory.

A stedfast Affection to the Protestant Religion and the Happy Government of His Majesty King George: or, Opposition to the Wicked Designs of the Present Rebellion. Recommended in a Sermon preached at Liverpool, etc., the 11th day of January 1715-16, at the Opening of the Special Commission of Oyer and Terminer, and the General Goal Delivery for Tryal of the Rebels taken at the late action at Preston. Published by the repeated desire of Thomas Crisp, Esq., High Sheriff, and the Gentlemen of the Grand Jury; as also at the request of William Squire, Esq., Mayor of Liverpool, and many other Gentlemen then present. By SAMUEL PEPLOE, M.A., and Vicar of Preston in Lancashire. London: printed for W. Taylor, at the shop in Paternoster Row. 1716. Price 3d.

Title as above, etc., 24 pp.

God's Peculiar Case in the Preservation of our Religion and Liberties. A Sermon preach'd at Lancaster Assizes, the 24th March 1716, before Judge Dormer, one of the Justices of the King's Bench, at Westminster. By SAMUEL PEPLOE, M.A., and Vicar of Preston in Lancashire.

London: printed for W. Taylor, at the shop in Paternoster Row. 1716. Price 4d. *Octavo.*

Title, Dedication (to Thomas Crispe, Esq., High Sheriff), and Sermon, 28 pp.

Samuel Peploe, M.A., was Vicar of Preston from 1700 to 1727, when he was created Bishop of Chester. In 1717 he was appointed Warden of the Manchester Collegiate Church. He died on the 21st February 1752, aged 84.

HENRY PIGOTT, Rector of Brindle, published an Assize Sermon (Preached at Lancaster) in 1676. *Small quarto.*

Two Sermons preached at the Assizes held at Lancaster on Sunday, Aug. 27th, 1710, and at several other places. By the Rev. HENRY RICHMOND, Rector of Leverpoole, and Chaplain to the Right Honourable Elizabeth, Countess Dowager of Derby. Published at the Request of the Gentry and Clergy, the Grand Jury being discharged on Saturday night. London: printed for Jonah Bowyer at the Rose in Ludgate Street, and sold by Joseph Eaton, bookseller in Leverpoole, 1710. *Octavo.*

Two Titles and two Sermons, 48 pp.

A copy of this is in the Author's Library.

A Sermon on the Death of Queen Anne, preached in St. Peter's Church, Leverpoole. Printed at Leverpoole 1714. *Octavo.*

An Assize Sermon, by the same Author, appeared. Liverpool, 1719. *Octavo.*

Of this a second edition was published.

The Institution and Efficacy of the Holy Eucharist. A Sermon preached at St. Peter's Church in Liverpool, 27th September, 1719. Printed by S. Terry in Dale Street for the booksellers in Liverpool. 1719. *Octavo.*

A copy of this is in the Library of J. A. Picton, Esq., F.S.A., Liverpool.

The Rev. Henry Richmond was Rector of Liverpool from 1706 to 1767.

Spiritual Wickedness in High Places; or, the Corruption and Oppression in the Spiritual Courts, laid open in the case of PETER SLYNEHEAD of the Parish of Prescot, in the County of Lancaster and Diocess of Chester. London: printed by R. Tookey, and are to be sold by [1] S. Malthus in London House Yard, near the west end of St. Paul's. 1704. Price 6d. *Foolscap Quarto.*

Title as above, and Contents, iii. pp. Spiritual Wickedness, 40 pp.

This work was written in consequence of a charge of adultery which was preferred against its author.

England's Misery, both Spiritually and Temporally, for want of a Godly Discipline. Humbly dedicated to the Queen and Parliament. By PETER SLYNEHEAD, of the Parish of Prescot, in the County of Lancaster and Diocess of Chester, in order to the restoring of a Godly discipline. London: printed by R. Tookey, and are to be sold by N. Eires, bookseller in Warrington, 1706. Price 6d. Where is also sold a former book of the same author's, entitled Spiritual Wickedness in High Places. Price 6d. *Small quarto.*

Title as above, and Contents, iv. pp. England's Misery, 40 pp.

A copy of this is in the Chetham Library.

The Damnable Doctrine of Church Discipline. By the Bishops Laws, and their Deputies in Spirituals, against the Health of our Souls. For they will pretend a Soul's Salvation, and thereby enforce a Soul Damnation. Who will pretend our Soul's Health, for to get our Worldly Wealth. Humbly dedicated to the Lords Spiritual of this our Soul Law. By PETER SLYNEHEAD of Sankey, in the Parish of Prescot, and County of Lancaster, and Diocess of Chester, in order to turn their cursed Deputies out of their office, unless they make Restitution, and satisfie the Church. London: printed in the year of our Lord, MDCCIX. *Small quarto.*

Title as above, Contents, and Damnable Doctrine, 20 pp.

A copy is in the Library of Dr. Kendrick of Warrington.

Peter Slynehead lived at Slynehead's Green in Sankey, in the parish

[1] Some copies have also the words "are to be sold by N. Eires, bookseller in Warrington.

of Prescot. For the publication of one of his works he was committed to the Fleet Prison, where he died. The law expenses ruined him, and his property at Sankey (consisting of 15 acres of land) was sold. Previous to his committal to the Fleet he was exposed in the stocks at Prescot and Warrington.

A Discourse of the Holy Spirit, His Workings and Impressions on the Souls of Men. [By RICHARD SHERLOCK.] London: printed by E. Cotes for R. Royston at the Angel in Ivie Lane. 1654. *Small octavo.*

Title and Discourse, 108 pp.

The Quaker's Wilde Questions objected against, etc. By R. SHERLOCK. *See* p. 363.

A Sermon preached at a Visitation held at Warrington in Lancashire, May 11th, 1669. By RIC. SHERLOCK, D.D., Rector of Winwick in Lancashire. Imprimatur June 18, 1669. Tho. Tomkyns Reverendissimo in Christo Patri ac Domino, Dom. Gibb. Arch. Cantuar a Sacr. Dom. London: printed by Rich. Royston, Bookseller to the King's most excellent Majesty. 1669. *Small quarto.*

Title, 1 p. Sermon, 19 pp.

Mercurius Christianus. The Practical Christian. A Treatise explaining the Duty of Self-examination. Together with Confessions, Meditations, and Prayers, in order to the Receiving of the Holy Communion of the Body and Blood of Christ. Composed for the use of Devout Persons. By R. SHERLOCK, D.D., Rector of Winwick. Lam. iii. 40. London: printed by R. Norton for R. Royston, Bookseller to His most sacred Majesty, MDCLXXIII. *Duodecimo.*

Title, Dedication, and Table of Contents, x pp. Mercurius, etc., 387 pp.

PLATES.

Frontispiece, David praying in the Temple.

After page of Contents, two plates facing each other.

1. Marie washing Christ's feet.
2. The Institution of His last Supper.

This work is dedicated to "my Parishioners at Winwick." It was reprinted in 18*mo* at Oxford in 1841.

A copy of this is in the British Museum.

The Practical Christian, or the Devout Penitent. A Book of Devotion, containing the whole Duty of a Christian in all occasions and Necessities. Fitted to the main Uses of a Holy Life. In four Parts. By R. SHERLOCK, D.D., late Rector of Winwick. The sixth Edition enlarged and corrected. To which is now added the Life of Dr. Sherlock, by the Right Reverend Father in God, Thomas, Lord Bishop of Soder and Man. London: printed by W. Pearson for W. Wotton, at the Three Daggers, in Fleet Street, and James Holland, at the Bible and Ball in St. Paul's Church-yard. 1713. *Octavo.*

Frontispiece and Portrait.

Richard Sherlock was born at Oxton in Cheshire, M.A. of Trinity College, Dublin, chaplain to Charles I.'s forces at Nantwich. He afterwards became chaplain to Sir Robert Bindlosse, of Borwick Hall, in Lancashire, and to the Earl of Derby, who nominated him to the Rectory of Winwick at the Restoration of Charles II. He died, and was buried in the Chancel of Winwick Church, June 1689, aged 76.

The Christian's Triumph over Death: A Sermon at the Funeral of Richard Legh, of Lime, in the County Palatine of Chester, Esq., at Winwick in the County Palatine of Lancaster, Sep. 6, 1687. By W. SHIPPEN, Rector of Stockport, in Cheshire, sometime Fellow of Univers. Coll. Oxon. Oxford: printed at the Theater. 1688. *Small quarto.*

Title and Sermon, 62 pp.

A dissuasive from Revenge; in a discourse upon these words, "Recompense to no man evil for evil," Rom. xii. 17. By NICHOLAS STRATFORD, D.D., Dean of S. Asap. London: printed for Richard Chiswell, at the Rose and Crown in St. Paul's Church-yard. 1684. *Duodecimo.*

Title and Epistle Dedication, xxxii. pp. Discourse, 126 pp.

Dr. Stratford was for some time Warden of Manchester Collegiate Church, and the above is dedicated "To my worthy and beloved Friends, the Inhabitants of Manchester and Salford."

A copy of it is in the Chetham Library.

He published several other Sermons, etc., which, however, do not refer to Lancashire.

The Death of the Righteous, or the Discriminating Circumstances that favour the Departure of a Pious Soul. Delivered at Wigan, April 18, 1695, at the obsequies of the Honourable and Vertuous Lady Elizabeth, the Relict of Sir Roger Bradshaigh, of Haigh, Knight and Baronet. By ZACH. TAYLOR, A.M., and Curate there of the Right Reverend Nicholas, Lord Bishop of Chester. In the Savoy: printed by E. Jones for Sam. Lowndes, over against Exeter-Change, in the Strand. 1695. *Small quarto.*

Half-title, Title as above, and Dedication, viii. pp. Sermon, 24 pp.

A copy of this rare Sermon is preserved in the Chetham Library.

Zachery Taylor was the son of the Rev. Zachery Taylor, M.A., Curate of Rochdale, and afterwards Head Master of Kirkham Free Grammar School. On the 9th March 1679 he was appointed Vicar of Ormskirk in Lancashire, which he resigned in 1693. In 1695 he became Rector of Croston in the same County; and in 1696 was Rector of Wigan. (*See* Surey " Demoniac Tracts," and p. 372.)[1]

The Way to the Trve Chvrch, wherein the principall Motiues perswading to Romanisme, and Questions touching the nature and authoritie of the Church and Scriptures, are familiarly disputed and driuen to their issues, where this day they sticke betweene the Papists and vs. Contriued into an answer to a Popish Discourse concerning the Rule of Faith and the marks of the Church. And published to admonish such as decline to Papistrie, of the weake and vncertaine grounds whereupon they haue ventured their soules. Directed to all that seeke for resolution, and especially to his louing countrimen of Lancashire. By JOHN WHITE, Minister of God's at Eccles. For finding out of the matter and questions handled, there are three Tables: two in the beginning and one in the end of the Booke.

De hoc inter Quæstio versatur vtrum apud nos an apud Illos vera Ecclesia sit.—August de vnit Eccles Cap. 2.

London: printed for Iohn Bill and William Barret. 1608. *Small quarto.*

Title as above, Dedication, Preface, and Tables, xlv. pp. (unpaged). Discourse. etc., 454 pp. Table, x. pp.

[1] For notice of this family, *see* Fishwick's "History of Kirkham" (Chet. Soc. xcii.), p. 146 *et. seq.*

A defence of the Way to the Trve Chvrch against A. D. His Reply, Wherein The Motives leading to Papistry,

The Qvestions touching the Rvle of Faith,
The Avthoritie of the Church,
The Svccession of the Truth, and
The Beginning of Romish Innouations are handled and fully disputed.

By IOHN WHITE, Docter of Diuinity, sometime of Gunwell and Caius Coll., in Cambridge.

[Quotation Chrysost. in 2 Cor. hom. 13].

London: printed for William Barret, dwelling in Paul's Church-yard at the signe of the Three Pigeons. 1614. *Small quarto.*

Title as above, Dedication, To the Reader, etc., xli. pp. (unpaged). The Defence, etc., 557 pp.

Copies of the two last works are in the Chetham Library.

The works of that learned and Reverend Divine JOHN WHITE, Docter of Diuinitie, together with a Defence of the Way to the Church, in answer to a Papist Treatise, written by T. W. O., entituled, White died Black. By FRANCIS WHITE, Docter in Diuinitie, and Dean of Carlisle. London: printed for W. Barret; and are to be sold by M. Lowndes and Rich. Moore. 1624. *Folio.*

Half-title, Title, Dedication, Preface, Contents, etc., 36 pp. A brief Discourse concerning Faith, and Index, 244 pp. Title to Defence of the Way, Dedication, and Contents, 22 pp. The Defence, 316 pp. Title to Sermons, and Dedication, iv. pp. Sermons, 36 pp. Title to Sermons and Dedication, 28 pp. Sermons, etc., 194 pp.

A copy of this Edition is in the Rev. Canon Raines' Library.

John White, D.D., was Vicar of Eccles from 1606 until his death in 1610. He was a Fellow of the Manchester College. His brother, Dr. Francis White, was Bishop of Ely.

"The Beauty of Unity; in a Sermon at Preston, in Lancashire, at the Opening of the Guild-Merchant held there, Sept. 4th, 1682, by RICHARD WROE, B.D., and Chaplain to the Lord Bishop of Chester." London:

printed for Benj. Tooke at the Ship, in St. Paul's Church-yard. 1682. *Quarto.*

Title as above and Sermon, 40 pp.

Righteousness Encouraged and Rewarded with an Everlasting Remembrancer. In a Sermon at the Funeral of the Rt. Worshipful Sir Roger Bradshaigh, of Haigh, Knt. and Baronet, who died at Chester on Monday, March 31st, and was buried at Wigan, Friday, April 4, 1684. By RICHARD WROE, B.D. London: printed for Benj. Tooke at the Ship, in St. Paul's Church-yard. 1684. *Quarto.*

Title as above and Sermon, 36 pp.

A Sermon preached at Bowden, in Cheshire, April 6th, 1691, at the Funeral of the Right Honourable Mary, Countess of Warrington. By RICHARD WROE, D.D., and Warden of Christ's College in Manchester. London: printed by T. D. for R. Clavell, at the Peacock in St. Paul's Church Yard. 1691.

Title and Dedication, iv. pp. Sermon, 26 pp.

A Sermon at the Funeral of Henry, Earl of Warrington, Lord Delamere, etc., preached at Bowden. By RICHARD WROE, etc. Printed for A. and J. Churchill at the Black Swan, in Pater-noster Row. MDCXCIV.

Half-title, Title, and Dedication, vi. pp. Sermon, 26 pp.

A Sermon preached in the Collegiate Church of Manchester March the 8th, 170¾. Being the Day of Her Majesty's Happy Accession to the Throne. By RICHARD WROE, D.D., and Warden of Christ's College in Manchester. Published at the Request of the Town. London: printed by J. H. for Henry Mortlock at the Phoenix, in St. Paul's Church-yard. 1704. *Quarto.*

Title as above and Sermon, 28 pp.

A copy is in the Chetham Library.

A Thanksgiving Sermon on Thessalonians iii. 10. [By R. WROE.] 1722.[1]

[1] This is mentioned by Baines (*see* Hist. Lanc.)

Richard Wroe, D.D., was a native of Radcliffe near Bury. In 1675 he was appointed a Fellow of the Collegiate Church, Manchester. In 1678 he was appointed prebendary to a stall of Chester Cathedral, and was for some time Vicar of Garstang in Lancashire, and Vicar of Bowdon in Cheshire. He died in 1718, and was buried in Manchester Cathedral.

Excommunicatio Excommunicata, or a CENSURE of the PRESBYTERIAN CENSURES and PROCEEDINGS in the CLASSES of MANCHESTER. Wherein is modestly examined what Ecclesiastical or Civil Sanction they pretend for their new and usurped Power. In a Discourse betwixt the Ministers of that Classes and some Dissenting Christians. London: printed for John Meacock; and are to be sold by Humphrey Moseley at the sign of the Prince's Arms, in St. Paul's Church Yard. 1658. *Quarto.*

Title as above, and Preface, x. pp. Censure, etc., 98 pp.

An important work. Amongst the signatures to the articles are those of Richard Heyricke (Moderator, *pro temp.*), Isaac Allen, Ferdinando Stanley, John Angier (Moderator), and Leonard Egerton.

A copy is in the Chetham Library.

ADDENDA.

PRESTON FIGHT; or, the Insurrection of 1715. A Tale. By WILLIAM HARRISON AINSWORTH.

> "My Lord Derwentwater he did swear,
> If that Proud Preston he came near,
> Ere the Right should starve, and the Wrong shall stand,
> He would drive them into some foreign land."
> *Old Lancashire Ballad.*

In three volumes. Vol. I. London: Tinsley Brothers, 18 Catherine Street, Strand. 1875. [Right of Translation reserved by the Author.] *Post octavo.*

Title as above, and Dedicatory Preface, vi. pp. Preston Fight, 287 pp.

VOL. II.

Title, 1 p. Preston Fight, 292 pp.

VOL. III.

Title, 1 p. Preston Fight, 265 pp.
Published at £1 : 11 : 6.

HISTORY of the BOROUGH of BURY and neighbourhood, in the County of Lancaster, by B. T. BARTON, Reporter.

> "Nothing extenuate, nor set down aught in malice."
> *Shakspeare.*

Bury: Wardleworth, Agur Street; Manchester: North of England Printing Society, Balloon Street; London: Smith and Sons. [1874.] *Octavo.*

Title as above, Preface, and Dedication, vii. pp. History, 320 pp. Illustrated with 12 Views.

ADDENDA.

PLATES.

Bury Parish Church, *Frontispiece.*
Derby Hotel, etc.
New Bank.
Birthplace of Sir Robert Peel.
Grammar School.
Cemetery.
Brunswick Chapel.
Presbyterian Church.
Elton Church.
Holcombe Hill.

Published at 5s.

Some remarks on LANCASHIRE FARMING, and on various subjects connected with the Agriculture of the County; with a few suggestions for remedying some of its defects. By LAW RAWSTORNE, Esq. London: Longman and Co., Paternoster Row, and Thomas Thomson, Bookseller, Preston. 1843. *Duodecimo.*

Title, Contents, and Introduction, vi. pp. Remarks, 118 pp. Errata, 1 p.
Published at 4s.

The WORKS of HENRY LIVERSEEGE. With a MEMOIR. By GEORGE RICHARDSON, Author of "Patriotism," "Miscellaneous Poems," etc. London: George Routledge and Sons, and L. C. Gent. 1875. *Imperial quarto.*

Engraved Title, 1 p. Title as above, Advertisement, List of Engravings, Memoir, and Reminiscences, 20 pp. Followed by 36 Engravings.
Frontispiece, Portrait of Henry Liverseege.

Published at £2 : 2s.

Henry Liverseege was born in Manchester 4th September 1802, and died 13th January 1832. The former edition of his works contains no Memoir.

Annales Caermoclenses, or ANNALS of CARTMEL. By JAMES STOCKDALE.

"Si vacet annales nostrorum audire laborum."—VIRG. Æn. I. 377.

Ulverston: William Kitchin, printer, Market Street; London: Simpkin, Marshall, and Co. 1872. All rights reserved. *Octavo.*

Title as above, and Preface, v. pp. Annales, 595 pp. Note, 1 p. Addenda and Errata, 2 pp. Index, vii. pp.

ADDENDA.

PLATES.

Cartmel Church, *Frontispiece.* Carke Hall.
Plate showing the Inhabitants of Carke Hall for several Generations.
South View of Wraysholm Tower.

Published at 10s. 6d.

MEMOIRS OF THE GEOLOGICAL SURVEY.—ENGLAND AND WALES.

The GEOLOGY of the BURNLEY COALFIELD, and the County around Clitheroe, Blackburn, Preston, Chorley, Haslingden, and Todmorden.

Quarter sheets, 88 N.W., 89 N.E., 89 N.W., and 92 S.W. of the 1-inch Geological Maps.

By EDWARD HULL, M.A., F.R.S.; J. R. DAKYNS, M.A.; R. H. TIDDEMAN, M.A.; J. C. WARD; W. GUNN; and C. E. DE RANCE. Table of Fossils by R. Etheridge, F.R.S., etc. etc.

Published by order of the Lords Commissioners of Her Majesty's Treasury. London: printed for Her Majesty's Stationery Office, and sold by Longman and Co., Paternoster Row, and Edward Stanford, 6 Charing Cross, S.W. 1875. Price 12s. *Octavo.*

Title as above, Addenda, and Notice, xi. pp. Geology and Index, p. 5 to p. 225. Illustrated with woodcuts.

The County Book of England and Official List. LANCASHIRE, 1875. Comprising every official Person in the County. London: Edward Stanford; Manchester: Edwin Slater; Liverpool: Adam Holden. 1875. *Post octavo.*

Title as above, Preface, The County of Lancashire, Corrections, etc., vii. pp. The County Book, 220 pp.

Published at 5s.

Transactions of the MANCHESTER LITERARY CLUB. Session 1874-5.

VOL. I.

Manchester: A. Ireland and Co., Pall Mall; London: Trübner and Co., Ludgate Hill. 1875. *Octavo.*

Title as above, List of Council, and Contents, vi. pp. Transactions, etc., 151 pp. List of Books, etc., xi. pp.

Published at 4s. Contains several papers of local interest.

GENERAL INDEX.

A

AB-O'-TH-YATE, B. Brierley, 245.
Adlington, Strange News from, 377.
Agreement (the) of the People, 374.
Agriculture in Lancashire—
A General View of, J. Holt, 62.
,, ,, R. W. Dickson, 55.
Notes on, J. Burns, 47.
Report on, G. Beesley, 47.
,, W. Rothwell, 69.
Aikin, Lucy, Memoir of, 190.
Alexis, a Narrative of the Rebellion, 240.
Amounderness. *See* Lonsdale.
Anderton, Henry, Life of (and Poems), 190.
Angier, John, Life of, 191.
Angus, Charles, Trial of, 114.
Appleby, Victory at (Civil War Tract), 334.
Archæologia, Lancashire Articles in, 290, 292.
Arkwright, Richard, Patent Trial, 191.
Arrowsmith, Edmund (Death of Two Catholics, etc.), 192.
Ashburner Family, Pedigree of, 192.
Ashton-under-Lyne, Account of, E. Butterworth, 1.
—— Black Knight, W. E. A. Axon, 3.
—— (Civil War Tract), 349.
—— Geological Sketches in the Parish of, C. Clay, 2.
—— History, J. Butterworth, 1.
—— Illustration of the Custom of a Manor, S. Hibbert, 2.
Assheton, Nicholas, Journal of, 192.
—— William, Life and Works of, 193.
Atmore, Eliza, Account of, 193.
Authors and Orators of Lancashire, J. Evans, 56.

B

BACUP, a sketch of the Rise of the Baptist Church in, 3.
Baines, Edward, Life of, 193.
Bamford, Samuel, Passages in the Life of a Radical, 193.
—— Early days of, 194.
Bancroft, Richard, Life of, 194.
Barber's Shop, the, R. W. Procter, 269.
Barnabee's Journal, 297, 298.
Barrow-in-Furness, its Rise and Progress, F. Leach, 3.
Barton, Sir Andrew, Memoir of, 175.
Bayley, H. V., Memoir of, 194.
—— T. B., Memoir of, 195.
Besom Ben, 282.
Bewsey, a Poem, 254.
Birch, a History of the Ancient Chapel of, J. Booker, 3.
Bispham. *See* Blackpool.
Blackburn, Chronological Notes of, W. Durham, 4.
—— a History of the rise of Congregational Union in, 4.
—— A Topographical, etc., Account of, P. Whittle, 4.
Blackley, History of the Chapel of, J. Booker, 5.
Blackpool, a Description of, W. Hutton, 5, 6.
—— an Historical Account of, W. Thornber, 6, 7.
—— an Historical Account of, P. Whittle, 7.
—— Guides to, 7.
Bobbin's, Tim, Cottage, E. Waugh, 116.
Bolton, Apparitions at (Civil War Tract), 334.
—— Chronological History of, 8.
—— Family, Account of, 195.

GENERAL INDEX.

Bolton, Handbook of, J. D. Briscoe, 8.
—— History of, J. Brown, 8.
—— Historical, etc., Account of, P. Whittle, 8, 9.
—— Massacre, at (Civil War Tract), 334.
—— Rise and Progress of Nonconformity in, F. Baker, 7.
—— Town Council Proceedings of, 9.
Booth, Barton, Life of, 195.
—— —— ,, Mr. Vincent, 196.
Bradforde, John, Examinations of, 196.
Bradford, John, History of, 196.
Bradford, John, Letters of, 198.
—— —— Memoir of, 197.
—— —— Writings of, 198.
Bradshaw's Manchester Journal, 296.
Bridgewater, Will of the Duke of, 198.
Britannia Magna, Thomas Cox, 54.
Broughton. *See* Fernyhalgh, 14.
Burnley, Ancient Mansions of, 10.
—— Coal Fields, 428.
—— History of the Grammar School, T. T. Wilkinson, 39.
—— History of the Parochial Church of, T. T. Wilkinson, 39.
Bury Grammar School, Statutes of, 10.
—— History of, B. T. Barton, 420.
Byrom, John, Private Journal of, 198.
—— Elizabeth, Journal of, 199.
—— Pedigrees, 199.

C

CAPPOCH, Thomas, History of, 200.
Cartmel Parish, W. Folliott, 10.
—— An Account of, T. D. Whitaker, 10.
—— Priory Church, 20.
—— Sketch of, 16.
Catholics, Condition of, under James I., 307.
—— Death of Two, etc., Lancaster, 1628, 192.
—— Roman, Names of Non-Jurors, 321.
Chadertoni Laurentii Vita, 200.
Chantries of Lancashire, History of, 67.
Charities of Lancashire, Commissioners' Reports on, 50-52.
Chatburn, Roman Coins at, 291.
Chester's Case, the Bishop of, 375.
Chetham, Humphrey, Will of, 201.
—— Miscellanies, 74-77.
Chorley, Historical and Descriptive Account of, 11.
Chorlton and Didsbury Chapels, J. Booker, 12.
Churches, our Country, Atticus, 61.
Civil War, the, R. Cattermole, 299.
—— —— Tracts, 332-352.
Clayton Family, Memorials of, 201.
Clitheroe, Ancient Charters of, J. Harland, 11.
Coniston Hall, or the Jacobites, 257.
Conspiracy, History of the late, J. Abbadie, 36.
—— in 1688, a True History of, 306.
Cotton Manufacture, History of, E. Baines, 293.
—— Manufacture, History of, R. Guest, 303.
—— Manufactories, R. Guest, 303.
—— Trade, a History of, E. Butterworth, 122.
Crompton, Samuel, a Brief Memoir of, J. Kennedy, 62.
—— —— Life and Times of, G. French, 201, 202.
—— —— Basis of his Claims, etc., 203.
Crumpsall, Memorials of Oldham's Tenement in, 12.
Currie, James, Memoir of, 203.
Cutler, Ann, Account of, 203.

D

DARNETON, or Rich and Poor, 284.
Darrell, Tracts, the, 355-358.
Declarations of Lords and Commons (Civil War Tracts), 336.
Derby Family. *See* Stanley.
—— Earls of, and verse writers of 16th and 17th centuries, 263.
—— the lady of Lathom 233.
—— Countess of, Memoirs of, 233.
—— Memoirs of, rescued by Truth, 235.
—— Memoirs, Testimony of Truth, 234.
—— family (Civil War Tracts), 335.
De Motu per Britanniam civico annis, MDCCXLV. *et.* MDCCXLVI., auctore, T. D. Whitakero, 73.
De Quincey, Confessions of an English Opium Eater, 204.
Didsbury and Chorlton Chapels, History of, J. Booker, 12.
Domestic Winter Piece, S. Law, 265.

GENERAL INDEX.

Doomsday Book, W. Bawden, 46.
—— —— W. Beamont, 47.
—— —— Col. Sir H. James, 62.
Drayton, John, J. Stonehouse, 278.
Droylsden, Historical, etc., Notices of, J. Higson, 12
Drunkard's, the, Prospective, J. Rigbie, 270.
Ducatus Lancastriæ, 78, 79.
Duddon, the River, W. Wordsworth, 284.

E

ECCLES, Parish Church of, J. Harland, 13.
—— on the find of pennies at, J. Harland, 11.
Eccles and Barton's Contentious Guising War, F. H** R** G** N., 13.
Eclipses, a Treatise, C. Leadbetter, 265.
Eggshibishun (th' greyt), etc., o Felley fro' Rachdi, 268.
England, a Journey through, 302.
Epistle (an), from the Rector of St. Anne, 287.
Everton, History of, R. Syers, 14.

F

FAIR EM the Miller's Daughter of Manchester, 285.
Fairfax, Sir Thomas, Memoirs of, 332.
Farington Papers, the, 204.
Far North, T. Kennedy, 264.
Feast (the) of Folly, 286.
Fell, Margaret, collection of passages, etc., in Life of, 205. *See* Fox.
Fell, Thomas, Account of, 204.
Fells (the) of Swarthmoor Hall, 205.
Fernyhalgh Chapel, Account of, P. Whittle, 14.
Fishwick, George, Memoir of, 206.
—— Mary, Memorials of, 206.
—— Mrs. Friendship's Tribute to the Memory of, 206.
—— Mrs., Memoirs of, 207.
Fleetwood, Guide to, 7.
Flixton Parish, E. Waugh, 15.
Folk Song and Folk Speech of Lancashire, 242.
Fothergill, Samuel, Memoir of, 207.
Fox, Margaret, Life of, 207.
Fruits of Retirement, M. Mollineux, 266.
Funeral-Certificates of Lancashire, T. W. King, 68.
Furness Abbey and Neighbourhood, J. Payn, 17.
—— a Guide to, from Blackpool, etc., and Furness Abbey, F. Evans, 16.
—— Annales Furniensis, T. A. Beck, 15, 16.
—— Antiquities of, T. West, 17.
—— Geological, Fragments of Rocks of, J. Bolton, 16.
—— Handbook to, G. H. Barber (?), 15.
—— Sketch of, C. M. Jopling, 16.
—— Words, a Glossary of, J. P. Morris, 17.

G

GIBSON *v.* Hargreaves, Report of Trial, 217.
Gleaston Castle, Celts found in, 290.
Good Old Times (the), a Story of Manchester, 239.
Goosnargh, History of, H. Fishwick, 19.
Gorton Historical Recorder, J. Higson, 19.
Grammar Schools in England and Wales, 298.
Grange, Guide to, 20.
Great Britain, a Tour through, 301.
Greenfield, a Poem, 243.
Greenhalgh Family, Memoranda of, 207.
Grimshaw, William, Life of, 208.
—— Life and Writings of, 208.

H

Halls, Ancient, of Lancashire, A. Rimmer, 69.
Hamilton, Duke of, the Case of, 377.
Hanson, Joseph, Letter to, 209.
—— —— Memoir of, 208.
—— —— Pamphlets relating to, 209.
Haydock, Roger, a Collection of Writings, Labours, etc., of, 209.
Hemans, Mrs., Life of, 210.
—— —— Memorials of, 210.
—— —— Works and Life of, 211.
Henry, Dr., a Biographical account of, 211.
Heroic Epistle (an), from the Obelisk, 285.
Heywood, Oliver, Life of, J. Hunter, 212.

GENERAL INDEX.

Heywood, Oliver, Memoir of, 212.
—— —— Works of, etc., 212.
—— Historical Description of, 20.
Hirst, John, Life of, 213.
History of Clemency, a vindication of the, 302.
Historical MSS., Reports of the Commission, 321.
Historic Society of Lancashire and Cheshire, 323-331.
Holt, David, Incidents in Life of, 213.
Homely Rhymes, S. Bamford, 243.
Hopwood (the), Will Case, Report of, 226.
Hornby, Tatham *v.* Wright, 20.
Horrox, Jeremiah, Memoir of, 213.
Houghton, Peter, Life of, 214.
Hours in the Bowers, S. Bamford, 243.
—— with the Muses, J. C. Prince, 269.
Houseman, Robert, Life of, 214.
Hunt, Henry, Trial of, 155.

I

IRKDALE, B. Brierley, 244.
Irwell, and Other Poems, 240.
Iter Lancastriense, a Poem, 263.
Itinerant, the, S. W. Ryley, 312.

J

JANNOCK, or the Bold Trencherman, 282.
Just, John, Memoir of, 215.

K

KAY, John, a Testimonial in behalf of, 215.
Kemble Family, the, 215.
—— J. P., Memoirs of, 216.
Kershaw, John, Autobiography of, 217.
Kirkham, History of, H. Fishwick, 20.
—— Miraculous Wonders at, 378.
Knowsley Menagerie, Gleanings from, 21.

L

LAKE Country, the, E. L. Linton, 29.
—— —— Lays and Legends of, 283.
Lake District, Ascents and Passes of, 33.
Lake District, Geology of, Mannex and Co., 115.
—— —— Scenery, J. B. Pyne, 32.
—— —— —— W. J. Loftie, 33.
—— —— —— J. W. Ford, 25.
—— —— —— and Poetry of, C. Mackay, 30.
—— —— Rambles in, H. Hardknot, 26.
Lakes (the), Companion to, G. Baines, 22.
—— Concise Description of, J. Ottley, 31.
—— Delineated, H. Horne, 27.
—— Description of, W. Green, 25.
—— Descriptive Tour, J. Housman, 28.
—— Fortnight's Ramble in, J. Budworth, 23.
—— Guide to, Allison's, 22.
—— —— Black's, 22.
—— —— E. T. Blanchard's, 23.
—— —— W. Green's, 25.
—— —— Jenkinson's, 29.
—— —— Leigh's, 29.
—— —— H. Martineau's, 30.
—— —— Murray's, 31.
—— —— J. Payn's, 31.
—— —— Peaks and Passes of, G. K. Matthews, 30.
—— —— J. Robinson's 32.
—— —— G. Tattersall's, 33.
—— —— M. E. C. Walcott's, 33.
—— —— T. West's, 34.
—— —— W. Wordsworth's, 36.
—— Picturesque Tour of, 21.
—— Plans and Description of, P. Crossthwaite, 25.
—— Survey of, J. Clarke, 24.
—— Tales and Legends of, L. Tuvar, 279.
—— Tour of, J. Denholm, 25.
—— Tour to, A. Radcliffe, 32.
—— Tours to (the British Mountains), T. Wilkinson, 35.
—— Views of, P. Holland, 27.
—— —— J. Wilkinson, 35.
Lancashire Agriculture, Report on, G. Beesley, 47.
—— —— Notes on, J. Binns, 47.
—— —— Report on, W. Rothwell, 69.
—— —— View of, R. W. Dickson, 55.
—— —— View of, J. Holt, 62.
—— Ancient Walls, A Rimmer, 69.
—— Anthology, 260.
—— Articles referring to, in Proceedings of Lanc. and Ches. Hist. Soc., 223-230.

GENERAL INDEX.

Lancashire Authors and Orators, J. Evans, 56.
Lancashire Ballads and Songs, J. Harland, 259, 260.
Lancashire, Beauties of, J. Britton, 48.
—— Book of County Rates, T. Battye, 120,
—— Chantries, a History of, 67.
—— Charities' Commissions, Reports on, 50-52.
—— County Book and Official List, 423.
—— and Cheshire, Past and Present, T. Baines, 44.
—— —— Historical Collection, T. W. Barlow, 45.
—— Churches, Exhortation to, 378.
—— Civil War Tracts of, G. Ormerod, 64.
—— —— —— relating to, 333-352.
—— Concise History of, E. Butterworth, 50.
—— Description of, G. A. Cooke, 53.
—— Dialect, Lectures on, W. Gaskell, 57.
—— —— Literature of, W. E. A. Axon, 38.
—— —— View of, Tim Bobbin, 248-256.
—— —— View of, Sequel to, P. Bobbin, 256.
—— Documents of 14th and 15th Centuries, J. Harland, 60.
—— Dom. Boc., W. Bawden, 46.
—— Domesday Book, W. Beamont, 47.
—— —— H. James, 62.
—— Duchy, 290.
—— —— Charters, W. Hardy, 60.
—— —— Observations on Title of the King to Escheats, 79.
—— —— Report of Select Committee, 80.
—— Expenditure of the County of, R. Hindle, 61.
—— Factory Folk, Home Life of, 281.
—— Farming, remarks on, L. Rawshorne, 422.
—— Folk Lore, J. Harland, 259.
—— Funeral Certificates, T. W. King, 68.
—— Gazetteer, J. Aston, 37.
—— —— S. T. Clarke, 52.
—— History of, E. Baines, 39-43.
—— —— and Directory of, E. Baines, 43, 44.
—— —— (Natural), C. Leigh, 63, 64.
—— —— Pictorial of, 78.
—— —— Legends, and Manufacture, G. N. Wright, 73.
Lancashire, History of, J. Corry, 53.
—— —— Illustrated, H. Ashworth, 50.
—— —— J. Austin, 37.
—— Illustrated Itinerary, 77.
—— Legends, J. Harland, 260.
—— —— 286.
—— Lieutenancy under the Tudors and Stuarts, J. Harland, 61.
—— Life, Sketches of, E. Waugh, 280.
—— Life, Tales, and Sketches of, 244.
—— Life, or Vicissitudes of Commerce, 257.
—— Lovers (the), 244.
—— Lyrics, J. Harland, 259.
—— Mansions, L. Twycross, 70-73.
—— Manufactures, J. Kennedy, 62.
—— Mid. History and Topography of, Mannex and Co., 64.
—— Ministers, deliberate resolution of, 335.
—— Murray's Handbook of, 307.
—— Pedigrees, J. Foster, 56.
—— Petition of 12,000 Freeholders of, 379.
—— Plot (the), J. Abbadie, 36.
—— Portfolio of Fragments, M. Gregson, 57-59.
—— Prints—Binns' Collection, 48.
—— Puritanism and Nonconformity, R. Halley, 59.
—— Races of, indicated by Local Names and Dialect, J. Davies, 55.
—— Rates, a book of, W. Crabtree, 54.
—— Rebellion, 1715, Memorials of, S. H. Ware, 77. *See* Rebellion.
—— South, Historical data relating to, H. Ashworth, 50.
—— South, Rural and Historical Gleanings in, J. Fielding, 56.
—— South, Walks in, S. Bamford, 45.
—— Statistical Sketches of, E. Butterworth, 49.
—— Summer Rambles in, 303.
—— Superstitions and Folk-Lore, C. Hardwick, 258.
—— Towns, Health of, Dr. Playfair, 65.
—— Topographical Survey, W. Tunnicliffe, 70.
—— Tracts relating to Military Proceedings during the Civil War, 64.
—— —— Civil War, 333-352.
—— Traditions, J. Roby, 271-274.
—— Valley of Achor (Civil War Tract), 340.

GENERAL INDEX.

Lancashire Visitations, 1567, 1613, 1664, 1665, 68, 69.
— War, a Discourse of, Major Robinson, 47.
— Wills (and Cheshire), G. J. Picope, 65.
— Witches, the, W. H. Ainsworth, 239.
— Witches, Plays on the, 262.
— Witches, the Famous, History of, 78.
— Witches, the late, 262.
— Worthies (and Yorkshire), 299.
— — F. Espinasse, 55.
Lancaster, Antiquities at, 290, 291, 292.
— Borough, List of Mayors, etc., 17, 68, 82.
— Castle, its History, J. Hall, 82.
— Charters, 81.
— Elections, List of the Poll, 1786, 82.
— — 1802, 82
— Electioneering Papers, 1802, 83.
— Guide to, 81.
— History and Antiquities of, 80.
— Historical and Descriptive Account of, 80.
— Lamentable and Sad News from, 338.
— Massacre (Civil War Tract), 344.
— Records, 1801-1850, 81.
Lancastriæ, Ducatus, 78, 79.
Lancastriensis Phthisiologia, C. Leigh, 63.
Latham Spaw, E. Borlase, 83.
Lathom House, a Journal of the Siege of, 83.
Law, Edmund, Life of, 217.
Lees, John, Inquest on, 155.
Legendary and Poetic Remains of J. Roby, 274.
Legends of Lancashire, 260, 286.
Leigh Parish Church, History of, 84.
Lever, Sir Darcy, Case of, 374.
Leyland, Amounderness, etc., Topography and Directory, Mannex and Co., 115.
Literary Reminiscences and Gleanings, 224.
Livesey, T., Life and Times of, 218.
Liverpool a few years since, C. Aspinall, 84.
— Ancient, J. A. Picton, 93.
— Ancient Pictorial Relics of, W. G. Herdman, 90.
— Arms and Seal, 292.
— as it was during the last Quarter of 18th Century, 87.
Liverpool Architectural and Archæological Society, 331.
— Bay, Submarine Forest on shores of, 86.
— Charters, 103.
— Churches and Chapels, D. Thom, 97.
— Clergy, Proceedings in Chancery, 104.
— Coal Trade, Export, 92.
— Commerce, B. Poole, 94.
— — H. Smithers, 95.
— Condition of, Religious and Social, 91.
— Corporation, Proceedings in an action at law, 104.
— Described, D. Thompson, 97.
— Descriptive History of, J. Wallace, 101.
— Descriptive Poem on, 279.
— Directories, 18th century, 105-107.
— Elections, 1710-1841, 107-114.
— Epidemic Fever in 1844 in, 100.
— Fight at (Civil War Tract), 344.
— Flora, 105.
— — T. B. Hall, 89.
— Geology of the Country round, 92.
— Guide to, Fraser's, 89.
— — W. Moss', 93.
— — New Practical, 102.
— — Stranger's, 102.
— — Whitby's, 100.
— Highways, Byeways, and Thoroughfares, 96.
— History and Antiquities of, 80.
— — of the Commerce of, E. Baines, 85.
— — of, an Essay towards the, W. Enfield, 88, 89.
— — of, T. Troughton, 97-99.
— in 1825, a Satire, 263.
— — Reply to, 264.
— Jews in, Letters sent to, 102.
— Lacy's Handbook of, 96.
— Letters from S. Derrick, 302.
— Literary and Philosophical Society, 331.
— Medical Survey of, W. Moss, 92.
— Memorials of, J. A. Picton, 93.
— Modern Views of, W. G. Herdman, 91.
— Pictorial; its Annals, J. Stonehouse, 96.
— a Poem, J. Grocott, 258.

GENERAL INDEX.

Liverpool Railway (and Manchester), J. S. Walker, 99.
—— Railway (and Manchester), T. Roscoe, 94.
—— Railway (and Manchester), H. Booth, 86.
—— Railway (and Manchester), Cornish's Guide to, 87.
—— Recollections of, a Nonagenarian, 96.
—— Report of an Inquiry into, 104.
—— Rise and Progress of, J. M. Walthew, 102.
—— Royal Picturesque Handbook of, 161.
—— Sailing Directions from Point Lynas to, H. M. Denham, 88.
—— Squib Book, 107, 109, 110-112.
—— Stranger in, 100, 101.
—— Stranger's Guide (Cornish's), 87.
—— ,, ,, (Smith's), 95.
—— Streets of, J. Stonehouse, 95.
—— Table Talk a Hundred Years ago, 85.
—— Topography, Speculations on, 86.
—— Tour to London from, E. Wood, 318.
—— Town Councillors, Pen and Ink Sketches of, 94.
—— Town Council Proceedings of, 103.
—— Town Hall Oath Book, 105.
—— Trial of C. Angus, 114.
Liverseege, Henry, Works of, 422.
Lonsdale Hundred, North of the Sands, History of, T. Wright, 116.
—— North and South, Amounderness, Leyland, and Southport, Topography of, Mannex and Co., 115, 116.

M

MAGNALIA DEI ANGLICANA, 314.
Manchester, Address to the Inhabitants of, T. Battye, 120.
—— A few pages about, B. Love, 132.
—— Annals of, C. Timperley, 138.
—— —— Waugh and Fawcett, 139.
—— as it is, B. Love, 152.
—— Armorial Bearings, W. R. Whatton, 141.
—— Art Treasures Exhibition, Catalogue of, 150.
—— —— Examiner, 151.
—— —— Examples from, J. R. Waring, 150.
—— —— Guide Books to, 151.
Manchester Art Treasures Exhibition, Report of Committee, 151.
—— Bards, Trial of, 286.
—— Blue Coat Hospital, Account of, W. Mullis, 132.
—— Botanical Guide to, R. Buxton, 123.
—— Characteristic Strictures, 149.
—— Charters Translated, J. Whitaker, 146.
—— Chetham Library, Catalogue of Popery Tracts in, 152.
—— Chetham Library, MSS. in, 152.
—— Cholera in, History of, 131.
—— Civil War Tracts, 344, 345, 346, 347, 348, 349.
—— Collectanea relating to, 130.
—— Collegiate Church, A. Aston, 119.
—— Collegiate Church from 1422, G. C. Clifton, 124.
—— Collegiate Church, why it was Collegiate, S. H. Ware, 140.
—— Collegiate Church Charters, etc., 153.
—— Collegiate Church, R. B. Winkles, 141.
—— Collegiate Church, Six Months Observations in, J. Neal, 132.
—— Collegiate Church (Handbook to the Cathedrals of England), 132.
—— Collegiate Church, the Warders of the, from 1422, 52.
—— Coronation at (Celebration of), 374.
—— Coronation of Charles II., 130.
—— Council, Proceedings of, 149.
—— Description of, J. Ogden, 133.
—— Description of the Country 40 miles round, J. Aitkin, 116-118.
—— Directories of 18th Century, 146-148.
—— Disclosures of Parochial abuse, T. Battye, 120.
—— Early Printed Book at, "A Guide to Heaven," 157.
—— Elector's Guide (1833), 148.
—— Exchange, Descriptive Account of, 153.
—— Fair Em the Miller's Daughter, 285.
—— Flora, L. H. Grindon, 128.
—— —— J. Wood, 146.
—— Foundation Charter, T. Wheeler, 144.
—— Foundations, History of, 141, 144.
—— Geological Society, 156.
—— Geology, J. Taylor, 138.

GENERAL INDEX.

Manchester Good (the) Old Times, W. H. Ainsworth, 271.
— Gimcrackiana, J. S. Gregson, 128.
— Guide to, 153.
— — Cornish's, 124.
— — New, 153.
— — the Stranger's, H. G. Duffield, 125.
— Handbook of, B. Love, 131.
— — J. Perrin, 134.
— Historical Sketch of, A. Prentice, 134.
— History of, J. Reilly, 136.
— — Political, Social, and Commercial, J. Wheeler, 144.
— History of, J. Whitaker, 144, 146.
— — Additional Remarks on, 124.
— — Curious Remarks on, 124.
— — of the Foundation of Christ's College, Chetham Hospital, and Free Grammar School, 141-146.
— — of the Towne, R. Hollingworth, 130.
— — of the Barony of (Mamecestre), J. Harland, 129.
— in Holiday Dress, R. W. Procter, 136.
— in 1844, L. Faucher, 127.
— Jacobite Trials at, W. Beamont, 121.
— Letters from a Gentleman in, 379.
— Literary and Philosophical Society, 156.
— Literary Club, Transactions of, 423.
— Local Acts, G. W. Ormerod, 133.
— and Manchester People, E. Easby, 125.
— Mamescestre, J. Harland, 129.
— Manor, Court Leet Records, J. Harland, 129.
— Mary Barton, a Tale, 257.
— Metrical Records of, J. Aston, 119.
— MSS. in the Chetham Library, 293.
— Natives, Biography of, E. Butterworth, 122.
— Obelisk, an Heroic Epistle, 285.
— Observations on Improvements of, W. Fairbairn, 127.
— Panorama of, J. Everett, 126.
— Peterloo Disturbances in, 1819, 154.
— — Exposure of Calumnies, 134.
— — Examination of the late dreadful occurrence, 154.
— — Coroner's Inquest, 155.
— — Meeting, 155.
Manchester Peterloo, Who Killed Cock Robin, 155.
— Pictorial History of, G. R. Catt, 123.
— Picture of, J. Aston, 119.
— Poetry, J. Wheeler, 283.
— Political Events in, T. Walker, 140.
— Prospect (a) of, from Chamber, 284.
— Railway (and Liverpool), T. Roscoe, 94.
— Railway (and Leeds), G. Butterworth, 121.
— Red Basil Book, T. Battye, 120.
— Represented or Misrepresented, 148.
— School, History of, W. R. Whatton, 143, 144.
— School, Admission Register, J. F. Smith, 137.
— Shells, D. Dyson, 125.
— Siege, History of, J. Palmer, 133.
— Siege that was to be, 287.
— Streets, Memorials of, R. W. Procter, 135.
— Tabula Mancuniensis, J. Butterworth, 123.
— Town of, E. Butterworth, 122.
— Trésors d'art, W. Burger, 121.
— Trials (the) at, in 1694, 127.
— Trial of Action, T. Walker, 154.
— Trial of an Indictment against Thomas Walker, 139.
— Turf, Stage, and Ring, R. W. Procter, 136.
— Vindicated, J. Byrom, 151.
— Vindication of, 149.
— Walks and Wild Flowers, L. Grindon, 128.
— Warehouse Boy, the, 266.
— Wesleyan Methodism, J. Everett, 126.
— Wonderful News from, 373.
— Worthies, E. Edwards, 125.
Manesty, John, the Liverpool Merchant, 265.
Manufacturing Districts, a Home Tour through, 304.
— — an Old Man's Wanderings in, W. C. Taylor, 314.
— — the State of, E. Baines, 293.
Marlocks of Merriton, B. Brierley, 244.
Marriot, John, a Short Account of, 218.
Marshe, George, Troubles and Martyrdom of, 218.
— — Life of, 197.

Martindale, Adam, Life of, 218.
Men and Measures, 286.
Meols. *See* Southport.
Middleton, Historical Notices of, E. Butterworth, 116.
Milnrow, and the Cottage of Tim Bobbin, 116.
Ministers of Lancashire, the Harmonious Consent of, 376.
—— —— Letter from the Duke of Hamilton to, 376.
Miscellanea Palatina, G. Ormerod, 308.
Miscellanies, Thomas Wilson, 283.
Monuments, Sepulchral, Committee of, Report of, 322.
Moore (the) Rental, 219.
Mosley, Sir O., Family Memoirs, 219.
Mount Pleasant, a Poem, 276.
Musings in many Lands, J. B. Rogerson, 275.
Mytton. *See* Stonyhurst.

N

NATURALISTS in Humble Life, J. Cash, 238.
Navigation, Inland, History of, 320.
Newcome, Henry, Autobiography of, 220.
—— —— Diary of, 219.
Noble and Gentlemen of England, 314.
Nonconformist's Remains, R. Slate, 212.
—— Memorial, S. Palmer, 309.
—— the Plea for Uniformity, 376.
Nonsubscribers, a Plea for, 373.
Norris (the), Papers, 220.
Northern Circuit, an Account of the, 314.
—— Counties, a Tour through, 315.
—— England, a Tour through, 320.
Notitia Cestriensis; or, Historical Notices of the Diocese of Chester, F. R. Raines, 66.
Nowell, Alexander, Life of, 220.
Nuttall, Josiah, Sketch of the Life of, 221.

O

OBSERVATIONS and Instructions, R. Heywood, 262.
Odes and Miscellanies, R. F. Chetham, 247.
Ogden, Amos, Account of, 221.
Old (the), Church Clock, R. Parkinson, 268.
Old Cronies, E. Waugh, 282.
Oldham, a Guide to, E. Butterworth, 157.
—— Historical and Descriptive Account of, J. Butterworth, 157.
Overborough Roman Antiquities, R. Rauthmel, 158.
Over Darwen, Antiquities at, 292.

P

PARK, Henry, Memoirs of, 221.
Peel, Sir Robert, a Critical Biography, 222.
—— —— Historical Sketch of, 221.
—— —— Life of, 223.
—— —— Life and Times, 223.
—— —— Memoirs of, 223.
—— —— Pamphlets relating to, 223.
—— —— Political Life of, 222.
—— —— Sketch of the Life of, 223.
Pendleton, Trial of, W. Holden, 158.
Pennington, Thomas, of Orrell, 372.
Pennystone, 278.
Penwortham, Documents relating to, W. A. Hulton, 159.
—— St. Mary's Church at, P. Whittle, 159.
Peterloo Riots, 154, 155. *See* Manchester.
Phases of Distress, J. Ramsbottom, 270.
Pilkington, James, Works of, 224.
Plebian Politics, 279.
Poetical Trifles, J. H. Mills, 266.
Poem, a [H. Clark], 289.
Poems, J. Byrom, 245, 246.
—— J. Heywood, 241.
—— J. Orrell, 268.
—— J. B. Rogerson, 275.
—— E. Rushton, 276.
—— E. Sherburne, 277.
—— B. Waller, 280.
—— [and Songs], E. Waugh, 281.
—— Thomas Wilson, 283.
Poetic Tales, M. Bishop, 243.
Poetical Works of E. Ridings, 270.
Poetry, Miscellaneous, S. Bamford, 242.
—— of Witchcraft, 262.
Political State of Great Britain, 295.
Poulton-le-Fylde, 5.

GENERAL INDEX.

Preston, a Brief Description of, J. Taylor, 160.
—— Charters, 165.
—— Churches and Chapels, A. Hewitson, 169.
—— Fight (Civil War Tract), 335.
—— Fight (the), W. H. Ainsworth, 421.
—— Guilds, 162-163.
—— History of, C. Hardwick, 159.
—— —— P. Whittle, 160-161.
—— —— and Directory (Mannex and Co.), 160.
—— Methodism, R. Allen, 159.
—— Preston Parliamentary Representation, 166.
—— Songster, 168.
—— Squib Books, 166-168.
—— Taking of (Civil War Tract), 334.
—— Town Council, Proceedings of, 168.
Prestoniad, a Poem, 267.
Prestwich Church, Memorials of, J. Booker, 169.
Public Records, Report of Deputy Keeper of, 322.

Q

QUAKERS, History of, W. Sewel, 313.
—— Sufferings of, J. Besse, 294.
—— Tracts, 358-371.

R

RAILWAY, North Union, History of, F. C. Buller, 49.
Rambles by Rivers, J. Thorne, 285.
Ranter's (the) Last Sermon, 378.
Richmond-Wills and Inventories, 311.
Richmondshire, History of, 316-318.
Rebellion (the) of 1715, History of, P. Rae, 309.
—— —— History of, R. Patten, 310.
—— —— Memorials of, S. H. Ware, 77.
—— of 1745, History of, J. Henderson, 304.
—— —— History of, J. Home, 304.
—— —— History of, J. Ray, 311.
—— —— Memoirs of, Chev. de Johnstone, 305.
—— —— a Poem, Rossendaliensis, 312.
Recusants, Humble Petition of, 337.
Ribble, the, Rambles by, 170.
Ribchester, Bronze Helmet found at, 291.
Rigby, Alex., Letter of (Civil War Tract), 335, 340.
—— —— Speech, 349, 350.
Rivington School Charters, 170.
Rochdale, a Fragment, W. Nuttall, 266.
—— Brass Instrument discovered at, 292.
—— Canal, Papers in Favour of (1791), 172.
—— Grammar School, F. R. Raines, 171.
—— Historical and Topographical Account of, J. Butterworth, 170.
—— in 1745, 171.
—— Leeds, and Liverpool Canal, J. Sutcliffe, 172.
—— Olden Times, Legends of, W. Nuttall, 267.
—— Past and Present, W. Robertson, 171.
Rocher Vale, J. Butterworth, 245.
Romney, Geo., Life of, 225.
Roscoe, William, Life of, 225.
—— Memoir of, 226.
Rossendale, Forest of, History of, T. Newbigging, 172.
Rothwell, Richard, Life of, 197.
Routh, Martha, Memoir of, 226.
Rushbearing (the) of, a Poem, 287.
Rustic Muse, the, J. Butterworth, 245.

S

SALFORD Charities, a History of, 173.
—— Directories, 18th Century's, 147.
—— Guide, New, 150.
—— Peel Park Museum, etc., 173. *See* Manchester.
Samlesbury Ancient Hall, History of, J. Croston, 174.
—— Higher Hall, Account of, 175.
Scarsdale, or Life on the Lancashire and Yorkshire Border, 277.
School Candidates, the, H. Clark, 247.
Seats of Gentlemen and Noblemen, J. P. Neale, 308.
Sefton Church, R. Bridgens, 175.
—— Earl of, *versus* Hopwood, 226.
Sermons and Theological Treatises, 380-420.
Sheriffs (High) of Lancashire, List of, 52.
Shuttleworth House and Farm Accounts, 227.

GENERAL INDEX.

Sieges and Battles in the North of England, a Description of, 331.
Simpson, William, Life of, 370.
Simple Records, J. Ashworth, 241.
Sketches from Life, W. Byrom, 246.
Smith, William (Bishop), Life of, 227.
Smithell's Hall, Description of, 175, 197.
Snowed Up, E. Waugh, 282.
Songs and Poems of Lancashire, 281.
—— of the Wilsons, 283.
Southport, a Guide to, T. K. Glazebrook, 176.
—— Handbook of, D. H. M'Nicoll, 176.
—— Historical Account of, P. Whittle, 17.
—— History of (Concise), 177.
—— —— P. Whittle, 177.
—— Illustrated Guide to, 177.
—— Topography and Directory. *See* Lonsdale.
Speke Hall, a Legend of, 289.
—— —— Carving at, 291.
Sports, Lawful, the King's Declaration about, 374.
Stanley Family (Civil War Tracts), 335-348.
—— Historical Sketch of the House of, 228.
—— History of the House of, 228-231.
—— Legend, the, 233.
—— of Knowsley, 230.
—— Papers, 229.
—— Private Devotions of 7th Earl, 229.
—— (the Derby), Household Book, 229.
—— Memoirs of the House of, 231, 232.
—— Sketch of the House of, 231.
—— Sir William's Garland, 278. *See* Derby.
—— the Great, 228.
Stonyhurst College, its Past and Present, 178.
Stonyhurst and Mytton, History of, 179.
Strange Tales, J. Ashworth, 241.
Stratford, William, Account of his Charities. 235.
Stydd Chapel, History of, 179.
Summer Rambles in Lancashire, etc., 303.
Surey Demoniac Tracts, 294, 295, 353, 354.
Swarthmoor Hall and its Associations, H. Barber, 180.

T

The Quack Doctor, 288.
The Spirit of the Doctor, J. Watson, 280.
Thorp, John, Memoirs of, 235.
Then and Now, W. Quarmby, 169.
Tim Bobbin's Toy Shop opened, 249,
—— Works, 248-256.
Titherington, Mary, Account of, 235.
Tour (a) from Downing to Alston Moor, 310.
Townley, Colonel, Trial and Execution of, 236.
Towns in Lancashire, Health of, L. Playfair, 65.
Toxteth Park, Topography of, J. Boult, 86.
Tracts for and against Popery in the Chetham Library Catalogue, T. Jones, 152.
Tracts, Miscellaneous, 371-379.
—— relating to Quakers, 358-371.
—— relating to Civil War, 332-352.
Trial of Henry Hunt, 155.
—— Redford against Birley, 1819, 155.
—— William Holden, 158.
Tufts of Heather from a Lancashire Moor, 281.
Turton-Goose Coal Hill, Record of, 180.
Turton and Gorton Church Libraries, 180.
Turton Fair, a Poem, 277.
Tyldesley (the) Diary, 246.

U

Upland Hall, a Tale, 242.

V

View (a) of the Lancashire Dialect, Tim Bobbin, 248-251.
Vision (the), E. Wood, 318.
Visitations of Lancashire, 1567, 1613, 1664, and 1665, T. R. Raines, 68, 69.

W

Walkden, Peter, Extracts from Diary of, 237.
Walney Island, 292.
Walton-le-dale Mock Corporation, 181.

GENERAL INDEX.

Warrington Civil War Tract, 349.
—— in 1565, W. Beamont, 181.
—— Local History, 182.
—— Lords, Annals of, 181, 182.
—— Squib Book, 183.
—— Worthies, J. Kendrick, 183.
Warton Parish, Antiquities in, 291.
Wenderholme, a Story, 258.
Whalley Coucher Book, the, 183.
—— History of the Parish, T. D. Whitaker, 184-189.
Whalley, Victory at (Civil War Tract), 349.
Winkley (the) Family, 237,
Win, the Festival of, 288.
Whitakeri Gvilielmi Vita et Opera, 237,
Wigan, the Mayor of, 245, 349.
—— (Civil War Tract), 349.
Witchcraft, the Displaying of, J. Webster, 315.
—— Magick, and Sorcery, History of, R. Boulton, 294.
—— etc., the Possibility of, R. Boulton, 295.
Witchcraft, Historical Essay on, F. Hutchinson, 305.
—— in Lancashire, seven persons possessed, 372.
Witches, Pott's Discovery of, 66.
—— —— Edited by James Crossley, 66.
—— the Lancashire, the Famous History of, 78.
Woolton Green, a Domestic Poem, 276.
Worston and Chatburn, Roman Coins found at, 291.
Worthington, John, Diary and Correspondence of, 237.
Worthies of England, 302.
—— of Lancashire and Yorkshire, 302.
—— Northern, 300.

Y

YELLAND, account of Barrow Hill, 291.

INDEX OF AUTHORS.

A

ABBADIE, JAMES, 36.
Abram, W. A., 331.
Adamson, William, 370.
Addamson, William, 369.
Addison, Leonard, 369.
Aikin, J., 117, 118.
Ainsworth, W. H., 240, 421.
Aldam, Thomas, 364.
Aldred, Jeremiah, 380.
Allen, Isaac, 420.
Allen, Richard, 159.
Ambrose, Isaac, 380-382.
Anderson, James, 384.
Angier, John, 382, 420.
Arbiter, Petronius, 233.
Armistead, Wilson, 89.
Ascroft, Thomas, 175.
Ashfield, C. J., 327, 328, 329.
Ashworth, Henry, 50.
—— John, 241, 242.
Aspden, Thomas, 228.
Aspinall, C., 84.
Assheton, William, 382.
Aston, Joseph, 37, 119, 285.
Atkinson, Thomas, 350, 351.
Atmore, E., 193.
Atticus, 61.
Austin, S., 37.
Aveling, T. W., 201.
Axon, W. E. A., 3, 38, 242.

B

BAINES, EDWARD, 22, 39, 40, 43, 193, 293.
Baines, Thomas, 44, 85, 325.
Baker, Franklin, 7.
—— T., 12.
Bamford, Samuel, 45, 193, 194, 242, 243.
Barber, Henry, 180.
Barker, H. H., 181.
Barlow, T. W., 45.
Barnet, Nehemiah, 383.
Barrington, Daines, 291.
Barton, B. T., 421.
Basnett, C., 383.
Battye, Thomas, 120.
Bawdwen, William, 46.
Bayley, William, 225.
Beamont, William, 47, 77, 121, 181, 182, 324, 330.
Beck, T. A., 15.
Beesley, William, 47.
Bell, William, 384.
Besse, Joseph, 294.
Binns, Jonathan, 47.
—— Thomas, 48.
Bishop, Mary, 243.
Blanchard, E. T., 23.
Boaden, James, 214.
Boardman, James, 85.
Bobbin, Tim. *See* Collier, J.
Bolton, John, 16.
—— Robert, 195.
Booker, John, 3, 4, 12, 75.
Booth, Henry, 86.
Borlase, Edmund, 83.
Bottomley, Mr., 243.
Boult, Joseph, 86, 329, 330, 331.
Boulton, Richard, 295.
Bowes, John, 330.
Boyer, A., 296.
Bradshaw, Ellis, 334.
—— John, 235.
Braithwait, R., 244.
Bramwell, William, 203.
Branthwait, John, 369.
Brathwait, Richard, 298.
Brereley, John, 384.

INDEX OF AUTHORS.

Bretton, Le, P. H., 190.
Bridgens, R., 175.
Brierley, Benjamin, 244, 245.
—— Samuel, 171.
Bright, H. A., 327.
Briscoe, J. D., 8.
Britton, John, 48.
Brooke, Richard, 87, 325.
Broome, Richard, 262.
Brown, Alexander, 95.
—— John, 8, 203.
Brownsword, William, 358.
Budworth, Joseph, 23.
Buller, E. C., 49.
Burger, W., 121.
Bushell, Seth, 385, 386.
Butler, Hillary, 189, 245.
Butterworth, Edwin, 1, 20, 49, 121, 122, 157.
—— James, 1, 122, 123, 157, 170, 245, 256.
Buxton, David, 326.
—— Richard, 123.
Byrom, John, 152, 245, 246.
—— William, 246.

C

CALDWELL, JOHN, 386.
Carlisle, Nicholas, 298.
Carrington, John, 353.
Carter, Oliver, 386.
Cash, James, 238.
Caton, William, 367, 368.
Cattermole, Richard, 299.
Catt, G. R., 123.
Chetham, R. F., 247.
Cheyney, John, 210, 369, 387, 388.
Chippendall, G., 288.
Chisenhall, Edward, 84.
Chorley, H. F., 210.
Chorlton, John, 387.
Churton, Ralph, 220.
Clarke, James, 24.
—— S. R., 52.
Clark, Henry, 247, 289.
Clarkson, R., 164.
Clay, Charles, 2.
Clegg, James, 8.
Clifton, G. C., 124.
Coleridge, Hartley, 299, 300.
Collier, John (Tim Bobbin), 52, 124, 248-256.
Comber, Thomas, 327.
Coningham, James, 387.
Cooke, G. A., 53.
Corey, Charles, 327.
Corry, J., 53.
Corser, Thomas, 263.
Corymœus. *See* Brathwait, R.
Cox, Thomas, 54.
Crabtree, William, 55, 214.
Crane, Thomas, 388.
Crofton, Zachariah, 370.
Crossfield, George, 207.
Crossley, James, 66, 237.
Crosthwaite, P., 24.
Croston, James, 174.
Cumming, J. G., 228.
Currie, W. W., 203.
Cust, Sir Edward, 328.

D

DAKYNS, J. R., 423.
Dalling, Lord, 221.
Darrell, John, 356.
Davies, John, 55.
Dawes, Matthew, 324.
Dawson, J. T., 326, 327, 328.
Deacon, John, 355, 357, 358.
Dearden, Joseph, 164.
De Foe, D., 301.
Denham, H. M., 88.
Denholm, James, 25.
De Quincey, T., 204.
Derby, Charles, Earl of, 388.
—— Earls of, 229.
—— James, Earl of, 229.
Derrick, Samuel, 302.
Dickenson, Jonathan, 368.
Dickson, R. W., 55.
Dillingham, William, 201.
Dixon, James, 331.
Dobson, William, 164, 165, 166, 170, 237.
Doubleday, Thomas, 222.
Dowling, J. A., 155.
Draper, Peter, 228.
Duffield, H. G., 125.
Dugdale, William, 68.
Durham, William, 4.

INDEX OF AUTHORS.

E

EARBURY, MATTHIAS, 302.
Easby, John, 125.
Eaton, Samuel, 389.
Edwards, Edward, 125.
Egerton, Leonard, 420.
Enfield, William, 88, 89.
Espinasse, Francis, 55.
Evans, Francis, 16.
—— John, 56.
Everett, James, 126.

F

FAIRBAIRN, WILLIAM, 44, 127.
Faucher, Leon, 127.
Fawcett, J., 211.
Fell, Leonard, 369, 371.
—— Margaret, 364, 366.
Ffarington, S. M., 204.
Fielding, Joseph, 56.
Fisher, H. S., 326, 328, 329.
Fishwick, Henry, 19, 20.
Fitchett, John, 256.
Fitzgerald, Percy, 215.
Fleetwood, Serjeant, 290.
Fleming, S., 277.
Flowers, William, 68.
Folliott, William, 10.
Ford, William, 25.
Foreness, E., 389.
Foster, Joseph, 56.
Fox, Margaret. *See* Fell.
Francis, G. H., 222.
Fraser, Alexander, 20, 217.
French, G. J., 180, 202.

G

GASKELL, Mrs., 257.
—— W., 57.
Gastrell, Francis, 66.
Gee, Edward, 390, 391.
Gibson, A. C., 327, 328, 329, 330.
Gillow, Joseph, 236.
Gipps, Thomas, 391, 392.
Glazebrook, T. K., 176.
Goss, Alexander, 127.
Greenhalgh, Joseph, 207.
—— Thomas, 257.
Green, William, 25, 26.
Gregson, C. S., 326, 327, 328.
—— J. S., 128.
—— Matthew, 57, 58, 59.
Gresley, William, 257.
Greswell, J., 144.
Grey, J. E., 21.
Grimshaw, James, 393.
Grindon, L. H., 128, 303.
Grocott, James, 258.
Gubb, E., 190.
Guest, Richard, 303, 304.
Guizot, M., 222.
Gunn, W., 423.
Gurney, Mr., 104, 154.

H

HALLEY, ROBERT, 59.
Halliwell, J. O., 260, 262.
Hall, J., 82.
—— Ralph, 369.
—— T. B., 89.
Hamerton, P. G., 258.
Hardknot, Harry, 26.
Hardwick, Charles, 159, 259, 326, 329.
Hardy, S. R., 208.
—— William, 60.
Hargreaves, James, 3, 213.
Harland, John, 11, 13, 43, 60, 61, 129, 130, 165, 215, 227, 259, 260, 324, 325, 330.
Harrison, John, 393.
—— William, 393, 394.
Harsnet, Samuel, 357.
Harvey, William, 222.
Haydock, Roger, 369.
Head, George, 304.
Heawood, William, 130, 374.
Henderson, Andrew, 304.
Henry, W. C., 211.
Herdman, W. G., 90, 91.
Herford, Brooke, 43.
Herle, Charles, 394-397.
Hewitson, A., 61, 168, 169, 178, 236
Hewlett, Alfred, 218.
Heyricke, Richard, 376, 397, 398, 420.
Heywood, James, 261.
—— Nathaniel, 398.
—— Oliver, 191.
—— Robert, 262.
—— Thomas, 219, 220, 229, 263, 324.

INDEX OF AUTHORS.

Hibbert, Samuel, 2.
—— T. D., 325.
Higgin, E., 323.
Higgins, H. H., 327.
Higson, John, 12, 19.
Hinchliffe, J. H., 291.
Hindle, Robert, 61.
—— William, 398.
Holland, P., 27.
Hollingworth, Richard, 131, 399, 400.
Holme, Edmond, 147, 173.
—— Thomas, 369.
Holt, David, 213.
—— John, 62.
Home, John, 304.
Hook, W. F., 194.
Horne, T. H., 27.
Horrobin, Robert, 400.
Housman, John, 28.
—— R. F., 214.
Howe, John, 400.
Hubberthorne, Richard, 362, 363.
Huddleston, Richard, 401.
—— John, 401.
Hughes, J. R., 327, 328.
Hull, Edward, 423.
Hulme, A., 91.
Hulton, W. A., 159, 183.
Hume, A., 324, 325, 329.
Hunter, Joseph, 212.
—— Richard, 401.
Hutchinson, Francis, 305.
—— William, 291.
Hutton, W., 6.

J

JAMES, Colonel Sir H., 62.
—— Richard, 263.
Jenkinson, 29.
Johnstone, De Chevalier, 305.
Jolly, Thomas, 353.
Jones, Thomas, 152.
Jopling, Charles M., 16.
Jumper, Jeremy, 263.
Just, John, 323, 324.

K

KENDRICK, JAMES, 183, 325, 326, 330.
Kennedy, James, 62.
Kennedy, Theo., 264.
Kenworthy, Charles, 264.
Kerr, James, 330.
King, W. T., 68.

L

LAHEE, N. R., 218.
Laird, William, 92.
Latham, William, 116.
—— George, 179.
—— R. G., 326.
Law, Samuel, 265.
Lawson, Thomas, 361.
Leach, Francis, 3.
Leadbetter, Charles, 265.
Lee, Francis, 291.
Leigh, Charles, 63, 64.
—— John, 131, 307.
—— William, 377.
—— —— 29.
Lettsom, J. C., 291.
Lewis, John, 401.
Leygh, William, 402.
Lilly, William, 358.
Lingard, John, 165.
Linton, E. Lyon, 29.
Livesey, John, 402, 403.
Loftie, W. J., 33.
Lort, Michael, 290.
Love, B., 131, 132.
Lyne, Charles, 307.
Lyons, Ponsonby A., 188.

M

MACKAY, CHARLES, 30, 224.
—— John, 302.
M'Leod, R. G., 329.
M'Nicoll, D. H., 176.
M'Owen, Peter, 206.
Maguire, W., 265.
Mannex and Co., 64, 115, 160.
Marsden, Thomas, 403.
Marsh, J. F., 326.
Martineau, Harriet, 30.
Matthew, G. K., 31.
Mayer, J., 325, 326.
Mills, J. H., 266.
Mollineux, Mary, 266.
—— Henry, 361.

INDEX OF AUTHORS.

Moon, John, 378.
Moore, George, 373.
—— Henry, 235.
—— John, 361.
—— Thomas, 325.
Morris, J. P., 17.
—— John, 307.
Morton, G. H., 92.
Mosley, Nicholas, 403.
Moss, W., 92, 93.
Mossom, R., 404.
Mott, A. J., 328.
Mottershead, J., 404.
Mounsey, Thomas, 204.
Mullis, William, 132.
Murray, John, 132.
Myles, William, 208.

N

NAYLOR, JAMES, 404.
Neale, J. P., 308.
Neal, John, 132.
Newbigging, Thomas, 172, 329.
Newcome, Henry, 404-406.
Nichols, J. G., 188, 324.
Nicholson, Thomas, 266.
Nuttall, William, 266.

O

OGDEN, JAMES, 133.
Oliver, Rowland, 267.
Ormerod, George, 64, 308, 324.
—— G. W., 133.
—— Oliver, 268.
Orrell, James, 268.
Otley, Jonathan, 31.
Owen, Charles, 406-409.
—— James, 410.

P

PALEY, W. B., 217.
Palmer, Samuel, 309.
—— John, 133, 142.
Park, M. J., 327.
Parkinson, Richard, 198, 199, 218, 220, 268.
Patchet, Francis, 360.
Patten, Robert, 309.
Payn, James, 17, 31.
Peel, Sir Lawrence, 223.
Pendlebury, Henry, 411, 412.
Pennant, Thomas, 310.
Peploe, Samuel, 412, 413.
Perceval, Samuel, 290.
Perrin, Joseph, 134.
Philips, Francis, 134.
—— John, 22.
Piccope, G. J., 65.
Picton, J. A., 93, 325.
Pidgeon, H. C., 324, 326.
Playfair, L., 65.
Pollard, William, 230.
Poole, Braithwaite, 94.
Pope, W. A., 207.
Price, Evan, 371.
Prince, J. C., 269.
Prior, Hermon, 32.
Procter, R. W., 135, 136, 224, 269.
Pyne, J. B., 31.

Q

QUARMBY, WILLIAM, 269.

R

RADCLIFFE, ANN, 32.
Rae, Peter, 311.
Raffald, Mrs., 147.
Raine, James, 311.
Raines, F. R., 66, 67, 68, 171, 192, 229, 230.
Ramsbottom, Joseph, 270.
Rance, De, C. E., 423.
Rauthmel, Richard, 158.
Rawstorne, Law, 422.
Ray, James, 311.
Reilly, John, 136.
Richardson, George, 422.
Richmond, Henry, 413.
Ridings, Elijah, 255, 270.
Rigbie, Joseph, 270.
Rimmer, Alfred, 69, 324, 325.
Robertson, William, 171.
Roberts, W. J., 323, 326.
Robinson, Edward, 47.
—— John, 32.
Robson, John, 324, 325, 327, 328.

INDEX OF AUTHORS.

Roby, John, 271, 272, 273, 274.
Rogerson, J. B., 275.
Roscoe, Henry, 225.
—— Thomas, 94.
—— William, 276.
Ross, David, 231.
Rossendaliensis, P., 312.
Rothwell, William, 69.
Rudd, Thomas, 360.
Ryley, S. W., 312.

S

ST. GEORGE, RICHARD, 68.
Scholefield, James, 324.
Seacome, John, 231, 232.
Sewel, William, 213.
Sharp, William, 313.
Shaw, John, 276.
Sheldrake, William, 277.
Shepherd, William, 276.
Sherburne, Edward, 277.
Sherlock, Richard, 363, 415, 416.
Shimmen, Hugh, 94, 95.
Shippen, W., 416.
Shirley, E. P., 314.
Shuttleworth-Kay, Sir James, 278.
Simpson, J. Y., 329.
—— Robert, 80.
—— William, 369.
Slate, R., 4, 212.
Slynehead, Peter, 414, 415.
Smithers, Henry, 95.
Smith, H. E., 329, 330, 331.
—— J. F., 137.
Stanley, Ferdinando, 420.
—— William, 278.
Stephenson, W., 55.
Stevens, William, 198.
Stockdale, James, 422.
Stonehouse, James, 87, 95, 96, 97, 278, 324, 326.
Stratford, Nicholas, 416.
Sutcliffe, John, 172.
—— Thomas, 215.
Syers, Robert, 14.

T

TATTERSALL, GEORGE, 33.
Taylor, George, 158.
Taylor, John, 138, 160.
—— Tim, 389.
—— W. C., 223, 314.
—— Zachery, 353, 354, 372, 417.
Tiddeman, R. H., 423.
Tilsley, John, 379.
Timperley, Charles H., 138.
Thom, D., 97, 325.
Thompson, David, 97.
Thornber, William, 6, 278, 324, 325.
Thorne, J., 285.
Townsend, Aubrey, 198.
Traill, T. S., 226.
Troughton, Thomas, 99.
Tunnicliffe, William, 70.
Tuvar, Lorenzo, 279.
Twycross, Edward, 70.
Tymms, Samuel, 314.

V

VICARS, John, 315.
Victor, Mr., 196.

W

WAGSTALL, Thomas, 372.
Walcott, Mackenzie E. C., 33, 329.
Walker, J. Scott, 99.
—— John, 279, 355.
—— Robert, 279.
—— Thomas, 140.
Wallace, J., 99.
Waller, Bryan, 280.
Walthew, J. M., 102.
Ward, J. C., 423.
Ware, S. Hibbert, 140.
Waring, J. R., 150.
Warner, Richard, 315.
Watson, G. C., 100.
—— James, 280.
—— John, 290.
Waugh, Edwin, 15, 33, 280-283.
Webb, Maria, 205.
Webster, John, 315.
Welton, T. A., 327.
Weston, Stephen, 291.
West, Thomas, 18, 34, 290.
Whatton, A. B., 213.
—— W. R., 43, 141, 143, 178.
Wheeler, James, 144, 283.

INDEX OF AUTHORS.

Wheeler, Thomas, 144.
Whitaker, John, 144-146.
—— J. W., 170.
—— T. D., 10, 73, 184-189, 316-318.
White, John, 417, 418.
—— J. P., 283.
Whittle, Peter, 5, 7, 9, 14, 115, 159, 161, 177, 179.
Wilcockson, J., 163.
Wilkinson, Joseph, 35.
—— Thomas, 35.
—— T. T., 9, 259, 260, 326, 327, 328, 329, 330.
Williams, J. A., 216
Willme, J., 102.
Wilson, R. C., 214.
—— Thomas, 283.
—— William, 284
Winkles, R. R., 141.
Winkley, William, 237.
Witt, W. G. de, 233.
Wood, Ephraim, 319.
—— J. E., 284.
—— John, 146.
—— K., 284.
Wordsworth, William, 36, 285.
Worsley, J. E., 84.
Wright, G. N., 73, 116.
Wroe, Richard, 418, 420.

Y

YEATS, John, 369.
Young, Arthur, 320.

ERRATA.

Page 8, line 19, *after* "John Brown," *read* "Author of the above."
,, 38, last line but two, "William and," *read* "William E. A."
,, 61, lines 15 and 20, "County Churches," *read* "Country Churches."
,, 73, line 11, "Unicus auctore," *read* "Unicus. Auctore."
,, 77, line 20, "MDCCXX." *read* "MDCCXV."
,, 83, line 5 from the bottom, "was the son of Sir John Borlase an," *reaa* "the son of Sir John Borlase was an."
,, 99, "A general and descriptive History of the antient and present state of the town of Liverpool," is the second edition of the work described on page 101.
,, 135, bottom line, *add* "Extra large Paper Edition, £3 : 3s. Only 50 printed."
,, 180, line 15, "or," *read* "in."